Vulnerability Assessment of Physical Protection Systems

Vulnerability Assessment of Physical Protection Systems

Mary Lynn Garcia, CPP

Sandia National Laboratories

ELSEVIER

AMSTERDAM • BOSTON • HEIDELBERG • LONDON
NEW YORK • OXFORD • PARIS • SAN DIEGO
SAN FRANCISCO • SINGAPORE • SYDNEY • TOKYO

Butterworth Heinemann is an imprint of Elsevier

The U.S. Government holds a non-exclusive copyright license in this work for government purposes. This book was authored by Sandia Corporation under Contract DE-AC04-94AL85000 with the U.S. Department of Energy.

Elsevier Butterworth–Heinemann
30 Corporate Drive, Suite 400, Burlington, MA 01803, USA
Linacre House, Jordan Hill, Oxford OX2 8DP, UK

Recognizing the importance of preserving what has been written, Elsevier prints its books on acid-free paper whenever possible.

Library of Congress Cataloging-in-Publication Data
Garcia, Mary Lynn.
    Vulnerability assessment of physical protection systems / Mary Lynn Garcia.
        p. cm.
    Includes bibliographical references.
    1. Security systems–Evaluation. I. Title.
    TH9705.G38 2005
    658.4′ 73–dc22   2005020032

British Library Cataloguing-in-Publication Data
A catalogue record for this book is available from the British Library.

ISBN 13: 978-0-7506-7788-2
ISBN 10: 0-7506-7788-0

For information on all Elsevier Butterworth–Heinemann publications visit our Web site at www.books.elsevier.com

Printed in the United States of America

05 06 07 08 09 10 10 9 8 7 6 5 4 3 2 1

For all those responsible for protecting our nation's assets

The search for static security, in the law and elsewhere, is misguided. The fact is, security can only be achieved through constant change, adapting old ideas that have outlived their usefulness to current facts. William O. Douglas, U.S. Supreme Court justice

Table of Contents

The companion material will give the reader additional resources that can be used in the planning, conduct, and reporting of a Vulnerability Assessment—specifically, project management reporting, threat and facility description worksheets, as well as templates for the initial and final briefings. In addition, sample data collection sheets for each technology area are included to aid in the evaluation and documentation of the pertinent data in each component technology and functional area. A collection of criteria for the alarm communication and display system evaluation is also provided, along with notes on how to use these criteria to compare candidate systems prior to purchase or installation.

Companion material available online at:
http://books.elsevier.com/companions/0750677880

Preface

This book is an extension of the *Design and Evaluation of Physical Protection Systems* text released in April 2001. That book introduced the overall process and principles of physical protection systems; this one describes the application of that process and principles to vulnerability assessment. As in the previous text, the underlying premise of this book is that overall system effectiveness is the objective of a physical security system, not merely the presence of nonintegrated equipment, personnel, and procedures. There is a need for such a text, despite the presence of many existing practices and publications that address vulnerability assessment. Many of these practices and publications rely on compliance-based approaches to security, even for critical assets. This is further constrained by the need to justify the business case for security to senior managers. The fundamental objective of a security system is to protect assets. It is agreed that investments in security should be justified, but protection system effectiveness must also be demonstrated for this investment. Therefore, the simple presence of people, procedures, or equipment does not necessarily provide protection. There is no reason why enterprises cannot have effective security that also complies with regulations or policies.

Because a vulnerability assessment is meant to identify security system weaknesses that can be exploited by malevolent human threats, the difference in performing the evaluation using a checklist that verifies presence of security components (compliance-based) versus an evaluation that shows system effectiveness (performance-based) is significant. The decision concerning which approach is used should be driven by the consequence of loss of the asset. Every enterprise, no matter the size, has critical assets. Critical assets must be protected from adversaries and require performance-based evaluation approaches to ensure effective protection. Low-value assets require less protection and compliance-based approaches are more appropriate in these cases. Since the attacks on 9/11, some progress has been made in improving physical security for critical or other important assets, but much remains to be done.

Some readers will find parts of this text, particularly analysis, to be overly simple in the scenarios and assumptions that are used in the examples. This is a valid point, but because vulnerability assessment is a sensitive process, caution prevails. The goal was to write a thorough but not overly detailed description of common vulnerabilities of physical protection systems. It is regrettable if this disappoints any readers; however, there are reasonable limits to the type of information that should be publicly available. (Managers who bear the responsibility and accountability for security systems may appreciate this thought more than other readers!)

Readers who are unfamiliar with the first book may find it useful to review the process before reading this text. Chapters 1, 14, and 15 should be sufficient to fill in most of the background, although some terms may still be unfamiliar. Chapter 1 in this text is an overview of risk management, the vulnerability assessment process, and systems engineering as applied in a vulnerability assessment. Chapter 2, which describes physical protection system principles, is a repeat of Chapter 5 in the Design book and includes a new section that specifically addresses vulnerability assessment. Chapter 3 on project management, team composition, and project kick-off was included to assist the many people we meet who need help in these aspects of security projects and as an aid in planning a vulnerability assessment. Protection objectives are reviewed in Chapter 4 for those who are unfamiliar with these process inputs and are described more fully in the first book. Chapters 5–10 are the core of the vulnerability assessment, where physical protection system components including people, procedures, and equipment are evaluated for their effectiveness and data on the various subsystems is collected. Chapter 11 describes analysis of all data and Chapter 12 discusses recommended reporting techniques and uses of the VA. The Appendices include various evaluation aids that can be used in a vulnerability assessment. This high-level process flow can be tailored to conform to internal and external expectations and practices.

As with the first text, there are many people who contributed to create this work. At Sandia National Laboratories, my sincere thanks to Mike Benson, Betty Biringer, Jim Blankenship, Frank Bouchier, Allen Camp, Lee Cunningham, Evangeline Delgado, Debi Eaglin, Ron Glaser, Steve Highland, John Hunter, Liz Jaramillo, Steve Jordan, Vern Koonce, Dan Keller, Carole Lojek, Dennis Miyoshi, Mike Moulton, Dale Murray, Sharon O'Connor, Randy Peterson, Charles Ringler, Diane Ross, JR Russell, Joe Sandoval, Steve Scott, Boris Starr, Basil Steele, Dave Swahlan, John Wharton, Ron Williams, John Wirsbinski, Tommy Woodall and Greg Wyse. Outside Sandia, Joe Carlon, Dennis Giever, Ernie Kun, Brad Rogers and Joe St Pierre provided additional assistance. The expert information presented in this text belongs to them; any errors are strictly mine. I am also grateful to Cindy Schifano of Smiths Detection and Don Utz of Kontek for permission to use the pictures that appear in Chapters 7 and 9.

At Elsevier, Pam Chester, Heather Furrow, Mark Listevnik, Chris Nolin, and Jenn Soucy provided me the gentle and competent guidance to meet publishing guidelines and schedules, and not go slowly crazy during the process. Finally, in keeping with the tradition established in the *Design* book, my special thanks to Doug, Fuzzy, and Kasey.

Since the attacks of 9/11, the world has changed in many ways. I hope this book helps students understand basic vulnerability assessment principles and security professionals achieve their goals while trying to do so much with limited resources.

Mary Lynn Garcia
May 2005

1

Introduction to Vulnerability Assessment

This text is a follow-on to the previously published *Design and Evaluation of Physical Protection Systems* (Garcia, 2001). That book (hereafter referred to as the *Design* textbook) provided an overview of the principles and concepts that must be considered when implementing a physical protection system (PPS); this one is a description of how to apply those principles and concepts to identify the vulnerabilities of an installed PPS and propose effective upgrades if needed. This is the basis of all vulnerability assessments (VAs) conducted by Sandia National Laboratories (SNL) during the last 30 years for a wide spectrum of customers including the U.S. Department of Energy (DOE), U.S. Department of Defense (DoD), North Atlantic Treaty Organization (NATO), U.S. Department of State (DOS), Government Services Administration (GSA), dam and water systems, prisons, schools, communities, and chemical companies.

A VA is a systematic evaluation in which quantitative or qualitative techniques are used to predict PPS component performance and overall system effectiveness by identifying exploitable weaknesses in asset protection for a defined threat. After the VA identifies weaknesses, it is used to establish the requirements for an upgraded PPS design. In addition, a VA is also used to support management decisions regarding protection system upgrades. Risk assessment and VA are closely related activities, to the point that many security professionals use the terms interchangeably. This may not present a huge problem in practice, but it does hinder communication between and among security service providers and customers.

The VA process can be broken into three distinct phases—planning, conducting the VA, and reporting and using the results. The process itself is part of the larger risk assessment process. Each of the phases will be described in detail in the remaining chapters of this text. The key points discussed in this chapter include:

- Risk Management and Vulnerability Assessment
- Risk Assessment and the Vulnerability Assessment Process
- Vulnerability Assessment Process Overview
- Vulnerability Assessment and Systems Engineering

This text is concerned with vulnerability assessment of a PPS, but the concepts can be applied to cyber protection, personnel protection, and overall security protection at a facility or across an enterprise. For the sake of clarity, throughout this text enterprise includes organizations, companies, agencies, governments, or any other entity with the need to manage security risks. Assets include people, property, information, or any other possession of an enterprise that has value.

It is important to differentiate security from safety when discussing vulnerability assessment. Safety is defined as the measures (people, procedures, or equipment) used to prevent or detect an abnormal condition that can endanger people, property, or the enterprise. These include accidents caused by human carelessness, inattentiveness, and lack of training or other unintentional events. Security, on the other hand, includes the measures used to protect people, property, or the enterprise from malevolent human threats. This includes civil disturbances, sabotage, pilferage, theft of critical property or information, workplace violence, extortion, or other intentional attacks on assets by a human. A good security VA will consider safety controls because some safety measures will aid in detection and response to security events (sprinklers will fight fires regardless of the cause), but some attacks require additional detection and response capability. For example, a disgruntled employee can sabotage critical manufacturing equipment and reduce production to a significant extent. Without security controls, it could be difficult to determine quickly enough whether this is an intentional act of sabotage and prevent a significant loss of revenue.

Risk Management and Vulnerability Assessment

Risk management is the set of actions an enterprise takes to address identified risks and includes avoidance, reduction, spreading, transfer, elimination, and acceptance options (Grose, 1987). Good risk management programs will likely include a combination of these options. Risk avoidance is accomplished by removing the source of the risk. For example, a company may choose to buy a critical component from another company, rather than manufacture it. This removes the production line as a sabotage target. Risk reduction is achieved by taking some actions to lower risk to the enterprise to reduce the severity of the loss. This is the goal of many security programs—lower risk by implementing at least some security measures. Risk can also be spread among multiple locations, perhaps by having similar production capability at more than one enterprise facility. Then, loss of capability at one site may be managed by increasing production at the other locations. Another example of risk spreading is the distribution of assets across a large industrial facility. By separating the assets, fewer assets may be at risk during any given adversary attack. Risk transfer is the use of insurance to cover the replacement or other costs incurred as a result of the loss. This is an important tool in many security systems. Risk acceptance is the recognition that there will always be some residual risk. The key is in knowingly determining an acceptable level, rather than unwitting acceptance. In security risk management, these decisions are based on the consequence of loss of the asset, the defined threat, and the risk tolerance of the enterprise. A tradeoff analysis must be performed to ensure that the dollars spent on physical security provide a cost-effective solution to security issues. If other risk management options provide equal or better results at lower cost, the use of a PPS may not be justified.

Security is only one facet of risk and therefore must be considered in the context of holistic risk management across the enterprise, along with other categories such as market, credit, operational, strategic, liquidity, and hazard risks. The relationships among risk management, risk assessment, and vulnerability assessment are shown in Figure 1-1.

To frame the relationship between risk assessment and risk management, consider definitions provided by Kaplan and Garrick (1981), who state that in risk assessment, the analyst attempts to answer the three questions: What can go wrong? What is the likelihood that it would go wrong? What are the consequences? The answers to these questions help identify, measure, quantify, and evaluate risks. Then, risk management builds on risk assessment by answering a second set of questions: What can be done? What options are available? What are their associated tradeoffs in terms of costs, benefits, and risks? What are the impacts of current management decisions on future options? The answer to the last question provides the optimal solution. Total risk management results from this process, where total risk management is defined as a systematic, statistically based, holistic process that builds on formal risk assessment and management by answering the two sets of questions and addressing the sources of system failures.

A security risk assessment is the process of answering the first three questions using threat, likelihood of attack, and consequence of loss as their benchmarks.

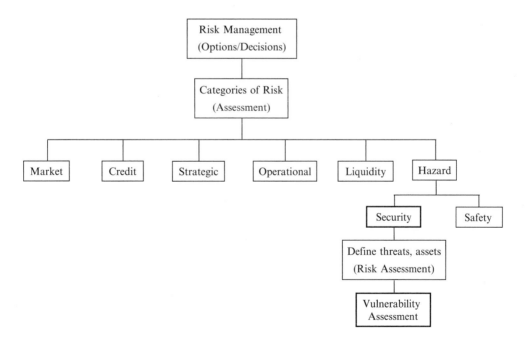

Figure 1-1 Relationship between Risk Management and Vulnerability Assessment. Risks across an enterprise must be managed holistically, and those that are identified as being above an acceptable level must be addressed. Vulnerability assessment is one of the constituent pieces of security risk assessment and is used to support risk management decisions.

A thorough security risk assessment would consider risks in the component parts of a security system (cyber, executive, transportation protection, etc.) to facilitate informed risk decisions across the enterprise. As applied to the VA of a PPS, risk assessment is an evaluation of the PPS supported by a number of analysis methodologies, including:

- Threat analysis
- Consequence analysis
- Event and fault tree analyses
- Vulnerability analysis

The first three techniques are reviewed in Chapter 4; vulnerability analysis is the subject of Chapter 11 of this text.

Risk Assessment and the Vulnerability Assessment Process

Most facilities or enterprises routinely conduct risk assessments of their security systems to verify that they are protecting corporate assets and to identify areas that may need additional attention. These assessments are defined differently for different enterprises, but in general they include consideration of the likelihood of a negative event, in this case a security incident and the consequence of that event. The *Design* textbook ended with a description of risk assessment and provided a formula that can be used to calculate risk, using qualitative or quantitative measures. That discussion, with one addition, is repeated here.

Security risk can be measured qualitatively or quantitatively through the use of the following equation:

$$R = P_A * (1 - P_E) * C$$

Where R = Risk to the facility (or stakeholders) of an adversary gaining access to, or stealing, critical assets. Range is 0 to 1.0, with 0 being no risk and 1.0 being maximum risk. Risk is calculated for a period of time, such as 1 year or 5 years.

P_A = Probability of an adversary attack during a period of time. This can be difficult to determine, but generally there are records available to assist in this effort. This probability ranges from 0 (no chance at all of an attack) to 1.0 (certainty of attack). Sometimes in the calculation of risk, we assume that there will be an attack, which mathematically sets P_A = 1.0. This is called a conditional risk, where the condition is that the adversary attacks. This does not mean that there will absolutely be an attack, but that the probability of attack is unknown or the asset is so valuable that it will be protected anyway. This approach can be used for any asset but is generally reserved for the most critical assets of a facility, where the consequence of loss is unacceptably high, even if P_A is low. For these assets, a PPS is generally required.

P_E = PI * PN, where P_I is the probability of interruption by responders, and P_N is the probability of neutralization of the adversary, given interruption. P_N can include a range of tactics from verbal commands up through deadly force. The appropriate response depends on the defined threat and consequence of loss of the asset. P_E represents the vulnerability of the PPS to the defined threat.

C = Consequence Value. A value from 0 to 1 that relates to the severity of the occurrence of the event. This is a normalizing factor, which allows the conditional risk value to be compared to other risks across the facility. A consequence table of all events can be created which covers the loss spectrum, from highest to lowest. By using this consequence table, risk can be normalized over all possible events. Then, limited PPS resources can be appropriately allocated to ensure that the highest consequence assets are protected and meet an acceptable risk.

Note that this equation introduces the use of a new term, the *probability of neutralization* (P_N). This was discussed only briefly in the *Design* book, because many facilities do not have an immediate response to security events. It is included here because response is a part of VA at all facilities and is discussed as part of the response subsystem evaluation in Chapter 10.

Using probabilistic risk assessment is more formal, scientific, technical, quantitative, and objective when compared to risk management, which involves value judgment and heuristics and is more subjective, qualitative, societal, and political. Ideally, the use of probabilities is based on objective likelihoods, but in security it is common to use more subjective likelihoods based on intuition, expertise, partial, defective, or erroneous data and occasionally, dubious theories. This is important because these are major sources of uncertainty, and uncertainty is a major element of risk. Additionally, these measures can reduce the credibility of the security risk assessment for senior management, who are used to seeing documented data in standard analysis models. In security systems, this uncertainty is even larger than normal, owing to the lack of dependable (that is, quantifiable) data for all types of adversary attacks.

An additional use of the risk equation is that the security risk life cycle can be viewed in context. When considering security systems and the attack timeline, the attack can be broken into three discrete phases: pre-attack, which is the time the adversary takes to plan the attack; the attack phase, when the adversary actually shows up to attack the facility, and the attack has started; and post-attack, when the adversary has completed the attack, and the consequences of a successful attack occur. If the problem is approached this way, each term in the equation is of primary importance during different phases of the attack. As such, P_A is most useful during the pre-attack phase. This is where intelligence agencies and deterrence have their biggest effect. Intelligence agencies gather information concerning threats and provide assessments about their likelihood of attack. These agencies

may even develop enough information to disrupt an attack by collecting enough legal evidence to arrest the adversary, through tips from inside sources, or by alerting targeted enterprises, allowing them to increase security protection. All of these activities will have an effect on P_A. Heightened security responses to intelligence assessments indicating potential attacks on Citibank and the stock exchange in New York, and the World Bank in Washington, DC, are recent examples of pre-attack influences.

If a quantitative approach is used, the P_A and C terms can be calculated using historical data and consequence criteria, respectively. In a qualitative analysis, these terms can be represented using descriptors such as likely, very likely, or not likely for P_A; and critical, severe, or minimal for the C term. This determination is based on the capability of the threat and the consequence of loss of the asset. If the likelihood of attack is high, but the consequence is low (think about shoplifting at one store in an enterprise), the problem to be solved is easier than if both P_A and C are high. (This ignores the cumulative effects of shoplifting across the enterprise. Many thefts of low-value items can add up to a high overall impact and this is part of the analysis.) There are times when either approach is appropriate, and the choice should be driven by the consequence of loss. This is based on the assumption that assets with a higher consequence of loss will attract more capable and motivated adversaries (threats), which in turn will require a PPS that is correspondingly more effective. Figure 1-2 represents the transition from qualitative to quantitative analysis, using consequence as the discriminator.

This section ends with definition of some terms that are used in risk assessments, particularly with respect to the probability of attack by an adversary. These are the proper definitions of these terms; some enterprises may use them differently. Probability is a number that is,

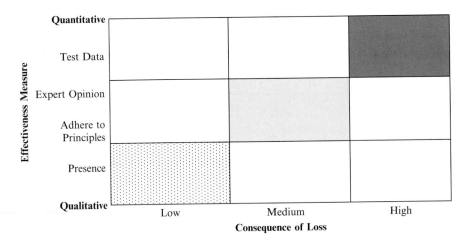

Figure 1-2 Application of Qualitative and Quantitative Analysis Approaches. Qualitative analysis uses presence of PPS components and adherence to PPS principles as system effectiveness measures. A quantitative analysis uses specific component performance measures derived from rigorous testing to predict overall system effectiveness. At any given facility, either or both techniques may be used depending on the consequence of loss of the asset. Relative value of PPS components based on expert opinion is another form of analysis of system effectiveness; however, the outcome depends heavily on the knowledge and experience of the expert.

by definition, between 0 and 1, and may or may not be time dependent. (As an example, the probability of snow on any given day in Ohio may be .25, but the probability of snow in Ohio is 1.0 over the next year.) This is discussed further in the next section. Although probability of attack is routinely cited as a threat measure, it is important to note that there frequently is not enough data to support a true probability. For example, there is no statistical data to support the probability of terrorist attacks. That fact, however, has not prevented the massive expenditure of dollars by governments and commercial enterprises to increase security at airports, seaports, critical infrastructures, and other facilities since 9/11. This is a good example of high-consequence, low-probability events and the use of conditional risk. For some assets, the consequence of loss is unacceptably high, and measures are taken to prevent successful adversary attacks, regardless of the low likelihood of

attack. Frequency refers to how many times an event has happened over a specified time and is also called a rate. Annual loss exposure (ALE) is an example of a frequency often used in security risk assessments. Likelihood may be a frequency, probability, or qualitative measure of occurrence. This is more of a catch-all term and generally implies a less rigorous treatment of the measure. Haimes (2004) has written a thorough discussion of risk modeling, assessment, and management techniques that can be used in security or general risk applications.

Statistics and Quantitative Analysis

In any discussion of quantitative security system effectiveness, the subject of statistics of security performance arises. To many, statistics is a subject that arouses suspicion and even dread; however, there are a few fairly simple concepts that form the basis of statistical analysis of security effectiveness. Most of these concepts are related to the possible outcomes of a security event. A security event occurs when a security component (people, procedures, or equipment) encounters a stimulus and performs its intended task; for example, when something, such as a human or small animal, enters the detection envelope of an intrusion sensor. There are four possible outcomes of this event:

1. The sensor successfully detects a human-size object.
2. The sensor fails to detect a human-size object.
3. The sensor successfully ignores a smaller-than-human size object.
4. The sensor fails to ignore a smaller-than-human size object.

The successes and failures are related such that when a human-size object is presented, there are two complementary results and when a smaller-than-human size object is presented, there are also two complementary results. This fact is used later in the discussion. Sensors are the example used here, but this principle applies to any of the probabilities used in this text—the success or failure of a PPS component or the system in performing its intended task can be measured.

Most statistical analysis of security performance is based on these four possible outcomes. The rate at which a sensor successfully detects objects is described as the detection rate. For example, if a sensor successfully detects a human-size object nine times out of ten events the detection rate for that group of ten events is 0.9 or 90%. This is a statistic but is not yet a probability. The detection rate can be turned into a probability when coupled with a confidence level. A confidence level is established based on the number of events that are analyzed; the more data available, the more confidence there is in the probability. This is easily understood when consider-

ing a common example. If a person tosses a coin and the outcome is heads, it would be unwise to assume that every coin toss will result in heads. However, if that person tosses a coin 100 times and 49 results are heads and 51 results are tails, there is a fairly high confidence that the outcomes will be about 50/50. If the experiment is continued to include 1,000 trials, the confidence in the estimate of the likely results is even higher. At this point the rate can be estimated with some statistical confidence, and this estimate is a probability. In other words, a probability is an estimate of predicted outcomes of identical trials stated with a confidence level. If 100% confidence is required, an infinite number of tests are required. In reality, when designing performance tests, a confidence level is chosen that requires performance of a reasonable number of trials.

It is not the intent of this section to teach readers how to calculate the statistics of security component effectiveness but, rather, to familiarize them with the terminology and underlying concepts as applied to a PPS. For example, if a metal detector is tested by carrying a gun through it 20 times and it detects all 20 times, the probability of detection can be calculated at a specified confidence level. Often the confidence level used for security component testing is 95%. Using this confidence level, the probability calculated for the metal detector based on the 20 trials is 0.85 (it is often said that the probability is 85% but in proper statistical terminology a probability is always a number between zero and one). In simpler language, there is a 95% confidence that the metal detector will detect the gun at least 85% of the time. The actual detection rate may be higher, but this is what can be supported given the amount of data collected. If the metal detector is tested 30 times at the same 95% confidence, the probability is now 0.9. Again restating into simpler language, there is a 95% confidence that the metal detector will detect the gun at least 90% of the time.

Sometimes it is more useful to classify PPS component performance into error rates rather than probabilities. These error rates are the mathematical complement of the success rates, which is the number of trials minus the number of successes (i.e., the number of failures). The error rates are stated as false accept and false reject rates. In the preceding sensor example, not detecting the human-size object is a false accept and detecting a smaller-than-human size object is a false reject. This example is used to show that these are the same possible outcomes; however, error rates are seldom used when describing the performance of detection sensor devices. Error rates are much more useful when characterizing the performance of entry control devices, particularly when evaluating the performance of biometric identity verification devices. These devices measure some biological feature, such as a fingerprint, to verify the identity of an individual. In this case, false acceptance of a fingerprint from someone who should not be allowed into a security area and false rejection of someone who should be allowed to enter a secured area are a useful way to view the data.

Other factors of interest in security component evaluation include discrimination and susceptibility to noise. Discrimination describes a sensor's ability to ignore an object that is of the appropriate magnitude but is not the intended target. Often, this is beyond the technical capability of the device. In the preceding sensor example, a human-size object may or may not have specific characteristics that allow the sensor to discriminate between a human and a human-size animal like a small deer or large dog. When the sensor does not have the ability to discriminate between stimuli of equal magnitude, another statistic, the nuisance alarm rate, is used. A nuisance alarm is caused when the sensor detects an object that is of sufficient magnitude but benign in nature. Anyone who has had a belt buckle cause an alarm in an airport metal

detector has experienced a nuisance alarm (assuming that person was not also carrying a gun!). The sources of nuisance alarms are easy to identify when the alarm is assessed by direct human observation or by viewing an image using a video camera. Understanding the causes of nuisance alarms is important in both design and analysis of a PPS. Installing a sensor that has low discrimination to an object or condition that is continually present in the sensor's operating environment will lead to a high nuisance alarm rate, thus lowering confidence in the system. In this scenario, human operators eventually discount alarms and may not pay sufficient attention to a real alarm when it occurs.

Some technologies are also susceptible to noise. Noise in the sensor includes sound, electromagnetic, or even chemical sources. This noise can be present in the background or internal to the system. Whenever a sensor alarms on external or internal noise, this is defined as a false alarm. In the same way that nuisance alarms reduce system effectiveness, false alarms also reduce system effectiveness. Indeed, false alarms can further erode confidence in the PPS because there is no observable alarm source present.

Throughout the discussions of security component performance in this text, it is important to remember that the four possible outcomes of any event are considered. This information, together with the concepts of discrimination and susceptibility to noise, form the basis of almost all security component performance evaluation. Combined with defeat analysis (which is discussed in other chapters), the full picture of PPS effectiveness emerges.

Vulnerability Assessment Process Overview

The evaluation techniques presented in this text use a system performance-based approach to meeting the PPS objectives.

Recall that the primary functions of a PPS are detection, delay, and response (see Figure 1-3). Each of these functional subsystems is described in the following chapters and includes a description of both quantitative and qualitative methods of evaluating PPS components at a facility. Quantitative techniques are recommended for facilities with high-consequence loss assets; qualitative techniques can be used if there is no quantitative data available or if the asset value is much lower. It is important to determine before the start of the VA whether a qualitative or quantitative analysis technique will be used. This ensures that the VA team collects the appropriate data and reports their results in a form that is useful for the analysis.

When performing a VA, the general purpose is to evaluate each component of the PPS to estimate their performance as installed at the facility. Once this is done, an estimate of overall system performance is made. The key to a good VA is accurately estimating component performance. When using a quantitative approach, this is done by starting with a tested performance value for a particular PPS component, such as a sensor, and degrading its performance based on how the device is installed, maintained, tested, and integrated into the overall PPS. For qualitative analysis, performance of each component is degraded based on the same conditions, but the performance of the device is assigned a level of effectiveness, such as high, medium, or low, rather than a number. In addition, component performance must be evaluated under all weather conditions, facility states, and considering all threats. The following sections introduce the various stages and activities of a VA.

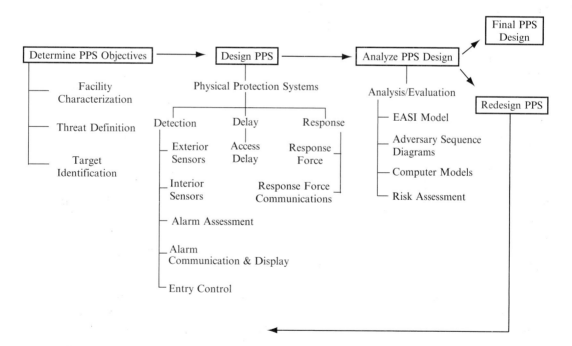

Figure 1-3 PPS Evaluation Process. As in the *Design* textbook, this process provides the framework for conducting a vulnerability assessment. Although frequently not part of the VA, the protection objectives must be known before evaluating the facility.

Planning the Vulnerability Assessment

Before a VA can be performed at a facility, a certain amount of preliminary work must be done to plan and manage the VA so that the customer is provided a useful product. The use of common project management principles and techniques provides a structure and a well-accepted method of approaching the technical, administrative, and business aspects of a VA. At a high level, a project can be broken into three major stages—planning, managing the work, and closeout.

Project Management

Projects, by their definition, have a defined start and end date. There is a point in time when the work did not exist (before the project), when it does exist (the project), and when it does not exist again (after the project). Many VA projects start with an initial customer contact, perhaps as a follow-on to existing work, a reference from another person or business, or as a result of a marketing activity. Project planning starts with understanding what the customer wants or needs. This stage of the project normally involves meetings with the customer to discuss what problems they are having or want to avoid, to understand why they are motivated to do this now, and to discover any specific constraints they may have. Defining the project includes determining the scope of work, as well as what needs to be done, over what period of time, and the cost of the final product. The project scope should state the project objectives and major constraints, such as dollars available or time to complete. Generally, the project is defined in a master document, statement of work, contract, memorandum of agreement, or some other equivalent document. This master document is usually supplemented by a requirements document, which is a summary of the technical specifications or performance required for the delivered product.

After the project has been approved, the customer has sent funding, the project team has been identified, and other administrative issues are set, the actual work can begin. Managing the project includes providing customer support; following the project plan; resolving major and minor project issues on a timely basis; and keeping the project on schedule, within budget and scope, and performing as expected. All of these aspects of the project are organized so that communication between the project leader and the customer and the project team occurs regularly, project risks are managed, product quality maintains an acceptable level, and all project metrics are monitored and remain in compliance.

At some point, all the direct project work is completed, all deliverables are in the customer's hands, the last status reports to the customer have been provided, and the project is complete; however, there are still some remaining issues that must be addressed before pronouncing the project complete. Project closeout can be broken into three areas: financial, administrative, and technical. Financial closeout of the project provides a final accounting of all project costs and allocation of funds to complete the project. Administrative closeout tasks include collecting all project documentation, storing it in an archive, destroying drafts or working papers that are no longer needed, returning any customer-owned equipment or documents, and verifying that all sensitive information is properly marked and stored securely. The technical closeout of the project can include a project closeout meeting, a lessons learned review, and a closeout report to the customer or internal management.

The use of good project management principles, tools, and skills will help scope, define, manage, and complete a successful VA project for both the VA provider and the customer. A combination of project planning and management techniques minimizes the effects of inevitable project problems and provides a framework to work through major project hurdles.

Establish the Vulnerability Assessment Team

The functional responsibilities of a VA team require a project leader and appropriate subject matter experts (SMEs). Many VA teams will use only a few personnel to serve these roles. Each team member may perform multiple functions, but all appropriate functions must be performed for a thorough VA. The major roles and responsibilities of the VA team include:

- Project Lead
- Systems Engineer
- Security System Engineer
- Subject Matter Expert (SME)—Sensors
- SME—Alarm Assessment
- SME—Alarm Communication and Display (AC&D)
- SME—Entry Control
- SME—Delay
- SME—Response
- SME—Communication Systems
- SME—Analyst
- SME—On-site Personnel

All members of the VA team should understand their roles and responsibilities, including what information or activities they are expected to contribute to the overall assessment.

Project Kick-Off Meetings

Before starting the VA, it is helpful to have kick-off meetings with the project team and the customer. The project team kick-off meeting is meant to familiarize all team members with the project scope, deliverables, schedule, funding, and to answer any questions. The project leader should provide the team with a detailed description of the project including the customer's objectives, the project schedule and budget, a review of any travel arrangements that must be made, the deliverables and their format, and how customer contact will be managed. This meeting is also the time to start planning the VA. An overview of the facility layout, geography, weather, and operations can be presented, along with any information concerning threats and targets. Usually, the tools that will be used in the analysis are known, but if not, this is a good time to initiate discussion about appropriate analysis tools.

It can be useful to summarize all of the known information about the project and facility in a VA team guide. This guide serves as a means of communicating information to all project team members and as a living document that captures facility information. The guide is a reasonably detailed description of the planned activities, but does not need to be extremely lengthy. It is expected that some portions of the guide will be common to all VAs and some portions will be unique to a specific facility. The team guide should include the background of the VA, how it will be conducted, team assignments, logistics, and administrative details.

Whatever the scope of the VA, a variety of site-specific data is required to complete the planning phase of the VA. This information is necessary to plan and carry out the VA in the most efficient and least intrusive manner possible. The more this information is known before the team gets to the facility, the easier and faster the VA will be, thus limiting the cost and duration of the team visit. Typical information that is required includes drawings of the facility, number of employees, operational hours, locations of critical assets, existing PPS equipment, weather conditions, on-site personnel contact information, and location of a workspace for the VA team. If known, this information is included in the team guide.

Another important aspect of the VA project is a briefing to senior management of the facility that will be evaluated. The better the purpose of the VA is communicated to management, the easier the evaluation will be, with few objections to team activities. This briefing should be clear about the goals and objectives of the VA, how it will be used, when it will be completed, and how the results will be communicated. For some facilities, senior management will receive the report directly. For others, the report may be submitted to another group, who will then distribute the results to the facility. Once the VA team arrives on-site, it may be necessary to have a kick-off meeting to explain the VA to lower level facility personnel. Senior management, facility points-of-contact, the facility security manager, operations and safety representatives, the entire VA team, and other stakeholders should be invited to this briefing. If facility management has already heard a briefing on the project, they may not attend, although it is probably good practice to invite them or a representative. It is always a welcome touch to invite the most senior manager at the facility to address the group and express her support of the process; at the very least, the security manager of the facility should be an active part of this briefing, especially if the VA team is from off-site. Every effort should be made to provide a kickoff meeting at the start of the VA, but if this is not possible, the project leader should be prepared to brief managers and staff at the facility before collecting data in each of the functional areas.

Protection Objectives

To successfully complete a good VA, it is critical that protection system objectives are well understood. These objectives include threat definition, target identification, and facility characterization. Each enterprise defines vulnerability assessment and risk assessment differently, and as a result some facilities may not have defined threats or identified assets. At facilities where the threat and assets have not already been defined, this task must be included as part of the VA project, although this is generally part of a risk assessment. This will likely add cost and time to the project; therefore, it is critical to understand this before finalizing these details in the project plan.

Knowing the threat is one of the required inputs to a VA because the threat establishes the performance that is required from the PPS. We would not evaluate a PPS protecting an asset from vandals the same way that we would for a system protecting an asset from terrorists. By describing the threat, the assumptions that were made to perform the assessment are documented and linked to the decisions that are made regarding the need for upgrades. As such, threat definition is a tool that helps facility managers understand how adversary capabilities impact asset protection and helps PPS designers understand the requirements of the final PPS.

In addition to threat definition, the VA team must also have an understanding of the assets to be protected at the facility. As with threat definition, some customers do not have their assets identified and prioritized before performing a VA. In this case, this must be accomplished before performing the VA. There are three methods for target identification including manual listing of targets, logic diagrams to identify vital areas for sabotage attacks, and use of consequence analysis to screen and prioritize targets. After threats have been defined and assets have been prioritized, a considerable amount of information will exist that is used to establish protection system objectives. The volume of information can be combined into a matrix that relates probability of attack, threat level and tactic, and consequence of loss of assets.

Facility Characterization

The major part of a VA is facility characterization, which consists of evaluating the PPS at the facility. The goal of a VA is to identify PPS components in the functional areas of detection, delay, and response and gather sufficient data to estimate their performance against specific threats. The PPS is characterized at the component and system level, and vulnerabilities to defeat by the threat are documented. Data collection is the core of PPS characterization; accurate data are the basis for conducting a true analysis of the ability of the PPS to meet its defined objectives. Accuracy, however, is only one of several factors to consider. The data gathered must be appropriate to the purpose and scope of the VA, and the quantity and form of the data must be sufficient based on available resources and desired confidence in the results.

A facility tour is usually conducted early in a VA. During the initial facility tour, the VA team begins to gather information regarding the general layout of the facility, the locations of key assets, information about facility operations and production capabilities, and locations and types of PPS components. Review of key documents and selected records are two important PPS characterization activities. These are useful in the evaluation of the effectiveness of a PPS and may begin during the planning phase of a VA. This step of a VA will also include interviews with key facility personnel. Interviews are critical to clarify information and to gain greater insight into specific facility operating procedures. Interviews with personnel at all organizational levels are recommended. Testing is the most valuable data-collection method for evaluating the effectiveness of a PPS. Evaluation testing can determine whether personnel have the skills and abilities to perform their duties, whether procedures work, and whether equipment is functional and appropriate. Evaluation tests include functional, operability, and performance tests. Functional tests verify that a device is on, and that it is performing as expected (i.e., a sensor still has a probability of detection of 0.9). Operability tests verify that a device is on and working (i.e., a sensor is on and detects, but has moved due to vibration, so is aimed at the wrong location). Performance testing is the characterization of a device by repeating the same test enough times to establish a measure of device capability against different threats. (A sensor is tested many times using crawling, walking, and running modes and under day, night, and varying weather conditions to fully characterize the probability of detection and nuisance alarm rate.) Because performance tests are fairly rigorous and require many repetitions over a period of time, they are generally impractical during a VA. Performance testing is typically performed in a laboratory or nonoperational facility.

One of the goals of the VA team before any system analysis is to identify the various facility states that can exist at the facility. A VA is used to establish vulnerabilities at a facility at all times of the day and at all times of the year. As such, the team must understand the various facility states, so they can determine if the PPS is more or less vulnerable at these times. If the team does not identify these states and determine system effectiveness during all of these different states, the VA will be incomplete and may lead to a false sense of protection. Examples of facility states include normal operating hours, nonoperational hours, a strike at the facility, emergencies such as fire or bomb threats, and shift changes. Once all project planning is complete and protection objectives are understood, the VA team is ready to visit the facility and start collecting data.

Data Collection—Detection

The detection function in a PPS includes exterior and interior intrusion sensors, alarm assessment, entry control, and the alarm communication and display subsystem all working together. Intrusion detection is defined as knowledge of a person or vehicle attempting to gain unauthorized entry into a protected area by someone who can authorize or initiate an appropriate response. An effective PPS must first detect an intrusion, generate an alarm, and then transmit that alarm to a location for assessment and appropriate response. The most reliable method of detecting an adversary intrusion is through the use of sensors, but this can also be accomplished by personnel working in the area or the on-site guard force. Exterior sensors are those used in an outdoor environment, and interior sensors are those used inside buildings.

Intrusion Sensors

Intrusion sensor performance is described by three fundamental characteristics: probability of detection (P_D), nuisance alarm rate (NAR), and vulnerability to defeat. These three fundamental characteristics are heavily dependent on the principle of operation of a sensor and the capability of the defined threat. An understanding of these characteristics and the principle of operation of a sensor is essential for evaluating the intrusion sensor subsystem at a facility. Different types and models of sensors have different vulnerabilities to defeat. Sensors can be defeated by spoofing or bypass, and consideration of these attack modes are part of the VA. Exterior sensors are grouped into three application types: freestanding, buried line, or fence associated sensors. Interior sensors are grouped as boundary penetration, interior motion, and proximity sensors.

Exterior perimeters are generally found only in high-security applications such as prisons, military bases, research facilities, critical infrastructure facilities, and industrial hazardous facilities (i.e., chemical plants). With a large percentage of the critical infrastructure in the United States owned and operated by the private sector, there is more interest in using exterior sensors in private industry since 9/11. If exterior sensors are not in use at a facility, this is an implicit indication that assets are low value or that the expected threat is low and no evaluation is necessary. The overall evaluation of exterior sensors will include attention to details such as sensor application, installation, testing, maintenance, nuisance alarm rate, and performance against the expected threats. If the threat is able to cut, climb, or bridge fences, this must be considered during the VA. The goal of exterior sensor evaluation is to provide an estimate of sensor performance (P_D) against defined threats, along with supporting notes, pictures, and observations that support this estimate. This will help establish the baseline performance of the overall PPS and, if not acceptable, will provide opportunities for upgrade improvements. Factors that will cause performance degradation include nuisance alarm rate and ease of defeat of the sensor through bypass or spoofing.

Interior sensors are used to aid detection of intrusions inside buildings or other structures. Unlike exterior sensors, interior sensors are commonly used at all types of commercial, private, and government facilities. Just as with exterior sensors, there are several factors that contribute to overall sensor performance. The most common interior sensors are balanced magnetic switches (BMS), glass-break sensors, passive infrared sensors (PIR), interior monostatic microwave sensors, video motion detectors (VMDs), and combinations of sensors, usually PIR and microwave sensors, in dual technology devices.

Interior boundary penetration sensors should detect someone penetrating the enclosure or shell through existing openings (doors, windows, and ventilation ducts) or by destroying walls, ceilings, and floors. Early detection gives more time for the response team to arrive; detection should occur during entry rather than afterward. Volumetric detection uses sensors to detect an intruder moving through interior space toward a target. The detection volume is usually an enclosed area, such as a room or hallway. Most interior volumes provide little delay other than the time required to move from the boundary to the target. Common sensors used for volumetric sensing are microwave and passive infrared radiation. Point sensors, also known as proximity sensors, are placed on or around the target to be protected. In a high-security application, point sensors usually form the final layer of protection, after boundary penetration sensors and volumetric sensors. Capacitance proximity, pressure, and strain sensors are commonly used for point protection, but a number of sensors previously discussed as boundary penetration and volumetric sensors are readily applicable to point protection.

Use of technology is not the only means of sensing intrusions into a facility or area. Employees working in the area, guards on patrol, or video surveillance are other commonly used techniques. These may be effective against very low threats, but testing has shown that these methods will not be effective against more capable threats or when protecting critical assets. Humans do not make good detectors, especially over a long period of time. The lack of firm criteria for what is an adversary intrusion, and the difficulty in recognizing this in time to prevent the attack, as well as safety concerns for employees, all contribute to this problem. Reliable intrusion sensing is best achieved through the use of sensors and is also less expensive than hiring guards. Another weakness of human sensing of intrusions is that it is easier to divert attention away from intrusions, particularly if they are engaged in other activities, such as doing their primary job, answering phones, or assisting visitors. If the defined threat or asset value is significant, sensing through human observation should be degraded during the VA.

When evaluating interior sensors, the goal is to make a determination of how well installed devices will perform against the expected threat. If sensors are present, there is an implicit expectation that they will be effective in protecting assets. Consideration must be given to the principle of operation of the sensor and its operating environment, installation and interconnection of equipment, NAR, maintenance, and the defined threat. The environment associated with interior areas is normally controlled and is, therefore, predictable and measurable. Consequently, it is possible to evaluate sensors for their performance in a particular environment.

After tours, interviews, and testing are complete, the VA team should document intrusion sensing subsystem strengths and weaknesses. Remember that intrusion detection is just one part of the VA, and the analysis cannot be completed until similar information is collected about the other protection subsystems. This part of the VA concentrates on the probability of detection (P_D) for each sensing type—exterior or interior sensors or sensing by humans. Estimates may be made using qualitative or quantitative criteria.

Alarm Assessment

After an alarm is generated using sensors or human observation, the alarm must be assessed to determine the cause and decide what, if any, response is needed. The detection function is not complete without alarm assessment. There are two purposes of assessment. The first is to determine the cause of each alarm, which includes deciding whether the alarm is due to an adversary attack or a nuisance alarm. The second purpose of assessment is to provide additional information about an intrusion that can be provided to responders. This information includes specific details such as who, what, where, and how many. The best assessment systems use video cameras to automatically capture images that show the cause of an alarm and then display these images to an operator who can assess the alarm. Assessment may also be accomplished through human observation, but this is much slower and not as effective.

It is important to differentiate video assessment from video surveillance when conducting a VA. Alarm assessment refers to direct observation of alarm sources by humans or to immediate image capture of a sensor detection zone at the time of an intrusion alarm. This assessment zone and the captured image can be reviewed to determine the cause of the alarm and initiate the proper response to the alarm. Video surveillance uses cameras to continually monitor all activity in an area, without benefit of an intrusion sensor to direct operator attention to a specific event or area. Many surveillance systems do not use human operators, but record activity on storage media for later review. The most effective security systems will use video assessment and not surveillance to determine causes of alarms.

A video assessment subsystem allows security personnel to rapidly determine whether an intrusion has taken place at a remote location. Major subsystem components include:

- Camera and lens
- Lighting system
- Transmission system
- Video recorder and/or storage
- Video monitor
- Video controller

At the end of this part of the VA, an estimate of the probability of assessment (P_{As}) must be provided for use in the system analysis. This probability is a result of the combined effects of video image quality and resolution, speed of capture of images, proper installation and maintenance of all components, and integration of sensor detection zones with camera field-of-view coverage. The most important factor in assessment subsystem

evaluation is to verify that video images containing the alarm source provide enough detail to an operator to allow an accurate determination of the cause of the alarm.

Entry Control

The entry control subsystem includes all the technologies, procedures, databases, and personnel that are used to monitor movement of people and materials into and out of a facility. An entry control system functions in a total PPS by allowing the movement of authorized personnel and material through normal access routes and by detecting and delaying unauthorized movement of personnel and material. Entry control elements may be found at a facility boundary or perimeter, such as personnel and vehicle portals, at building entry points, or at doors into rooms or other special areas within a building. In addition to checks for authorized personnel, certain prohibited items or other materials may also be of interest on entry or exit. For evaluation purposes, entry control is defined as the physical equipment used to control the movement of people or material into an area. Access control refers to the process of managing databases or other records, determining the parameters of authorized entry, such as whom or what will be granted access, when they may enter, and where access will occur. Access controls are an important part of the entry control subsystem.

The primary objective of controlling entry to facilities or areas is to ensure that only authorized persons are allowed to enter and to log these events for documentation purposes. The objective of searching vehicles, personnel, and packages before entry into these areas is to prevent the introduction of contraband materials that could be used to commit sabotage or to aid in the theft of valuable assets. The primary objective of exit control is to conduct searches of personnel, vehicles, and packages to ensure that assets are not removed without proper authorization. A secondary objective of entry and exit control is to provide a means of accounting for personnel during and after an emergency. There are several methods an adversary may use to defeat an entry control point. These include bypass, physical attack, deceit, and technical attacks. Any or all of these methods may be used by the defined threat, and consideration of this is an important prerequisite to entry control subsystem evaluation.

Under operational loads, the entry control subsystem's performance should not adversely impact security or user operations. The system can be divided into two areas with regard to performance—on-line and off-line functions. On-line functions should be treated as a higher priority by the system. On-line functions are those such as alarm annunciation, portal access requests, and alarm assessment that require an immediate response to the user. Off-line functions include generation of preformatted alarm history reports or ad-hoc database queries.

In addition to the system software, the access control software that commands the entry control subsystem hardware and maintains and manages the data and logic necessary for system operation must be evaluated as part of the VA. In general, the software must receive electronic information from the installed entry control devices, compare this information to data stored in a database, and generate unlock signals to the portal locking device when the data comparison results in a match. Failure to achieve a successful data match will result in a signal that will not unlock the portal.

Many individual entry control technologies are available, as well as many combinations of them that are used in a PPS. In general, these devices are used to control personnel, contraband material, and vehicle entry or exit and include manual, machine-aided manual, and automated operation. The entry control subsystem uses probability of detection as the primary measure of effectiveness. In the security industry the terms false accept rate and false reject rate are also used to characterize entry control device performance. The false accept rate is the complement of the probability of detection and is equal to $1 - P_D$. This is a key measurement of subsystem performance because it represents the probability of defeat of the device. The entry control subsystem can be broken into two major categories: personnel and vehicle control. Contraband material control, such as metal or explosives detection, is a subset of each of these categories.

Alarm Communication and Display

Alarm communication and display (AC&D) is the PPS subsystem that transports alarm and video information to a central location and presents the information to a human operator. The two critical elements of an AC&D subsystem are the speed of data transmission to specified locations and the meaningful presentation of that data. Most AC&D subsystems integrate the functions of detection (detect and assess a potential intrusion) and response (initiate either immediate or delayed response procedures), as well as other subsystems such as radio communications and entry control. Although an AC&D subsystem is a complex integration of people, procedures, and equipment, evaluation by the VA team can be reduced to a handful of performance indicators. Effective AC&D subsystems are robust, reliable, redundant, fast, secure, and easy to use.

The AC&D communications system moves data from collection points (sensor and tamper alarms, video, self-test signals) to a central repository (database, server) and then to a control room and display. If the central repository is physically located in the control room, it may consist of multiple computers or displays, and the communication system may also move data throughout the repository and control room. Alarm communication has several characteristics that compel the evaluation. These characteristics include the amount of alarm data, speed of delivery, and high system reliability.

The control and display interfaces of the AC&D subsystem present information to an operator and enable the operator to enter commands affecting the operation of the AC&D subsystem and its components. The ultimate goal of this subsystem is to promote the rapid evaluation of alarms. An effective control and display system presents information to an operator rapidly and in a straightforward manner. The subsystem also responds quickly to operator commands. The control and display system must be evaluated with the human operator in mind; therefore, operation under conditions not directly related to the AC&D subsystem must be observed during evaluations. The console design should facilitate the exchange of information between the system and the operator, such as alarm reports, status indications, and commands. A good human interface improves the mechanics of issuing commands and of deciphering the information presented. Thus, the amount of data displayed should be limited to only what is required by the operator.

The overriding evaluation principle for the AC&D subsystem must be operator first, and the operator must always be in command of the system. The primary purpose of any AC&D subsystem is to enhance facility security. This is accomplished by making operators more efficient and effective in their duties, thus providing the best protection for the cost of subsystem implementation. An easy-to-use system is much more likely to succeed than an unnecessarily complex one.

The primary performance measure for an AC&D subsystem is the probability of assessed detection (P_{AD}). It is a basic principle of an effective PPS that detection is not complete until an alarm has been assessed, which is why P_{AD} is used as the

performance measure for the AC&D subsystem. Factors that contribute to this include time for alarm receipt, time to assess the alarm, ease of system use and control by the operator, and operator workload. This term is the product of probability of detection of the sensor subsystem and the probability of alarm assessment. This formula can be used qualitatively or quantitatively—the key is to verify that both sensors and assessment work together to protect assets. The VA team establishes performance of the intrusion sensing and alarm assessment subsystems individually and then evaluates the AC&D subsystem to show how all subsystems work as an integrated system. P_{AD} is then degraded further based on the results of the evaluation of individual AC&D components. These include:

- Operator workload
- Displays (input/output and ergonomics)
- Video system integration
- Maintenance
- Communications systems for moving sensor data to a display
- Processing systems (computers)
- Other functions (such as entry control)
- Physical infrastructure (power, environmental, cabling, etc.)
- System administration

Poorly integrated AC&D subsystems impact overall system effectiveness by causing decreases in performance in each of the individual components.

Data Collection—Delay

The second function of an effective PPS is delay, which slows down the adversary and allows time for the desired assessment and response. This delay is effective only if it follows detection, which can take different forms. The most obvious form of detection is through the use of electronic sensor systems which relay information back to a monitoring station. When dealing with truly massive delay barriers such as 15 feet of heavily reinforced concrete or underground bunkers, it may be perfectly acceptable to use human beings as the one and only sensor system. Security patrols conducting scheduled or random inspections will be capable of detecting any manual entry attempt with sufficient time to neutralize the adversaries. Increases in adversary task time are accomplished by introducing impediments along all possible adversary paths to provide sufficient delay for any suitable response. In general, estimates of delay times are made using literature searches, actual testing, or approximations made using data from literature or tests. The delay time of any barrier depends on adversary tools and the barrier material. Adversaries have the option of using tactics of force, stealth, deceit, or combinations of these tactics during an attack. Delay evaluation during a VA is primarily directed toward adversary tactics of force or stealth; the entry control subsystem addresses deceit.

To aid alarm assessment and interruption of the adversary at predictable locations, consideration must be given to installing barriers and detection systems adjacent to each other so that the barrier is encountered immediately after the sensor. This delays the adversary at the point of an alarm, increases the probability of accurate assessment, and allows for an effective response. Barrier effectiveness is supported through the use of the principle of balance, which ensures that each aspect of a specific barrier configuration are of equal strength.

A barrier is normally considered as penetrated when an adversary reaches a point three feet beyond the barrier. In contrast, defeat is a much broader term, which implies that the barrier is no longer effective in delaying the adversary. This distinction is important because it is quite often easier to defeat a barrier via stealth or other means than it is to penetrate it. Most security barriers at industrial facilities are designed to deter or defeat sporadic acts of vandalism, inadvertent entry, or casual thievery. For more motivated or capable threats, however, these traditional fences, buildings, doors, and locks may present little deterrence or delay.

A close examination of the large variety of scenarios and tools an adversary can select to penetrate a given facility will likely indicate that existing barriers do not ensure that adversary delay time will always be sufficient for the system. Further, if the adversary has not been detected before encountering a particular barrier, or during penetration, the effectiveness of that barrier will be negligible. Most conventional barriers such as distance, fences, locks, doors, and windows provide short penetration delay against forcible (and perhaps stealthy) attack methods that use readily available hand or power tools. Against thick, reinforced concrete walls and other equally impressive-looking barriers, explosives become an effective, rapid, and more likely method of penetration by a determined adversary. An example is the use of vehicle bombs. In addition, recall that security guards are not an effective delay unless they are located in protected positions and are equipped as well as the adversary (i.e., armed adversary and unarmed guards).

An important concept in delay evaluation is that delay is a strong function of the defined threat and the adversaries' skill. Stealth, cunning, and surprise can be valuable assets to any adversaries. The VA team should not only look at the physical delay elements present in a PPS, but also look at their condition and integration with the rest of the PPS. The team must consider unique ways that an adversary team could and most likely would exploit weaknesses in the PPS. One of the often overlooked aspects of a VA is how the adversary can, and will, use existing tools and materials within the facility to achieve their goals.

There are a variety of active or passive barriers that can be used to provide delay, and many are present in the normal course of building construction. Depending on adversary tools and capabilities, these barriers will have different delay times. Location of the barrier also plays an important role in the delay time and effectiveness of a barrier. A thick concrete wall on the exterior of a building may be susceptible to rapid breaching with explosives. The same wall, however, when incorporated into an interior underground vault may provide substantial delay, as the adversaries may not be able to use large quantities of explosives without collapsing the entire structure around them. Typical barriers include fences, gates, turnstiles, vehicle barriers, walls, floors, roofs, doors, windows, grilles, utility ports, and other barriers.

Data Collection—Response

Response is the third and final function of a PPS that is evaluated during a VA. There are many ways to respond to a security event; the appropriate response depends on the defined threat, the value of the asset, and the use of risk management options other than a physical protection system at the facility. At any given facility, one or more response strategies may be in use, and this will affect data collection activities accordingly. In addition to the response strategy, security communication is a critical part of any response function and must also be considered during the VA.

The key information collected during the VA relates to two important and interrelated factors. The first is the time it takes for the desired response to be placed into effect; the second is the effectiveness of that response. These aspects of response are facilitated by reliable communication among the responders and with others. A related matter is whether there is an immediate on- or off-site response. During the initial design and implementation of a PPS, each facility must decide if the response goal is to react after a successful attack or to stop the adversary from completing a successful attack. The misalignment of response goals and protection objectives at a facility will cause serious degradation of PPS effectiveness.

Response goals can be broadly categorized as delayed or immediate, respectively. Delayed response refers to any after-the-event reaction, where preventing a successful attack is less important than initiating asset recovery or investigation procedures, or where evacuation of the facility is the response to an attack. Examples of delayed response include review of surveillance tapes after an asset has been lost or damaged, incident investigation, asset tracking and recovery, criminal prosecution, or any combination of these. Immediate response refers to the timely deployment of any personnel to an intrusion to prevent undesirable events from occurring or to the immediate implementation of a mitigation procedure, such as evacuation, after a successful attack, to limit the effects of undesirable events. Generally speaking, if there is no immediate response to security events, there is a basic assumption that the asset can be lost and that this risk is acceptable. This may be true when the asset value is low, the threat is not very capable or motivated, the frequency of the event (i.e., the probability of attack) is low, the asset is protected using another risk management alternative (i.e., insurance) rather than physical protection, or if liability concerns limit the use of an immediate response. For critical assets, however, the lack of an immediate response to a malevolent intrusion increases the risk of asset loss and therefore must be carefully considered during the VA.

The two measures of an immediate response are the time for arrival and neutralization. The time to arrive is used to establish interruption; neutralization is a measure of response effectiveness, given arrival. Interruption is a measure of the detection, delay, communication, and response functions of the PPS and is represented by the probability of interruption (P_I). Neutralization measures response force numbers, training, tactics, and use of any weapons or equipment and is represented by the probability of neutralization (P_N) In addition, the VA team must estimate the probability of communication (P_C), which is essential for an effective immediate response.

Several general response strategies can be used at any given facility; some high-security sites with multiple critical assets may use more than one strategy and the response strategy plays a major role in how a facility is evaluated during a VA. Response strategies include deterrence, denial, containment, and recovery. Deterrence is used to discourage some low-level threats from attacking a facility by presenting the appearance of tight security, thereby suggesting that an attack would not be successful. This strategy is used at almost all private and government facilities. Because this strategy relies on the adversary's perception that they are not likely to succeed, this approach will work only against less capable or motivated threats.

For some critical assets or production facilities, such as hazardous chemical, biological, and nuclear materials or toxic waste, where release of these agents into the environment through sabotage would cause many injuries, deaths, or contamination, a denial strategy is required. Denial refers to the protection of material by preventing adversary access to areas where materials are stored or to vital equipment used to process the material. For a successful sabotage event to occur, the adversary only has to complete the attack on the target and cause the release; capture of the adversary after a successful release does not prevent the consequence of the attack.

A containment strategy is generally used when the adversary goal is theft of an asset. Containment means that the adversary is not allowed to leave the facility with the asset; that is, they are contained on-site and the theft attempt is not successful. This strategy is usually reserved for facilities with high-value or high-consequence assets, such as mints that store large quantities of currency, museums, precious gem or metal repositories, or hazardous material storage locations. Prisons also use a containment strategy, but they are attempting to prevent inmates from leaving a facility, not the theft of assets.

In the event that deterrence or containment strategies fail, a backup approach is recovery of the stolen asset. In some recovery strategies, the recovery is immediate (i.e., hot pursuit of the adversary as he/she speeds away in a car). For most facilities, there is an acceptance that assets may be lost for a period of time, and recovery of the assets at some point in the future is the primary response. Recovery responses include investigation, tracking of assets, and follow-up using criminal prosecution.

Security communications consist of the people, procedures, and technology used to transmit communications among members of the response force during both normal and response operations. During normal operations, security communications may be required for conducting entry control, escort, patrols, and other security functions (for an on-site security group). During response to an attack, communications are essential for organizing responders, directing them to the scene of the emergency, and successfully interrupting or neutralizing the adversary. Accurate and reliable communication is required for interruption and neutralization. The overall performance measure used is the P_C, which is a measure of confidence that information will flow through the system, starting with alarm reporting and ending with deployment and engagement with the adversary. For a delayed response using video surveillance or assessment, P_C

will depend on the transmission system used to capture and store alarm and video information for later review.

The actual performance measures and estimates used depend on the response strategy and the presence of an immediate response. For delayed responses, it is sufficient to ensure that there is timely and accurate detection, and that legally admissible and usable video information is captured as evidence. This requires a fully functional communication system, limited in this case to integrated sensing and video assessment, and transmission of this information to a storage location. This can be approximated using the probability of assessed detection. For any immediate response, response force time, neutralization capability, and the probability of communication will be the key aspects of the evaluation.

Analysis

After all the appropriate data have been collected, analysis of the PPS can begin. There are two basic analysis approaches used in a VA—compliance- or performance-based. Compliance-based approaches depend on conformance to specified policies or regulations; the metric for this analysis is the presence of the specified equipment and procedures. Performance-based approaches actually evaluate how each element of the PPS operates and what it contributes to overall system effectiveness. The use of compliance- (or feature-) based systems is only effective against low threats, when assets have a low consequence of loss, or when cost-benefit analyses have been performed that document that physical protection measures are not the most cost-effective risk management option. A compliance-based analysis is easier to perform because the measure of system effectiveness is presence of prescribed PPS equipment, procedures, and people. The analysis consists of a review of facility conformance to the compliance

requirements, the use of checklists to document presence or absence of components, and a deficiency report that notes where the facility is out of compliance. The VA report summarizes these findings and the facility makes improvements according to enterprise policy. Because the premise of this text is that overall system effectiveness is the goal of a VA, and that all dollars spent on PPS elements should result in improved protection while also complying with requirements, this text primarily addresses performance-based analysis. Performance-based analysis can use either qualitative or quantitative techniques.

When conducting either a qualitative or quantitative performance-based analysis, the following six-step process is used:

1. Create an adversary sequence diagram (ASD) for all asset locations
2. Conduct a path analysis, which provides P_I
3. Perform a scenario analysis
4. Complete a neutralization analysis, if appropriate, which provides P_N
5. Determine system effectiveness, P_E
6. Develop and analyze system effectiveness upgrades, if system effectiveness (or risk) is not acceptable

If desired, a facility may also choose to evaluate the PPS using risk as a metric, although this method is more commonly used in risk assessment and not in vulnerability assessment.

An ASD is a functional representation of the PPS at a facility that is used to describe the specific protection elements that are present. It illustrates the paths that adversaries can follow to accomplish sabotage or theft goals. Because a path analysis determines whether a system has sufficient detection and delay to result in interruption, it is conducted first. The path analysis uses estimated performance measures, based on the defined threat tools and tactics, to predict weaknesses in the PPS along all credible adversary paths into the facility, measured by the probability of interruption. This step is facilitated through the use of an ASD of the facility to be analyzed.

A scenario analysis is conducted to determine whether the system has vulnerabilities that could be exploited by adversaries using varying tactics, resulting in lower effectiveness of the PPS. Scenario analysis considers specific tactics along the path, as well as attacks on the PPS itself or on the response force. These tactics include stealth, force, and deceit, and they may be used individually or combined during a scenario. As in path analysis, an important aspect of scenario analysis is consideration of different operating states at the facility or near the asset. There are usually at least two facility states—open and closed. As a part of scenario analysis, an effort is made to identify the worst cases of attack scenarios. Although analysis is not limited to these situations, they are very useful because they define the adversary attacks that test the limits of PPS effectiveness.

After weak paths and suitable attack scenarios have been determined, a neutralization analysis can be performed. This part of the analysis is performed only at facilities where there is an immediate response resulting in a face-to-face confrontation with adversaries. Neutralization analysis provides information about how effective the response function will be under different scenarios and is a measure of response force capability, proficiency, training, and tactics.

At this point PPS effectiveness can be calculated, using qualitative or quantitative techniques. System effectiveness is represented using only P_I (as in the case of a delayed response using review of video and investigation, when mere presence of an immediate response will chase an adversary away, or when an adversary will surrender if interrupted), or through the use of both P_I and P_N (at facilities where an immediate response will engage with the adversary).

If the baseline analysis of the PPS shows that the system does not meet its protection objectives, the VA team can suggest upgrades that will address these issues. Usually, these upgrades are not specific technical recommendations, but are functional improvements that can be achieved by increasing performance at certain locations. The analysis is then repeated using these performance increases to estimate the overall increase in the ability of the system to meet its objectives. These results are provided to security system designers who will determine which specific equipment or other upgrades will provide the required performance. Once the analysis is completed, it is important to present both the baseline and upgrade analyses to establish the need for improvements and show the return on investment in upgrades.

Reporting and Using the Vulnerability Assessment

After analysis of facility data is complete, the VA team reports the results in a manner that is useful to the managers at the facility. The goal of the report is to provide accurate, unbiased information that clearly defines the current effectiveness of the PPS, along with potential solutions if the current system is not effective. The VA informs facility management of the state of the PPS and supports upgrade decisions. In general, the VA report is then used in successive projects that address the identified vulnerabilities and improve the PPS at the facility.

Reporting can be formal or informal, verbal or written, and may take the form of a short overview, or a longer, more detailed approach. The choice of reporting form and content is an aspect of the project agreement and generally follows the conventions of the customer or facility being evaluated. Regardless of how reporting is presented and documented, certain content must be included to make the report understandable and useful to the facility. By its very nature, a VA report is a powerful document and should not be shared indiscriminately. Protection of the final report, as well as the appropriate distribution, should be defined as part of the master project agreement. It is recommended that one organization have final control of the document and who it is shared with, even though other organizations may have copies.

Once the VA report is completed, a variety of responses or next steps can take place. By far, the most common approach is for the facility to pursue improving the PPS and following the recommendations of the VA team. A VA can be thought of as the analysis of system requirements that must occur before system design and implementation. The same things that made a particular PPS weak in the first place can limit the effectiveness of any upgrades if they are not carefully considered. This process may be relatively short and easy if the recommendations involve only procedural or minor equipment changes, such as replacing one type of CCTV camera with another. If the system requires major equipment upgrades, however, the proper approach to the upgrade design will ensure a cost- and performance-effective result.

The goal of the design team is to create upgrades that meet the performance predicted in the upgrade analysis phase of the VA. This can be difficult to accomplish, and it can take several iterations between the designers and the facility to clarify goals and constraints and to create the best system that can be installed for the available funding. The three general stages of design activity include conceptual, preliminary, and final design. Although this discussion is focused on the VA of an existing facility, the same process is used for evaluation of a new facility. For new facilities, VA analysts and designers work together closely to model the proposed PPS at the facility, and then iterate on which PPS elements will give the most cost-effective solution. Once they agree, the system designers work through the design stages to define how the final design will be implemented to meet the specified performance.

Systems Engineering and Vulnerability Assessment

This section introduces the systems engineering process and describes how this process is used in a VA. Before discussing this relationship, a few definitions and a brief introduction to systems engineering are provided.

In the *Design* text, a system was defined as "an integrated collection of components or elements designed to achieve an objective according to a plan." Systems may be small (a microwave oven) or large (a city), and all systems are composed of other smaller systems (or subsystems). In some applications, a collection of many systems into a functional whole is called a system of systems or a family of systems. Further, systems are not found only in engineering, but exist in other disciplines as well. For example, there is a criminal justice system that includes law enforcement, the courts, and corrections. Biological systems can be microorganisms, a pond, or a human. A social system includes the culture, behaviors, and mores of a society. Systems engineering "is an interdisciplinary approach and means to enable the realization of successful systems. It focuses on defining customer needs and required functionality early in the development cycle, documenting requirements, and then proceeding with design synthesis and system validation while considering the complete problem. Systems engineering considers both the business and the technical needs of customers with the goal of providing a quality product that meets user needs" (International Council on Systems Engineering (INCOSE), 2005). It is concerned with the integration of functional, technical, and operational requirements within the business goals and environment of the customer. Integration refers not only to physical or electrical integration (although these are important aspects of system performance), but the integration of customer needs, technical performance, safety, reliability, procedures, personnel, maintenance, training, testing, and life cycle costs of the proposed solution. The systems engineering process flow is shown in Figure 1-4.

Systems engineering is not about being a good engineer—everyone is a systems engineer in his/her area of expertise. Rather, systems engineering is a logical and structured process that starts by defining the problem to be solved, considering multiple potential solutions, and then analyzing these solutions to support selection and implementation of the most balanced and robust design that meets requirements and goals. Implementation of the design includes proper installation, maintenance, testing, and training of per-

sonnel to preserve optimal system function. Systems engineering also addresses the final disposition, retirement, or replacement of the system after its useful lifetime has been reached. The information presented in this section is an overview of systems engineering based on principles developed by the International Council on Systems Engineering (INCOSE, 2005) and a text by Martin (2003). An effective VA follows basic systems engineering principles.

A common model of systems development is one that considers both systems and component engineering. These two areas are both science-based, where science determines what is, component engineering determines what can be, and systems engineering determines what should be. The systems engineering domain includes user requirements (define the problem) and system requirements (boundaries and constraints), which lead to the component engineering domain. This domain includes component selection, design, analysis,

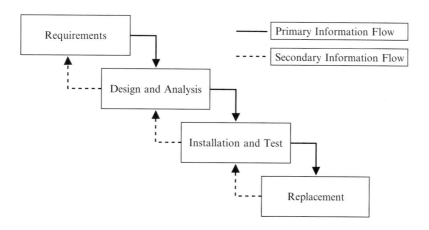

Figure 1-4 Systems Engineering Process. The process is iterative and should begin at the requirements stage. A VA fits into this stage of the cycle, which guides the other stages. The results of the VA are used to establish the requirements for an upgraded system design, which are validated through the use of analysis and testing. Once installed, the system should be tested and maintained to optimize system performance and allow for some expansion. At some point, requirements may change or the system reaches the end of its usable lifetime, and replacement of the system or components must be addressed.

integration, and testing. During a VA, the project leader generally serves as the systems engineer who ensures that the final product meets customer needs, although large projects may include a systems engineer as a separate team member. Component engineers are the subject matter experts on the VA team who bring technical depth in engineering, adversary and response tactics, explosives, analysis, and other areas to evaluation activities.

Because the VA process described in this text is performance-based, it embraces all the areas of system development described previously: science, systems, and component engineering. The science-based nature of this approach cannot be ignored. An example may clarify the distinction between compliance- and performance-based approaches. A compliance-based approach might select a radar to provide exterior intrusion detection instead of other sensors, such as microwave, active infrared, fence-associated, or buried cable, based on past use, a large inventory of available devices, approved lists, or vendor-provided information. In contrast, a performance-based approach would begin by ensuring that all system requirements are identified and that the selected device is the one that best meets all requirements. Then, performance of the device is based solely on the trade-off analysis of which devices meet all requirements. Examples of exterior intrusion detection requirements include probability of detection, nuisance alarm rate, vulnerability to defeat by the defined threat, integration with other PPS components, expansion capability, and life cycle cost of implementation and operation. This example emphasizes the need for good systems engineering, so that the VA and any necessary upgrades provide the best PPS for the cost. As a result, customer desires often must be bound by explaining what realistically can and cannot be achieved using PPS components. This rationale is included in the Requirements stage of systems engineering, which is described next and is a part of VA project management, which is described in Chapter 3. A brief comparison of compliance- and performance-based approaches is shown in Table 1-1.

Table 1-1 *Comparison of Compliance- and Performance-Based Vulnerability Assessment Approaches.*[*]

Criterion	Compliance-Based Approach	Performance-Based Approach
Asset value	Low	All assets
Requirement basis	Policy	Overall system performance
Component performance measure	Presence	Effectiveness and integration
Data collection methodology	Site survey	Site evaluation testing
Analysis	Checklist	System effectiveness
Reporting	Deficiency report	Path effectiveness and vulnerabilities
Upgrade design	Address deficiencies	Functional performance estimates
Component selection	Component engineering	Systems engineering
Underlying process	Satisfy policy requirement	Systems engineering

[*]Compliance-based approaches are less rigorous and easier to perform than performance-based approaches. Compliance-based approaches are most appropriate for low-value assets, while a performance-based process can be used for assets of any value.

Given this background, Figure 1-3 illustrates the systems engineering process as applied in a VA, which will be discussed in other chapters. The remaining sections of this chapter describe the phases of systems engineering in more detail and how they relate to a VA, and include references to specific chapters in the book that contain further information. The purpose of this discussion is not to thoroughly describe the systems engineering process, but to show how a VA is based on the process.

System Requirements

As shown in Figure 1-3, evaluation of a PPS begins with an understanding of the problem that is to be solved. This includes facility characterization, defining the threat, and target identification. In systems engineering, these PPS objectives are a subset of system requirements, and they serve as the primary basis for appropriate PPS evaluation by subject matter experts from a variety of disciplines.

A requirement is a characteristic that identifies the levels needed to achieve specific objectives under a given set of conditions and is a binding statement in a contract or regulatory document. In formal systems engineering documents, requirements can be thresholds or goals, with thresholds being something that must be achieved, whereas goals have some degree of usefulness or desirability, but are not necessarily mandatory. Requirements are generally stated as "shall," whereas goals are stated as "should." This is a major point to consider when establishing system requirements. There are many customer, user, and stakeholder wants, needs, and expectations. Early in the evaluation process, these imprecise statements must be reduced to an actionable and measurable set of mandatory requirements, so that the final product delivers what the customer expects. It is not uncommon to skip this step in the process and jump immediately into system evaluation. This

approach almost always leads to dissatisfied customers and incomplete products and should be avoided. There are three types of requirements in a system—functional, constraint, and performance.

A functional requirement describes the product and level of detail, including component interfaces and what the PPS will do. These requirements address the integration of people, procedures, and equipment that provide the desired end product. They also address stakeholder, customer, and user needs, desires, and expectations. There is a difference in the needs of stakeholders (those who have a role in or expectations of the product), customers (those who pay for the system), and users (those who will operate and maintain the final product). A requirements analysis considers these different needs. Questions such as: What needs are we trying to meet? What is wrong with the current system? Is the need clearly articulated? are appropriate for customers and stakeholders. Other questions concerning who the intended users are, how they will use the product, and how this is different from the present operation are appropriate for users.

Constraint requirements include any external or internal compliance condition or stipulation that must be met. They include external laws and regulations, legal liabilities, standards, and enterprise policies and procedures. Examples are federal safety requirements, labor law, fire and electrical codes, enterprise-defined infrastructure, and project management processes. In a VA, additional constraints are a function of the specific site, such as terrain, weather, facility layout and footprint, the presence of a response force, and other unique conditions. These constraints are part of the operational environment that must be considered in the VA. Other constraints may be imposed by the limits of available technology, such as the radar example given previously.

Performance requirements define how well a capability must operate and under what conditions. These are stated in clear, unambiguous, and measurable terms. Examples of performance measures are earned value, monthly financial status, milestones met, other business or administrative measures, and security performance measures such as probability of detection, delay times, probability of assessment, and probability of interruption. Performance requirements are derived from functional requirements and specify the metrics that are used to judge component and system effectiveness in meeting requirements.

There are many reasons to perform a VA, and these underlying needs must be understood by the VA team before beginning the evaluation. For example, periodic VAs may be required by an enterprise policy or regulatory agency (a constraint requirement), even though the system is still performing as required. Or, the facility may have recently been attacked and lost a critical asset, and there is a desire to improve protection of assets (a functional requirement). Since 9/11, many private companies and government agencies have issued new threat guidance concerning the use of weapons of mass destruction (WMD) and need to perform VAs to verify that existing PPSs are still effective (a performance requirement). These examples emphasize the need to understand customer goals in asking for a VA. In addition, the customer's intended use of the VA must be considered. If the VA is performed only to satisfy a regulatory requirement, but there is no intention of implementing any changes in response to identified vulnerabilities, this is important for the VA team to understand. If the customer is unwilling or unable to allocate additional funding or other resources to improving the PPS if required, this is part of the operating environment that constrains the VA. Identifying customer needs, motivation, and desires is a part of VA project management, which is described in Chapter 3.

In a VA, functional requirements can be equated to defining the protection objectives—what is to be protected (assets) and from whom (threat). A high-level functional requirement in security is "protect the secret rocket fuel formula from theft by a competitor." In addition to these requirements, it is also important to characterize the enterprise in terms of its mission and the external and enterprise operating environments, particularly with respect to any compliance constraints that must be met. For example, since 9/11 a variety of laws and mandates have been enacted by the U.S. government that have had a significant impact on security at airports and seaports. These new constraint requirements must be considered during VAs at these sites, so that their affect on overall system effectiveness is considered.

The performance requirements of the security system are related to the capability of the defined threat. For example, a PPS that protects assets from vandals requires lower performance than one against a group of highly motivated and well-equipped environmental activists. This is why it is so important to define protection objectives before starting the VA and not jump right into design, or worse, procurement, of PPS components. In many instances, an enterprise has responded to a security incident or regulatory requirement by buying more cameras, with no analysis of what capability the new cameras will add to the current system. This relates to the earlier point concerning thresholds and goals. As applied to a VA, a threshold is used to specify the minimum acceptable performance of the PPS that must be achieved (i.e., probability of detection must be 0.9 for running, walking, and crawling intruders). If the threshold cannot be met by an improved PPS within the constraints, the system is not implemented or requirements are reduced because analysis does not support making an additional investment in a system or upgrade that cannot meet the minimum functional requirements. Put in different terms, the return-on-investment (ROI) is zero—additional money was spent with no corresponding increase in the ability of the PPS to protect assets. This is not the traditional interpretation of ROI, where there is a direct financial gain as a result of system improvement. Rather, this ROI is the proactive protection of assets in a structured and reasoned manner. This may pay off indirectly in financial gain by protecting the enterprise's reputation, ensure business continuity in case of an attack, and show external auditors or agencies that reasonable steps were taken to protect high-value assets. If a PPS that meets customer needs and system requirements cannot be implemented, other risk management alternatives should be considered, perhaps in combination. There are often other ways to achieve the customer's goals that are cheaper and more effective than reducing risk using a PPS.

The basic PPS evaluation principles used during a VA are described in Chapter 2. Project management techniques which address user, customer, and stakeholder requirements; the final product that will be delivered; and manage the customer relationship are described in Chapter 3, as noted previously. Chapter 4 reviews PPS Protection Objectives, which establish the functional and performance requirements for VA data collection and analysis. Facility characterization is also described in this chapter and establishes additional constraints, such as political, regulatory, financial, and physical limitations that are imposed on the VA.

System Design and Analysis

At this point, a clear set of requirements exist and have been agreed to by the customer, and the VA can begin. The system is evaluated by subject matter experts (i.e., component engineers) considering the defined threats and identified assets, and all constraints are factored into the evaluation. Team composition and their roles and responsibilities are listed in Chapter 3. A VA on a PPS considers the functions of detection, delay, and response, and evaluates how well people, procedures, and equipment meet all requirements. It is implicit in this approach that the defined threat must physically enter the facility to attack. As a result, standoff attacks from off-site or cyber attacks on networks are not part of the VA of a PPS; these are legitimate security concerns that are addressed in the overall security system for the facility. During a VA, the current system is evaluated based on the system requirements, and analysis is used to show whether the system meets the requirements. If the baseline analysis shows that the system does not meet requirements, potential upgrades are analyzed, but only to a functional level (i.e., specific devices that achieve this performance are not identified). In this case, the VA then establishes a new set of system requirements that is passed to designers for upgrade improvements using the new functional and performance requirements. The upgrade design process is described later in this section.

VA analysis is supported through the use of evaluation tests on installed PPS components, which documents PPS component performance and how this affects the overall system. Any performance deficiencies are documented and used in the analysis. These component deficiencies lead to system weaknesses that can be exploited by adversaries, which is the definition of a vulnerability. For many PPS components, historical test data already exist that are used in analysis. The principles and techniques used to evaluate the detection, delay, and response subsystems and components of the PPS are described in Chapters 5-10 and form the core of this text.

The VA analysis process includes the use of trade-off analyses that consider the performance that can be expected for various combinations of PPS elements and assist in selection of performance options that best meet all requirements. A robust design will also look beyond the requirements (i.e., thresholds) and determine how effective the system is in meeting customer desires. For example, analysis of a PPS must show effectiveness against the defined threat; in addition, analyses showing how well the system will perform against higher threats can also be performed to give an indication of system effectiveness beyond requirements. This additional performance documents how effective the PPS will be as threats increase, and if this performance can be obtained for little increased cost, it can be a viable option. This is an example of a customer goal, as compared to a requirement. The analysis shows how an investment in the PPS can be leveraged to add system capability at a low cost; for example, installing larger, high-resolution CCTV monitors in the alarm monitoring station. It may cost a little more to buy better monitors, but better monitors will make operators faster and more effective at assessing intrusion alarms caused by small objects. As a result, a small additional investment in better monitors will provide more effective alarm assessment capability. This relates to the earlier point about meeting customer goals—implementation of this option should be discussed with and approved by the customer, and consider all impacts to the PPS, such as any increased cost of installation, normal and backup power specifications, and operator viewing distance.

At the end of the VA, analysis either shows that the current PPS is effective in meeting requirements, or it isn't. If not, the VA team will propose various functional and performance upgrades to the PPS that will meet requirements. At this point, the VA is complete, and the final report is written. If the facility chooses to follow the VA recommendations, and assuming that many equipment improvements are needed, another separate group of PPS designers is assigned to design the upgraded PPS. The design of a PPS is a complex subject that could easily fill another book; however, the process is summarized in the remainder of this section.

The design stage of the systems engineering process is often iterative, starting with conceptual design, proceeding to a preliminary design, and ending with the final system design that is deployed. As the design progresses, a multidisciplinary team (much like the team that performed the VA) reviews potential design options to converge on the best solution. In many cases, the existing requirements may not completely specify the performance required of the upgraded system, and this is part of the reason for an iterative design cycle. This process is facilitated by the use of design reviews, modeling and simulation tools, test data, and discussions with the customer to verify that the proposed solution is in alignment with their needs (shall requirements) and desires (should requirements). The final design ends in a detailed description of the product and how it is implemented (a detailed final drawing package). Upgrade design activities after the VA are described in Chapter 12. Before implementing the final design, the system components are analyzed to validate and verify system operation. Validation is the process of checking satisfaction of stakeholders (have we done the right job?) and verification checks that the design meets the specified technical requirements and the components are properly integrated (have we done the job right?).

Validation checks to ensure that no requirements were missed and that there are no extraneous requirements. This is called requirements traceability and is frequently used in large, costly systems (and may be required by some customers). Traceability shows that the product is just what the customer wanted, no more and no less. It also serves to document and explain selection of specific components during the system design stages and links requirements to these components and the overall system. If there is no link between a component and a requirement, the customer was given more than they needed. This is important because it clarifies to a customer why one device was used over another in the final design. Consider the example of specifying a camera in a PPS design. Many types of cameras are available, and selection of the appropriate camera depends on the functional, constraint, and performance requirements of the system. If the defined threat includes an adversary crawling across a perimeter at night, camera resolution, lighting, video recording, and storage must be specified to meet this performance requirement. Contrast this with a defined threat that includes a vehicle crashing the perimeter. The larger profile of a vehicle will not require the same camera resolution as a crawling attacker, and thus the specific camera that is selected may be different. However, the vehicle will be moving at a faster rate of speed than a crawler, and this constraint will influence what other devices are incorporated into the system design. Validation often uses acceptance tests under local conditions to check that the system meets the needs and expectations of stakeholders. If formal documentation is needed, the use of traceability software, as noted previously, may be warranted (go to www.telelogic.com for an example). The software documents the link between requirements, system design, implementation, and test.

System Installation and Test

At this stage of the upgrade process, the new design is implemented as described in the drawings and specifications of the final design package. Deviations from these specifications should be approved by knowledgeable experts who understand their effects on component and overall system performance. Some changes may be relatively transparent, but others may seriously affect system performance. For example, changing the distance between or height of light fixtures may change the amount of light that is available in an area. System installation is supplemented by on-site operational, functional, and performance tests to ensure that the system is working as predicted and the customer's needs are met. Operational tests confirm that an installed device is working (i.e., it sends a signal), and functional tests show that the device is working and performing as expected (i.e., a sensor still has the expected P_D). It is also recommended that final acceptance tests are performed before the customer accepts the delivered system. An acceptance test is the final stage of system delivery, and test results are used to either justify or withhold final payments to vendors, depending on whether the system passes or fails the test. The use of acceptance testing is described in Chapter 12.

Because the PPS is expected to continue to perform after initial installation, proper maintenance and periodic testing of components and the system are required to maintain optimal system function. These are aspects of the overall system and system design also includes recommendations on the maintenance, testing, and training procedures that should be used to keep the system operating reliably and as expected. These details are aided by complete system documentation, a preliminary training program to acquaint users with the proper ways to maintain the system, and recommended procedures and processes that will ensure continued acceptable system performance. Component installation, maintenance, testing, and staff training procedures are evaluated during the VA (described for each subsystem in Chapters 5-10) and can have a significant affect on overall system performance. Procedural improvements can also be low-cost system upgrades.

System Replacement

It is good systems engineering practice to include planning for the retirement and replacement of the system in the system design, after its expected lifetime has been reached. The final design that is implemented should allow for system expansion and growth, up to a certain point. Typically, this point allows for 50% expansion above the current capability. This advance planning allows for expansion of systems in response to changes without excessive cost or loss of protection. Examples of system expansion include the installation of fiber optic cable bundles with more conductors than currently needed at initial installation. It only costs a little more to buy a fiber bundle with twice as many conductors; installation costs are the same. Alternatively, a conduit with a larger diameter could be used to allow room for additional wiring at a later date. In the same way, adding power drops or junction boxes will allow for rapid expansion of the PPS in the future. It is expected that technology will advance, threats will change, facilities may grow or shrink, or equipment will fail, any of which can create a need for new components that meet existing or new requirements. Although retirement and replacement are not part of a VA, expansion capability of the PPS is one criterion that is considered during a VA. This is specifically addressed in Chapter 8 but is a part of all subsystem evaluations.

Summary

This chapter described risk management, vulnerability assessment, and systems engineering and explained how these processes support security system evaluation. Risk management and risk assessment were reviewed. Both qualitative and quantitative techniques to measure system effectiveness in a vulnerability assessment were described, as well as when each technique is appropriate. The use of statistical measures was discussed to introduce this topic and to show how statistics are used to support system evaluation. The

vulnerability assessment process was also introduced by dividing the process into three stages—planning, conducting, and reporting—and using the results. The chapter ended with a brief description of how the evaluation process described in this text follows a system engineering process to enable the realization of successful systems. This process focuses on defining customer requirements and then evaluating the system while considering the complete problem. Systems engineering integrates disciplines and groups into a team effort, following a structured development process that proceeds from problem definition to evaluation and analysis to implementation of any required system upgrades, while considering both the business and the technical needs of customers with the goal of providing a quality product that meets user needs.

References

Flynn, S., *America the Vulnerable*, New York: HarperCollins, 2004.

Garcia, M.L., *The Design and Evaluation of Physical Protection Systems*, Boston: Butterworth-Heinemann, 2001.

Grose, V.L., *Managing Risk: Systematic Loss Prevention for Executives*, Arlington, VA: Omega Systems Group, 1987, 47–48.

Haimes, Y.Y., *Risk Modeling, Assessment, and Management*, 2nd ed., Hoboken, NJ: Wiley and Sons, 2004.

International Council on Systems Engineering (INCOSE), definition available at http://www.incose.org/practice/whatis-systemseng.aspx, April 18, 2005.

Kaplan, S., and Garrick, B.J., On the Quantitative Definition of Risk, *Risk Analysis*, Vol. 1, No. 1, 1981, 11–27.

Martin, J.N., *Systems Engineering Guidebook, A Process for Developing Systems and Products*, Boca Raton, FL: CRC Press, 2003.

2
Physical Protection Systems Principles and Concepts

This chapter is nearly identical to Chapter 5 in the *Design* text, but it includes one rewritten section that introduces how we use the principles and concepts described here when conducting a VA. The main purpose of this chapter is to review:

- PPS functions of detection, delay, and response
- Basic principles of an effective PPS design
- Performance measures used for each PPS function

Readers who are familiar with this information can skip to the section on Design and Evaluation Criteria and read the high-level description of how a VA is used to evaluate PPS functions and components. Because this chapter is an overview of PPS design and evaluation, its background information can be found in Chapters 6-12 (Part Two) of the *Design* text.

Physical Protection Systems Overview

Whether designing a new PPS or upgrades to an existing system, the designer must determine how best to combine such elements as fences, barriers, sensors, procedures, communication devices, and security personnel into a PPS that can achieve the protection objectives. Protection objectives and their use in a VA are discussed thoroughly in Chapter 4. The resulting PPS design should meet these objectives within the operational, safety, legal, and economic constraints of the facility. The primary functions of a PPS are detection of an adversary, delay of that adversary, and response by security personnel (guard force). These functions and some of their components are shown in Figure 2-1.

Certain guidelines should be observed during the PPS design. A PPS performs

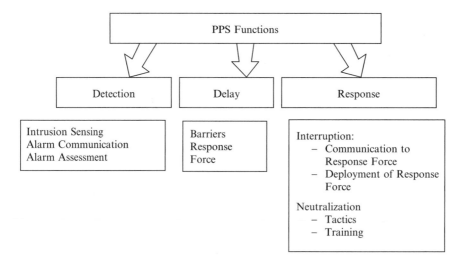

Figure 2-1 Functions of a Physical Protection System. The PPS functions include detection, delay, and response. These functions must occur in this order and can be evaluated to determine the vulnerability of an existing or proposed PPS to a specified threat.

better if detection is as far from the target as possible and delays are near the target. In addition, there is close association between detection (exterior or interior) and assessment. It is a basic principle of security system design that detection without assessment is not detection, because without assessment, the operator does not know the cause of an alarm. If the alarm is the result of trash blowing across an exterior area or lights being turned off in an interior area, there is no need for a response, because there is no valid intrusion (i.e., by an adversary). Another close association is the relationship between response and response force communications. A response force cannot respond unless it receives a communication call for a response. These and many other particular features of PPS components help to ensure that the designer takes advantage of the strengths of each piece of equipment and uses equipment in combinations that complement each other and protect any weaknesses.

Design of the PPS begins with a review and thorough understanding of the protection objectives the designed system must meet. This can be done simply by checking for required features of a PPS, such as intrusion detection, entry control, access delay, response communications, and a protective force. A PPS design based on required features, however, cannot be expected to lead to a high-performance system unless those features, when used together, are sufficient to ensure adequate levels of protection. Feature-based designs check only for the presence of a particular number or type of component, with no consideration for how effectively the component will perform during an adversary attack. A good PPS is designed using components that have validated performance measures established for operation. Component performance measures are combined into system performance measures by the application of system modeling techniques.

Physical Protection System Design

A system may be defined as a collection of components or elements designed to achieve an objective according to a plan. The ultimate objective of a PPS is to prevent the accomplishment of overt or covert malevolent human actions. Typical objectives are to prevent sabotage of critical equipment, theft of assets or information from within the facility, and protection of people. A PPS must accomplish its objectives by either deterrence or a combination of detection, delay, and response. Listed here are the component subsystems that perform these functions.

Detection

- Exterior/Interior Intrusion Sensors
- Alarm Assessment
- Alarm Communication and Display
- Entry Control Systems

Delay

- Access Delay

Response

- Response Force
- Response Force Communications

The system functions of detection and delay can be accomplished by the use of either hardware or guards. Guards usually handle response, although automated response technologies are under development. There is always a balance between the use of hardware and the use of guards. In different conditions and applications, one is often the preferable choice. The key to a successful system is the integration of people, procedures, and equipment into a system that protects the targets from the threats. This integration requires a trade-off analysis of cost versus performance, so if a designer decides to use more guards and less hardware, there should be a corresponding analysis that supports this decision. Keep in mind that humans are generally not good detectors, but equipment performs well with the repetition and boredom associated with constant close monitoring.

Detection, delay, and response are all required functions of an effective PPS. These functions must be performed in this order and within a length of time that is less than the time required for the adversary to complete his task. A well-designed system provides protection-in-depth, minimizes the consequence of component failures, and exhibits balanced protection. In addition, a design process based on performance criteria rather than feature criteria will select elements and procedures according to the contribution they make to overall system performance. Performance criteria are also measurable and can thus be helpful in the analysis of the designed system.

PPS Functions

The primary PPS functions are detection, delay, and response. It is essential to consider the system functions in detail, as a thorough understanding of the definitions of these functions and the measure of effectiveness of each is required to evaluate the system. It is important to note that detection must be accomplished for delay to be effective. As noted previously, the system goal is to protect critical assets from theft or sabotage by a malevolent human adversary. For a system to be effective at this objective, there must be notification of an attack (detection), and then adversary progress must be slowed (delay), which will allow the response force time to interrupt or stop the adversary (response).

Detection

Detection is the discovery of an adversary action. It includes sensing of covert or overt actions. To discover an adversary action, the following events need to occur:

1. A sensor reacts to a stimulus and initiates an alarm.
2. Information from the sensor and assessment subsystems is reported and displayed.
3. A person assesses information and judges the alarm to be valid or invalid. If assessed as a nuisance alarm, detection has not occurred. Therefore, detection without assessment is not considered detection. Assessment is the process of determining whether the source of the alarm is due to an attack or a nuisance alarm.

These events are depicted in Figure 2-2 and show that detection is not an instantaneous event. Included in the detection function of physical protection is entry control. Entry control allows entry to authorized personnel and detects the attempted entry of unauthorized personnel and material. The measures of effectiveness of entry control are throughput, false acceptance rate, and false rejection rate. Throughput is defined as the number of authorized personnel that are allowed access per unit time, assuming that all personnel who attempt entry are authorized for entrance. False acceptance is the rate at which false identities or credentials are allowed entry, and false rejection rate is the frequency of denying access to authorized personnel.

The measures of effectiveness for the detection function are the probability of sensing adversary action, the time required for reporting and assessing the alarm, and nuisance alarm rate. A sensor activates at time T_0, and then at a later time a person receives information from the sensor and assessment subsystems. If the time delay between when the sensor activates and when the alarm is assessed is short, the probability of detection, P_D, will be close to the probability that the sensor will sense the unauthorized action, P_S. The probability of detection decreases as the time before assessment increases. Figure 2-3 shows that a long time delay between detection and assessment lowers the probability of detection, because the more time required to make an accurate assessment, the less likely it will be that the cause of the alarm is still present. For example, if sensor alarms are assessed by sending a guard to the sensor location, by the time the guard arrives, there may no longer be an obvious alarm source. In this case, the delay between sensor initiation and assessment can be so lengthy that no assessment could be made. This is why P_D decreases. In addition, the delay between detection and assessment favors the adversary because of the further progression of the adversary toward the target before the response force has been notified of an attack.

Response force personnel can also accomplish detection. Guards at fixed posts or on patrol may serve a vital role in sensing an intrusion. An effective assessment system provides two types of information associated with detection: information about whether the alarm is a valid alarm or a nuisance alarm and details about the cause of the alarm—what, who, where, and how many. Even when assisted by a video assessment sys-

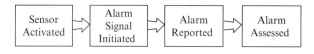

Figure 2-2 Detection Functions in a PPS. Detection starts with sensor activation and ends with assessment of the alarm to determine the cause.

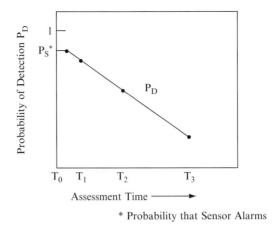

* Probability that Sensor Alarms

Figure 2-3 Relationship between Assessment Time and Probability of Detection. The probability of detection will decrease as assessment time increases.

tem, however, humans do not make good detectors. Studies have shown that brief instances of movement are missed by 48% of human observers using video monitors (Tickner and Poulton, 1973).

An additional performance measure of sensors is the nuisance alarm rate. A nuisance alarm is any alarm that is not caused by an intrusion. In an ideal sensor system, the nuisance alarm rate would be zero. In the real world, however, all sensors interact with their environment, and they cannot discriminate between intrusions and other events in their detection zone. This is why an alarm assessment system is needed; not all sensor alarms are caused by intrusions.

Usually nuisance alarms are further classified by source. Both natural and industrial environments can cause nuisance alarms. Common sources of natural noise are vegetation (trees and weeds), wildlife (animals and birds), and weather conditions (wind, rain, snow, fog, lightning). Industrial sources of noise include ground vibration, debris moved by wind, and electromagnetic interference. False alarms are those nuisance alarms generated by the equipment itself (whether by poor design, inadequate maintenance, or component failure).

Delay

Delay, the second function of a PPS, is the slowing down of adversary progress. Delay can be accomplished by people, barriers, locks, and activated delays. The response force can be considered elements of delay if they are in fixed and well-protected positions. The measure of delay effectiveness is the time required by the adversary (after detection) to bypass each delay element. Although the adversary may be delayed before detection, this delay is of no value to the effectiveness of the PPS, as it does not provide additional time to respond to the adversary. Delay before detection is primarily a deterrent. In some situations, barriers are placed before detection; however, this application is meant to force an adversary to change or abandon his/her tactic. For example, the use of speed bumps or placement of jersey bounce barriers along the sides of a road will slow down or prevent an adversary in a vehicle from leaving the road. Figure 2-4 summarizes the function of delay in a PPS.

Response

The response function consists of the actions taken by the response force to

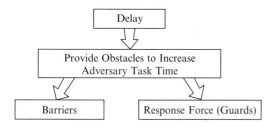

Figure 2-4 Delay Function. Delay components include barriers and members of the response force. Barriers include active and passive barriers.

prevent adversary success. Response, as it is used here, consists of interruption. Interruption is defined as a sufficient number of response force personnel arriving at the appropriate location to stop the adversary's progress. It includes the communication to the protection force of accurate information about adversary actions and the deployment of the response force. The measure of response force effectiveness is the time between receipt of a communication of adversary action and the interruption of the adversary action (response force time). The PPS response function is shown in Figure 2-5. An additional measure of response force effectiveness, neutralization, is also used in some high-security applications. Neutralization is a measure of the outcome of a force-on-force confrontation between the response force and adversaries. This type of response is rarely seen in industrial applications; however, there are other aspects of response that may

qualify as neutralization in these applications. Examples include use of verbal commands, intermediate force, and arrival of local law enforcement. This concept is discussed further in Chapter 10.

The effectiveness measures for response communication are the probability of accurate communication and the time required for communication. The time after information is initially transmitted may vary considerably depending on the method of communication. After the initial period, the probability of valid communication begins to increase rapidly. As shown in Figure 2-6, with each repeat, the probability of correct and current data being communicated is increased. There can be some delay in establishing accurate communication caused by human behavior. On the first attempt to communicate, the operator is alerted that there is a call, but may not have heard all the relevant information. Then a request for a second transmission is made to repeat the information, and finally, the operator understands the call and asks for clarification.

Deployment describes the actions of the protective force from the time communication is received until the force is in position to interrupt the adversary. The effectiveness measure of this function is the probability of deployment to the adversary location and the time required to deploy the response force.

Relationship of PPS Functions

Figure 2-5 Response Function. Response components include communication, proper deployment of the response force, and interruption of the adversary before attack completion. For some threats, interruption by the response force may not be enough to counter the attack.

Figure 2-7 shows the relationships between adversary task time and the time required for the PPS to do its job. The total time required for the adversary to accomplish the goal has been labeled adversary task time. It depends on the delay provided by the PPS. The adversary may begin the task at some time before the first alarm occurs, labeled T_0 in the figure. The adversary task time is shown by a dashed line up to this point because delay is not effective

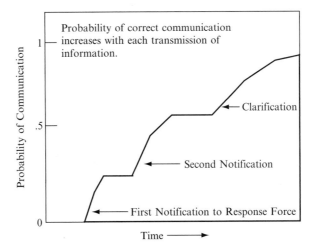

Figure 2-6 Variation of Probability of Communication with Time. As the time to establish accurate communication increases, the probability of communication increases. This is primarily due to human behavior, but can be exacerbated by radio communications problems.

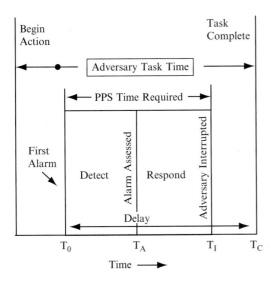

Figure 2-7 Interrelationships of PPS Functions. Detection begins on receipt of the first alarm and ends when the alarm is assessed. The delay function slows down the adversary to allow the response force time to deploy. The PPS must provide detection and enough delay for the response force to stop the adversary from successfully completing their task.

before detection. After the alarm, the alarm information must be reported and assessed to determine if the alarm is valid. The time at which the alarm is assessed to be valid is labeled T_A, and at this time the location of the alarm must be communicated to the members of the response force. Further time is then required for the response force to respond in adequate numbers and with adequate equipment to interrupt adversary actions. The time at which the response force interrupts adversary actions is labeled T_I, and adversary task completion time is labeled T_C. Clearly, for the PPS to accomplish its objectives, T_I must occur before T_C. It is equally clear that detection (the first alarm) should occur as early as possible, and T_0 (as well as T_A and T_I) should be as far to the left on the time axis as possible.

Characteristics of an Effective PPS

The effectiveness measures of the PPS functions of detection, delay, and response and their relationships were discussed previously. In addition, all of the hardware elements of the system must be installed, maintained, and operated properly. The procedures of the PPS must be compatible with the facility procedures and integrated into the PPS design. Training of personnel in policies, procedures, and operation of equipment is also important to system effectiveness. Security, safety, and operational objectives must be accomplished at all times. A well-engineered PPS will exhibit the following characteristics:

- Protection-in-depth
- Minimum consequence of component failure
- Balanced protection

Protection-in-Depth

Protection-in-depth means that, to accomplish the goal, an adversary should be required to avoid or defeat a number of protective devices in sequence. For example, an adversary might have to defeat one sensor and penetrate two separate barriers before gaining entry to a process control room or a filing cabinet in the project costing area. The actions and times required to penetrate each of these layers may not necessarily be equal, and the effectiveness of each may be quite different, but each will require a separate and distinct act by the adversary moving along the path. The effects on the adversary by a system that provides protection-in-depth will be to:

- Increase uncertainty about the system
- Require more extensive preparations prior to attacking the system
- Create additional steps where the adversary may fail or abort the mission

Minimum Consequence of Component Failure

It is unlikely that a complex system will ever be developed and operated that does not experience some component failure during its lifetime. Causes of component failure in a PPS are numerous and can range from environmental factors (which may be expected) to adversary actions beyond the scope of the threat used in the system design. Although it is important to know the cause of component failure to restore the system to normal operation, it is more important to provide contingency plans so that the system can continue to operate. Requiring portions of these contingency plans to be carried out automatically (so that redundant equipment automatically takes over the function of disabled equipment) may be highly desirable in some cases, for example, the presence of back-up power at a facility. In the event that an adversary disables the primary power source, generators or batteries can be used to power the security system. Some component failures may require aid from sources outside of the facility to minimize the impact of the failure. One example of this was the use of National Guard units to supplement airport security personnel after the terrorist attacks at the World Trade Center and the Pentagon on 9/11. In this case, the component failure was the temporary lack of sufficient response forces under new threat conditions. Another example is the failure of the primary alarm communications and display (AC&D) system. This is why many sites implement a secondary AC&D system that will still provide a monitoring capability in the event of a primary system failure. This approach also allows for the switching of system control during a duress situation at either monitoring station.

Balanced Protection

Balanced protection means that no matter how an adversary attempts to accomplish a goal, effective elements of the PPS will be encountered. Consider, for example, the barrier surface that surrounds a room. This surface may consist of:

- Walls, floors, and ceilings of several types
- Doors of several types; equipment hatches in floors and ceilings
- Heating, ventilating, and air conditioning openings with various types of grilles

For a completely balanced system, the minimum time to penetrate each of these barriers would be equal, and the minimum probability of detecting penetration of each of these barriers should be equal; however, complete balance is probably not possible or desirable. Certain elements, such as walls, may be extremely resistant to penetration, not because of physical protection requirements, but because of structural or safety requirements. Door, hatch, and grille delays may be considerably less than wall delays and still be adequate. There is no advantage in over-designing by installing a costly door that would take several minutes to penetrate with explosives, if the wall with the door were corrugated metal, which could be penetrated in a few seconds with hand tools.

Finally, features designed to protect against one form of threat should not be eliminated because they overprotect against another threat. The objective should be to provide adequate protection against all threats on all possible paths and to maintain a balance with other considerations, such as cost, safety, or structural integrity.

Design and Evaluation Criteria

Any design process must have criteria against which elements of the design will be evaluated. A design process based on performance criteria will select elements and procedures according to the contribution they make to overall system performance, which is the effectiveness measure of the system. By establishing a measure of overall system performance, these values may be compared for existing (baseline) systems and upgraded systems and the amount of improvement determined. This increase in system effectiveness can then be compared to the cost of implementation of the proposed upgrades and a cost/benefit analysis can be supported.

A feature criteria (or compliance-based) approach selects elements or procedures to satisfy requirements that certain items are present. The effectiveness measure is the presence of those features. The use of a feature criteria approach in regulations or requirements that apply to a PPS should generally be avoided or handled with extreme care. Unless such care is exercised, the feature criteria approach can lead to the use of a checklist method to determine system adequacy, based on the presence or absence of required features. This is clearly not desirable, as overall system performance is of interest, rather than the mere presence or absence of system features or components. For example, a performance criterion for a perimeter detection system would be that the system be able to detect a running intruder using any attack method. A feature criterion for the same detection system might be that the system includes two specific sensor types such as motion detection and a fence sensor.

A feature criteria approach is acceptable when protecting low-value assets from low threats, such as retail store shoplifting. In this case, a thorough quantitative analysis of security features may not be required; however, security elements can still be designed and integrated together to aid in the detection and prosecution of shoplifters. This is why even feature-based systems can use the principles described in this text to get the best protection possible for the dollars invested. In this way, the compliance requirements of a regulatory organization can be met, while at the same time the system can be optimized to actually protect assets. In our retail example, the hope that deterrence or the use of nonintegrated security measures will prevent shoplifting is not effective, given the continuing losses suffered by the retail industry despite significant investment in security measures.

The evaluation techniques presented in this text use a total system performance-based approach to meeting the PPS objectives. Each of the functional subsystems described in the following chapters will include a description of both quantitative and qualitative methods of evaluating PPS components at a facility. Quantitative techniques are recommended for facilities with high-consequence loss assets; qualitative techniques can be used if there is no quantitative data available or if the asset value is much lower. It is important to determine before the start of the VA whether a qualitative or quantitative analysis technique will be used. This ensures that the VA team collects the appropriate data and reports their results in a form that is useful for the analysis. In addition, we recommend that an adversary sequence diagram be used to facilitate either a qualitative or quantitative analysis (adversary sequence diagrams are discussed in Chapter 14 of the *Design* text, and in later in Chapter 11 of this text). As noted in Chapter 1, an effective design or evaluation of a PPS incorporates good systems engineering principles. A VA is often the initial stage of a conceptual design meant to improve protection of assets at a facility.

The performance measures for the PPS functions are:

Detection

- Probability of detection
- Time for communication and assessment
- Frequency of nuisance alarms

Delay

- Time to defeat obstacles

Response

- Probability of accurate communication to response force

- Time to communicate
- Probability of deployment to the correct location
- Time to deploy
- Response force effectiveness after arrival at the correct location

When performing a VA, the general purpose is to evaluate each element (people, procedures, and technology) of the PPS to estimate its performance as installed at the site. Once this is done, an estimate of overall system performance is made. The key to a good VA is accurately estimating element performance by considering specific degradation factors for each element. When using a quantitative approach, this can be done by starting with a tested performance value for a particular PPS element, such as a sensor, and degrading its performance based on how the device is installed, maintained, tested, and integrated into the overall PPS. For qualitative analysis, we would degrade performance of each element based on the same conditions, but we would represent the performance of the device by assigning a level of effectiveness such as high, medium, or low, rather than a number. Operation of all elements must be evaluated under all weather conditions, facility states, and considering all threats. The specific means of evaluating and degrading elements for each function of the PPS is described in more detail in Chapters 5-10.

Additional Design Elements

An effective PPS will combine people, procedures, and equipment into an integrated system that will protect assets from the defined threat. People and technology components are important design tools that often form the basis for protection systems. The use of procedures as protection elements cannot be overstated. Procedural changes can be cost-effective solutions to physical protection issues, although, when used by themselves, they will protect assets from only the lowest threats.

Procedures include not only operational and maintenance procedures but also training of facility personnel in security awareness and of guards or other response forces on when and how to stop an adversary. Another procedural design tool is the use of investigations. Investigation may be used to respond to a loss event or to anticipate a threat, such as in background investigations of potential employees. Regardless of how the investigation tool is used, it is an important design element in a PPS and should be used when appropriate. Of course, for critical high-consequence loss assets, an investigation after-the-fact may be too late. In these cases, more immediate responses are required to prevent loss of or damage to the critical asset. If the PPS is unsuccessful at preventing a successful attack, an investigation may be the only remaining method of responding to the attack. Although this will not eliminate the consequence of loss resulting from the attack, it can still be useful to apprehend the guilty party or prevent other successful attacks. It is important to note that, in this event, there is an implicit acceptance that the asset can be lost and the PPS is not expected to protect the asset.

In addition to use of the investigative tool, some corporations are applying more resources to the use of technical surveillance countermeasures, such as sweeps and searches for electronic bugging devices. This is an additional aspect of a security system that, like executive protection, can be part of an integrated approach to asset protection. The use of hotels and other nonproprietary sites for seminars or meetings provides the opportunity for industrial espionage. For these threats, a security manager may choose to send security personnel to the meeting location and ensure that a room or area is free of any recording or other surveillance equipment. Technical surveillance techniques may also be used within a facility, either on a daily basis or for some special events, such as on-site Board of Directors meetings, to prevent theft of information.

The performance measures for investigative and technical surveillance techniques do not lend themselves to quantification as readily as physical protection elements. In these cases, discovery of the person responsible for theft or damage or of the presence of surveillance devices serves as the measure of performance for the design element. These tools are useful but may not be sufficient for protection of critical assets at sites. As with any protection system, the design elements used to achieve system objectives depend on the threat, the likelihood of an attack, and the consequence of loss of the asset.

A wide variety of other procedural elements can be incorporated into an effective system design at a facility. These are too numerous to be listed in detail here, but as a general guideline, procedures should supplement a good technical design and training. Procedures that can be considered, depending on the threat and the value of the asset, include shredding of all papers before disposal, locking procedures for safes, password control and update for computer systems, random drug searches in accordance with company policies and legal requirements, periodic audits of employee computer files, and issuing parking permits to employees and authorized visitors. No matter the type of procedure used, they are another design tool that falls into one of the three functions of a good PPS—detection, delay, and response.

Summary

This chapter described the use of a systematic and measurable approach to the design of a PPS. The functions of detection, followed by delay and response, the effective integration of these functions, and a brief description of the relationship of these functions were presented. Specific performance measures of various components of a PPS were described.

Additional desired characteristics of a good PPS, including protection-in-depth, minimum consequence of component failures, and balanced protection, were also described. The process stresses the use of integrated systems combining people, procedures, and equipment to meet the protection objectives. Emphasis was placed on the use of performance-based systems, rather than feature based, because systems based on performance indicate how successful the design is at meeting the protection objectives, not just the presence or absence of components. Performance may be estimated using qualitative or quantitative techniques. The use of performance measures also facilitates a cost/benefit analysis that can compare increased system effectiveness to cost of implementation. The goal of a VA is to assess performance of the installed equipment, procedures, and personnel at the site to accurately estimate detection, delay, and response functions and to determine how well the installed PPS meets specified protection objectives.

Reference

Tickner A.H., and Poulton E.C., Monitoring up to 16 television pictures showing a great deal of movement, *Ergonomics* 16(4), 1973, 381–401.

3

Getting Started

This chapter discusses how to plan a VA and manage it as a project. There are many good sources of information on how to manage projects and as many different ways to accomplish this. Because this text is meant primarily as a description of how to conduct the technical evaluation that constitutes the VA, the material presented here is only an overview of the process; references are provided for any reader who would like additional details. The assumption is that the reader is new to vulnerability assessments in general and project management in particular, and more information is provided than experienced VA personnel might need. Readers who are more experienced in project management should skip to the section on VA team composition and roles and responsibilities. The key concepts covered in this chapter include:

- Project management fundamentals
- VA team composition, roles, and responsibilities

- Project kick off for the team and the customer

There is no equivalent chapter in the *Design* textbook for this chapter; however, the process overview provided in Chapter 1 of that book may be helpful.

Project Management

Before a VA can be performed at a site, a certain amount of preliminary work must be completed to plan out the site evaluation. The use of common project management principles and techniques provides a structure and a well-accepted method of approaching the administrative and business aspects of a VA. At a high level, a project can be broken into three major stages—planning, managing the work, and closeout. Each of these phases is described in the following paragraphs. As the organization doing the work or the project size gets smaller, there can be significant variation in the formality or explicit documentation used. It is true that smaller projects will likely have a lower risk of failure, but for a small company this can have a large impact on future work opportunities. This is why project management principles are applied to all projects. The following information is drawn from project management information provided by commercial vendors (Jones, 2005 and Ten Step, 2005) and project management textbooks (Mochal and Mochal, 2003). Additional information on project management techniques, tools, and references can be found at the Project Management Institute homepage at www.pmi.org. Because different companies designate the person in charge of the day-to-day management of a project by different names, we use the term *project leader* to describe this position. The term *project manager* is used to describe the first level of management that may supervise the project on a periodic basis. Also, the general term *customer* is used to represent the organization, agency, sponsor, or client being served by the VA. In a like manner, the organization, company, agency, or other group conducting the VA is called the *VA provider.*

Phase One—Project Planning

When preparing to start a VA, or any project, there are some general rules that provide guidance for what to expect. The first law of projects is: The only thing constant is change. If all projects actually proceeded the way they were planned, there would be no need for project management, software tools, or even signed contracts. The basic fact is that if we don't plan for change, we are taking a significant risk. Although some projects may be accomplished with no unexpected problems, this should not be the planning assumption. Having a good project plan and managing according to the plan is a

risk management technique that allows consideration of what could go wrong and how to adapt when it does. Consideration of how to manage unexpected changes will protect both the customer and the VA provider when a crisis occurs by having an agreed-upon course of action already documented. There are two corollaries to the first law of projects: Life's not fair, and we can't have more than there is. Understanding that these operating conditions are a normal part of the project provides the overarching guidance needed to successfully plan and manage the project.

A reasonable person might ask why the first law of projects is true. Typical reasons for project failure or crisis include planning done by the wrong people (marketing, management, procurement, not the project team), unclear project objectives or goals causing project personnel to not work toward the same goal, too much work planned for too short a time, unknown project milestones or other data, unrealistic cost estimates, project personnel moving on and off the project without consideration of schedule impact, and changes in project scope. To avoid these common problems, a complete project plan is needed that will address project cost, performance of the work, and schedule for completion of major and minor tasks, as well as final product deliverables.

Initial Customer Contact
Projects, by their definition, have a defined start and end date. There is a point when the work did not exist (before the project), when it does exist (the project), and when it does not exist again (after the project). Most VA projects start with an initial customer contact, perhaps as a follow-on to existing work, a reference from another person or business, or as a result of a marketing activity. However the initial contact is made, project planning starts with understanding what the customer wants or needs. It is

assumed that the VA provider is competent in this area and has the ability to provide the desired product. Clearly, if the expertise required to conduct a VA is not present, no amount of project planning can mitigate this basic flaw.

This stage of the project normally involves meetings with the customer to discuss what problems they are having or want to avoid, why they are motivated to do this now, and to discover any specific constraints they may have. For example, they may need the result in two months, or they may have only a limited budget available. As much as possible, these details must be elicited from the customer before conducting the VA. Be careful—the customer may not always know or want to share these details. It is critical to project success that the true needs of the customer are known and understood. The customer should provide information on the sensitive issues that may arise during the project. If they do not volunteer this information, it can be obtained through the use of open-ended probing questions during discussions. This step can be facilitated through the use of a nondisclosure agreement, so the customer will have some reassurance about protection of their sensitive information. It is also important to understand the politics and culture of the organization that is responsible for the site; failure to understand these issues can seriously affect project success. It is useful to interview the key stakeholders in the project; perhaps senior management, the security director, project personnel, or even a regulatory agency all have a stake in the outcome. Interview as many of these stakeholders as possible (this can be difficult to achieve but is an ideal goal) and try to gain an understanding of what they really want. Be sure to also consider any political ramifications to the VA provider or other complications that may occur during the project. In addition to clarifying customer needs for the project team, this step helps establish a close relationship between you and the customer. A key component of a successful project is having good rapport with your customer. This will allow a true partnership between the two parties, with each group working toward project success. This process is part of the Requirements stage of the systems engineering process described in Chapter 1.

It may take several meetings with the customer to clarify these details, but once this step is complete, the project can be defined at a high level. Most organizations use a proposal or preproposal process to define the project and get agreement from senior management to proceed. Smaller companies may combine these steps using fewer personnel and less formal processes, but they should achieve the same result. In some organizations, the approval step will occur even before the initial project discussions with the client; the general point is that this approval, however informal and whenever it happens, is an important part of the project management process.

Define the Project

Defining the project includes determining the scope of work, as well as what needs to be done, over what period of time, and the cost of the final product. The project scope should state the project objectives and major constraints, such as available funding or time to complete. The organization of the project should be considered at this point, including who will lead the project, how many and which staff members will support the project, and at least an estimated budget and schedule. Although VAs are generally conducted fairly quickly at the site (from a few days to a few weeks, depending on scope), the planning before arrival at the site, and analysis and reporting after the on-site visit can extend the project several months.

Generally, the project is defined in a master document, statement of work, contract, memorandum of agreement, or some other equivalent document. The master document is usually supplemented by a requirements document, which is a summary of the technical specifications, project constraints, and performance required for the delivered product.

The master document should include information concerning project scope, costs, schedule, deliverables, required legal terms and conditions, specific tasks to be performed, and any other administrative details. Additional information to be included is identification of key project personnel and a description of how the project will be organized. Project organization addresses who will lead the project and the customer point of contact, as well as the schedule of project interface or status meetings between the project team and customer, specific measures that define project success or acceptable performance, required project documentation including financial and technical status reporting to the customer, and the frequency of these reports. For most VAs, protection of project data and results must also be addressed. As a general rule, the final VA report should be classified or have limited distribution; the specific approach used to deal with this depends on the customer. Government agencies generally have specific classification guidance that must be followed, whereas private industry may or may not have this guidance developed. The master document should specify which details or products of the VA require protection; often, individual details are less sensitive than the combination of details and analysis.

One aspect of project planning documentation that is often omitted is the process for resolving unexpected project changes, such as a technical failure, reducing project cost, adding new tasks, or getting back on schedule. We recommend that the approach used when projects are not proceeding as planned should be incorporated into the master document as a specific condition. Later, if this process must be used, it will be easier to go back to the master document than to try to create the process spontaneously. Thoughtful planning of project recovery will remove the emotional element that arises when progress declines and provides an agreed-upon structure to resolve issues effectively.

Project scope includes all of the preceding information and defines the boundaries of the project. For example, if a site is very large, the VA to be conducted might not cover the whole site, but only parts of it. Or, the customer may already have a threat definition and asset identification and prioritization that will be used, so this information will not be a required task in the VA. Project scope identifies what is included and what is not included in the project. At a minimum, this should include describing what deliverables, organizations, business processes, tools, data, and capabilities are in or out of scope. A limited scope VA may not require the use of complex computer analysis tools, large teams, lengthy on-site visits, or detailed formal reports, whereas a complete scope VA may include threat definition, consequence analysis to identify critical assets, a large team on-site for several days, use of multiple complex computer models to predict system performance, and a lengthy, detailed report documenting the VA team's observations, test results, and analysis.

Often, a VA is the first stage of a longer project addressing PPS upgrades. If the project is very large and will cover several years, it is important to specify which products will be delivered in this stage of the project and which will be delivered in later stages. A related aspect of this may be clear definition of who will get copies of the final report and other groups that specifically can or cannot see the final report.

As part of project planning, the risks associated with the VA project should also be considered. Project risks include cost, performance, and schedule, as well as political, technical, safety, and staffing aspects. The more areas of the project that have risk, or uncertainty, associated with them, the more the project plan should address these risks. One method of doing this is to add money to the cost estimate for each task, where tasks that are more uncertain are estimated at higher costs than those that are better understood.

The description of project planning described here assumes that all members of the VA project team have been identified and are part of the overall project planning. This is the ideal state when setting up the project plan; however, it is likely that the time to make proposals to customers to perform a VA is limited, so deviations from the ideal are expected. If there is appropriate time to gather the project team and work the plan as a group, this will give the best opportunity to identify project issues, define tasks, construct the schedule, and make good cost estimates. If this is not possible, it is imperative that an experienced project leader develop the project plan so that an accurate assessment of the project can be generated in a timely manner.

When operating in this more constrained mode, assessment of project risk becomes all the more important. There are a few tips that can be used to reduce project risk in the planning stage. Consideration of the uncertainty associated with each task was already described. In addition, it is vital that the project leader be very realistic in the planning. A common error in project planning is in underestimating the cost of labor to complete a task. This can be due to many factors, but a common one is to assume that a project team member will spend 100% of his/her time on a project. Even if this person was assigned to the project full-time, he/she will not spend all that time working only on project tasks. People spend at least some portion of their time attending corporate training or meetings, reading email, and doing other administrative work. As a result, a good project manger will use a degradation factor for staff time spent on the project, for example 30%. This means that of the available work hours for a team member, that person will really spend only 70% of the time doing direct project work. This factor depends on the size of the company, the availability of resources, existing workload, and corporate management style. Conservative estimates should always be used; it is easier to ask for money in the initial stages of the project (and return unused money) than to try to get additional funding during the project. It is also recommended that contingency money be added to cost estimates, either as a separate task or as a small add-on cost to each task. This is another method of managing project uncertainties.

At this point, the project should be defined well enough so that senior management of the VA provider can review it and decide whether the project should be approved, delayed, or modified. Normally, by the time the project has reached this stage, there is already informal approval to proceed; however, there are times when this may not be true. There are a number of reasons why senior management might not approve a VA project, including lack of personnel, questions about technical feasibility given project constraints, legal prohibitions, or past experience with a customer. To expedite management review and approval of VA projects, standard forms can be used that summarize the project. Sample project summary and risk assessment forms are provided in Appendix A.

Phase Two—Managing the Project

After the project has been approved, the customer has sent funding, the project team has been identified, and other administrative issues are decided, the actual work can begin. Managing the project includes customer support, following the project plan, resolving major and minor project issues on a timely basis, and keeping the project on schedule, within budget and scope, and performing as expected. All of these aspects of the project are organized so that communication between the project leader and the customer and the project team occurs regularly, project risks are managed, product quality maintains an acceptable level, and all project metrics are monitored and remain in compliance. As one might guess, this isn't always easy.

Many project leaders believe that remaining on budget is really all that has to happen for a project to be successful. The better ones know that it is the balance among cost, performance, and schedule that is the heart of project management. The very best project leaders know that neither of these is really sufficient. It is not enough to know how much money was spent in a week (or any period of time); it isn't even enough to know what work was accomplished and if the project is on schedule. The real issue is knowing what work is planned to support the project. Although each enterprise will have different time periods for formal monitoring of a project, a weekly project review cycle is recommended. This means that the project leader knows each week how much money was spent, what work was completed, how closely the project is following the schedule, and what work is planned for the next week. This can be facilitated through the use of project status reports, because early identification of project issues allows more time to correct any problems. Generally, customers require status reports on some periodic basis (detailed in the master document for the project), so it only follows that the project leader needs to know the status of each project team member to report to the customer.

Project Status and Reporting

The most important reason for weekly status reports from project personnel is that it will be much easier to manage deviations from expected cost, performance, or schedule if they are identified early and when they are still small. What project leader wouldn't want to know, as soon as possible, that a project is exceeding the planned spend rate or a team member is falling behind on his/her work? As soon as an anomaly appears, it can be addressed and minor variations can be quickly dealt with, and larger issues can be identified and monitored for further action. Failure to identify deviations early and devote appropriate attention to them when they are still small can allow them to escalate into major issues that can have a substantial detrimental effect on the overall project. Weekly status reports provide the project leader the information needed to manage the project effectively and to keep in touch with the people who are doing the project work. As noted previously, smaller, shorter-duration projects that are less complex may report less formally than large, complex, or longer projects. The amount and formality of reporting are a function of the project size, scope, and risk. A sample project status report is shown in Table 3-1. Templates for many project documents are also available on a CD that is included in the Mochal book on project management.

Note that the project staff status report example in Table 3-1 gives a good amount of information in a simple, easy-to-use form. The staff member reported cost, performance, and schedule information, and also noted some issues that she is concerned about. This is one of the project staff responsibilities—to identify any problems that may be developing. If each person on the project lets the project leader know about concerns, the issues can be addressed before major problems arise. It is also worth noting that this status report includes more than one project. The objective is not to burden staff with constant status reporting, but to give them a chance to communicate with their project leaders. There is no reason why the same report can't be sent to several project leaders,

Table 3-1 *Sample Staff Project Report.*

Week: 2/5/99	Accomplishments	Status	Issues
VA1 Hours worked: 8	Reviewed drawing of site exterior sensors, created test plan for on-site evaluation, made travel arrangements to go to site. Planned next week—meet with Joe and Sue to discuss how they will test and see how we can combine efforts.	On schedule	Big new project coming in, I may be moved off this project by my manager.
VA2 Hours worked: 20	Worked on input to final report, assisted in upgrade analysis of site. Planned next week—Continue writing my section of final report.	About 2 days behind schedule	I don't have time to do all this writing, plus other stuff.
Project A Hours worked: 12	Still working conceptual design, due next week. Planned next week—Meet with project team and review design.	On schedule	None.

Note that the report includes which week is being reported, the number of hours she worked on each project, her activities this week and expected activities for next week, how she is doing compared to schedule, and a place for notes on issues she is concerned about.

who only review the pertinent information. Sometimes seeing what else the person is working on helps identify the source of any problems. Each project leader should make a point of periodically visiting each person on the team to allow an opportunity for face-to-face contact. The use of email has reduced the need to reuse a paper form, but reports should be collected at the end of each month and placed in the project file (either in electronic or paper form).

In addition to the project leader, there are others who are interested in project status. Customer reporting is defined in the master document and establishes the frequency and format of the report. It is likely that internal management will also want periodic updates on projects. Because internal management has a different purpose than customers when reviewing project status, different report formats may be required. Internal managers are not only interested in the stan-

dard triple-constraint of cost, performance, and schedule, but also in understanding project risks, what new products are being developed, how other staff or projects could benefit from the VA, and if there are any emerging issues that require their assistance. Examples of internal management reporting forms and how they are used are provided in Table 3-2 and Figure 3-1.

The forms shown in Table 3-2 and Figure 3-1 include similar information, but Table 3-2 may lend itself better to written project status reports, whereas the form in Figure 3-1 may be more useful when presenting project status orally. Some companies use arrows or colors to indicate cost, performance, and schedule status; others use earned value. Up or down arrows can be used to represent better- or worse-than-expected status, respectively. A horizontal arrow indicates that status is as expected. Colors of red, green, and yellow can also be used, where green indicates expected

Table 3-2 *Written Project Leader Status Report for Internal Management.*

Project Name	Status
Project W—One of my four projects	Cost, performance, and schedule all as expected. All milestones have been met. Customer is satisfied, but some potential for negative impact because of other commitments by key staff. Project meeting with customer scheduled for next week.
Project X—My second project	Over cost, but performance as expected.
Project X—My third	Cost, performance, and schedule as expected. Some increased risk because of change in customer point-of-contact.
Project Z—My fourth	Ahead of schedule, cost and performance as expected.

Note that the report is concise; addresses cost, performance, and schedule at a high level; and provides information on possible emerging issues. The form summarizes all the projects a project leader is responsible for and should be submitted on a periodic basis.

Project Title

[ ]   **Objective**

                                       Milestones/Deliverables

Budget
FY05 $K
FY06 $K (if applicable)
FY07 $K (if applicable)
Project #   Task #

Points of Contact   **Risk/Issues**
Project Leader:
Project Manager:
Sponsor:

Figure 3-1 Project Status Report Format for Presentations to Internal Management. Known as a quad chart, this form allows the project leader to summarize all the pertinent information about the project on one slide.

performance, red indicates a problem, and yellow indicates a potential issue. Some companies combine arrows and colors to communicate a lot of information con- cisely. For example, a red down arrow in cost would indicate that the project is over- running its budget, while a green horizon- tal arrow in performance would mean that this aspect of the project is performing as expected.

Earned value is another method of showing current project status that is used by many government agencies. This method allows for a comparison of cost and schedule factors to provide a measure of project performance. To compute earned value, cost variances are monitored by taking the ratio of budgeted costs to actual cost; schedule variations use the ratio of milestones achieved to milestones scheduled. In each case, the closer the measure is to 1.0, the better. An excellent tutorial on earned value has been created for the U.S. DOE and is available on the Web (DOE, 2005).

Recovery Plans

Even the best-planned and managed projects can run into serious problems at times. When this happens, remain calm. Many projects experience a crisis because of unpredictable events such as turnover of customer contacts, construction delays, a sudden reduction of project funding resulting from cost overruns in other areas of the customer's program, unexpected technical problems, or (for some military facilities) the outbreak of war or a regional conflict. This leads to the second law of projects: The customer is not always right. This is not to say that we won't do everything we can to make a customer happy and provide the desired product, but at the same time, we need to manage customer expectations to reduce any negative consequences to either party. After all, left to his/her own judgment, the customer wants the VA provider to take all the risk and the customer to reap all the benefits. Despite the desire to please the customer, the customer may sometimes ask more than can reasonably be provided or more than is contractually required. This is when a properly written master document will show its value.

When the project is in crisis, review with the customer the section of the master document that describes how prob-

lems will be resolved; reassure the customer that, by working together, an acceptable option will be created; gather any new or unknown information; and set up a face-to-face meeting. At the meeting, be firm, come prepared with multiple options, and don't be afraid to tell the customer (diplomatically, of course) that some changes are too big to be easily accommodated without a major impact. One option includes doing the work in more phases, so that existing resources are used most effectively and give the customer as much of what is needed as possible. Other phases can be funded after the initial phase is complete. For example, if a VA was scheduled to be performed at a site, but the customer must cancel because the funding was reprogrammed, work with the customer to keep enough funding to stabilize all the existing facility information that has already been collected, and then store the information until the customer can fund the rest of the project. This is an instance where the corollary "Life's not fair" may apply.

For some major crises (maybe disaster is more appropriate), the project must be rescoped because the environment has changed (a new senior manager is in place at the customer's site), a major problem has occurred (a successful attack like 9/11), or a new set of customer requirements has been identified (new laws since 9/11). Many security projects change scope because someone complains about the cost or operational impact. This is an opportunity to go back to the master document, review the agreed-upon success metrics, and decide how to proceed. Seek assistance in these details—that is the reason the master agreement was written.

The expected outcome of problem discussion and resolution is a recovery plan, which describes what steps will be taken to get back on track. Often this results in a reduction of work to be performed so that the dollars remaining can be used best; sometimes it requires movement of personnel off the project. It is also important to review the success metrics for the project in this case, as they may need to change. In fact, there are only a few things you can do to get back on track—do less work, take more time, or accept less capable products. This is an example of the other project law corollary—we can't have more than there is.

Project Management Tools

Several tools are available to aid in project management. Project management software that combines cost, performance, schedule, and personnel assigned (Microsoft Project®, Scitor Project Scheduler®, Primavera®); reporting tools, mostly in the form of word processing or publishing software (Microsoft Word®, Adobe Pagemaker®); financial reporting tools (Business Objects®); and project tools used at an enterprise level (Oracle®, SAP®). Every company will likely have its own desired tool set, or there may be a customer requirement to use certain tools. The tools are useful, but they are only tools and do not replace good project leaders. Once again, depending on the size of the VA provider or the VA project, varying levels of formality will be required. In larger organizations, a dedicated financial staff may be available to assist the project leader with financial or status reporting, and software tool experts may be available to support the project.

Project Closeout

At some point, all the direct project work is completed, all deliverables are in the customer's hands, the last status reports to the customer have been provided, and the project is complete. This is not entirely true; there are still some remaining issues that the best project leaders will address before closing the project. Project closeout can be broken into three areas: financial, administrative, and technical. At a minimum,

financial closeout must be completed; the other aspects are strongly recommended.

Financial closeout of the project provides a final accounting of all project costs and allocation of funds to complete the project. This includes verifying that enough funding remains to cover all outstanding financial commitments for the VA, capturing the final cost of the project, and returning any unused funds to the customer. Administrative closeout tasks include collecting all project documentation, storing it in an archive, destroying drafts or working papers no longer needed, returning any customer-owned equipment or documents, and verifying that all sensitive information is properly marked and protected appropriately. The technical closeout of the project can include a project closeout meeting, a lessons learned review, and a closeout report to the customer or internal management. Additional details about project closeout are discussed in Chapter 12.

Project Management Summary

The use of good project management principles, tools, and skills will help scope, define, manage, and complete a successful VA project for both the VA provider and the customer. A master document should be constructed that specifies project details, especially concerning cost, performance, and schedule, but also defining what is and isn't included in the project scope, how and what information will be communicated, success metrics, and a description of the conflict resolution process that will be followed in case of project deficiencies. A combination of project planning and management techniques will minimize the effect of inevitable project problems and provide a framework to work through major project hurdles. Most important, build and maintain a good relationship with the customer so that both parties can work together effectively during stressful times.

Establish a Vulnerability Assessment Team

The following information describes the roles, responsibilities, and functions of VA team members. The description is fairly detailed so as to provide a complete explanation of VA team roles and responsibilities. The major functional responsibilities of a VA team require a project leader and appropriate subject matter experts (SMEs). Many VA teams will use only a few personnel to serve these roles. Each team member may perform multiple functions, but all appropriate functions must be performed for a thorough VA. Completion of the primary functions may require other support personnel (for example, simulation operators, technical writers). Note that this section addresses only the actual VA team. The contributions of facility operational, safety, and other representatives are described later in the section "Participation of On-site Personnel"? Depending on whether the VA team is composed of employees from inside the company or outside contractors hired by the company, the number of on-site personnel assisting in the VA can vary.

Vulnerability Assessment Project Leader

As with any project, the VA team needs a person who will lead the project and handle the day-to-day administrative and financial aspects, as well as the technical evaluation activities. The key responsibility of the VA project leader is management of the VA. The project leader should perform the following tasks that support this role:

- Ensure the team is properly prepared and equipped.
- Oversee the predeployment collection of information necessary to support the assessment.
- Develop/implement the VA schedule.
- Assist in the initial site briefings to customer representatives and key personnel.
- Oversee control of sensitive or proprietary information.
- Interact with and support the team SMEs to ensure successful completion of the VA and resolve issues that may arise to present barriers to the successful completion of the VA.
- Serve as the team's primary point of contact with facility management and staff.
- Ensure completion of required briefing materials, analysis, and VA reports documenting the results of the VA.
- Provide final site briefings to customers' senior management.
- Conduct follow-on activities after the VA is completed to meet project objectives.

Systems Engineer

For some very large teams, projects, or programs, a systems engineer may be needed. The key responsibilities of the systems engineer are to maintain a broad view of the VA and to ensure that the results support short- and long-term goals of all stakeholders. This includes customer relations, managing political agendas, technical system quality, trade-off analysis, and project management. The systems engineer works at the highest level of system integration. Often, this person is also the project or program manager. The systems engineer has the following duties:

- Ensure that good systems engineering principles and processes are applied during the VA within the context of the larger program or system. These include technical management, requirements definition, design, implementation, and technical evaluation.

- Represent higher level management interface to the VA team and other related activities.
- Connect the activities of the VA with other related activities for the same customer or program by facilitating communication between the VA team and the appropriate program.
- Define, clarify, and document requirements of program and VA.
- Oversee (or perform) appropriate trade-off analyses.
- Manage impacts to or conflicts between the VA and Program/Customer and take early action to avoid problems.
- Present conceptual framework to VA team to help them interpret and understand requirements.
- Ensure smooth technical project with no surprises or adverse consequences to Program/Customer.
- Work closely with the VA project leader to meet project and program goals in a consistent and seamless manner.

Security System Engineer

The key responsibilities of the security system engineer are to ensure integration and evaluation of the individual components of the PPS that contribute to the functions of detection, delay, and response, and to identify vulnerabilities. The security system engineer is usually an SME in some aspect of physical security, with broader knowledge and experience in other areas of a PPS. The security system engineer performs the following duties:

- Coordinate with other SMEs to ensure completeness in evaluation of PPS components.
- Consult with SMEs to estimate performance of PPS components.

- Assist with system evaluation tests for comparison to existing performance measures.
- Focus on PPS integration and performance, based on component performance estimates.
- Ensure that people, procedures, and technology are all evaluated during the VA and that no major gaps are left.
- Assist VA team in deciding rigor of evaluation testing required appropriate to system and objectives of VA.
- Assist analyst in preparing the site adversary sequence diagram (ASD).
- Evaluate the system for exploitable weaknesses that may degrade the performance of the system as a whole.
- Work with other VA team members to explore possible solutions to problems identified in the analysis of system effectiveness.
- Provide evaluation results to the VA project leader for inclusion in the site analysis, final VA report, and associated briefing materials.

SME—Intrusion Sensing Subsystem

The key responsibilities of the sensor expert are to provide estimates of exterior and interior sensor performance and identify their integration with other components of the PPS. For high-value or very complex sites, there may be separate members to cover exterior and interior sensors. The sensor expert performs the following duties:

- Characterize the various exterior and interior sensors installed at the site or the use of human observation for detection. Document notable characteristics of the installed components with notes, pictures, sketches, etc.
- Determine which evaluation tests are appropriate to support performance estimates and conduct these tests.
- Estimate the detection probabilities of the detection system at each path

element in the ASD against each applicable threat.

- Provide notes and observations on other aspects of the PPS to other VA team members.
- Evaluate the sensor subsystem for exploitable weaknesses that may degrade the performance of the system.
- Assist analyst in preparing the site ASD.
- Work with other VA team members to explore possible solutions to problems identified in the analysis of system effectiveness.
- Provide results to the VA project leader for inclusion in analysis, the final VA report, and associated briefing materials.

SME—Alarm Assessment Subsystem

The key responsibilities of the alarm assessment expert are directed at the alarm assessment subsystem in use at the site. The alarm assessment expert performs the following duties:

- Document method of alarm assessment—manual or video.
- If manual (human) assessment, note time to make assessment and provide time and probability estimate to analyst.
- Review video assessment subsystem and determine appropriate tests needed to support performance measure estimates.
- Conduct evaluation tests of system for comparison to documented performance measures.
- Verify video integration with sensors.
- Characterize video assessment subsystem including resolution, recording capability, time for video display, efficiency of operator actions, ease of system operation, maintenance, lighting, placement and type of cameras, archiving procedures, assessment procedures, and other details.

- Evaluate the video assessment subsystem for exploitable weaknesses that may degrade the performance of the system as a whole.
- Assist analyst in preparing the site ASD.
- Work with other VA team members to explore possible solutions to problems identified in the analysis of system effectiveness.
- Provide alarm assessment results to the VA project leader for inclusion in the site analysis, final VA report, and associated briefing materials.

SME—Alarm Communication & Display (AC&D) Subsystem

The major responsibilities of the AC&D expert are to evaluate and document subsystem operation. The AC&D expert performs the following duties:

- Observe subsystem operators and determine effectiveness of operator, console layout, time to assess alarms, and other duties of operator under a range of conditions.
- Review subsystem and determine appropriate evaluation tests to estimate performance.
- Document subsystem including console layout, procedures, equipment and uses, and operator training.
- Determine effect of subsystem on overall system integration and performance.
- Evaluate the subsystem for exploitable weaknesses that may degrade the performance of the system.
- Assist analyst in preparation of site ASD.
- Work with other VA team members to explore possible solutions to problems identified in the analysis of system effectiveness.
- Provide results to the VA project leader for inclusion in the site analysis, final VA report, and associated briefing materials.

SME—Entry Control Subsystem

The responsibilities of the entry control expert are to evaluate entry control technology and access control procedures for entry and exit of personnel and material. The entry control expert performs the following duties:

- Review entry and access controls and determine appropriate tests (if any) required to evaluate system.
- Observe entry and exit procedures and document entry control equipment, maximum throughput, differences in procedures during operational and nonoperational times, and related details.
- Evaluate access control procedures, databases, and database protection.
- Evaluate the entry control subsystem for probability of deceit for outsiders or insiders to gain entry to the site or limited access areas within the site.
- Assist analyst in preparation of site ASD.
- Work with other VA team members to explore possible solutions to problems identified in the analysis of system effectiveness.
- Provide results to the VA project leader for inclusion in the site analysis, final VA report, and associated briefing materials.

SME—Delay Subsystem

The main responsibilities of the delay expert include providing estimates of barrier delay, describing potential facility damage during an attack, and developing potential solutions to identified problems in this area. The delay expert performs the following duties:

- Estimate the delay times of each barrier at the site against each applicable threat by conducting evaluation tests and reviewing historical data.

- Estimate traversal time across site areas listed in the ASD by each selected threat type (vehicle, foot, aircraft, other) based on the localized topography.
- Assess potential damage from air blast, debris, and shock produced by explosives, if part of threat capability.
- Assist analyst in preparation of site ASD.
- Work with other VA team members to explore possible solutions to problems identified in the analysis of system effectiveness.
- Provide delay times to the VA project leader for inclusion in the site analysis, final VA report, and associated briefing materials.

SME—Response Subsystem

The key responsibilities of the response expert include estimating the response time to deploy to assigned locations and the ability of responders to prevent adversaries from completing a malevolent act. For many facilities, response is from off-site, such as law enforcement; for some, responders will be emergency personnel, such as fire and medical. Whatever response will be used for a security incident, the response expert must determine how effective the response will be. The response expert performs the following duties:

- Review guard post orders, procedures, plans, and enterprise or facility requirements.
- Observe the response force in the performance of routine and incident responses (if possible).
- Conduct interviews with members of the response force.
- Conduct evaluation tests to determine whether response force personnel have the skills and abilities necessary to perform their duties, whether procedures are effective,

and whether equipment is functional and appropriate.

- Conduct tests to determine the time required to respond to attacks on all assets.
- Assist other VA team members in testing.
- Assist analyst in preparation of site ASD.
- Determine the effectiveness of the response force to neutralize potential adversaries, once deployed, to an asset location, if applicable.
- Provide results to the project leader for inclusion in the site analysis, final VA report, and associated briefing materials.

SME—Communications Subsystem

The major responsibilities of the communications expert are to provide performance estimates of the communications systems in use at the site and their integration with other components of the PPS. The communications expert performs the following duties:

- Review communication systems technology and procedures in use and determine appropriate testing to evaluate performance.
- Identify all communication end points and estimate probability of successful communication between nodes. Examples include communications between patrols and main dispatch, between guards at post and main dispatch, and between deployed response elements.
- Conduct jamming tests to determine communication effectiveness, if appropriate.
- Locate and evaluate equipment locations for elements of the communication system, such as repeaters, communication hubs, and main dispatch.
- Evaluate the communication subsystem for exploitable weaknesses that

may degrade the performance of the system.

- Assist analyst in preparation of site ASD.
- Work with other VA team members to explore possible solutions to problems identified in the analysis of system effectiveness.
- Provide results to the VA project leader for inclusion in the site analysis, final VA report, and associated briefing materials.

SME—Analyst

The key responsibilities of the analyst include oversight of the analysis phase of the VA process to ensure that the results of the VA are conceptually meaningful, technically defensible, discriminating, and consistent. The analyst has the following duties:

- Ensure that data are accurately and adequately collected and that the analysis is conducted and reported in a manner that supports customer understanding.
- Validate any experimental strategy used so that, given the time and resources available, it yields analytical results that are correct, understandable, defensible, and as replicable as possible.
- Construct the site ASD of the facility and provide it to other members of the VA team to support their data collection efforts.
- Given the data collected by the VA team, conduct an analysis of the effectiveness of the system for the defined threat and identified targets.
- Work with other VA team members to identify potential upgrades. These should be functional improvements to detection, delay, or response.
- Develop and ensure adherence to and use of a standard simulation protocol if conducting simulations in support of an analysis.

- Identify the scenarios selected by the VA team to be used in the analysis. If any simulations are performed, identify the number of simulations required for each scenario to achieve an acceptable level of confidence in the results.
- Identify assumptions made, input data used, and other information used in the analysis (e.g., detection values, assessment capabilities, and delay times).
- Ensure information required to recreate the analysis is saved.
- Provide analysis results to the VA project leader for inclusion in the site analysis, final VA report, and associated briefing materials.

Special Note for Response Force Simulations

In some VAs, most notably those done for the military or other government agencies with highly critical assets and an immediate armed response, a neutralization analysis using simulation software tools is performed. This expert is accomplished in the use of certain force-on-force modeling tools. These tools are used only where an actual force-on-force confrontation between an on-site response force and the adversaries is possible. In private industry, neutralization will more likely include a force spectrum, which may range from presence through use of deadly force by local law enforcement or the site security force. It is unlikely that neutralization simulations will be used in these cases. The key responsibility of the neutralization technical is to determine the effectiveness of the response force in any engagement confrontation with the adversary. The neutralization analysis expert performs the following duties:

- Recruit, manage, and lead simulation tool operators.
- Work with the project leader and analyst to effectively support the VA.

- Collect and create terrain files and other required data for simulation tools.
- Oversee actual simulation tool evaluation runs.
- Oversee training of on-site personnel in the simulation tool, if necessary.
- Work with other VA team members to characterize the PPS in the simulation.
- Assist in the conduct of modeling and simulation to measure the effectiveness of the security force to neutralize potential adversaries after arrival at a location.
- Provide the results of the neutralization simulation to the VA project leader for inclusion in the final VA report and associated briefing materials.

Participation of On-Site Personnel

Whether direct employees of the enterprise or an outside contractor conducts the VA, the assistance of personnel familiar with the operational aspects of the facility being evaluated will be required. An exception to this requirement occurs when the VA is to be conducted by personnel normally assigned to the facility. In this case, the VA team may have complete knowledge of all operational aspects of the site; however, it is still possible that the assistance of other facility personnel will be necessary.

At a minimum, the participation of facility safety, operations, process, and security personnel will be needed. If there is an on-site response force, they will also be an important part of the VA. If off-site law enforcement or other groups provide response, a representative of that group should be included. Normally, points-of-contact at the site are established for the VA team to assist in preparation and planning of the VA, as well as for support when the team is on-site. It is expected that some clarification will also be necessary after the VA team has left the facility and is performing their analysis. It is critical that facility personnel understand their role in the VA and are given the appropriate time to support the VA team. For this reason, there is often a senior management liaison to the VA team. This person generally ensures that facility personnel are assigned to the VA team and their work assignments are adjusted to allow them to support the team, particularly during on-site activities. The key point is that participation of facility personnel will be required, and this aspect of assistance should be emphasized to the customer before starting the VA.

Kick-Off Meetings for Project Team and Customer

Before starting the VA project, it is helpful to have kick-off meetings with the project team and the customer. These meetings often can't be held because of cost concerns, time limitations, or practicality. This step may not be necessary if the VA is done by employees of the company that owns the facility or if the team is experienced. Customer kick-off meetings are a necessity and can be held either as a series of meetings with senior managers or as one meeting just before the VA team starts on-site work.

Project Team Kick-Off Meeting

The project team kick-off meeting is meant to familiarize all team members with the project scope, deliverables, schedule, and funding, as well as to answer any questions. It is not crucial that every project detail be covered at this time (all details may not be known), but presumably team members are relatively easy to contact. If not, the team may need to agree to a periodic meeting schedule via teleconference or email. At a minimum, the project leader should provide the team a detailed description of the project including the customer's objectives, the project sched-

ule and budget, a review of any travel arrangements that must be made, the deliverables and their format, and how customer contact will be managed.

This meeting is also the time to start planning the VA. An overview of the site layout, geography, weather, and operations can be presented, along with any information concerning threats and targets. The tools that will be used in the analysis are usually known, but if not, this is a good time to initiate discussion about appropriate analysis tools. Using the scope of the VA as a guide, team members should also start to identify the data that should be collected, any tests that should be completed at the site, equipment needed to support tests, and how data will be reported. Depending on the scope of the VA, a considerable amount of information can be required to facilitate the VA. Additional details about the data to be collected are addressed in subsequent chapters on conducting the VA; this discussion is limited to the administrative start of the project. Summary and sharing of this information can be expedited through the use of a team guide.

VA Team Guide

It can be useful to summarize all of the known information about the project and site in a VA team guide, which serves as a means of communicating information to all project team members and as a living document that captures site information. The guide is a reasonably detailed description of the planned activities, but does not need to be extremely lengthy. It is expected that some portions of the guide will be common to all VAs and other portions will be unique to a specific site. The team guide should include a description of the background of the VA, how it will be conducted, team assignments, logistics, and administrative details.

The background section should discuss the objectives and scope of the VA, the site to be visited, the mission or purpose of the site or facility to be assessed, and other pertinent information. This information should include such things as the need to define threats or identify targets, the specific data required from team members and the form of this data, and dates for delivery of preliminary and final reports from each team member. A description of what data are to be protected and how they should be protected should also be included in this section.

The conduct section should describe in detail the evaluation activities to be performed in each area; that is, detection, delay and response functions, analysis, and reporting. This section should include a description of the data to be collected and review of the data collection sheets introduced in Chapter 5. Analysis review should include the level of analysis to be provided, the responsible personnel for various analysis elements, and how team inputs to analysis activities will occur. The method of reporting, primary personnel providing reports and briefings, and report format should also be reviewed.

Depending on the project, the project leader may write the final report, all members of the team may contribute, or a technical writer may be responsible for this. If a team approach is chosen, certain decisions must be made before writing. Understanding the report format before VA initiation will significantly reduce production time and allow team members to focus their attention on their specific areas of responsibility. Issues that should be considered when discussing reporting include the format of the report, protection of the data and report, how individual sections will be incorporated, how photos and pictures will be included, and how editing will be handled. Discussion regarding these aspects of the report early in the project will ensure smooth integration of all team member sections and a faster completion of the report.

The next section should list VA team assignments and the roles and responsi-

bilities of each team member. Often a particular team member is present to collect information in a number of areas, particularly with respect to the technical evaluation of the system, so these guidelines will remind team members of their specific contributions.

A logistics section should also be included that should provide information on travel arrangements (if necessary), communications among the team, and how the team will get onto the site. Travel arrangements would include flight information for each team member, hotel arrangements, and availability of rental cars within the team. Communications details include having a list of pager, cell phone, and email addresses for each team member, in case one member is delayed or a change is required. For some sites, there is an access procedure that must be followed. One member of the team will need to be responsible for collecting appropriate personal information on all team members and providing this to the host site. Logistics information may not be required if most of the team is assigned to the site being evaluated.

The logistics section should also contain a rough schedule for the VA. The schedule should be broken down by day, which will help the team and the site plan for the activities that need to be accomplished and identify team members who can assist others at times. A sample schedule is shown in Table 3-3. One final piece of information that should be included is a list of the site points of contact and their phone numbers, departments, and locations. This list may also include site management, in the event that their support is needed.

Site Information

Whatever the scope of the VA, a variety of site-specific data is required to complete the planning phase of the VA. This information is necessary to plan and carry out the VA in the most efficient and least intrusive manner possible. The more this

Table 3-3 *Sample VA Schedule.*

Day/Time	Activity	Responsible Contact
Monday morning	Briefing to facility managers and staff	Ms. Doe, Project Leader
Monday afternoon	Set up VA team work area	Mr. T. Dog, Security Manager
	Facility tour	
Tuesday morning	Sensor Evaluation	Mr. S. Mann
	Entry Control Evaluation	
Tuesday afternoon	Video and alarm assessment	Mr. T. Vee
After full sunset	night evaluation	
Wednesday morning	Alarm Communication and Display	Mr. Vee
Wednesday afternoon	Access Delay Evaluation	Mr. Mann
	Begin analysis	Ms. Doe
Thursday morning	Response Evaluation	Mr. S. Bullit
	Continue analysis	
Thursday afternoon	Revisit any areas of interest	TBD
	Final analysis	
	Prepare briefing	
Friday morning	Briefing to facility managers	Ms. Doe & Project team
Friday afternoon	Clear work area, pack up equipment	
	Depart site	

This schedule shows the anticipated evaluation activities for each half day and the responsible point of contact. The schedule may take more or less time, and have fewer or more team members, depending on the scope of the VA and the complexity of the site.

information is known before the team arrives at the facility, the easier and faster the VA will be, thus limiting the cost and duration of the team visit. The VA project leader, or his/her delegate, usually sends an initial data request to the site. The following list is a guide to the data that may be included in the initial request; items may be added or deleted based on the scope of the VA. Information requested generally includes:

- Drawings showing perimeter, buried utilities, buildings, site layout, and detailed blueprints of appropriate areas. It can be easier to have these drawings in electronic form, but this is not always possible. Maps of the surrounding terrain are also useful.
- Site details such as number of personnel, shift schedules, locations of critical assets, locations of PPS equipment in use, positions of guards, patrol routes, and any guard weapons. Unusual weather condi-

tions and other environmental details are also required.

- All on-site personnel who will assist the VA team, including physical and email addresses, and phone and fax numbers.
- Request for workspace for the VA team to use while on-site. The size of the workspace depends on the size of the VA team and should include access to power for computers and network access if the VA team members are employees of the enterprise.
- Technical specifications of PPS components currently in use at the site, including make and model number, as well as maintenance procedures for these elements. It is also useful to have copies of installation, maintenance, and testing logs.

Customer Kick-Off Meeting

An important aspect of the VA project is a briefing to senior management at the site that will be evaluated. The better the goals of the VA are communicated to management, the easier the evaluation, with few objections to team activities. The management briefing should be accomplished using Microsoft PowerPoint or a similar software tool to create electronic slides. For most companies today, electronic briefings are the expected norm; however, for some companies or agencies, transparencies or even index cards are the norm. Be sure to use a briefing style and format that meets customer expectations and practice, or that is described in the project master document. This briefing clearly describes the goals and objectives of the VA, how it will be used, when it will be completed, and how the results will be communicated. For some sites, senior management will receive the report directly. For others, the report may be submitted to another group, who will then distribute the results to the site. Be sure to leave time to answer questions and don't overschedule this event. Be flexible enough to skip over parts of the briefing if senior mangers have many questions, or bring them back on schedule by suggesting that their questions will be addressed in future slides. A sample briefing template is available in Appendix B.

Once the VA team arrives on-site, it is useful to have a kick-off meeting to explain the VA to lower level facility personnel. Senior management, site points-of-contact, the site security manager, operations and safety representatives, the entire VA team, and others should be invited to this briefing. If facility senior management has already heard a briefing on the project, they may not attend, although it is good practice to invite them or a representative. It is always a welcome touch to invite the most senior manager at the facility to address the group and express support of the process; at the very least, the security manager of the site should be an active part of this briefing, especially if the VA team is from off-site. Every effort should be made to provide a kick-off meeting at the start of the site evaluation, but if this is not possible, the project leader should be prepared to brief managers and staff at the facility before collecting data in each of the functional areas. There will be questions by facility personnel before the VA, so be prepared to answer them, possibly many times.

Summary

This chapter discussed preparing for the VA by addressing project management, VA team composition, and kick-off briefings to the project team and customer. A brief overview of project management principles and techniques was provided, along with notes on how these apply to a VA. Roles and responsibilities of each VA team member were presented, as well as additional notes on the participation of facility personnel who are most familiar with operations at the site. Notes on conducting kick-off meetings with the VA team and the customer were presented. The chapter also included a sample VA schedule and a briefing template for customer presentations.

References

Erika Jones and Associates, information available at http://www.ejaprojects. com, April 18, 2005.

Mochal, T., and Mochal, J., *Lessons in Project Management*, Berkeley, CA: Apress, 2003.

TenStep Incorporated, available at http:// wwwtenstep.com/open/0.0.0TenStep Homepage.htm, April 18, 2005.

U.S. Department of Energy, available at http://oecm.energy.gov/Default.aspx? tabid=79, April 18, 2005.

4
VA Process Inputs—Establish Protection Objectives

Before starting a VA, it is critical to understand protection system objectives. These objectives include threat definition, asset identification, and facility characterization. Each enterprise defines vulnerability assessment and risk assessment differently. Rather than focusing on the semantics of what is included in each of these evaluations, suffice it to say that because a VA concentrates on determining PPS effectiveness, defined threats and prioritized assets are required inputs to the process. This chapter provides an overview of determining protection objectives before performing a VA. In addition, there are some basic facility functions, operations, and other characteristics that must be considered during the VA. The background information for this chapter can be found in Chapters 2-4 of the *Design* text. The key concepts discussed in this chapter include:

- Defining the threat
- Identifying assets and prioritizing them by consequence of loss

- Creating a matrix relating threats and assets
- Characterizing a facility to perform a VA

At sites where the threat and assets have not already been defined, this task must be included as part of the VA project. This will likely add cost and time to the project; therefore, it is critical to know if this information exists before finalizing these details in the project plan.

Defining the Threat

Threat definition establishes the performance that is required from the PPS. We would not evaluate a PPS protecting an asset from vandals the same way as a system protecting an asset from armed criminals. By describing the threat, the assumptions that were made to perform the assessment are documented and are used to show how they influence required upgrades. As such, threat definition is a tool that helps site managers understand the impact of successful attacks by defined adversaries and helps PPS designers understand the requirements of the PPS.

The following is a brief summary of the threat definition process described in the *Design* text. After this review of the overall process, some of the methods that are used to define threats are discussed. The process for threat definition consists of three basic activities:

1. Listing the information needed to define the threat
2. Collecting information on the potential threat
3. Organizing the information to make it usable

Listing Information Needed

Before the threat can be defined, information that would be most useful to know about the adversary must be understood. Typically, this information includes the adversary class (insider, outsider, collusion between insiders and outsiders), and their goals, motivation, and capabilities. Adversary goals include theft, sabotage, or other goals, such as workplace violence, sale of illegal drugs on-site, and creating negative publicity about activities or ownership at the facility. Theft can include removing physical items or information. Sabotage may involve damaging critical equipment, release of hazardous material, or modification of data or proprietary information. Some adversaries' goal is to draw attention to a site because of philosophical objections. The key concept is that by defining this information about the expected adversary, the PPS can be designed to assist in protection of the appropriate assets. For example, a protestor may want to climb the fence at a company that raises and supplies laboratory animals for scientific research to express their concern about animal cruelty. This is

a much lower threat than an employee who brings a gun to work to shoot a manager or co-worker. If a gun is one of the expected tools of the adversary, there are ways to design a PPS to detect entry of weapons. A threat definition often includes a spectrum of threats that reflects the presence of a variety of assets at the facility.

Collecting Information

The collection of threat information is accomplished by reviewing available documentation and by contacting agencies that may have useful threat information. These organizations could include local, state, federal, or military law enforcement agencies and related intelligence agencies. The following types of information may be reviewed for their use in defining threats:

- Incident reports at the site. This could include criminal reports, intelligence reports, and other historical data.
- A list of contacts for law enforcement activities.
- The number of personnel at the facility and types of positions. Employee numbers versus the number of contractors, visitors, and vendors. Any problems that may have occurred with any of these groups and incidents such as domestic violence, union disputes, downsizing, and other problems should be identified.
- Reports of criminal or terrorist activities in the area.
- Review publicly available information from sources such as the Internet, local newspapers, professional associations, and government sources. The U.S. Department of State compiles lists of terrorist activities each year that are available to the public (Department of State, 2005a and 2005b). The Department of Homeland Security is also a source of threat

information for many critical infrastructure segments (SWERN, 2005). The U.S. Department of Justice, Office of Justice programs also provides crime statistics online at http://www.ojp.usdoj.gov/bjs/.

Organizing Information

After potential threat information has been gathered, it should be organized to make it usable, and to facilitate decisions concerning which threats will be included in the threat spectrum used to assess the effectiveness of the existing PPS. A table to assist in the organization of the data was provided in the *Design* text.

Because the threat definition will likely consider both insiders and outsiders, characteristics of both types of adversary should be part of the threat definition. A determination is also made concerning an insider's desire and capability to collude with an outsider to accomplish their theft or other goal. At a minimum, a single insider should be considered in collusion with an outsider. An insider's actions depend on a number of factors, including their access to the asset, position in the organization, ability to carry weapons onto the site, and their knowledge of security at the site. Insiders generally include groups such as contractors, vendors, and visitors.

Threat Definition Methods

We have seen four methods used to define threats, and each is useful in specific applications.

1. Develop threat from historical or intelligence data.
2. Use a policy-based threat issued by an appropriate agency or organization.
3. Create a range of potential threats (threat spectrum).

4. Use defined scenarios of adversary attack.

In some cases, there is sufficient historical data to develop an accurate profile of the likely threats facing a site or enterprise. An example of this might be vandals or criminals who damage or steal lower value assets. There are usually crime statistics available for these types of attacks, and this information can be used to help define these threats, in addition to the site's own internal incident data. This is common practice at medium to large U.S. corporations.

In other cases, there is little historical data, but intelligence data indicate the likelihood of a specific threat. An example is the terrorist threat to many critical U.S. facilities. The intelligence community makes every effort possible to gather current and relevant information to provide early warning of a malevolent act at a specific location. This information often forms the basis for PPS design at critical government facilities and some private industry sites, particularly those identified as critical infrastructures.

Some organizations, including the U.S. DoE and Department of Defense (DoD), as well as large multinational U.S. corporations, use a policy-based threat as their threat definition. In these cases, a specific group within the organization creates the threat definition that is used by all other groups within the organization. The group defining the threat generally has access to intelligence information and has studied various attacks on their sites or other sites that are similar in some aspect, and use this information to create a credible threat definition. For some organizations, this threat is a single threat statement, and for others, it includes a threat spectrum. In either case, the threat that is created is called the design basis threat (DBT) and is used in all VAs conducted across the organization. In addition, local attributes are commonly used to modify the threat as needed. It is important to emphasize that the DBT may not represent the real threat; it is an assessment by informed and qualified people that represents credible threat capabilities. The real threat may be higher or lower than the DBT; thus the DBT is used as a management and design tool to document one assumption of the PPS design or evaluation.

In some cases, there is little historical or intelligence data available to assist an analyst in the development of a threat profile. In this case, the organization might just select and define a range of threats and capabilities, for example, vandals, criminals, and competitors, and use these as benchmarks for the VA of their PPS.

In addition to the methods listed previously, some organizations take a slightly different approach to threat, which is to use certain defined scenarios. This method can achieve the same goal as threat definition as long as the scenario provides enough detail about adversary tools, capabilities, and tactics so that the VA team has enough information to be able to complete their analysis. For example, one scenario at a facility located along a waterfront might be that adversaries use a boat to access the site, enter a building, damage a hazardous chemical control valve so that the chemical will slowly drain from a tank, and then run back to the boat and escape. While this seems like a fairly detailed scenario, it would be much more effective for the VA team to know how many people are part of the attack, whether they are carrying weapons, what tools they are carrying, and whether they would actually use their weapons. In addition, this adversary group could have insider assistance in the form of information so that the adversaries would know where to find the tools on-site needed to damage the valve. Although the threat is generally defined first and then used to create credible attack scenarios, the use of scenarios in place of a threat definition can be useful, as long as the scenario description is detailed enough to allow the

VA team to analyze the PPS and determine vulnerabilities. A range of scenarios is often created, and each site is left to select those that are applicable; this leaves open the possibility that some sites will only select one scenario, whereas others may select several, often occurring simultaneously. This variation can cause different sites with similar assets to implement different protection schemes, which could be counterproductive to the protection objectives of the larger enterprise. In this case, an asset that is similarly valued by an organization could actually have different levels of protection, which could create attack opportunities for an adversary.

It is worth pointing out that recent malevolent attacks, such as the sarin gas attack in the Tokyo subway, 9/11, the anthrax attacks in Florida and New York, and the Madrid train bombings, demonstrate that some adversary groups are developing new capabilities in chemical, biological, and explosives weapons of mass destruction. As a result, a number of recent U.S. laws have established new expectations with respect to security at some facilities. These include the U.S. Patriot Act, the Bioterrorism Preparedness Act, and the Maritime Transportation Security Act of 2002. These laws are having some effect on threat definition at certain facilities, and there is a corresponding expectation that security at these sites will be appropriate for these threats. One example is the requirement to improve security at ports, rail stations, airports, and other transportation systems (Transportation Research Board, 2005).

Insider Threat

One category of threat that causes considerable problems when designing a security system is insiders. Reports consistently show that insiders are responsible for the many security events that occur at all sites overall (Hoffman et al., 1990; CSI/FBI, 2005). Because insiders already have authorized access to a site, many PPS elements cannot be used to detect insider intrusions. For example, exterior perimeters will not be effective against insiders, because they will enter the site through entry control points using legitimate photo badges or electronic credentials, and detection won't be possible. As a group, insiders can exploit their knowledge of the facility and its operations, including security elements, can choose the best time and strategies for a successful attack, may have access to the most critical areas of a site, and may have access to the PPS itself, which can be used to conceal an attack.

Depending on the particular site and their policies and procedures, it can be difficult to collect all the pertinent information required to define insiders. Examples of issues include the disparity in reporting and categorizing insider crimes and the lack of prosecutor feedback after case disposition. Insider attacks can include theft of equipment, money, proprietary or classified information, high-value products such as precious metals, or embezzlement. Acts of sabotage include such things as vandalism, arson, bomb threats or actual bombings, and equipment tampering. One study (Hoffman et al., 1990) showed that insider criminals are among the most difficult adversaries to protect against and that financial gain was their primary motivation, although other factors such as family ties, intimate relationships, dissatisfaction, and ideological beliefs also played a role. This study also showed that guard forces present a special and troublesome problem. Insider acts can be accomplished by individuals, in cooperation with other insiders, or as allies of outsiders. A more recent study, although focused on computer security, provides additional insights into insider capabilities and motivation (U.S. Secret Service, 2005).

Just as with outsiders, insiders may be willing to kill or be killed, may abort an attack to avoid capture if they suspect they have been detected, and may use covert or overt actions as tactics. The insider can be divided into four categories, as shown in Figure 4-1. Insiders may be passive or active, with active insiders further broken down into rational and irrational groups. The rational group can then be subdivided into violent or nonviolent types.

Passive insiders provide information to other insiders or outsiders; active adversaries actually participate in the attack in some way. An irrational insider may not follow a clear decision process and can use violence indiscriminately. This group could include employees who are mentally unstable or under the influence of illegal substances or alcohol. Rational nonviolent insiders may tamper with, and use limited covert force against, PPS elements and are likely to try to avoid identification; rational violent insiders use force, weapons, and possibly explosives against PPS hardware, barriers, or personnel to ensure success. Characteristics of each insider threat category are shown in Figure 4-2.

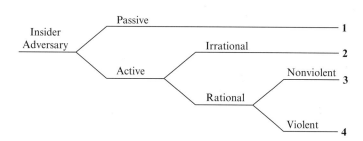

Figure 4-1 Insider Threat Categories. All categories may not exist at a site, but each group has special characteristics that are important to consider when evaluating the PPS.

Insider category	Characteristic
1. Passive	Provides information to a colluding adversary or an outside group
2. Irrational	Does not follow a clear decision rule; uses violence indiscriminately
3. Rational Nonviolent	May tamper with and use limited covert force against protection elements; is not willing to be identified
4. Rational Violent	Uses overt force, weapons, and explosives against hardware, barriers, or personnel to increase chances of success

Figure 4-2 Characteristics of Insiders. Note that passive insiders only provide information; the other categories are all subsets of an active insider threat. Irrational threats may be a result of mental illness or drug or alcohol abuse.

Insiders complicate the evaluation (and thus the design of upgrades) of a PPS for a number of reasons. In some cases, the insider threat is not even considered because of cultural values. For example, the Japanese, until recently, would not include insiders as part of their threat spectrum at critical sites. In other cases, it can be hard to convince senior management that insiders are a threat to critical assets. This view is often accompanied by the belief that some levels of employees are more trusted than others; for example, senior managers versus production personnel. Protection is needed against all insiders, regardless of their level of access, authority, or knowledge. In addition, PPS measures to detect insiders often have an adverse operational impact, such as the use of two-person rules or requiring security clearances.

In general, insider threats are addressed by removing them from the employee population, reducing their opportunities for theft, preventing any actual attempted thefts, recovering stolen material, and by material controls to verify that thefts have not occurred. These techniques are incorporated into the PPS through the use of background investigations, varying access controls across a site, inventories of critical assets, reduction and consolidation of some critical assets at a site, and periodic drug testing at some sites. All aspects of insider protection are required to be integrated into the overall PPS to be effective, which is one reason why this is such a complex problem. When conducting a VA, it is important to note the PPS elements in place to prevent insider attacks, assuming insiders are part of the threat spectrum. This choice can be made by individual clients and customers, but we have yet to visit a site where insiders were not an actual threat, so we recommend including them in any VA.

Other Notes on Threat Definition

Many companies and agencies have a DBT that describes the threat applied at a facility. Although these may exist, they often do not contain sufficient detail, or they may need to be modified for some locations. For instance, the use of explosives by some threats is a concern since the attacks on 9/11. When considering the use of explosives, it is important to specify the quantity that will be used. The amount of explosives in a backpack will have a different effect than the amount that can be carried in a large vehicle, such as a dump truck. The use of a vehicle bomb should specify the amount of explosives and the vehicle type and weight. In the past, vehicle attacks were limited to vehicles that weighed 4,000 pounds; however, this has recently been increased to 15,000 pounds by some government agencies. This is why threat definition should be as specific as possible—the vulnerability of the PPS depends on the adversary and their tools. By thoroughly defining the threat, we are establishing the required performance of the final PPS.

If a large company or a government agency is planning to do VAs at their facilities, it should agree on the threat before the evaluations begin. One of the biggest benefits of using a defined threat in a VA is that multiple sites can be compared to each other based on the same set of assumptions. In this way, senior management can see an "apples to apples" comparison of all sites and a more accurate view of the current vulnerabilities can be presented. This controlled comparison will assist senior managers in making informed decisions about which sites need the most attention and help them prioritize the application of their limited resources. Constant changing of the threat at different sites will make it difficult to make meaningful comparisons of the results of all the VAs and use the results to optimum advantage.

Whichever process is used to define threats, it is critical that customers concur with the threat definition that will be used. Occasionally, at sites that have no existing threat definition, this concurrence does not occur until the end of the on-site part of the VA, because the threat is developed in parallel with the VA. To mitigate the difficulty created by this arrangement, a variety of threats should be analyzed to cover a threat spectrum that will include all credible threats under consideration. It should be noted that time to develop the DBT on-site will delay the start of site evaluation activities and may delay delivery of the final report.

Estimating Likelihood of Attack

Another aspect of threat definition that has proven to be difficult to accomplish at times is determining the probability of attack by the defined threat. As noted previously, historical data can be used to define the adversary; it can also be used to predict the probability of attack. Criminal statistics exist for different crimes in different geographic locations, so this is a ready source of data (National Law Enforcement and Corrections Technology Center (NLECTC), 2005). As noted in Chapter 1, probability of attack is really a part of risk assessment, but many organizations want to know this as part of the VA. Figure 4-3 shows a crude but simple method of estimating the probability of attack, in a qualitative manner. Appendix C contains a worksheet that can also be used to estimate the probability of attack.

The probability of attack may also be expressed as a frequency or likelihood. These terms are often used interchangeably, although there are some differences. Probability is the likelihood that a specific event will occur, expressed as the ratio of the number of actual occurrences to the number of possible occurrences. Frequency is the number of times a specified periodic phenomenon occurs within a specified interval. A probability provides a quantitative description of the likely occurrence of a particular event; frequency includes a time element. Either term can be useful in threat definition. At some point, the likelihood of attack may be less important than the value of a highly critical asset. In the largest sense, this is a function of the asset owner's risk tolerance, but all businesses have some critical assets, and they must be protected. In these cases, it can be more useful to consider how well protected the asset is assuming an adversary attacks.

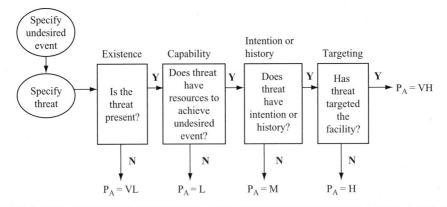

Figure 4-3 Simple Method to Estimate Probability of Attack. By following the flow of criteria, a crude determination of the probability of attack can be made. If desired, a conversion from a qualitative to quantitative estimate can be made by selecting a numerical value to represent the qualitative level, although this is not a mathematically rigorous approach.

This concept is captured through the use of conditional risk, where the condition is that there is an attack. The use of conditional risk was discussed in Chapter 15 of the *Design* text and in Chapter 1 of this text. The use of conditional risk allows the organization to focus on the protection around the asset, rather than spend a lot of time debating the likelihood of attack. This is most useful for highly valued or unique assets, which probably require protection irrespective of the likelihood an adversary will attack. Customers occasionally misinterpret conditional risk to mean that the likelihood of attack is 1.0 (i.e., it is a certainty that the asset will be attacked). This is not the case at all; more accurately, this means that we don't know the likelihood of attack and that the consequence of loss of the asset is high enough so that the estimate is not required. No matter what the likelihood of attack, loss of the asset is an unacceptably high consequence, and it will be protected. This is a subtle but important point.

Asset Identification

In addition to threat definition, the VA team must have an understanding of the assets to be protected at the site. As with threat definition, some customers do not have their assets identified and prioritized before performing a VA. In this case, this step must be accomplished before performing the VA. The following discussion is a brief overview of the asset identification process. For additional information on this process, refer to Chapter 3 of the *Design* text. Once assets have been identified, this information must be shared with the VA team. Occasionally, local management at a site will add assets to the already prioritized list, which can complicate the VA. In this case, we recommend including the new assets, while still focusing on the agreed list.

Asset Identification Methods

Asset identification is an evaluation of what to protect by considering the value of the asset to the facility or enterprise. There are three steps for identification of assets: (1) specify undesirable consequences; (2) select asset identification technique; and (3) identify areas, components, or material to be protected.

Three methods for asset identification are reviewed in this section. They include manual listing, logic diagrams to identify vital areas for sabotage attacks, and the use of consequence analysis to screen and prioritize assets. The first two techniques were covered in the *Design* text and so will only be summarized here, whereas the use of consequence analysis is described in more detail later. Other methods of asset identification can also be found in Fisher and Green (1998) and Hess and Wrobleski (1996).

Other aspects of asset identification include consideration of the form of the asset and adversary tactics. The form of the asset cannot be ignored—once a particular asset is identified as valuable enough to protect, it must be protected in all forms. For example, if the asset is a trade secret that is stored on paper in a safe and also in an electronic file on a network, the protection must be equal. This is another example of balanced protection— all paths to the asset must be equally difficult for the adversary. At a high level, this implies that network and physical protection must be roughly equal. If they are not, the asset may still be vulnerable, even if the PPS is very effective. In addition, there are several adversary tactics that can be used to steal information. Insiders can memorize details over a period of time, fax the information off-site, or carry it out on small electronic media, such as USB drives. Some of these attacks are difficult to detect and prevent, but are worth considering in the overall protection scheme. Another insider tactic is protracted theft. In this case, a knowledgeable insider may steal low quantities of tangible assets, such as computer chips, drugs, or other valuable items, and accumulate larger quantities over time. This can be difficult to detect, even in cases where process controls are used, and it is another example of why the form of the asset is important. While it is a given that there can never be absolute security, the form of the asset should be considered when defining threats, identifying assets, and evaluating the effectiveness of a PPS.

Manual Listing

For theft of localized items such as computers, tools, proprietary information, or work-in-process, the manual listing of assets is an appropriate technique. Because these are theft targets, the undesirable consequence to be avoided is loss of the asset. This technique consists of listing the assets of concern and their locations. The list provides the assets to be protected. The manual technique can also be applied to theft of product-in-process (such as semiconductors or drugs) or sabotage of critical components if the facility is small or processing is very simple. Product-in-process may also include individual pills before packaging or filled bottles waiting to be loaded into cases. Intermediate process steps may be good theft targets, particularly for insiders. If a production line is very complex or if multiple production lines are at work, the opportunities for theft of these assets may be broadly distributed throughout the plant, not limited to the end of the production line. In addition, storage and shipping areas are also locations of interest. Or, consider a large petrochemical plant with sabotage as a concern. Many complex systems, each with hundreds of components, interact to produce, route, and store the finished products. Furthermore, many support systems such as electrical power, ventilation, and instrumentation are interconnected to primary components, such as pump motors, in a complex manner. Asset identification must consider which systems and components to protect, as well as their interaction with other support systems.

Logic Diagrams

The logic diagram is a useful tool for determining potential theft and sabotage targets for a complex facility. Because of the complex nature of this process, experienced experts in the use of logic diagrams should be consulted before initiating this activity. Because logic diagrams are used to ensure there is a thorough understanding of where theft or sabotage can occur, the undesirable consequences may vary. Theft assets may have loss of revenue or competitive advantage as undesired consequences, whereas sabotage targets may use loss of life or environmental damage as the undesired consequence. Excellent resources on the use and construction of logic diagrams are provided in Kumamoto and Henley (1996) and by the Nuclear Regulatory Commission (NRC, 1981).

Consequence Analysis For some large organizations or facilities, there may be too many targets of attack to use manual listing or logic diagrams to identify assets. In these cases, it may be more appropriate to use a screening methodology to help reduce the number of assets to a more manageable number. Over time, all assets can be evaluated using a VA, but by using a screening methodology, assets can be prioritized, with the highest ranked assets receiving the most immediate attention. Asset screening using consequence analysis is described in this section.

Consequence of Loss It is not possible or practical to protect everything at a site at the same level. Effective security protects what needs to be protected to prevent undesirable consequences. Much of this determination will be a function of the risk tolerance of the enterprise that owns the assets, but some assets have an unacceptably high consequence of loss and must be protected. Some examples of undesirable consequences are:

- Damage to national security
- Successful terrorist attacks
- Loss of control of nuclear material or weapons
- Loss of life as a result of hazardous material release
- Loss of market position

Note that the undesired consequence is the final result of a successful adversary attack and not just the completion of the attack tasks. For example, in the boat attack on the chemical valve, the adversary completes the attack when the valve is damaged; the undesired consequence is leakage of enough hazardous chemical to cause environmental damage, injuries to people, or loss of life.

Depending on the undesired consequences that the site is trying to avoid, different adversary tactics need to be considered, and an analysis of the potential harm that will occur is required. For example, if the undesired consequence is loss of life because of release of a toxic gas by a saboteur, a consequence analysis is conducted to determine the potential effect of this malevolent event. Some sites may have multiple undesirable consequences and, therefore, may need to capture all of these states in a single overarching statement of undesirable consequence, such as loss of facility, and then list under this all the consequences that could cause this outcome. In some government agencies, the assets to be protected range from low-value items, such as laptop computers, to unique national resources, such as the Statue of Liberty or the Brooklyn Bridge. Because of this diversity of assets and their corresponding diversity of value, a screening methodology is used to help identify the most critical assets that need protection. This screening approach is accomplished through the use of consequence analysis. A good example of this is the problem faced by the U.S. Department of Homeland Security—with so many potential targets available across the nation, some screening process must be developed that will identify a prioritized list of assets. This allows the application of limited resources to the most critical assets first, then attention to other assets over time. The key to a good consequence analysis is development of a set of criteria.

Criteria

The most critical part of screening is to develop a small set of criteria that can be used to judge which assets have the highest potential of causing the undesirable consequences if lost. Screening identifies undesired events, evaluates the consequences of these events, and uses the results to decide whether a particular facility or asset should be included in the assessment. The outcome of the screening methodology is a list of assets that are designated as high, medium, or low consequence.

The VA project leader is responsible for facilitating the screening process with appropriate personnel, which will include facility safety, operations, management, and security staff, and may also include local, state, or federal government agencies, depending on the site to be evaluated. It is worth noting that some industrial sites are now designated as part of the national critical infrastructure, and as such they are receiving greater scrutiny by various elements of the government. As a result, there is a greater need for these sites to perform VAs that are accepted by these agencies. It is likely that future VAs at these sites will use common threats and asset criteria so that the results can be compiled and compared. The asset screening process is composed of five steps:

1. Identify undesired events. Indicate which undesired events are most important to the site owner or which will have the greatest potential impact on their continuing operation.
2. Determine consequence criteria. For each undesired event, determine one or more measures of consequence. We recommend making these quantifiable, not subjective, criteria. The use of quantifiable criteria will be easier to defend under external scrutiny and will prevent manipulation of the criteria to achieve a desired answer.
3. Determine measures for consequence criteria. For each criterion, determine what values would constitute a high, medium, or low measure of consequence. This establishes the screening matrix.
4. Consequence analysis. Evaluate each asset that can produce the undesired consequence if attacked, using the criteria and measures.
5. Prioritize assets. Using the completed consequence analysis, rank order assets from highest to lowest and determine what level will be used to identify assets for the VA.

The screening process flow is summarized in Figure 4-4.

An example of the screening matrix that includes undesirable consequences, criteria, and measures is shown in Table 4-1. Note that this is not a table from an actual site, but shows a variety of undesirable consequences and criteria and what measures define high, medium, and low effects. Once the matrix is constructed, different site assets are compared and judged using the matrix. The more "highs" the asset scores, the higher its priority. Once this exercise is completed, decisions can be made about how far down the list the VA team will go for its site evaluation.

Threat/Asset Matrix

After threats have been defined and assets have been prioritized, a considerable amount of information will be generated that can be used to establish protection system objectives. The volume of information can be combined into a matrix that relates probability of attack, threat level and tactic, and consequence of loss of assets. Figure 4-5 shows an example of how this chart is constructed. Presentation of data to senior managers of the enterprise using this technique will quickly summarize and relate these details to each other. This is a good way to reduce information

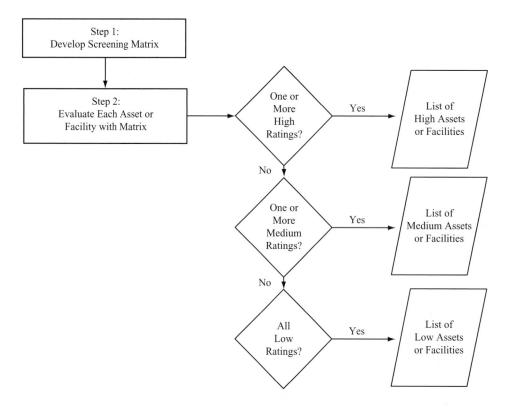

Figure 4-4 Asset Screening Flowchart. This is a summary of the asset identification screening process. First the criteria for screening are developed, then assets are rated using the criteria. Assets are prioritized based on the overall rating of the asset.

Table 4-1 *Sample Screening Matrix for Asset Identification.*

Undesired Event	Criteria	High	Medium	Low
Damage to national security	Loss of classified information	Loss of top secret	Loss of secret	Loss of unclassified
Terrorist attack	Loss of life	>3,000	100–3,000	<100
	Number of injured	>5,000	1,000–5,000	<1,000
	Property damage	>$1B	$100M–1B	<$100M
Hazardous material release	Loss of life	>1,000	10–1,000	<10
	Environmental damage	>$20M	$1–20M	<$1M
Loss of customer confidence	Customers lost	>50	10–50	<10
Loss of major function	Revenue loss	>$10M	$1–10M	<$1M

By specifying the undesired event, criteria, and a range of consequences, critical assets can be identified and prioritized for protection.

High Consequence	Terrorist (sabotage)		Insider (theft)
Medium Consequence		Insider (sabotage)	
Low Consequence	Vandal (graffiti)		Hacker (Web deface)
	Low Probability	**Medium Probability**	**High Probability**

Figure 4-5 Threat and Asset Matrix. This is a useful presentation tool that summarizes much of the information collected when establishing protection system objectives. Note that it relates threat level, tactics, and probability of attack to consequence of loss of assets.

to an understandable matrix and focus management attention on the highest risk events. The different shading is used to emphasize the areas of highest risk (i.e., where the probability of attack and consequence of loss are both high) and lowest risk. The highest risks must be addressed to protect assets; lower risk assets may be addressed through procedural changes or other risk management alternatives. The decisions about which combinations of probability of attack and consequence of loss represent the highest risk are a reflection of the enterprise's risk tolerance.

Facility Characterization

The major part of a VA is facility characterization, which primarily consists of evaluating the PPS at the site. Considerable detail about how this is done will be provided in following chapters, but an overview of the process is described here. The goal of a VA is to identify PPS components in the functional areas of detection, delay, and response and gather sufficient data to estimate their performance against specific threats. The PPS is characterized at the component and system levels, and vulnerabilities to defeat by the defined threat are documented.

Data collection is the core of PPS characterization; accurate data are the basis for conducting a true analysis of the ability of the PPS to meet its defined objectives. Accuracy, however, is only one of several factors to consider. The data gathered must be appropriate to the purpose and scope of the VA, and the quantity and form of the data must be sufficient to support analysis based on available resources and desired confidence in the results.

An ideal assessment uses statistically significant data derived from a series of tests that evaluate the system and individual components under all expected conditions. In almost all cases, this is not practical because of time or resource constraints and the desire to minimize the disruption caused by the VA team. To address this issue, historical performance test data are used in lieu of actual performance tests, although specific installation and maintenance of components, along with many other factors at a site, influence the actual performance of those components. For example, a specific type of sensor installed at a site may have a significantly different actual detection probability than the detection probability developed by a testing organization under controlled conditions. The historical performance data are then modified by security system experts based on conditions at the facility that cause degradation in performance of the installed component.

Methods used to collect PPS characterization data for a VA include site tours and observations, document reviews, and interviews. Evaluation testing is another valuable data-collection method for determining the effectiveness of the installed PPS. A detailed discussion of these activities is provided next.

Characterization Tools

A site tour is usually conducted early in a VA. During the initial site tour, the VA team begins to gather information regarding the general layout of the facility, the locations of key assets, information about facility operations and production capabilities, and locations and types of PPS components. Subsequent tours and observations of facility operations are conducted by VA team members to:

- Become familiar with specific facility layouts
- Examine the locations of PPS components
- Verify that documentation accurately reflects the current condition and configuration of the site
- Identify anomalies or deficiencies that require further investigation
- Select specific areas or components as candidates for evaluation testing

Group and individual tours allow the VA team to observe the actual operating environment at the site and note details that affect system performance. This is often one of the most productive activities of the VA team because of the nature of the information that can be obtained. To quickly gather information and obtain maximum benefit from these tours, the following should be considered:

- Observe procedures during normal operations whenever possible. For example, observe vehicle search procedures while interviewing entry control personnel.
- Observe actual operations. For example, ask the people who normally conduct operations to demonstrate procedures rather than having other staff describe or demonstrate how they think a procedure is performed.
- Note areas that require further review.

The review of key documents and selected records are two important PPS characterization activities. These are useful in the evaluation of the effectiveness of a PPS and may begin during the planning phase of a VA. PPS documentation reflects the site's philosophy and approach to implementation and maintenance of the system. Information obtained from document reviews will verify information received from briefings, site tours, and interviews; gather information about the existence and performance of PPS components; support PPS analysis; and give an overall view of the PPS at a facility.

The PPS characterization step of a VA includes interviews with key site personnel. Interviews are critical to clarify impressions or contents of document reviews and to gain greater insight into specific facility operating procedures. Interviews with personnel at all organizational levels are recommended. Frequently, interviews with key personnel will reveal whether policies and directives are effectively communicated and implemented and whether systems actually function as described in documentation. Interviews are not necessarily formal and will frequently take the form of discussions that occur during site tours and evaluation testing.

The VA team should ensure that the personnel being interviewed understand the question and answer accordingly and that the right questions are asked of the right people. One useful technique is to ask personnel in one group how other groups perform. For example, ask alarm operators how long it takes to get equipment repaired. Another useful technique is to ask questions while observing personnel perform routine activities. These are some questions to consider when using this technique:

- Is this a normal procedure?
- How long has it been this way?
- Are there alternatives to this procedure and when are they used?
- Is there training on this procedure?

Testing is the most valuable data-collection method for evaluating the effectiveness of a PPS. Evaluation testing can determine whether personnel have the skills and abilities to perform their duties, whether procedures work, and whether equipment is functional and appropriate. Evaluation tests include functional, operability, and performance tests. Functional tests verify that a device is on, and that it is performing as expected (i.e., a sensor still has a probability of detection of 0.9). Operability tests verify that a device is on and working (i.e., a sensor is on and detects, but has moved because of vibration and so is aimed at the wrong location). Performance testing is the characterization of a device by repeating the same test enough times to establish a measure of device capability against different threats. (A sensor is tested many times using crawling, walking, and running tactics and under day, night, and varying weather conditions to fully characterize the probability of detection and nuisance alarm rate.) Performance tests may be conducted on individual PPS components or on the overall PPS. Because performance testing is fairly rigorous and requires many repetitions over time, they are generally impractical during a VA. Performance testing is typically performed in a lab or nonoperational facility.

Evaluation tests may vary in complexity from a simple test of a sensor through an attempt to carry a contraband item into

a facility, and up to a tactical response exercise involving adversaries and large numbers of security response personnel. Some tests can be conducted under normal conditions, in which the component, system, or person is not affected or alerted. Other tests must be conducted under artificial conditions, although realism is always a primary planning consideration. The project leader works with team members and on-site staff to coordinate the planning and conduct of tests. This process can be informal for simple technical evaluation tests, or very structured for more complex tests requiring more coordination, such as response force exercises.

Facility States

One of the goals of the VA team before any system analysis is performed is to identify the various facility states that can exist at the site. A VA is used to establish vulnerabilities at a site at all times of the day and at all times of the year. As such, the team must understand the various facility states, so that they can determine whether the PPS is more or less vulnerable at these times. If the team does not identify these states and determine system effectiveness during all of these different states, the VA will be incomplete and may lead to a false sense of protection. Examples of facility states include normal operating hours, nonoperational hours, a strike at the site, emergencies such as fire or bomb threats, and shift changes. For example, it is common practice to turn off interior intrusion alarms in work areas during operational hours. This eliminates constant alarms as personnel carry out their work and is called access. Other facility states that address the status of intrusion sensors include secure (all sensors are operating) and alarm (sensors are activated by something). The status of other PPS elements also should be considered. If vaults, safes, gates, or doors are open and unlocked at different times of the day, they will have different performance against malevolent threats than if they are closed and locked. In addition, performance of all PPS elements must be considered under daylight or nighttime, and the expected weather conditions at the site. Exterior sensors and cameras are affected by fog, rain, snow, and wind; interior cameras may not work well if the lights are turned off in rooms. It should be clear that these facility states and combinations must be considered to truly determine how vulnerable the site is to an attack.

Security Checklists

Most, if not all, security textbooks use a security survey to support the evaluation of a site when establishing vulnerabilities (Fisher and Green, 1998; Hess and Wrobleski, 1996). These can be useful starting points, but should not be relied on for a thorough evaluation. One problem is that these surveys do not document the effects of the observed state of equipment. Asking if there are fences or cameras or access controls present is not sufficient to determine if they are working properly. Another problem is that these lists are somewhat vague in their criteria. For example, almost every checklist asks if lighting is adequate, but it is unclear what adequate means. Is it adequate if lights are present? What if lights are present, but they don't light areas where cameras are located? Or, what if lights are present with cameras, but the light-to-dark ratio is too high or too low? These aspects of the VA are discussed in more detail in Chapters 5-10, but the general point is that checklists are only a starting point. The VA is used to establish what PPS components are installed at a site, and how vulnerable they are to an adversary attack. Checklists may document presence, but not effectiveness, of installed components. As noted in Chapter 2, documenting presence of components is not the recommended approach to evaluating a PPS, particularly when pro-

tecting critical assets. A form that can be used to document protection objectives, characterize the facility, and summarize analysis is provided in Appendix C.

Summary

This chapter discussed the protection objectives of a VA, especially the importance of defining the threat, identifying assets, and characterizing the PPS at the site. Threat definition was reviewed, along with some resources to help define threats in preparation for a VA. Asset identification methods were also reviewed, and additional details given about how to screen many assets and reduce them to a prioritized list. This is useful when dealing with very large enterprises with a variety of assets. The chapter ended with an introduction to facility characterization, particularly focusing on the PPS at the site. This section introduced some of the activities and techniques used by the VA team when performing their evaluation. Considerable additional detail on this aspect of a VA is described in the next chapters.

References

Federal Bureau of Investigation/Computer Security Institute, Annual Computer Security Survey, available at www.go CSI.com, April 20, 2005.

Fisher, R.J., and Green, G., *Introduction to Security*, 6th ed., Boston: Butterworth-Heinemann, 1998, 168–171.

Hess, K., and Wrobleski, H., *Introduction to Private Security*, 4th ed., Minneapolis/St. Paul: West Publishing, 1996, 423–429.

Hoffman, B., Meyer, C., Schwarz, B., and Duncan, J., *Insider Crime: The Threat to Nuclear Facilities and Programs*, RAND Report to U.S. Department of Energy, February 1990.

Kumamoto, H., and Henley, E.J., *Probabilistic Risk Assessment and Management for Engineers and Scientists*, 2nd ed., Piscataway, NJ: IEEE Press, 1996, 165–226.

National Law Enforcement and Corrections Technology Center (NLECTC), Criminal Justice links, available at http://www.nlectc.org/links/justnet.html, July 15, 2005.

Nuclear Regulatory Commission (NRC), 1981, W.E. Vesely, F.F. Goldberg, N.H. Roberts, and D.F. Haasl, Fault Tree Handbook (NUREG-0492), available at http://www.nrc.gov/reading-rm/doc-collections/nuregs/staff/sr0492/, April 20, 2005.

Southwest Emergency Response Network (SWERN), available at www.SWERN.gov, April 18, 2005.

U.S. Department of State, Significant Terrorist Incidents, 1961–2003: A Brief Chronology, available at http://www.state.gov/r/pa/ho/pubs/fs/5902.htm, April 19, 2005a.

U.S. Department of State, Country Reports on Terrorism 2004, available at http://www.state.gov/documents/organization/45313.pdf, April 29, 2005b.

U.S. Secret Service, 2005, National Treat Assessment Center (NTAC), Insider Threat Study: Illicit Cyber Activity in the Banking and Finance Sector, available at http://www.secretservice.gov/ntac_its.shtml, April 19, 2005.

Transportation Research Board, available at http://www4.trb.org/trb/homepage.nsf/web/security, April 20, 2005.

5

Data Collection—Intrusion Detection Subsystem

The detection function in a PPS includes exterior and interior intrusion sensors, alarm assessment, entry control, and the alarm communication subsystem all working together. Intrusion detection is defined as knowledge of a person or vehicle attempting to gain unauthorized entry into a protected area by someone who can authorize or initiate an appropriate response. As shown in Figure 2-2, an effective PPS must first detect an intrusion, generate an alarm, and then transmit that alarm to a location for assessment and appropriate response. The most reliable method of detecting an adversary intrusion is through the use of sensors, but this can also be accomplished by personnel working in the area or an on-site guard force. Exterior sensors are those used in an outdoor environment, and interior sensors are those used inside buildings.

The key concepts discussed in this chapter include:

- Review of sensor technologies and performance measures
- Description of the classification of sensor technologies
- In-depth notes on representative types of sensors and how they are evaluated
- Estimating intrusion detection performance

The background information for this chapter can be found in Chapters 6 and 7 of the *Design* textbook, but a brief review follows. This chapter focuses on the use of sensors to initiate detection; a section on the effectiveness of human observation is also included. As noted in Chapter 1, we do not recommend or even use checklists when we conduct VAs at sites. We do, however, recognize that there is a lot to know and do to characterize a PPS and document the VA in the analysis and final report. A series of data collection sheets is provided in Appendix D that can be used by the VA team to document observations and important points about sensors (and other technologies and PPS elements described later). These are not checklists but can be used to remind VA team members of what to look for and provide a tool for taking notes on PPS components. These notes can then be used in the analysis of the system and as documentation for the final report.

Sensor Overview

Intrusion sensor performance is described by three fundamental characteristics: probability of detection (P_D), nuisance alarm rate, and vulnerability to defeat. These three fundamental characteristics are heavily dependent on the principle of operation of a sensor and the capability of the defined threat. An understanding of these characteristics and the principle of operation of a sensor is essential for evaluating the intrusion sensor subsystem at a facility.

The probability of detection depends primarily on:

- Threat to be detected (i.e., walking/running/crawling intruder, tunneling, etc.)
- Sensor hardware design
- Installation conditions
- Sensitivity adjustment
- Weather conditions
- Condition of the equipment
- Maintenance/testing

An intrusion sensor may have one P_D for a low-level threat, such as a vandal, and another lower P_D against a more sophisticated threat. This is an area where the threat drives the VA. If the defined threat is three criminals with considerable knowledge and skill, a sensor with a higher P_D is required because the adversary is more capable. If the threat is teenagers vandalizing property, a lower P_D can be tolerated, because the threat is correspondingly less. Similarly, it would be impractical to use a microwave sensor in an area that received deep snow accumulation during the winter, as this could allow an adversary to tunnel undetected into the facility through the snow. When a high P_D is required 24 hours a day under all expected weather conditions to protect assets, sensor evaluation must consider both the threat and the operating environment.

A nuisance alarm is any alarm that is not caused by an adversary intrusion. Nuisance alarm rate (NAR) is a function of the number of nuisance alarms over a given time period. In an ideal sensor system, the NAR would be zero (0.0); however, in the real world all sensors interact with their environment, and they cannot discriminate between adversary intrusions and other events in the detection zone. This is why an alarm assessment subsystem is also needed: Not all sensor alarms are caused by intrusions. Alarm assessment is used to determine the source of the alarm and whether it requires a response, which is why one basic principle of security is that detection is not complete without assessment. It is not useful or effective to send guards to assess alarms, because many alarms will be due to nuisance sources. Alarm assessment is discussed in detail in the next chapter. False alarms are those nuisance alarms generated by the equipment itself (whether by poor design, inadequate maintenance, or component failure) and the false alarm rate (FAR) is a function of these over a given period. Different types of intrusion sensors have different sensitivities to these nuisance or false alarm sources, and a high NAR or FAR will degrade overall PPS effectiveness. Note that these definitions differ from those commonly used in security.

Different types and models of sensors have different vulnerabilities to defeat. There are two general ways to defeat sensors:

- Bypass—Because all intrusion sensors have a finite detection zone, any sensor can be defeated by going around its detection volume. Examples of this include bridging over or digging under perimeter sensors, or entry through a door that has no sensor.

- Spoof—Spoofing is any technique that allows the adversary to pass through the sensor's normal detection zone without generating an alarm. Use of this technique depends on threat capability and installation and maintenance of the sensor. An example would be moving very slowly through a sensor's detection area to defeat the automatic gain control that is designed into most exterior sensors to reduce nuisance alarms.

There are several ways to classify the many types of intrusion sensors. In this discussion, five methods of classification are used:

- Passive or active
- Covert or visible
- Line of sight or terrain following
- Volumetric or line detection
- Application—exterior or interior

Exterior sensors are grouped into three application types: freestanding, buried line, or fence-associated sensors. Interior sensors are grouped as boundary penetration, interior motion, and proximity sensors.

Before the three fundamental characteristics of any intrusion sensors can be determined, it is important to understand the principle of operation of the sensor. This step is most important during the initial system design, when local environmental and operational conditions must be considered to minimize nuisance alarms and optimize sensor performance. Unfortunately, this careful consideration does not always occur, which has the dual effect of wasting dollars spent on technology, and creating opportunities for suc-

cessful adversary intrusions. Each sensor technology will perform within the limits of the laws of physics, and interactions between sensor hardware and the physical environment are part of the evaluation, along with proper installation, maintenance, and operating procedures, and an understanding of the expected threat. Because the number of products available is too large to describe fully in this book, some common sensors and their principles of operation are described next to show how information is gathered and used during a VA. The performance required of each component and the overall system depends on the capability and motivation of the threat, along with the value of the asset.

Exterior Intrusion Sensor Technologies and Evaluation

Exterior perimeters are generally found only in high-security applications such as prisons, military bases, research facilities, critical infrastructure facilities, and industrial hazardous facilities (i.e., chemical plants). With a large percentage of U.S. critical infrastructure owned and operated by the private sector, there is more interest in using exterior sensors in private industry since the attacks of 9/11. If exterior sensors are not in use at a facility, this is an implicit indication that assets are low value or that the expected threat is low and no evaluation is necessary. In this case, the reader may skip to the section on Interior Intrusion Sensor Technologies and Evaluation. If a facility is using exterior sensors, there is an explicit expectation that these sensors will contribute to overall physical protection at the site, and they should be evaluated.

Examples of each category of exterior sensor application are discussed later to demonstrate the VA process for these components. Specific notes on these technologies, as well as data that should be collected during the VA for exterior sensors in general, are reviewed. The overall effectiveness of each sensor can be affected by the application, theory of operation, installation, environment, testing, maintenance, training, probability of detection, probability of assessment, NAR, and vulnerabilities. These key performance parameters help determine the degradation factors that the VA team will consider in their evaluation.

Some of the most common sensors used in fixed exterior perimeter applications are freestanding microwave and e-field, buried line ported coaxial cable and fiber optic cables, and fence-associated taut wire and fiber optic fence cables. Other technologies that are applied to wide area detection include exterior video motion and radars. Exterior sensors can be used individually, but are generally used in combinations to provide effective intrusion information under a variety of weather and threat conditions.

Freestanding Sensors

Freestanding sensors are neither buried nor associated with a fence. They are usually mounted above ground on their own supports. Microwave and e-field sensors are examples of this type of application.

Exterior Microwave Sensors

Exterior microwave sensors include bistatic and monostatic devices. Bistatic sensors consist of transmitting and receiving antennas at opposite ends of a microwave link in long, flat detection zones. Monostatic sensors use the same antenna or nearly coincident antennas for the transmitter and receiver and are typically used for detection in a relatively confined volume compared to bistatic sensors. This is why monostatic sensors are used most often in interior applications and are described in the Interior Intrusion Sensor Technologies section.

The basic theory of operation of a bistatic microwave sensor influences the key performance parameters to be considered in the VA process. A bistatic microwave sensor uses a modulated transmitter and receiver separated by a limited line-of-sight (LOS) distance. The received signal is the vector sum of the direct transmitted signal and reflected signals from the ground and nearby elevated structures, such as buildings, fences, camera towers, junction boxes, and other sensors. Sensing is based on the fact that a moving object will cause a change in the net vector sum of the received signal compared to the transmitted signal, resulting in varying signal strengths. When an intruder approaches the sensor, changes occur to the overall received signal because of reflections from the intruder or because an existing signal path is blocked. Depending on the phasing of the signal, it can cause an increase or decrease in the received signal. These signal changes are monitored with a threshold detector and an alarm occurs when the signal variation exceeds a preset threshold limit. An automatic gain control (AGC) circuit allows the sensor to adapt to slow environmental changes. Although these devices are LOS, their detection zone encompasses a significant volume because of spreading of the microwave beam between the two ends. Because the receiving and transmitting antennas are the same, the detection zone is widest and highest at mid-range, as shown in Figure 5-1.

Installation concerns are derived from the basic theory of operation of the bistatic microwave. Because the microwave beam increases in size as it leaves the antennas, the beam does not touch the ground for a certain distance, depending on the angular beam width. This distance is called the offset and is shown in Figure 5-1. The detection height is also lower at this point and performance can be degraded for a jumping adversary in a poorly designed microwave sensor system. Bistatic microwave sensors must be installed so that the offset cannot be used as an intrusion method by a crawling

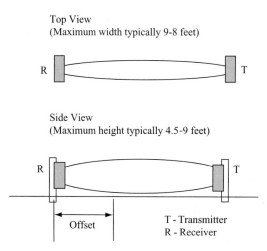

Figure 5-1 Bistatic Microwave Sensor Pattern. Note the wide detection volume shown by the top view and the offset distance between the antenna and where the signal first touches the ground shown in the side view. Installing bistatic sensors so that adjacent pairs protect the offset and electronics of each unit reduces the vulnerability of this device.

adversary. This is prevented by installing bistatic microwave sensors so that there is a crossover between adjacent sets of sensors, as shown in Figure 5-2. This installation technique also prevents tampering with the receiver, by placing the sensor electronics inside the detection volume of the adjacent sensor set. The optimal installation uses a basket-weave pattern to eliminate offset vulnerabilities and prevent the s-crawl that can be used to bypass other installation patterns (see Chapter 6 of the *Design* text for a full description of these techniques). Special attention should be paid to areas where exterior microwave detection zones end at buildings. It is imperative that the detection pattern be tested at these locations to verify that there are no gaps in coverage that will allow an adversary to penetrate the perimeter undetected.

Installation of bistatic microwave sensors is best accomplished using vertical pipes as mounting posts set in a permanent concrete footing. Conduit included

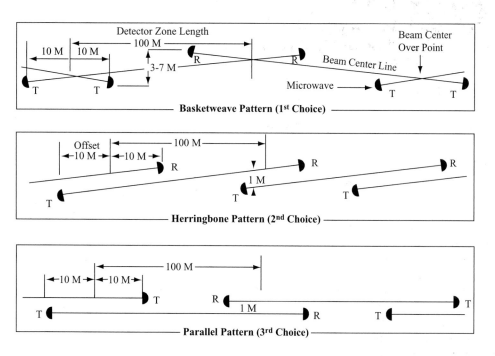

Figure 5-2 Exterior Bistatic Microwave Installation Patterns. The most desirable installation pattern is the basket-weave configuration. Other patterns may also be used, but they require considerable attention to placement and spacing of antennas.

in the footing for electrical wiring should be sized to accommodate the necessary power and signal wiring. If both sensors are not installed to be stable in wind or other environments, misalignment of the antennas will result, causing nuisance alarms and degrading sensing performance. Bistatic microwave sensors must be properly aligned to obtain good detection, and even minor misalignments can greatly affect detection, particularly at lower sensitivity settings (see Figure 5-3). In addition, tamper switches are included with the transmitter and receiver equipment provided by the manufacturer. These tamper switches can be connected in series with the alarm relay (with a resistor divider network, so a tamper alarm can be uniquely identified) or monitored separately. The transmitter power is sometimes wired through the tamper

Figure 5-3 Example of Poor Exterior Bistatic Microwave Installation. As currently installed, these stacked microwave sensors (on right post) are looking through the fence, which will cause nuisance alarms and be hard to assess. The empty post next to the installed sensor is the proposed new location for the sensor; however, this installation will be too close to the outer fence and the coils of barbed wire on the ground, and nuisance alarms will still be a problem. These conditions are partially due to the narrow zone between the fences.

switch so that any attempt to tamper with the transmitter results in a loss of signal. This type of wiring is not as desirable, because the receiver reports the event as a standard alarm rather than a true tamper event.

Because bistatic microwave sensors are LOS devices, they must be installed so that there is a flat, reflective surface between antennas to get reliable detection of crawling intruders. At most sites this requires extensive grading to provide a surface that is plus zero, minus six inches so the beam is not blocked, creating a hole to crawl through. If erosion is present in the detection zone, the adversary can crawl through a low spot, further decreasing performance. By using bistatic short- or long-range models, the length and width of the detection zone can be varied to provide the appropriate detection between fences or at vehicle, personnel, or rail portals through perimeters. In addition, bistatic microwave sensors may also be stacked, which provides protection from both crawling and jumping attack methods. When multiple units are stacked to provide this protection, the units should be installed using different microwave frequencies.

Environmental conditions that affect bistatic microwave sensor performance will usually depend on the reflection characteristics of the surface below the microwave signal, distance between and height of the transmitting and receiving antennas, alignment, the microwave frequency of operation, and the terrain flatness and surface irregularity between the antennas. Too much variation in these parameters causes degraded signal strength, increases NAR, and creates vulnerabilities in the microwave detection volume.

The NAR for a well-designed microwave sensor system is directly affected by the installation and environment. Standing or running water in the detection zone is a major source of nuisance alarms. Puddles provide a near-perfect reflector for the microwave signal, and when the wind ripples the surface of the puddle, major changes in signal occur and nuisance alarms are generated. Heavy rain can also cause nuisance alarms, particularly if the surface is concrete or asphalt. Birds and small animals (particularly rabbits) are also major nuisance alarm sources. Wet, heavy snow can create unique problems for bistatic microwave sensors as a result of beam reflectance off the surface of the snow and attenuation by the snow. This can result in degraded performance against a crawling adversary in deep snow. If the snow begins to build up to the depth of the antennas, the sensor could go into constant alarm. Wind can cause nuisance alarms if the sensor is not properly aligned and the signal is reflected off moving fences. In single fence perimeters, the NAR will be very high as a result of blowing trash or other debris, animals, or unintentional intrusion by site personnel. For this reason, microwave sensors should be used only in double fence perimeters, where the microwave detection zone can be protected through the use of an outer fence to block blowing debris, some animals, and inadvertent entry. A high NAR generally indicates either improper installation or misapplication of microwave technology at the specific site. Either will result in degraded performance of the sensor and can create vulnerabilities. Thus, the NAR and installation conditions are part of the VA, as appropriate for the defined threat.

Basic vulnerabilities in an exterior microwave sensor are a result of improper installation and environmental conditions. Crawling and jumping vulnerabilities are introduced from improper offset distances or antenna mounting heights. Irregular terrain and washouts will also introduce crawling vulnerabilities. Heavy snow can create a path for an intruder that is difficult to assess and will reduce overall system performance. Environmental conditions, such as standing water, will increase the NAR and decrease the proba-

bility of detection at these times, which creates a vulnerability. Heavy fog will not decrease probability of detection, but it will decrease the probability of alarm assessment. If cameras are used for alarm assessment, a vulnerability will also exist during these times.

To ensure the integrity of a microwave sensor's intrusion detection capability, periodic testing and maintenance must be performed. Normal maintenance procedures recommended by the supplier should be documented by the site and verified by the VA team. To check sensor operation, exercising any device self-test on a predictable and periodic basis is recommended and should be documented. If testing is not performed on a routine basis, degradation of the sensor is appropriate, because of the possibility of sensor failure during an adversary attack. Evaluation of maintenance should include verifying that the area between the transmitter and receiver is not blocked by debris or weeds, no erosion has occurred in the zone, nearby fences are not loose, and the surface still drains standing water.

When evaluating exterior microwave sensors, tests that verify the offset, detection pattern, and sensitivity of the device should be used to establish the performance of the device against defined threats. Probability of detection, probability of assessment, nuisance alarm rate, and vulnerabilities are affected by installation pattern, grade between the antennas, standing or running water, poor alignment, antenna height, and spacing. The more the microwave sensors deviate from the installation, maintenance, and testing recommended in this section, the more the overall sensor performance should be degraded by the VA team.

Electric-Field Sensors

Electric-field sensor operation is based on detecting an intruder by means of an electric field disturbance. Their detection mechanism involves sensing changes in capacitance between sensor wires or between sensor wires and earth ground. Capacitance is a measure of the ability to store electrical charge. In a parallel plate capacitor, two conductors (flat plates of metal) are separated by a distance that contains a dielectric, which is a material that is a poor electrical conductor, such as dry air. When an electrical current is applied, electrons accumulate on one plate, causing a negative charge, and then repel the electrons from the other plate, leaving a positive charge. When the electric current is removed, the charge remains for a time. The capacity to store this charge depends on the area of the parallel plates and the dielectric between the plates. An electric-field sensor uses sensor wires, wire supports, a signal processor, and mechanical hardware as shown in Figure 5-4. One or more wires, uniformly spaced and stretched above the ground, form the conductors. The dielec-

Figure 5-4 Typical Freestanding Electric Field Sensor. This sensor is installed in a test field and is undergoing some adjustment before testing. Note the consistent distances between the sensor wires and lengths of each section. These installation details are critical to effective detection.

tric is the air around the wires. The capacitance between the wires remains relatively constant until an intruder approaches the wires. Humans are composed mostly of water, which has a dielectric constant about 100 times that of air. An approaching intruder changes the capacitance between the wires by the presence of his/her high dielectric body. The closer an intruder gets to the wires, the more the capacitance changes. This capacitance change is what the processor of an electric field sensor senses. The configuration of the sensor wires and the way in which the signal is processed vary among the manufacturers of electric-field sensors.

One model of electric-field sensor consists of one or two field wires and two or more sense wires. Filtering is used so that the signal can vary with conditions other than an intrusion. Cutting off low frequencies allows slow environmental changes, such as increasing humidity, to occur without causing an alarm. High-frequency cutoff reduces alarms caused by rapidly changing environmental conditions that occur too fast to be an intruder. The filtered signal is applied to a threshold detector to determine whether an alarm should be declared.

Other electric-field sensor models deploy an array of sensor wire capacitors. These sensors ignore signals that occur either equally on various pairs or in a distributed fashion rather than locally. Some sensors also use digital processing to handle more complex algorithms. The spacing of the wires on such models is generally closer than the type previously described. Depending on their configuration, these models may use many more wires, although they do not have separate field and sense wires. A signal is applied to a sensor wire and changes in the signal caused by changes in capacitance between the wire and earth ground are monitored. Generally, their detection volumes are much more confined to the near vicinity of the wires.

An electric-field sensor can be installed to provide volume coverage; however, it is usually adjusted to detect intruder penetration rather than being adjusted for a specific detection distance. The manufacturer's installation and operating instructions give detailed procedures for connecting and adjusting the electric-field sensor. Proper installation should be verified by the VA team during their evaluation. Bends in sectors can be accommodated and the terrain can be irregular, but the terrain must be of uniform grade between posts so that the sensing wires are installed parallel to the ground. Experience indicates that the soil under the electric-field sensor should be graded, leveled, and prepared before installation of equipment and cable. The area within two meters of the sensor needs to be clear of vegetation. The sensor should be examined for proper wire tension, properly soldered and sealed connections, and the absence of moving objects such as tree branches, grass, weeds, and fence mesh near the sensor. If the sensor is installed with considerable curvature, insulator friction may cause uneven wire tension, which can cause nuisance alarms or create penetration areas. Each zone must have the appropriate electrical ground to ensure proper sensor performance, normally accomplished through the use of a ground rod driven into the ground at the processor box. All exposed electrical connections should be coated with a silicone rubber sealant to provide moisture protection and eliminate any tampering by adversaries. All sensor wire inputs should be equipped with lightning arrestors to protect equipment in areas where lightning is expected. The sensitivity setting should not be greater than required because higher sensitivity increases the NAR. Deviation from these installation guidelines results in degraded performance of the sensor.

All electric-field sensors detect changes in capacitance. Therefore, these sensors are all potentially sensitive to environmental factors that can cause changes in capacitance between the wires or between the wires and ground. The various wire configurations and processing methods used by the different models are attempts to minimize environmental effects while achieving adequate detection.

Electric-field sensors can have very high probability of detection against certain threats. Their wires form a barrier to an intruder who is rapidly penetrating the detection zone. Because the wires are generally mounted to a significant height, the detection zone can be quite high and is uniform if properly installed. Electric-field sensors have detection volumes that vary depending on the specific model and the wire configuration. Some models have a narrow detection volume that is only an inch or so from the wires. Such wires are closely spaced and are intended to detect an intruder attempting to penetrate between the wires. Another model exhibits a detection volume that depends on how the sensor is approached, the size of the intruder, and how fast the intruder is moving. On some models the detection volume is difficult to define because of the wire configurations used and because the detection algorithm requires a signal of sufficient strength from more than one wire. These sensors are all volumetric detectors, and the exact location of the area where an alarm is generated is not easily distinguished.

The NAR for electric-field sensors is increased by environmental factors such as rain, snow, wind-blown debris, lightning, birds, and small animals. The magnitude of the NAR also depends on the specific sensor, installation method, sensor maintenance practices, and the sensitivity setting. Testing data indicate that a properly installed and operating free-standing electric-field sensor is nearly unaffected by wind. If the electric-field sensor is mounted on a chain-link fence, the fence fabric should be tight enough to prevent nuisance alarms. If the fabric is not tight, a higher than normal NAR can be expected in winds exceeding 22 mph. On early model electric-field sensors, favorable walk-test results were obtained with the bottom sense wire covered by snow. Tunneling through the snow is possible against some models. As noted above, periodic testing and maintenance should be performed and documented, and these results should be reviewed by the VA team to verify sensor performance.

Common vulnerabilities for electric-field sensors involve bridging or tunneling attempts. Since this system is similar to a fence line, video alarm assessment will be degraded on one side of the sensor (normally the side opposite the camera). If the system is not installed correctly, a higher NAR will also introduce vulnerabilities and decrease probability of detection.

Evaluation of an electric-field sensor should include crawl, walk, and shuffle walk tests (a very slow walk with no swinging arm movement), as appropriate for the expected threat. Proper grounding is a very important parameter for probability of detection, NAR, and vulnerabilities. The VA team should pay very close attention to how the sensor is installed and grounded to insure proper operations. Records describing periodic functional and performance tests should be reviewed. All maintenance logs should also be reviewed for sensor problems and the resolution of these problems. If periodic testing and maintenance is not performed, or if maintenance is slow to correct deficiencies, sensor performance should be degraded. Training records should also be reviewed to confirm that personnel have the required skills and understanding to maintain and operate all sensors effectively.

Freestanding Sensors Summary

In general, freestanding sensors should be evaluated for their proper application to the environment, proper installation including structural stability and alignment, functional operation (i.e., they give an alarm when expected), and NAR. If the NAR is high, this can be an indication of either improper sensor selection for the application or improper installation and maintenance. If the surrounding environment has a lot of vegetation, small animals, soil erosion, or interference, there will be a high NAR. This condition will be exacerbated by the lack of immediate alarm assessment, which is addressed in the next chapter. When conducting a VA, discuss nuisance alarms with site personnel and ask how many there are and what causes them. Discolored rocks and small piles of grass are clues that there may be low spots that fill with standing water at times. These details will assist in making upgrade recommendations. Be sure to note other nuisance alarm sources or sensor bypass aids such as other sensors or PPS components, nearby roads, power lines, culverts, underground pipe chases that may be covered with manholes, and any trees or structures that can be used to avoid the sensors.

During the VA, sample a few representative zones, select suspicious ones for more testing, and verify detection for defined threats. As appropriate for the expected threat, walk, run, jump, or crawl tests may be needed, as well as verification that the sensor will trigger when expected and that an alarm is reported to the monitoring location. Tests should be conducted at each end and the middle of the detection zone at a minimum. The speed of the test should be documented (i.e., how fast the run, walk, or crawl is), as well as the time of day, weather conditions, and results. These tests indicate either proper performance of the device, and substantiate this in the final report, or penetration areas in the detection zone, which will create vulnerabilities.

Buried-Line Sensors

A buried-line sensor consists of a transducer that is sensitive to seismic and/or magnetic disturbances and a processor that evaluates signals generated in the transducer. Detection logic in the processor activates an alarm when the sensor signal exceeds a specified threshold. Four types are generally used in PPS designs, including seismic, magnetic, seismic-magnetic, and ported coaxial sensors. The most common type is a ported coaxial sensor, also known as leaky coax or radiating cable sensors. This type of sensor responds to motion of a material with a high dielectric constant or high conductivity near the cables. These materials include both the human body and metal vehicles.

Ported Coaxial Sensors

The basic theory of operation for a ported coaxial (coax) cable sensor is based on the radio frequency (RF) energy between two or three identical leaky cables buried parallel in the ground. A transmitter is connected to one cable, and a receiver is connected to the other(s). The outer conductor of the cables is ported, which means it contains closely spaced small holes or gaps in the shield that allow RF energy to radiate. As a result, any electrical energy injected into the transmit cable is radiated into the surrounding medium, and some of this energy is coupled into the receive cable through its ported shield. Thus, a static field of coupling is established between the cable pair. When an intruder enters the established field, the coupling is perturbed, and the change in received signal is processed for an alarm condition. Either pulsed or continuous-wave RF energy can be used. The pulsed system operates much like a guided radar, and thus both detection and location of the intruder are determined. The continuous wave system detects the intruder but does not localize the presence along the cable length.

A pulsed ported coax sensor consists of a processor and a pair of sensor cables. If the length of the cable pairs must be more

than 0.5 mile, power amplifiers are used to extend the cable set to up to 1 mile. The processor contains a transmitter, a receiver, various amplifier and filter circuits, and a microprocessor with associated hardware and software. In operation, the processor sends a pulse of RF energy at a frequency of about 60 MHz down the transmit cable. Some of this RF energy leaks out of the transmit cable and into the receive cable. The received signal is time divided into range cells with a typical length of 36.5 yards; in some cases, the lengths of the cells can be adjusted. Each cell has a unique threshold that is established during calibration. The cells are generally grouped into alarm zones such that, when the received signal exceeds the threshold in a particular cell, its zone reports an alarm.

Continuous wave (CW) ported coax sensors perform no range processing; therefore, they transmit continuously or during specified times. The frequency of operation is around 40 MHz or 60 MHz. There is only one threshold per set of sensor cables, and the cables are the length of the sector, typically 328 feet. In one of the two processor arrangement types, both the transmitter and the receiver are located at the same end of the sensor cables. In this case, the ports in the sensor cables are graded; that is, the ports vary in size by regular gradations to compensate for signal attenuation at the far end. The other arrangement locates the transmitter at one end of the sensor cables and the receiver at the opposite end. The port size is constant for a cable using such a processor arrangement.

Cable installation can have a major impact on P_D, NAR, and vulnerabilities. Installation factors that affect detection will also affect the NAR. Buried-line sensors can follow irregular terrain and irregular fence lines, requiring minimum site preparation. Areas that permit standing water will cause nuisance alarms. Separation distances from potential seismic sources will vary among the sensor types.

If a potential source of numerous nuisance alarms cannot be removed, then another type of sensor should be used. If the buried-line sensor is to be installed with another type of sensor, then the site requirements for both sensors must be met. Nuisance alarms can be generated in some buried-line sensors by electromagnetic interference (EMI) caused by line transients in power lines and in signal cables, such as telephone cables. When the sensor must be located near such lines, it is necessary to position the transducer and/or shield the utility lines for minimum noise pickup. Because the sensor cables are buried 4 to 9 inches deep, the precise location of the sensor cables, and hence the detection zone, can be concealed. Test data have shown that both detection zone size and detection sensitivity vary along the sensor cables. This variance may result from several causes, such as phase cancellations, buried metallic objects, changes in cable separation or burial depth, and soil composition. Therefore, it is important to both identify the sensitivity areas and the installation to achieve adequate detection. Soil characteristics have an effect on the signal strength of the ported coax receiver signal, but even at sites where soil attenuation is relatively large, operational ported coax systems have been achieved. Variations in soil moisture are reflected in changes in ported coax signal attenuation. Wet soil attenuates signal strength more than dry or frozen soil; therefore, seasonal changes may be accompanied by changes in ported coax detection sensitivity.

Probability of detection can also vary with regard to cable length. The cross section of the detection zone is somewhat elliptical and can be up to 3 feet high and 9 to 12 feet wide above and, to some extent, below the ground. Intrusion detection by most buried-line sensors is confined to the area close to the sensor transducer. Detection depends on the seismic characteristics of the soil, burial depth of the sensor, manner in which the sensor is approached, and the attenuation or sensitivity setting of the processor. In addition, magnetic detection depends on the amount of ferromagnetic material carried by the intruder. Detection sensitivity can also be affected by changes of dielectric or conductivity within the detection zone and insensitivity to seismic noise. Large amounts of salt or metals in the soil will also degrade performance of this sensor.

The NAR for buried-line sensors varies greatly according to the model and the manufacturer. Environmental factors, such as rain, thunder, wind, animals, and sources of seismic noise, such as trains, nearby vehicular traffic, and industrial noise, can affect the NAR. The NAR also depends on the intensity and the rate of occurrence of those factors. The NAR for magnetic sensors is also subject to lightning and electromagnetic interference/radio frequency interference (EMI/RFI). The major source of nuisance alarms is surface water from rain or melting snow, making proper drainage essential. Either flowing water or standing water will generate signals similar to movement detected by the sensor. Movement of metallic objects (e.g., automobiles and fences) or dielectric objects (e.g., animals, people, and plants) in the vicinity of the sensor cables can cause nuisance alarms, depending on the speed and size of the objects. In addition to these noise sources, railroads within a few kilometers of the installation can be another source of seismic noise. Small animals weighing less than 9 pounds generally do not cause alarms unless they cross the sensor cables in groups. The magnitude of the NAR also depends on the type of sensor, installation method, maintenance practices, and sensitivity setting. Nuisance alarms can be caused by unbalanced currents being switched in the cables. Because it will not be obvious that electrical signals are causing the alarm, these types of nuisance alarms will probably be assessed as false alarms.

Maintenance guidelines have been established by each manufacturer. The self-test feature should be exercised and documented by the site, and confirmed by the VA team. Because of the covert nature of these devices, performance tests should be conducted at 6-month intervals and more often if performance degradation of the sensor is suspected. Terrain maintenance is essential for proper sensor performance and adequate alarm assessment. This includes mowing grass and weeds and filling in areas eroded by water runoff.

Buried-Line Sensors Summary

When evaluating buried-line sensors in general, the VA team should first ask whether buried sensors are in use at the facility—this may not be immediately obvious or known to the team. If present, the team should verify that the device is functional by causing an alarm in the detection zone and that the alarm is received at the monitoring location. Installation, maintenance, and testing should be verified to ensure that the sensor detects the defined threat and with a NAR that does not reduce the sensor's P_D and overall performance. Zones should be examined to determine if there are any objects that might interfere with sensor operation. Rusty nails and rocks with a high mineral content can affect the sensor performance. Sources of strong electrical interference that could degrade sensor performance, including switching substations, electric welders, RF communications antennas, electric gates, and solenoid-operated locks, should also be identified. Depending on the results of the preceding data gathering, the performance of the buried sensor should be degraded to reflect the decrease in probability of detection or increase in vulnerabilities.

Fence-Associated Sensors

Examples of fence-associated sensors include taut wire, which can also be a freestanding sensor or fiber optic sensors mounted on the fence. A taut wire sensor fence is composed of steel wires, usually barbed, that are stretched above the ground and securely anchored to posts. As with a chain-link fence, a taut wire sensor fence acts as a barrier to delay an intruder. In addition, each wire functions as an intrusion-sensing mechanism that generates an alarm if it is cut or climbed on. Taut wire fences can be installed directly in front of an existing fence or on top of an existing fence. In the former case, the sensor is usually installed to detect cutting intrusions, and in the latter, it is installed to detect climb-over attempts. In both cases, if the sensor is cut or climbed, an alarm will be generated. Recent advances in technology have allowed the use of fiber optic sensors as intrusion detection sensors in perimeter and interior applications. Fiber optic cable sensors will detect both cutting and climbing intrusions and are usually mounted right on the fence fabric of an existing fence.

An important aspect of fence-associated sensors that must be addressed in a VA is the location of the sensor in multiple fence systems. A typical high-security perimeter includes two fences, separated by a constant distance, which establishes an isolation zone (also referred to as a clear zone). In this configuration, freestanding sensors are usually combined with buried and fence-associated sensors to provide multiple, complementary lines of sensing. It is strongly recommended that fence-mounted sensors be on the innermost fence of a double fence isolation zone, but some facilities use three fences. There is little improvement in performance in three-fence systems, but considerably more expense. These systems are designed against skilled outsider adversaries, and care must be used to ensure effectiveness of all installed components into an integrated subsystem. If not designed and implemented properly, a three-fence system can actually degrade performance of the isolation zone.

Taut Wire Sensors

A taut wire sensor fence senses motion of its wires through the fundamental operating principle that steel wire, when subjected to tension, acts like a spring over its entire length. Closely spaced steel wires are stretched between two anchor posts. If an intruder steps on the wire, it stretches further. If the wire is cut, it contracts like a released spring. In either case, a sensing device attached to the wire detects the motion by means of a switch, a strain gauge, or other passive transducer. A high P_D for a taut wire sensor fence requires an alarm to be generated before a sufficient gap can be created that permits an intruder to pass through the wires. The allowable gap size is related to the wire spacing, the deflection required to alarm, and other factors related to the difficulty that an intruder encounters when using the gap. Thus, the probability of detection of the sensor is a function of the measured gap size required for an alarm.

Installation of each taut wire sensor fence section consists of horizontal wires stretched between two anchor posts, usually to a tension of at least 80 pounds, with a sensor post centered between the anchor posts. The anchor post also functions as a sensor post in one model. Intermediate slider posts used to support the wires are generally spaced at 10-foot intervals between the sensor and anchor posts. The wires are attached to the slider posts so that the wire cannot be clamped easily to allow manipulation and bypass. The slider posts maintain proper wire spacing and convert a vertical deflection of the taut wire, caused by an intruder stepping on the wire, into the horizontal motion required by the sensing device. Friction between the mounting hardware and wire movement limits the zone length to 170 or 200 feet for some models. The posts should be appropriately sized and anchored so they remain plumb after the taut wire system is attached and operational (Figure 5-5).

Taut wire sensor fences are designed to be erected as freestanding fences; however, they may also be mounted on an existing chain-link fence or a wall. The chain-link fabric need not cover the full fence height, but it must reach a height suitable for the application. Top and bottom rails are not necessary; the fabric may be supported by tensioned wires laced through the fabric. The chain-link fabric should be mounted on the opposite side of the fence from the taut wire sensor. Slant outriggers should also face away from the protected area to make undetected entry by climbing difficult. A Y-configuration of inriggers and outriggers on top of the fence will make it equally difficult for a climber entering or exiting the perimeter.

A taut wire sensor fence can accommodate only limited changes in terrain within each zone. The cumulative change in alignment (elevation or direction) for a sensor section portion must not exceed 15 degrees on either side of its sensor post (thus, a half section). In a taut wire perimeter, an anchor post should be located at any point of discontinuity, such as a corner or a sharp change in terrain. The space around the sensor fence should be cleared of all vegetation, tree branches, and other debris. The ground surface within 3 feet on each side of the fence should be scraped and graded to keep the spacing between the bottom wire and the ground surface uniform. For higher security, a concrete curb under the sensor fence is recommended to discourage tunneling or trenching.

The NAR for a taut wire sensor is very low because either a large force must be exerted on one of the wires or a wire must be broken to cause an alarm. Some environmental conditions that can cause alarms are ice storms, melting snow (causing an ice coating that pulls down the lower wires), and movement of the fence posts caused by frost heave in the soil. Achieving and maintaining a low NAR depend on the type of sensor, the quality of installation, and adequate maintenance.

Figure 5-5 Typical Taut Wire Sensor Installation. A taut wire sensor can accommodate some degree of change in terrain elevations. The concrete pad in front of the fence makes it difficult to dig under the fence and provides a good background for video assessment. Note the heavy mounting poles and consistent section lengths, which are critical installation details needed to ensure performance in adverse weather and maintain constant sensor sensitivity.

Because a taut wire sensor fence is a line detection sensor and the mechanism for detection is easy to perceive, its potential defeat modes must be considered along with its detection ability. Taut wire sensors can be defeated by either bridging over or trenching under the fence. Clamping and cutting the sensor wires are also a potential vulnerability and are a function of threat capability, tools, and motivation.

Maintenance on a taut wire fence is mostly mechanical and the hardware should be inspected for physical damage or evidence of movement during the VA. If a fence post has obviously tilted, it may not be braced properly and can introduce a vulnerability. The wire tension should be checked to ensure that it meets manufacturer specifications. Maintenance logs also should be reviewed by the VA team to verify that periodic adjustments are made on wire tension and clamps to keep the sensor operating optimally.

When the VA team is evaluating a taut wire sensor, it is recommended that operational tests include, but not be limited to, verification of sensor operation and detection tests to verify detection level. Such tests indicate trends or changes and the need for recalibration. Operational tests should verify the operation of each sensor zone on a frequent schedule, perhaps daily, and should verify detection level on a regular schedule, at least every 6 months and whenever there are indications that detection performance has changed. To verify operation of the sensor zones, sample zones should be walk-tested; an alarm from each zone indicates correct operation.

The VA team should directly observe the sensor to determine the occurrence and causes of nuisance alarms during a period of little or no activity in the protected area, as well as the site response to these alarms. Each alarm occurrence and its cause, and all other pertinent information, should be recorded for use in analysis and the final report. Each fence part should be inspected for compliance with applicable materials, forming, welding, fit, coating, and other installation requirements. Each sensor switch assembly should be inspected for accurate fabrication, satisfactory prewiring, and the appropriate installation of antitamper switches and devices.

Penetration detection of the sensor by the VA team is verified by wire deflection testing performed for each wire or wire gap. The gap between sensor wires created by deflection of a wire can be measured using wooden blocks constructed to the required gap sizes. When a block is inserted between a wire pair, an alarm should occur. A second method uses a scale near the wire. The wire is pulled until an alarm occurs, and the distance on the scale is recorded. Before testing by this method, a maximum deflection should be selected to prevent damage caused by overdeflection. A third method can be used to test the operation of the top wire. In this test, a person weighing no more than 150 pounds climbs a ladder leaning against the top wire until his/her knees reach the top barbed wire. The allowable gap size is subjectively determined based on applicable regulations, the perceived threat, and the user's best judgment. Adequate detection resulting from penetration, as verified by the wire deflection test, also verifies that cutting and climbing on the sensor wires will cause an alarm. Actual cutting or climbing on the wires would damage the sensor and would not provide any useful information. Tests should also verify that break-off anchoring tabs (if used) will not support a fence climber. Excessive wire deflection during testing should be avoided because of potential damage to either the sensor or the supporting hardware. The wire deflection test should be repeated at both ends and in the middle of each zone. The data collected related to

the installation, maintenance, and testing will determine the overall sensor performance and how it should be degraded by the VA team.

Fiber Optic Sensors

A fiber optic sensor is composed of a fiber optic sensing cable, light source, light receiver, and signal alarm processing unit. Figure 5-6 shows a fiber optic sensor installed on a fence. An optical fiber is monitored to verify that the fiber is transmitting light and also to assess the level of change in that light. A light source, such as an LED or laser diode, is coupled to one end of the fiber, and a receiver such as a photo transistor or similar device is coupled to the other end of the fiber. The photo diode detects the level of light that passes through the optical fiber. There are two major categories of fiber optic sensors: continuity and micro-bending. Major advantages of fiber optic cable include immunity to radio and electromagnetic interference and durability to changes in temperature and humidity. The fiber optic sensing cable is virtually undetectable electronically because it does not produce any electronic signature.

A fiber optic continuity sensor depends on a break in the fiber loop that causes a loss of signal at the receiver. When the signal alarm processor detects this event, a change in the logic level or relay actuation occurs to signal an alarm. Fiber optics have been used as continuity sensors for several years and, when properly installed, provide reliable intrusion detection as structural boundary penetration sensors, such as in building walls or ceilings.

The theory of operation using micro-bending technology is very different than the theory using continuity. This sensor will detect slight micro-bending of the fiber, which causes a phase shift of the transmitted light signal. This phase shift is recognized by the alarm processor and becomes the basis for an alarm signal.

A

B

Figure 5-6 Fiber Optic Fence Sensor and Splices. Figure A on the left shows a splice using electrical tape. Figure B on the right is a putty splice. Neither is appropriate and both will cause nuisance alarms and degraded sensor performance over time. Sensor vendors recommend specific splice kits for repairs, and all splices should be examined by the VA team.

Fiber optic sensors that use micro-bending technology have sensitivity adjustments that allow alarms on different levels of disturbance. Fiber optic sensors using micro-bend technology will detect an intruder without physically damaging the fiber. Micro-bend fiber optic sensors are very difficult, if not impossible, to tap into because the processor is looking for a small change in the fiber from movement or pressure.

Continuity fiber optic sensors, though less expensive than micro-bend fiber optic sensors, do not detect an intruder until the fiber is broken. For exterior fence-associated applications, these sensors are usually applied as a netting barrier to detect cutting and climbing, depending on the sensor configuration. Installation is normally accomplished by attaching the fiber directly to the fence fabric using cable ties. These ties must withstand the environmental conditions at the site and be rated for ultraviolet (UV) exposure from the sun. Another installation technique is to install the fiber in conduit and attach the conduit to the fence. The more common technique is to attach the fiber to the fence, and this is

the subject of the remainder of this section.

The NAR for micro-bend fiber optic sensors depend on the sensitivity settings. Small vibrations, movement, or pressure on or near the sensing fiber will cause an alarm. Installation and setup are important for reducing the nuisance alarm rate while maintaining adequate intrusion detection capabilities and this aspect of sensor performance must be evaluated during the VA. The NAR for continuity fiber optic sensors is very low; only a nuisance source that breaks the cable will cause an alarm. Other nuisance sources, such as RF and signal disturbance, will be the same as for any electronic system.

Technical methods such as time-of-flight techniques and synchronous detection, which are based on injecting pulses of light into the fiber, may recognize attempts to splice or bridge portions of the optical fiber. Optical fiber is difficult, but not impossible, to tap. By observing the amplitude of the light transmitted down the fiber, tapping or bridging can be detected; nevertheless, sensitive measurements are required because the associated changes are usually small. Monitoring light in the fiber from measurements taken near the fiber is difficult, unlike similar measurements for wire conductors.

Key evaluation considerations for the performance of a fiber optic fence-associated sensor depend on the type of sensor and how it is applied. The most common type uses micro-bending, and a higher NAR can be expected because of the higher sensitivity compared to a continuity type.

Fence-Associated Sensors Summary

For any fence-associated sensor, the construction of the fence will have the biggest impact on sensor performance. Loose fence fabric will be the major source of nuisance alarms; most industrial fence installation specifications do not result in proper tension. If the fence installation does not address common bypass vulnerabilities, such as tunneling and bridging, sensor performance should be degraded. As with all other sensors, installation, maintenance, and testing will determine overall sensor performance and how it should be degraded by the VA team.

Other Exterior Intrusion Sensing Technologies

Other exterior intrusion sensors include radars, video motion detectors (VMDs), special applications of the preceding technologies for steam pipe and storm sewer drains, and portable sensors; but these are not recommended because of high NAR, low performance under adverse weather conditions, problems assessing alarms, lack of detection early enough to facilitate a response (for portable sensors), and cost. For a site with low threats or low-value assets, some of these sensors are not appropriate. VMDs are frequently used at industrial sites, but they are not recommended for exterior use because of the high NAR and diffi-

culty assessing alarms under adverse weather conditions, and because they require fixed, not pan-tilt-zoom (PTZ), cameras to perform best, which is not usually the case at these sites.

General Exterior Intrusion Sensing Evaluation

The VA team should document observations that provide the basis for estimates of performance to aid in analysis. These observations can often play a role in recommended upgrades by providing some low- or no-cost opportunities for improvement. The team should make full use of photos, videotape, and sketches to help support observations; these visual descriptions are also useful for follow-up consultations with technical experts. Where possible, the VA team should take pictures and videos of the same location during the day and at night. This will provide a visual record and a method of comparing these varying states. Often, a sensor will perform well during the day but not at night and pictures can more easily show these differences.

It is a basic principle of VAs that each site requiring physical protection has a unique combination of asset configuration and physical environment; thus, a PPS designed for one site cannot be wholly transferred to another. As described previously, the physical environment and defined threat will influence sensor selection for a perimeter. Both natural and industrial environments provide site-specific nuisance alarm sources, and the topography of the perimeter determines the space available for the clear zone width and whether terrain is flat or irregular. These factors are part of the evaluation of sensor performance.

Many perimeter security systems use cameras to perform alarm assessment. For both the sensor and video systems to perform well, care must be taken to ensure that the designs of the two systems are compatible. Compromise is required in deciding isolation zone width. Sensor experts desire a wide area to reduce nuisance alarms, and video experts desire a narrow assessment area to achieve better camera coverage. An acceptable isolation zone width is 30 to 50 feet. Isolation zones of less than 30 feet may not provide enough space to detect intruders and assess an alarm, which would translate to a lack of performance for a fairly high cost.

The VA team should focus attention on which sensors are used at the facility and whether they are installed and maintained properly. Certain installation conditions, such as sensor stability and alignment, no exposed wiring, true detection overlap for complementary sensors, and tamper protection for both the sensor and junction boxes, are indicators of proper sensor installation and should be documented. If there is an isolation zone, the VA team should ensure that it is well maintained and a constant width around the entire facility, and that there are no low spots between or under fences. If there are freestanding sensors in the clear

zone, their layout should be verified. A basket-weave pattern is the recommended layout for all but taut wire sensors, and badly implemented herringbone or parallel layouts will degrade sensor performance. Noting the number of fences and sensors on or near these fences will also affect sensor performance, and these locations may explain high-nuisance alarms or other interference with the sensors. Trees, buildings, or other structures (culverts, overhead pipes, power lines, bus stop structures, etc.) near or in the isolation zone that could help an adversary defeat the perimeter should be noted and will result in significantly degraded sensor performance (see Figure 5-7).

Another aspect of the VA focuses on testing and maintenance procedures and training of site personnel. The VA team should ask facility staff how often they test sensors, how testing is performed and documented, and what kind of failure rate they have. The team should ask questions regarding how the sensor operates to determine how well maintenance personnel understand the system. If it is clear

Figure 5-7 Fence Bypass. Note that the structure allows for easy bypass of the fence and any associated sensor. Because the isolation zone is so narrow (barely visible in photo), sensors in the area between the fences may also be bypassed from the structure.

that they do not understand how the system works or are not doing the proper tests, this should be noted and used to justify lower performance estimates during system analysis. If they have a good understanding of the sensors, the VA can focus more on the usual trouble spots such as nuisance alarm sources and the number of zones that have low spots.

Maintenance sensors, fences, and the isolation zone, if present, also have an effect on performance. The VA team should determine how personnel are trained on maintenance, or whether this activity is contracted out to others. If contract maintenance is used, it is expected that after-maintenance testing will be performed by facility personnel to verify that the sensor is working as expected and hasn't been tampered with to allow undetected intrusions. Failures at certain times of day or night may indicate improper installation or maintenance, or may indicate a mismatch between the sensor technology and the environment. This may also indicate an adversary attack that is meant to cause the site to ignore or turn off sensors. Maintenance logs should be reviewed to support the information provided by site personnel. Special note should be made of time to repair or replace bad components and the number and type of spares that are available on-site. If there is a long time between discovery of a problem and repair or if there is no contingency plan for operation without a component, sensor performance should be degraded.

Related information that will be required for analysis and the final report includes knowledge of who has access to the junction boxes that control sensor signals and power, who performs sensor tests, and what equipment is used to test sensors. Each of these is an opportunity for an insider to aid in defeat of the sensors. The VA team should also open a few junction boxes and verify that they are well sealed, tamper protected, and how power is supplied to the sensors and battery backups. If

sensors all share a single power supply or do not have reliable battery backup power, performance should be degraded.

An isolation zone improves perimeter sensor performance by increasing detection, decreasing nuisance alarms, preventing bridging or similar defeat tactics, and providing a well-lighted, clear area for alarm assessment and surveillance. The width of the clear zone should be defined by two parallel fences extending the entire length of the perimeter, the area between the fences cleared of all above-ground structures, including overhead utility lines, and neutral gray gravel used to provide drainage for sensors and constant background for video assessment. The fences are intended to keep out people, animals, and vehicles; vegetation in this area is also removed. Only the detection and assessment hardware and associated power and data lines are installed in this isolation zone. Personnel gates are usually located in the inner fence to allow access for maintenance. The isolation zone and its associated protection elements must form a continuous line of detection around the facility. Any breaks (aside from required personnel and vehicle entry points, which are discussed more in Chapter 7) or bypasses caused by trees, structures, vehicles parked near fences, or other climbing or bridging aids will result in degraded performance of the perimeter.

The configuration of multiple sensors within the clear zone also affects system performance. Overlapping the detection volume of two different sensors within each sector enhances performance by producing an overall detection envelope. Thus, sensor pair defeat is less probable because either a larger volume must be bypassed or two different technologies must be spoofed simultaneously. A third sensor, however, can further enhance performance, not by overlapping with the first two but by forming a separate line of detection. Physically separate lines of detection can reveal information useful for determining alarm priority during multiple simultaneous alarms; the order of alarms in a sector or in adjacent sectors may or may not correspond to the logical sequence for an intrusion. If a fourth sensor is used, dual sensor line pairs are a reliable configuration.

Fences alone are not effective protection for either low-value assets or low threats. Although they do provide excellent boundary definition and prevent accidental intrusions, they can easily be cut or climbed with minimal tools or experience (see Figure 5-8). Most exterior perimeters are used at high-security facilities, such as prisons, military or government installations, or nuclear power plants. Most of these facilities use the multiple fence configurations described previously. There are many industrial applications in which limitations of space or dollars result in the use of a single fence and a sensor being installed. This may be effective against low-level threats, but will result in many nuisance alarms and, if not integrated with video assessment, will result in performance that may not be justified for the cost. Integration with cameras is discussed further in the next chapter, but note that camera placement is important because cameras cannot see through fence fabric that is parallel to the camera field-of view, which is another degradation factor. Use of fence-mounted sensors on a single fence is a source of additional degradation of any exterior sensors during a VA, especially for medium- to high-level threats.

The VA team's evaluation of fence-mounted sensors should consider several factors that degrade sensor performance. Sensors actually installed on the fence must consider the installation of the fence fabric. A quick technique for checking fence tension is to grab the fence, then jerk on it; if the fence moves or sends a ripple of motion down the fence, the fabric is too loose and will cause too many nuisance alarms. Look for loose signs, wires, cable

Figure 5-8 Single Fence with Sensor. Note the gap under the fence, allowing for easy undetected entry by crawling under the fence (bypassing the sensor). This vulnerability was addressed by adding a metal barrier across the gap, but the barrier had no sensor. This configuration still allows undetected entry by crawling under the fence.

ties, or other material on the fence or fence posts. If these move, they will also cause nuisance alarms. The most important issue is how the fence sounds. If the fence rattles when hit, there are probably objects like loose ties that will cause nuisance alarms. In addition, the length of each fabric panel should be checked. If they are not the same, it will be almost impossible to adjust the sensitivity of the fence sensor to get consistent detection and NAR for the entire perimeter. In a like manner, the shape of the diamonds made by chain-link fabric should also be checked. Distortion of the diamond shape indicates that fence tension is too high, which can generate nuisance alarms. One of the most important tests of a fence-mounted sensor is to verify when an alarm is sent. Most fence-mounted sensors are set to cause an alarm after a specific number of hits, normally three, but this number is adjustable. When verifying sensor performance, first determine the setting for the sensor, then hit it one less time than this setting and check that there is no alarm. After the sensor has had time to reset, try this test again, hitting it the number of times it is set to trigger the alarm and verify that an alarm is sent. This is a quick way to verify both the sensitivity setting and the function of the sensor. If the sensor sends an alarm on the wrong number of hits or sends no alarm on the correct number, performance of the sensor should be significantly degraded.

Summary of Exterior Intrusion Sensing

Overall evaluation of exterior sensors includes attention to details such as sensor application, installation, testing, maintenance, nuisance alarm rate, and performance against defined threats. If the threat is able to cut, climb, or bridge fences, this must be considered during the evaluation. The goal of exterior sensor evaluation is to provide an estimate of P_D

against each defined threat, along with supporting notes, pictures, and observations that support these estimates. This establishes the baseline performance of the overall PPS and, if not acceptable, provides opportunities for upgrade improvements. Other factors that cause degradation include nuisance alarm rate and ease of defeat of the sensor by bypass or spoofing.

Some basic performance evaluation concepts for exterior sensors include:

- Continuous line of detection
- Protection-in-depth
- Complementary sensors
- Alarm combination/priority schemes
- Clear zone
- Sensor configuration
- Site-specific system
- Tamper protection
- Self-test
- Integration with a video assessment system

Additional information on exterior sensing technology testing is available from the Department of Energy (DOE, 2005).

Interior Intrusion Sensor Technologies and Evaluation

Interior sensors are used to aid detection of intrusions inside buildings or other structures. Unlike exterior sensors, interior sensors are commonly used at all types of commercial, private, and government facilities. Just as with exterior sensors, there are several factors that contribute to overall sensor performance, and these are discussed next. The most common interior sensors are balanced magnetic switches (BMS), glass-break sensors, interior monostatic microwave sensors, passive infrared sensors (PIR), video motion detectors (VMDs), and combinations of sensors, usually PIR/microwave sensors, in dual technology devices. Just as with exterior sensors, interior sensing technologies are discussed based on their area of application (boundary penetration, volumetric, and proximity).

Boundary Penetration Sensors

Boundary penetration sensors should detect someone penetrating the enclosure or shell through existing openings (doors, windows, and ventilation ducts) or by destroying walls, ceilings, and floors. Early detection gives more time for the response team to arrive; therefore detection should occur during entry rather than afterward.

Magnetic Switches

Magnetic switches are commonly used to detect opening of doors or windows. Two types of magnetic switches are commercially available—simple and balanced. The simple magnetic switch is used both as a tamper switch and as an in-the-door sensor. A simple magnetic switch consists of a switch unit and a magnet unit. The magnet unit includes a permanent magnet in a housing that permits mounting on a door or a window. The switch unit, mounted on the frame, incorporates a steel armature connected to an electrical contact. When the steel armature is near the magnet unit, the armature is attracted to the magnet. When the magnet is removed by opening the door or window, the motion of the armature causes the switch contact to be transferred from one position to another. Some magnetic contacts use a small magnetic reed switch in place of the steel armature in the switch unit. The reed switch changes position between its rest condition and under the influence of a magnet, resulting in the same output as the armature, that is, a switch actuation when the associated door or window is opened.

A BMS, the most commonly used door sensor, uses a magnet in both the switch and magnet units. The BMS is especially effective for high-security applications. The switch unit, which contains a magnetic reed switch, a bias magnet, and tamper/supervisory circuitry, is mounted on the stationary part of the door or window. The magnet unit containing the larger permanent magnet is mounted on the movable part of the door or window, adjacent to the switch unit. With the door or window closed, the magnetic fields are adjusted to create a magnetic loop causing a magnetic field of almost zero. In some models, this magnetic field is generated by adjusting the bias magnet; in other models the adjustment is made by varying the position of the magnetic unit with respect to the switch unit. Any action that causes the magnetic field to become unbalanced, such as opening the door or window, results in the transfer of the reed switch and an alarm output. The same result is obtained if an external magnet is brought into the vicinity of the BMS, thus changing the magnetic field. Because the BMS is the most commonly used magnetic switch, the following performance characteristics, installation guidelines, and maintenance guidelines specifically address the BMS. A newer BMS codes multiple magnets in each unit; thus each BMS is matched and the defeat of the BMS is nearly impossible. Repairing a failed switch, however, requires that the BMS must be replaced completely with another matched pair.

A BMS is installed by mounting the switch assembly on the protected side of the fixed surface. The magnetic assembly is mounted on the movable surface at the top of the fixed surface near the edge that is on the opposite side of the hinge. If the mounting surface is ferrous material, spacers of plastic or other nonferrous material must be used to prevent interference with switch operation. For the same reason, new brackets made of aluminum instead of steel will be required. A rigid mount maintains switch alignment and prevents a high NAR. To minimize induced residual magnetism, the switch and magnet assemblies must not be allowed any closer to the steel parts of the mounting surface than they will be in the final mounting position (determined by moving one unit with respect to the other unit or by internal adjustments, according to manufacturer instructions). Installing the BMS with a continuously monitored tamper switch, supervised wiring in conduit, fail-safe operation, and standby power is essential for effective protection. These installation details must be considered by the VA team during the evaluation.

The BMS probability of detection can be decreased by an externally introduced magnetic field. The vulnerability of physically bypassing or shunting the switch also exists. Manufacturers reduce the vulnerability of magnetic switches to external magnetic fields by: (1) using multiple magnets, various magnetic orientations, and magnetic shielding, such as Mumetal; (2) creating standoff distances; and (3) adding magnetic tamper indicators. The newest switches on the market have narrowly defined magnetic field paths, making them immune to external magnets. Additional reed switches, installed in a supervisory loop, will detect tampering by an external magnetic field. Encasing the switch in a magnetically permeable material, excluding the side facing the field magnet, diverts an external field from the switch. Materials with high-magnetic permeability, such as Mumetal, are preferable for the shielding; however, steel can also be used.

The NAR for a properly installed and maintained BMS is very low. The most common nuisance sources are loose mounting hardware and misalignment of the units. If the units are mounted on a large roll-up door, misalignment and nuisance alarms will be generated if the doors do not close properly or if high winds can cause motion in the door (see Figure 5-9). If the door hardware for the BMS applications is not maintained, it will also degrade the performance of the sensor.

A BMS should be tested by opening and closing the protected object (door, window, gate, or other). If the switch is not operating properly, further alignment and adjustment may be necessary. To ensure that proper switch performance continues, periodic testing and monitoring of the sensor installation are recommended. The BMS evaluation should verify that sensors are installed on the protected side of the door and that there is tamper protection to detect surreptitious entry attempts.

Periodic maintenance is necessary to maintain an effective switch installation. Loose bolts and screws and worn hinges can cause switch misalignment. Frequent shock as a result of door closing causes wiring and connection failures and intermittent signals. Along with regular performance testing, a periodic visual inspection of the switch is recommended, particularly after maintenance. Maintenance intervals depend on the severity of the environment in which the switch is operated. Replacing standby batteries based on a conservative schedule ensures uninterrupted service. A log of each service call should be maintained, including the date and time of corrective action and an assessment of the cause of the problem.

The VA team's evaluation of a BMS should focus on the type of sensor, installation, maintenance, and testing. The sensor performance should be degraded if a simple switch is used in high-security applications. If a high NAR is observed, performance should be degraded because a properly installed sensor should only cause an alarm on a change in the sensor position. Exposed wiring can introduce vulnerabilities to the system and should be documented by the VA team (see Figure 5-10). If switches are installed on the unprotected side of the door or window, performance should be degraded to almost zero for most threats. Performance tests should include measuring the distance the door or window is moved before an alarm

Figure 5-9 Balanced Magnetic Switch on Rollup Door. This is a good use of a BMS, but the door material is very weak, allowing for bypass of the sensor by cutting or breaking through the door.

Figure 5-10 BMS Exposed Wiring. The exposed wiring of this BMS makes this sensor vulnerable to attack, by even a low threat, and reduces probability of detection.

is generated. Depending on the application, this distance could be critical for overall system performance. These requirements are normally addressed in the security requirements documentation for a particular agency or site.

Glass-Break Sensors

A glass-break sensor is mounted directly on the glass surface, window frame, or other surfaces in a room to detect breaking glass, as in a forced entry. Several technologies are used to detect glass breaking. The technologies are passive sonic, vibration (piezoelectric or inertia), and active glass-break sensors. A brief discussion of each of these technologies follows. The remainder of this section focuses on active glass-break sensors.

The passive sonic sensor, also called a sound discriminator, is a covert listening device that uses a microphone to detect sounds generated by breaking and entering. This sensor is used in many security applications and is generally low cost because of its simplicity. If the area to be protected is noisy, however, a passive sonic sensor may not be applicable. These sensors are not recommended for use in high-security applications.

Vibration glass-break sensors may use piezoelectric sensing elements or electromechanical inertial sensing elements. Both technologies use a reference mass that does not move when the mounting surface moves. Sensitivity adjustments and pulse-counting logic are features designed to tailor the sensor to its installation environment. Although glass appears to break with a single burst, multiple impacts occur as falling pieces strike each other; thus, a multiple-impact counting device can be used. Usually, both piezoelectric and inertia sensors count bursts of vibration, allowing the sensor to be adjusted to compensate for a noisy surface. When the proper signature is sensed, the sensor generates an alarm.

Active glass-break sensors use a transmitting transducer to inject an ultrasonic signal into the glass (usually a sheet of glass). The receiver may be located at another place on the sheet of glass, or it may be located in a common housing with the transmitter. The received signal is a combination of a direct signal from the transmitter and a reflected signal from discontinuities in the sheet of glass, primarily the edges. When the glass is impacted but not broken, the discontinuities essentially remain the same. When the glass is broken, the discontinuities and thus the received signal are changed. The receiver analyzes the complex phase/amplitude relationships of the received signal as compared to the transmitted signal. When breaking glass is detected, the sensor produces a logic-level output or a relay actuation signal. The structural discontinuity between the window and its frame limits the area of detection to the glass itself. Because a glass cutter functions by breaking a small portion of the glass where it scratches the surface, an attempt to cut the glass will usually be detected if the sensor sensitivity is set appropriately. Although an active glass-break sensor is more expensive than other glass-break sensors, nuisance alarms caused by nonbreaking impacts on the glass are avoided. Active glass-break sensors are installed directly on the glass inside the protected area. The sensors are often glued to the surface and multiple active sensors mounted on the same window can interact.

The VA team's evaluation of an active glass-break sensor should focus on its installation, maintenance, and testing. The sensor performance should be degraded if the sensor is not installed securely to ensure that motion does not occur during normal operation. If a high NAR is observed, overall performance should also be degraded, as a properly installed sensor should alarm only when the glass is broken. Exposed wiring can introduce vulnerabilities to the system and should be documented by the VA team. If sensors are installed on the unprotected side of the glass, the performance should be degraded for high-security threats. Testing will be difficult because the glass would be damaged so as to induce a valid signal for an alarm. Any data collected by the site as a result of actual glass breakage, either by an intruder or accident, should be documented by the VA team as an indication of performance.

Boundary Penetration Sensors Summary

For any boundary penetration sensor, the construction of the volume to be protected will have a major impact on sensor performance. The VA team should examine all six sides of the volume looking for common penetration paths for the defined threat. For high-security applications, the walls, floor, and ceiling may also need sensors. Poor installation is one of the major sources of nuisance alarms. Because some of the nuisance sources can be outside the volume being protected, how the alarms are assessed and the type of response will also affect overall system performance. If sensor installation does not address common vulnerabilities, such as substituting magnets in a BMS sensor or cutting holes in soft walls to bypass a glass-break sensor, performance should be degraded. As with all other sensors, the installation, maintenance, and testing of a boundary penetration sensor will determine the overall sensor performance and how it should be degraded by the VA team.

Volumetric Sensing Technologies

Volumetric detection uses sensors to detect an intruder moving through an interior space toward a target. The detection volume is usually an enclosed area, such as a room or hallway. Common sensors used for volumetric sensing are microwave and PIR. If closed-circuit television (CCTV) cameras are present, VMDs are increasingly being used to detect changes in video signal characteristics.

Volumetric sensors may be active or passive. Passive sensors are always monostatic, meaning there is only one sensor housing. Active sensors may be monosta-

tic, bistatic, or multistatic. A monostatic sensor uses the same housing for both transmitter and receiver, and a bistatic sensor uses separate housings for the transmitter and receiver. A multistatic sensor has one main transmitter, with additional transmitters slaved to the same oscillator; multiple receivers can also be used.

Dual technology, or combination sensors, refers to motion detectors that combine a passive sensor, such as an infrared sensor, with an active sensor, such as a microwave sensor. Ideally, absolute alarm confirmation is achieved by combining two technologies that individually have a high probability of detection and do not have common nuisance alarm sources, but in practice this is not the case.

Microwave Sensors

Typical interior microwave sensors are monostatic volumetric sensors that operate on the Doppler principle, using either a single antenna for both transmitting and receiving or separate, collocated transmitting and receiving antennas. In addition to surveillance of a fairly large enclosed volume, a microwave sensor is useful for monitoring a limited area as a point sensor. Examples of this sensor are the automatic door openers used in supermarkets and airports.

Monostatic microwave sensors transmit electromagnetic signals in the range of 10 GHz. Detection is based on the Doppler shift between the transmitted signal and the reflected signal. The magnitude and frequency shift of the Doppler signal depend on the size and velocity of the object causing the return signal. The sensor's processor measures the frequency shift of the Doppler signal and determines if it falls within the range appropriate for the defined threat. Logic can be used to reject signals representing oscillating motion, such as those exhibited by curtains moving in air currents or other freely swinging objects. The shape of the detection volume is governed by the design of the antenna. The antenna is usually a microwave horn but may be a printed circuit planar or phased-array antenna. This shape, which resembles a tear drop, can also be range gated to set the maximum detection length.

Because microwave energy is difficult to constrain, special care should be taken when installing, locating, and directing the energy within the area requiring protection. Because of high operating frequencies, microwave sensors are capable of penetrating many building materials, such as glass, plastic, Plexiglas, wallboard, and wood; however, building materials such as concrete, brick, and metal will block a microwave signal. A protected volume surrounded by masonry or metal construction confines microwave energy and prevents detection outside the protected volume. To prevent eye damage, the sensor antenna should be placed so that personnel cannot look into it at very close ranges (less than 1 foot).

Nuisance alarms may be generated by water moving in plastic plumbing behind wallboard, vehicles moving outside a protected room, the movement of fans, or even small animals, such as mice. Deploying multiple microwave sensors in the same area can result in crosstalk and nuisance alarms. A microwave oven can also cause nuisance alarms. For some sensor models, fluorescent lights are a source of nuisance alarms. If the fluorescent light is located in the sensor detection envelope, especially at distances of less than 10 feet, reflections from the ionized gas within the fluorescent tubes may cause low-frequency Doppler shifts. Blocking the line-of-sight path to the light by installing either metal mesh having less than 0.25-inch holes or an RF absorber should eliminate this nuisance source. The signal can reflect off metallic surfaces and cause detection outside the protected area. Metal air ducts can direct the signal into areas outside the protected volume. Detecting objects outside the protected volume will normally create false alarms,

as the source of the signal is difficult to assess.

Moving an object into the detection envelope of the sensor can effectively block the sensor's field-of-view and create vulnerabilities. Shadow zones may be created by metal bookcases, desks, and wall partitions. Metal furniture near the sensor can also cause a strong reflected signal that masks the weaker signals from an intruder elsewhere in the protected area. A signal-level sensing device would detect an object moved into its detection envelope if the sensing were absolute. Most microwave sensors, however, have a long-term automatic level-adapting circuit that causes stationary objects to gradually disappear over time. A microwave sensor has reduced sensitivity for either motion across its field-of-view or very slow intruder motion.

The VA team should confirm that the microwave sensor is properly maintained. The sensor hardware should be examined for signs of damage, alterations, or tampering. Mounting hardware should be inspected to verify that the microwave sensor has not been moved or is not loose. The location of furniture and equipment with respect to the sensor should also be examined and documented. Placement of items, especially metal objects such as file cabinets, in a microwave sensor zone could affect the detection pattern by creating blind spots and potential vulnerabilities. These objects can also cause more nuisance alarms as a result of microwave signal reflections.

Testing of the effectiveness of an interior microwave sensor should include a tamper circuit test and walk tests. The tamper circuit test checks that the tamper circuitry on the microwave sensor is operational and separate from the alarm signal. Walk tests are performed to verify alarm probability of detection and detection patterns. Before testing, the test indicator in the sensor can be reconnected to aid in testing; after the test, this lamp should be disconnected again. If this lamp is always connected, sensor performance could be severely degraded because of the indication of detection this gives to an adversary, particularly an insider. The results of these tests should be documented by the VA team to assist in determining the overall sensor performance.

Passive Infrared Sensors

The PIR sensor is the most commonly used volumetric detector today. Infrared (IR) radiation emitted by an object is directly related to its temperature. IR radiation is invisible to the eye. The visible region encompasses only those wavelengths between 0.45 and 0.75 micrometers. The IR region lies between 0.75 and 1,000 micrometers. The human body radiates IR energy in the 8 to 14 micrometer region. Even apparently cold objects, such as dry ice and liquid oxygen, emit IR radiation.

The PIR sensor basic principle of operation depends on the difference in IR energy between an intruder and the background. The sensor detects the presence of an object when its field-of-view is blocked by an object that has a different temperature than the background. As a passive device, the sensor does not transmit a signal. Instead, the sensor responds to the energy emitted by a human intruder, which is approximately equivalent to the heat radiated by a 50-watt light-bulb. The PIR sensor responds to either the heat energy emitted by a human body or changes in background radiation caused by a person blocking the background in the sensor's field-of-view. Using a variety of lenses, the detection pattern is subdivided into the solid angular segments. The electrical signal varies when a heat source moves out of one solid angular segment into the next, providing detection of a heat source in motion. Logic circuitry is usually applied to the received signal to differentiate among various situations. If the signal pattern matches that of a person in motion rather than generalized heating and cooling, an alarm is generated. The PIR sensor is more sensitive to motion across the field-of-view than to motion toward or away from the sensor. By properly designing the optics, the PIR sensor's field-of-view can be tailored to provide various coverage patterns, such as a single segment, a curtain, or a hemisphere. A sensor having a single sensitive zone has a range of 15 to 18 meters and is well suited for use in a hallway or a corridor.

A PIR sensor's probability of detection is a function of the magnitude of the difference between intruder temperature and background. Below the minimum magnitude of this difference, detection becomes difficult and unreliable. This minimum difference is usually referred to as the minimum resolvable temperature (MRT) difference and is usually quantified as:

$$MRT = [T_1 - T_2]$$

where T_1 is the temperature of the intruder and T_2 is the ambient or background temperature. Probability of detection depends on other factors as well, such as the rate at which a temperature differential is introduced to the sensor detection zone and also intruder and background temperature gradients. Because the sensor is concerned only with temperature differences, intruders with a temperature colder than the background are detected as easily as intruders that are warmer than the background.

Any object causing an appropriate temperature differential can generate nuisance alarms in a PIR sensor. The sensor adapts to nuisance alarm sources that last a few minutes or longer, but it may respond to short duration changes. In practice, nuisance alarms are seldom generated by localized heating and cooling because these temperature changes do not happen rapidly. Any hot spots that generate IR energy should be removed or shielded. Radiant energy from such sources may produce thermal gradients that change the background energy pattern.

Hot spots include open heating elements, incandescent lightbulbs, convective heat currents, and direct sunlight on windows, floors, and walls. Sunlight can enter the protected area directly through openings, such as broken window panes, ventilation grids, and poorly fitting doors. Small animals or insects moving in the PIR sensor field-of-view may also be detected. Devices that meet the required temperature differential and sway into the sensor field-of-view may generate nuisance alarms. Vibration of the sensor may also cause nuisance alarms by causing a heat source to appear as movement. Insects crawling on the lens or elements inside the sensor, and condensation in the sensor, may also cause nuisance alarms. The detector elements in a PIR sensor can be subject to interference from various electromagnetic fields generated by equipment, such as hand-held radios; however, they are not generally subject to nuisance alarms caused by sound, vibration, and electrical or radio disturbances.

An intruder who appears to be the same temperature as the background is invisible to the sensor and could create a vulnerability. Good housekeeping in the detection area must be practiced to prevent the accumulation of clothing or other covering materials that are at room temperature; otherwise, these articles could be used as a screen to spoof the sensor. The sensor also can be defeated by very slow intruder motion. Because PIR sensor operation is primarily geometric, its field-of-view can be masked by applying tape to portions of the optics. Tape is legitimately used to eliminate trouble-causing spots in the field-of-view, but tape could also be applied covertly to prevent proper sensor operation.

Maintenance of the PIR sensor should be observed and documented by the VA team. The sensor hardware should be examined for signs of damage, alterations, or tampering. Mounting hardware should be inspected to verify that the microwave sensor has not been moved or is not loose. The location of furniture and equipment with respect to the sensor should also be examined and documented. Any solid item in the PIR sensor zone could affect the detection pattern by creating blind spots and potential vulnerabilities.

Performance testing of the effectiveness of an interior PIR sensor should include a tamper circuit test and walk tests. The tamper circuit test checks that the tamper circuitry on the sensor is operational and separate from the alarm signal. Walk tests are performed to verify alarm probability of detection and detection patterns. The same advice regarding the test lamp indicator provided for microwave sensors applies to PIR sensors. The results of these tests should be documented by the VA team to assist in determining the overall sensor performance.

Video Motion Detection Sensors

A VMD is a sensor that processes the video signal from a CCTV camera. In theory, a single camera can be used for detection, surveillance, and alarm assessment. As noted previously, VMD performance is compromised by the use of PTZ, not fixed, cameras at most facilities. Artificial lighting is required for continuous 24-hour operation. A VMD is an electronic device that monitors a video camera signal and detects changes in the characteristics of a video scene. During setup of a typical VMD system, an area is defined for motion detection. The detection area's size can usually be varied over a wide range as a percentage of the total camera field-of-view. A change is detected when scene characteristic changes are different than the characteristics of a stored reference scene. Depending on the complexity of the VMD system, an alarm is generated when the processor sees enough changes or after other programmable conditions are satisfied. Once an alarm is generated, the section where detection has occurred can be highlighted on a CCTV monitor, which aids in assessing the alarm. A variety of commercial VMDs are available, each with its own unique operational characteristics.

VMDs can be divided into two basic types: analog and digital. Analog VMDs have been in existence longer than digital VMDs and are simpler and less expensive. Digital VMDs are more complex but have greater performance capability. Analog VMDs typically monitor changes in one entire detection area. The video signal level in the detection area is averaged and then compared to a previously stored average reference level. The reference level is obtained by the VMD at startup and is continuously updated in small increments to compensate for very slow changes in scene illumination. An alarm is generated if the average signal level is suddenly lower or higher than the reference level. The sensitivity or threshold setting is defined as the amount of change required for the VMD to generate an alarm. Digital systems divide the motion detection area into sections, referred to as cells, zones, dots, or boxes. On an individual basis, these small sections are monitored for changes in signals by using digital processing. In most digital systems, a change in one small section does not generate an alarm; additional digital processing is usually performed before an alarm is declared. This additional processing is used to determine the size, speed, and direction of a defined threat.

VMDs can be set up and adjusted to provide a high probability of detection. During setup, the minimum relative contrast and the size of the object to be detected should be considered. Because of camera lens perspective, objects appear smaller as they move away from the camera. In less sophisticated VMD systems, this creates varying sensitivity with respect to distance from the camera. In sophisticated digital systems, compensation for lens perspective results in fairly even sensitivity throughout a detection area. The detection area is dependent on

the type of VMD, but it generally accounts for 20% to 100% of the monitor screen.

A high NAR rate is one of the main degradation factors for VMD applications. Many digital VMDs use prealarm processing to reduce the NAR. An example of prealarm processing is tracking changes through a number of the small sections for logical intruder movement, requiring a specified number of small sections to change over time. Some systems determine the object size by processing the number of small sections that change during the intruder motion. Most digital systems will determine if a global change occurred by checking whether all small areas changed at the same time. More complex systems use filtering algorithms to reduce the NAR caused by high-velocity objects, such as birds and flying insects. If an intruder must follow a well-defined path to a target, some VMDs can be programmed to detect direction of travel through specific cells. Prealarm processing is aimed at reducing the NAR while maintaining good probability of detection. The amount of prealarm processing varies widely among the available systems.

The assessment camera is an integral part of a VMD. Camera characteristics affect both the detection capability and the NAR. A low-contrast output from a camera reduces detection capability; high noise levels from a camera can increase nuisance alarms. CCTV cameras require enough light for proper operation, and this light must be uniform enough to avoid excessively dark or light areas. Because a VMD detects changes in the video signal characteristics, any change can cause an alarm. Flickering lights, camera movement, or similar changes can lead to excessively high NARs. As a result, use of VMDs with exterior cameras generally have a higher NAR than in interior applications.

When the camera view is obscured by dirty lenses, bad weather, or lighting failure, a VMD can have severe vulnerabilities. During these times, the system could be defeated. Other defeat methods do exist, but they require technical knowledge of the particular system in use and so depend on the defined threat capabilities. Very slow movement through the detection area can defeat most VMDs. This slow movement requires that an intruder remain in the detection/assessment area for a long time, which would perhaps allow detection by another method.

The performance of a VMD is directly affected by the maintenance of the sensor and CCTV system. A high-quality video signal from the CCTV system is required to get maximum operation from the VMD. All of the standard maintenance procedures for a CCTV system should be followed. The VA team needs to spend time observing and documenting the maintenance of the CCTV system and VMD. Basic procedures including lens cleaning and periodic replacement of lightbulbs should be completed by the maintenance staff. If not, the performance of the system could be degraded.

Evaluation testing of the VMD should be done to determine the P_D and NAR. Walk, run, and crawl tests should be conducted at the far field-of-view. A period of time should be identified when the VMD can be monitored when there is no motion in the area. The VA team should also examine previous logs to determine whether there has been an historical problem with NAR. The overall VMD performance is degraded partly based on the results of these tests.

Volumetric Sensors Summary

Volumetric sensors are used in all levels of security applications including homes, industry, and government facilities. For volumetric sensors, the environment of the volume to be protected has a major impact on sensor performance. The VA team should determine key environmental parameters that affect the sensor based on its theory of operation. They should also look for objects in the volume that

might create blind spots or vulnerabilities. For high-security applications, multiple sensors may need to be installed to obtain complete coverage of the volume, if required. As with all other sensors, the installation, maintenance, and testing of a volumetric sensor will determine the overall sensor performance and how it should be degraded by the VA team.

Manufacturers are currently combining the outputs of volumetric sensors into dual technology sensors using a logical AND configuration that requires nearly simultaneous alarms from the combined sensors to produce a valid alarm. If the technology of one sensor is defeated or fails, then the whole sensor is defeated. Using a time window to evaluate sensor outputs according to the received interval decreases the NAR of the dual technology sensor. Newer models OR the two sensors, which will address the defeat of an ANDed device, but still reduces sensing of one device, since their placement is not optimized.

When sensors are combined in a logical AND configuration, the probability of detection for the combined detectors is less than the P_D of the individual detectors. If a microwave sensor with a 0.95 P_D is combined with a PIR sensor having a 0.95 P_D, the resulting 0.90 P_D for the dual technology sensor is the product of the individual P_Ds.

Assuming a single direction of intrusion, a higher P_D can be obtained from separately mounted logically combined sensors than from a dual technology sensor. Microwave sensors have their highest P_D for radial motion either toward or away from the sensor; a PIR sensor has its highest P_D for motion across its field-of-view. Thus, the P_D for the sensors combined in a single unit and aimed in the same direction is less than the P_D for individual detectors mounted perpendicular to each other with overlapping detection envelopes, as both devices can't be optimized at the same time. The highest overall system P_D is achieved by annunciating the individual sensors separately. This is primarily due to the vulnerabilities that are introduced with an AND configuration, which only requires defeat of one sensor to defeat the device. An OR configuration will have a higher NAR but it does not allow the same easy defeat methods; an OR configuration will still not optimize placement of both sensor technologies simultaneously.

Proximity Sensing Technologies

Point sensors, also known as proximity sensors, are placed on or around the target to be protected. In a high-security application, point sensors usually form the final layer of protection, after boundary penetration sensors and volumetric sensors. Capacitance proximity, pressure, and strain sensors are commonly used for point protection, but a number of sensors previously discussed as boundary penetration and volumetric sensors are readily applicable to point protection. A brief description of examples of these technologies follows. A detailed description of a pressure sensor is also included in this section.

Point protection can be accomplished by surrounding a given object with an enclosure that is protected by a boundary penetration sensor. An alarm is generated by the sensor when the enclosure is breached. Enclosing an object in a glass case and either mounting a glass-break sensor on the case or embedding a fiber optic continuity sensor in a blanket or under a floor stand provides point protection for the object. A mechanical switch, such as a spring-loaded switch affixed to a display or mounting platform, also provides point protection. The object to be protected is placed so that its weight or position maintains switch closure. Removal of the object causes the switch state to change and thus produces an alarm. A volumetric sensor can be set with a very limited range, perhaps only a few inches, so that detection occurs only when touching the protected object. An invisible curtain generated by either a PIR or VMD can provide point protection for a relatively small object. Any attempt to touch the object changes the signal characteristics in the curtain and generates an intrusion alarm. Museums often use volumetric sensors in this way to protect their displays.

Pressure Sensors

A pressure sensor is a proximity sensor that detects the presence of a load placed on it or removed from it. The pressure sensor may be a spring-loaded switch or a pressure mat activated by the weight of the protected object. Removing the object results in a switch actuation, which generates an intrusion alarm. Alternatively, the pressure sensor may be a pressure mat placed beside the protected object to detect the weight of an intruder.

A pressure sensor uses a sensing device that responds to distortion of the sensor caused by adding weight. The operation of a pressure mat is generally similar to the operation of pressure sensors. An electrical pressure mat contains a long electrical switch consisting of two ribbon conductors that are separated by compressible foam pads spaced at intervals along the length of the switch. When pressure is applied to the pad, the foam compresses, and the ribbon conductors touch each other. Contact between the pads results in a switch closure that can be used to operate an annunciation device.

Pressure sensors should have a very low NAR. If installed and maintained properly, the only source of alarms should be objects that weigh as much as defined threats. As very few normal environmental changes fall in this category, equipment failure is a more probable cause of alarms. A pressure sensor also is subject to considerable wear from normal traffic, and periodic tests should be performed to ensure that the sensor is operating effectively. The sensor pad can be installed in a depression in the floor or under a cover. If the pad is placed under a protective cover, such as a rug or a rubber doormat, the cover must be fastened down around the edges to prevent the pad from moving or removal. A pressure sensor is vulnerable to either bridging by a board placed on bricks or jumping or stepping across it. The VA team should observe how the sensor is installed, maintained, and tested to determine overall sensor performance.

Proximity Sensors Summary

Proximity sensors are usually the last line of detection in a high-security application. There are many technologies that can be applied to perform this function. The key to overall performance will be a very low NAR. If an alarm is generated, immediate response is normally required because the intruder is now very near the target. Immediate response will be reliable only if the sensor has a very low NAR. The exact location and operation of a proximity sensor should be kept as covert as possible, as there will be several vulnerabilities if the intruder knows all the details about this sensor. The VA team should degrade the overall effectiveness of the proximity sensor based on these factors.

Other Technologies

Other interior intrusion sensors that are in use include fiber optic cable in walls or other enclosed spaces (as shown in Figure 5-11) or other continuity sensors, vibration, seismic, sonic and infrasonic, sound wave, and light beam sensors. Depending on the age of the facility, the defined threat, and value of the asset, these sensor types are still in use and may be appropriate for protection. They should be evaluated by reviewing the appropriateness of the sensor for the threat and operating environment, installation, maintenance

Figure 5-11 Fiber Optic Cable Used on Interior Wall. The cable detects cutting through the wall by checking sensor continuity. This is a covert sensor, generally used in high-security systems or close to valuable assets.

and testing, performance against the defined threat, and integration with other PPS elements.

General Interior Intrusion Sensing Evaluation

Just as with exterior sensors several factors must be considered when estimating sensor performance. Principles of operation, installation, maintenance, and integration with other sensors and PPS components all contribute to the evaluation of installed interior sensors at a site. Data collection sheets are provided in Appendix D to aid in the characterization and evaluation testing of interior sensors.

Sensors should be installed so that they provide their best sensitivity along expected paths of entry by an intruder or so that they cover the actual asset being protected and there is no exposed wiring, the sensor is stable, and the detection zone is not blocked by doors, other structures, or furniture. Once the sensor has been aimed at the appropriate location, the test lamp that indicates detection by the sensor should be disconnected, and this should be verified during the VA. Each sensor reports to an alarm interface panel, and these panels should be inspected to ensure that it is operational and tamper protected (see Figure 5-12). Tamper alarm reporting should also be verified at the central monitoring station and should be a separate alarm from intrusion sensors.

As with exterior sensors, the NAR of interior sensors is a major indicator of sensor performance. The VA team should inquire as to nuisance alarm rates and sources and the appropriate procedural

response to these events. If there are multiple interior sensors in use in an area, they should be tested to verify that they are complementary if they are expected to reinforce each other. If the sensors are dual technology sensors, the evaluation should consider their placement and whether they are logically ANDed. Unless the threat is very low, this will result in degraded performance of the device. The detection pattern and volume should be verified for each device, along with the initial determination that the device is functional.

Interior sensors are often in access during normal operational shifts. Questions should be asked regarding when and how the sensors are accessed, who controls this function, and whether they are walk-tested when turned back on. The VA team should determine when and which interior sensors are in access and verify that sensor tamper alarms are still reported during this state. In addition, alternate paths, such as ductwork, should

Figure 5-12 Interior Alarm Panel. This is the alarm panel where interior sensors relay alarm information to the monitoring subsystem. Note the exposed wiring, which introduces a simple vulnerability. This was exacerbated by the lack of a tamper alarm on the box enclosure.

be examined for sensors to determine how difficult it would be to bypass most of the more visible sensor coverage. This aspect of sensor degradation depends on the expected threat and paths of entry. All procedures for sensor maintenance, operation, and control should be documented by the VA team and evaluated for how well they address insider threats and provide reliable detection. Sensors should be tightly integrated with CCTV cameras. This is described further in the next chapter, but it is an important aspect of sensor integration into the overall PPS. After all these factors have been considered, an estimate of performance for each sensor in use at the site can be made, and documentation to support this assessment should be created using notes, photos, sketches, and other methods.

Summary of Interior Sensing Technologies

When evaluating interior sensors, the goal is to make a determination of how well installed devices will perform against the expected threat. If sensors are present, there is an implicit expectation that they will be effective in protecting assets. Consideration must be given to the principle of operation of the sensor and its operating environment, installation and interconnection of equipment, NAR, maintenance, testing, training, and the defined threat. The environment associated with interior areas is normally controlled and is, therefore, predictable and measurable. Consequently, it is possible to evaluate sensors for their performance in a particular environment.

Intrusion Sensing by Humans

Use of technology is not the only means of sensing intrusions into a site or area. Employees working in the area, guards on patrol, or video surveillance are other commonly used techniques. Although human observation may be effective against very low threats, testing has shown that these methods will not be very effective against more capable threats or when protecting critical assets. Humans do not make good detectors, especially over a long time. The lack of firm criteria for what is an adversary intrusion, the difficulty in recognizing this in time to prevent the attack, as well as safety concerns for employees, all contribute to this problem. We have done more than 20 VAs at one customer's sites, and test intrusions have never been detected where sensing depends on human observation. Reliable intrusion sensing is best achieved through the use of sensors and is less expensive than hiring guards. Another weakness of human observation is that it is easier to divert their attention away from intrusions, particularly if they are engaged in other activities, such as doing their primary job, answering phones, or assisting visitors. If the defined threat or asset value is significant, sensing through human observation should be degraded. The VA team can usually run a few tests to demonstrate to a customer how easy it is to defeat a human detection system. This should be a well-coordinated test with the site to prevent any accidents or unfavorable reactions to the VA team.

Estimating Intrusion Sensing Performance

Once tours, interviews, and testing are complete, the VA team should document intrusion sensing subsystem strengths and weaknesses. The method of presenting these results is discussed in detail in Chapter 12. This can be done qualitatively or quantitatively, using the following guidance. Remember that intrusion detection is just one part of the VA, and the analysis cannot be completed until similar information is collected about the other protection subsystems. This part of the VA concentrates on the probability of detection for each sensing type—exterior or interior sensors or sensing by humans.

In general, the data collection aspect of the evaluation should note areas where component performance was degraded and why, as well as the effect this has on the component, subsystem, or overall system. At this stage, vulnerabilities are not addressed directly; rather, information is collected to support an analysis that will show overall system effectiveness. Too often, VA teams jump right from observations to vulnerabilities and can overlook many potential opportunities for optimization after all aspects of the PPS have been characterized. It is important to review all aspects of a PPS, document all data collected, and then analyze the cumulative effects of this data to determine system effectiveness. Once this is done, a determination can be made as to whether upgrades are needed, and just as important, which upgrades will produce the best performance for the dollars spent.

If a qualitative analysis technique is used, observations and their effects should be recorded, using indicators such as high, medium, or low to represent each component of the intrusion sensing system, including sensors, people, and procedures. Avoid reliance on expert opinion alone; all observations should be supported by test data, pictures, or third-party reports. If the consequence of loss is low, or other risk management alternatives provide primary protection for the asset (for example, insurance to replace items, not physical security to protect them), analysis will be easier. Establishing presence of PPS components is not the goal of a VA; the goal is to determine how well the installed components work together to protect the asset and justify the dollars spent on physical security.

For a qualitative analysis, five categories and associated criteria are used to help determine a qualitative score for P_D.

The five categories, and evaluation criteria, are:

1. Proper sensor selection for environment
   a. Correct sensor for terrain, soil, weather, operating environment, and threat
2. Installation
   a. Sensors are stable and have no exposed wiring
   b. Compliance with manufacturer's specifications and local electrical and fire codes
   c. Protection against water, extreme heat or cold, humidity, snow or ice damage
   d. Tamper alarms are included and monitored as separate alarm sources
3. Maintenance
   a. Periodic testing to verify required operation
   b. Expansion capability is available
   c. Critical spares on hand
   d. Maintenance logs show timely repairs or contingency plans to allow continued operation
   e. Training of personnel is appropriate and current
   f. After maintenance, tests performed to verify no insider tampering
4. Performance against defined threats
   a. Varies with expected threat—crawling, walking, running, jumping, bridging, bypass, and spoofing methods are prevented
   b. Detection using sensors, not personnel
   c. Operation 24/7 with consistent P_D across all facility states
5. Intrusion sensing integration with other PPS components
   a. Sensors are integrated with cameras, not just surveillance
   b. Sensors placed before barriers
   c. Immediate on-site response of any kind to alarms
   d. Sensor alarms are assessed

e. If multiple sensors are used, they are complementary

Unless all categories are rated as high, and this is supported by documentation, P_D will be no more than medium. If multiple categories are weak or deficient, intrusion sensing will be low. Because it is expected that evaluation can result in similar ratings for each category, Table 5-1 shows a quick method of comparing results that can be used to raise or lower estimates and resolve "ties." This guidance can also be used for estimates of various performance factors for other PPS subsystems. The guidelines can be modified as desired, but a standard set should be used across an enterprise and facility, so that meaningful comparisons can be made. When estimates in all categories are very close, the performance and integration categories are the primary drivers of sensing performance.

Analysis using a quantitative technique will consider the same categories as described previously, but will represent P_D as a mathematical probability. This is a more rigorous treatment of intrusion sensing and should be supported by test data from a credible source. Although P_D is the desired result, this estimate is usually accompanied by a NAR, either expressed as the number of nuisance alarms per zone per a period of time or as a percent of alarms. For example, an exterior sensor might have an average NAR of two alarms per zone per day, or this could be expressed as "2% of the 50 exterior alarms each week are due to nuisance sources." We often also include an estimate of the probability of communication of the alarm to a monitoring station. This is normally quite high (>0.9), but can be degraded if wiring or other interconnections slow down reporting of sensor alarms.

A few fairly simple concepts form the basis of statistical analysis of security technology components. Most of these concepts deal with the possible outcomes of a security event. In this discussion, a security event is said to occur when a security component encounters a stimulus and performs its intended task, for example when something enters the detection envelope of an intrusion sensor such as a human or a small animal. There are four possible outcomes of this event:

1. The sensor successfully detects a human-size stimulus.
2. The sensor fails to detect a human-size stimulus.
3. The sensor successfully ignores a smaller-than-human stimulus.
4. The sensor fails to ignore a smaller-than-human stimulus

Successes and failures are related such that when a human-size object is presented, there are two complementary results; and when a smaller-than-human object is presented, there are also two complementary results. This fact will be used later in the discussion. Sensors are the example used here, but this principle applies to any of the probabilities used in this text—the success or failure of a PPS component or the system in performing its intended task can be measured.

Most statistical analysis of security performance is based on these four possible

Table 5-1 *Qualitative Evaluation Characteristics.*

Qualitative Description
Very High (Always)
High (Almost always)
Moderate (More often than not)
Low (Occasionally)
Very Low (Almost never or never)

These levels can be used to help raise or lower a performance estimate, by category or overall. This secondary step can be used to support higher or lower performance if the preliminary estimate has many medium to high categories.

outcomes. The rate at which a sensor successfully detects objects is described as the detection rate. For example, if a sensor successfully detects a human-size object nine times out of ten events, the detection rate for that group of ten events is 0.9 or 90%. This is a statistic but is not yet a probability. The detection rate can be turned into a probability when coupled with a confidence level. A confidence level is established based on the number of events that are analyzed; the more data available, the more confidence in the probability. This is easily understood when considering a common example. If a person tosses a coin and the outcome is heads, it would be unwise to assume that every coin toss will result in heads; however, if that person tosses a coin 100 times and 49 results are heads and 51 results are tails, there is a fairly high confidence that the outcomes will be about 50/50. If the experiment is continued to include 1,000 trials, the confidence in the estimate of the likely results is even higher. At this point the rate can be estimated with some statistical confidence, and this estimate is a probability. In other words, a probability is an estimate of predicted outcomes of identical trials stated with a confidence level. If 100% confidence is required, an infinite number of tests are required. In reality, when designing performance tests, a confidence level is chosen that requires performance of a reasonable number of trials.

For example, if a sensor is tested by crawling through it 20 times and it detects all 20 times, we can calculate the probability of detection at a specified confidence level. The confidence level used for most security system effectiveness analysis is 95%. Using this confidence (and statistical tables), the probability of detection calculated for the sensors based on the 20 trials is 0.85 (often we hear it said that the probability is 85%, but in proper statistical terminology a probability is always a number between zero and 1). In

simpler language, this means that testing shows a 95% confidence that the sensor will detect a crawling intruder at least 85% of the time. The actual detection rate may be higher, but this result is all that can be supported given the data. If the sensor is tested 30 times for the same confidence level of 95%, the probability of detection is now 0.9. Again restating into simple language, there is a 95% confidence that the sensor will detect a crawling adversary at least 90% of the time. This statistical overview is provided for enterprises that are considering collecting their own performance data for use in evaluating specific security devices before purchasing or installing them at facilities.

Summary

This chapter discussed the use of exterior and interior sensors in a PPS. For each category, a representative technology was discussed to show how they are evaluated during a VA. Each sensor technology performs within the limits of the laws of physics, and interactions between sensor hardware and the physical environment are part of the evaluation, along with proper installation, maintenance, and operating procedures, and an understanding of the expected threat. Human observation may also be used for intrusion sensing, but human performance is more limited. If the defined threat or asset value is significant, sensing that relies on human observation should be degraded. The intrusion sensing subsystem evaluation should note areas where component performance was degraded, and the effect this has on the component, subsystem, or overall system. The performance measure of intrusion sensing at a facility is the probability of detection (P_D), and this estimate can be made qualitatively or qualitatively using five evaluation categories and associated criteria.

Because the goal of a VA is to establish how well the installed components work together to protect the asset, P_D is used in an analysis to establish overall system effectiveness and then justify the funding required to upgrade the PPS if necessary.

Reference

DOE, 2005, Exterior Sensor Testing, available at http://www.oa.doe.gov/guide-docs/0009pssig/AppA.pdf, April 21, 2005.

6

Data Collection—Alarm Assessment Subsystem

After an alarm is generated through either sensors or human observation, the alarm must be assessed to determine the cause and decide what response, if any, is needed. As shown in Figure 2-2, the detection function is not complete without alarm assessment, which will be shortened to assessment in the remainder of this text. The key points covered in this chapter include:

- Methods of alarm assessment
- Effectiveness of video surveillance versus video assessment
- Components of a video alarm assessment subsystem
- Degradation factors for the alarm assessment subsystem
- Estimating alarm assessment performance

The background information for this chapter can be found in Chapter 8 of the *Design* textbook. As described previously in Chapter 5, exterior or interior sensors best accomplish intrusion detection; humans are better at assessing an event.

There are two purposes of assessment. The first is to determine the cause of each alarm, which includes deciding whether the alarm is due to an adversary attack or a nuisance alarm. The second purpose of assessment is to provide additional information about an intrusion that can be provided to responders. This information includes specific details such as who, what, where, and how many. The best assessment subsystems use video cameras to automatically capture images that show the cause of an alarm and display these images to an operator who can then assess the alarm. Assessment may also be accomplished through human observation, but this is slower than, and not as effective as, the use of video assessment (see Figure 2-3).

Alarm Assessment Overview

A key principle in the evaluation of a PPS is that detection is not complete without

123

assessment. This principle is based on the premise that the primary goal of a security system is to protect assets from loss or damage. As explained in Chapter 2, to effectively meet this objective, a facility must detect that an attack has started and delay the adversary long enough to allow an appropriate response to the attack. There is an important distinction between detection and assessment. Detection is the notification that a possible security event is occurring; assessment is the act of determining whether the event is an attack or a nuisance alarm. The method of assessment will have a major impact on the performance that can be expected from the assessment subsystem.

Assessment can be provided using visual checks by personnel or by CCTV camera coverage of each sensor sector. Visual checks using personnel will take much longer to dispatch a patrol or other staff, and by the time they arrive, the alarm source may no longer be present. Unless there is visible damage to structures or other objects in the area, accurate assessment of the alarm can be problematic. Because of this severe limitation in human assessment, subsystems that rely on this method are generally rated very low for the probability of alarm assessment. Using cameras in a video assessment subsystem, operators can rapidly assess sensor alarms at remote locations and avoid unnecessarily sending guards or other responders to an area. In low security applications, the use of humans for both detection and assessment may be accepted, but this will result in lower estimates of performance by the VA team. Evaluation of a human assessment subsystem focuses on the procedures used to notify and dispatch people, the timeliness of their arrival, and how they report once they arrive at the location. Because the use of human assessment results in such low performance and is easier to evaluate, the remainder of this chapter focuses on video assessment.

The key parameters that determine video assessment subsystem effectiveness include:

- Minimum time between sensor alarm and video display
- Complete video coverage of the sensor detection zone (called the assessment zone when sensors and video are integrated)
- Ability to classify a 1-foot target at the far edge of the assessment zone. *Classification* means that an object in the video image can be accurately differentiated as human, animal, blowing debris, or other category. Some protection systems must *identify* the object in the image, which is the ability to differentiate between people, for example, John not Jim. These capabilities are a function of image quality, which is measured using video resolution.
- Vertical field-of-view at far edge of exterior detection zone to account for the height of a standard fence (if present), and a person climbing over the top of the fence
- Continuous operation 24 hours per day, 7 days per week
- Minimal sensitivity to environmental conditions for all cameras
- Minimal obscuration of the assessment zone, that is, trees, fences, or junction boxes in exterior areas or furniture that blocks camera view in interior areas
- Camera field-of-view and video recording system integration that displays the alarm source to an operator

The more the assessment subsystem deviates from these requirements, the lower the quality of the video image and the more the VA team will degrade subsystem performance.

Assessment versus Surveillance

It is important to differentiate video assessment from video surveillance when conducting a VA. Video assessment refers to immediate image capture of a sensor at the time of an intrusion alarm such that the source of the alarm can be determined. Once an alarm is assessed, the proper response to the alarm can be initiated. Video surveillance, on the other hand, uses cameras to continually monitor all activity in an area, without benefit of an intrusion sensor to direct operator attention to a specific event or area. Many surveillance systems do not use human operators, but record activity on storage media for later review. The most effective security systems use video assessment and not surveillance to determine causes of alarms.

The use of video assessment or surveillance relates to the value of the asset and the timeliness of the response that is required. If the asset to be protected has a low value or a consequence of loss that can be tolerated, use of surveillance systems may be appropriate. If the consequence of loss of the asset is unacceptably high, however, assessment subsystems are the better alternative. As an example, if a clerk in a gas station is killed during the commission of a robbery, the video surveillance system in place to monitor the store using videotape recording (if properly designed) may collect information as to the identity of the felon, but did nothing to prevent the death of the employee (Arnold, 2005). Although the surveillance tape may provide evidence to help identify, capture, and prosecute the felon, the system failed to prevent the death of the employee, resulting in a high-consequence loss. It is hard to see how this arrangement protects either the money or the clerk. This is why it is so important to consider the threat and consequence of loss of an asset before the VA begins—so that the appropriate level of protection needed to prevent unacceptable outcomes can be determined.

Video Assessment Performance Factors

At the end of this part of the VA, an estimate of the probability of assessment (P_{As})

must be provided for use in the system analysis. This probability is a result of the combined effects of video image quality and resolution, capture speed of images, and integration of sensor detection zones with camera field-of-view coverage. The most important factor in assessment subsystem evaluation is to verify that video images containing the alarm source provide enough detail to an operator to allow an accurate determination of the cause of the alarm. There are many components of a video subsystem, and any one can be appropriate in a given application. The key is to understand what performance is required of the assessment subsystem, and then evaluate how the components contribute to this performance. In general, a facility will see many more nuisance alarms then intruder attacks, so the NAR should be minimized to maintain effective assessment subsystem performance. The NAR is a function of the sensors used at the facility, which was discussed in Chapter 5 on sensors. Factors that affect video image quality, such as camera resolution and sensitivity, use of color or black-and-white cameras, lighting, surface reflectance, recording and storage media, signal strength, switching, signal transmission and conditioning, and monitor performance are all aspects of the evaluation. The evaluation should also verify that the assessment subsystem will work under all expected environmental conditions and facility states expected at the site. Weather is a major consideration for exterior cameras, and interior camera performance can be affected by objects that block the camera's view, blind spots in the camera field-of-view, operational conditions inside the room, and automated lighting controls in a building.

Evaluation of these performance factors vary with the threat, value of the asset, the presence of an immediate on-site response, and the use of other risk management alternatives to protect assets. In general, this comes down to two basic protection approaches—immediate or delayed response to an adversary attack. If the asset to be protected is critical, and a capable threat is anticipated, an immediate response may be the only way to protect the asset from loss through sabotage or theft. If the asset is less valuable, the threat is not very capable or other risk management alternatives provide primary protection (i.e., insurance), a delayed response can be used. Either approach requires an effective video assessment subsystem to support the protection objectives; the only difference is how quickly the video images will be reviewed. For this reason, we recommend that the VA consider these assessment subsystem evaluation factors regardless of the response strategy.

Although the video assessment subsystem is a complex integration of components, there are several fast and easy ways to evaluate the subsystem that do not require extensive knowledge of the technical parameters in order to estimate performance. The fastest qualitative method is to view video images on a monitor at the alarm monitoring and display location. If the images provide the required detail, to support the protection objectives, the subsystem can be said to be adequate. If not, further tests or evaluation may be required to isolate and document the degradation to specific components of the subsystem. The required image detail depends on threat actions, such as whether they are crawling, running, walking, jumping, or bridging; whether assessment must be at the classification or identification levels; the environmental conditions that exist at the facility; and the expected nuisance alarm sources.

Evaluation Testing

To support testing of the video assessment subsystem, test targets can be used to verify video image quality. As shown in Figure 6-1, these targets are simple geometric shapes that include a 1-foot square, circle, and triangle. The test target sizes

are based on a horizontal field-of-view of 6 horizontal television lines (HTVL) per foot as the required resolution, which is sufficient to classify a crawling intruder under appropriate lighting. If the expected threat will always provide a larger profile to the video system, a lower horizontal resolution is acceptable. Using the test targets is appropriate in both cases. The test targets are painted black and white so that they can be used to check image resolution in dark and bright spots, respectively. Because the evaluation must consider component performance under a variety of changing conditions, this is a simple way to test whether the test targets can be seen at lighting extremes in the area. In bright spots the white side faces the camera, and in dark spots the black side faces the camera. These targets are used for testing both black-and-white and color cameras.

The targets are placed at various points in assessment zones (or across the camera field of view, if using a surveillance system), and the subsystem operator is asked to distinguish the different targets. The more targets that can be clearly differentiated, the more confidence the VA team has in the quality of the video image. Locations selected for testing are those that do not appear to make target identification easy, such as dark or bright spots, places where the camera view is obstructed, or where the surface may not be level. The tests can be performed for both exterior and interior cameras, although some locations may be more useful for exterior testing. These targets test the extremes of the black-and-white capabilities of the assessment subsystem against the background color of the assessment zone. Other aspects of video image quality that must be considered are lighting, camera mounting, the transmission system used, and the integration of switchers and controllers into the subsystem to facilitate alarm assessment.

The test targets are also used to check the far-field resolution, particularly in

Figure 6-1 Video Test Targets. The targets can be used to quickly determine video subsystem resolution. If the different shapes can be recognized, video resolution is sufficient to classify an object in the scene. In this picture, the shapes are circle, square, triangle from left to right, and the black side is facing the camera. Human testers dressed in clothing that blends into the background can also be used to simulate an actual intruder, but the test targets are generally more efficient for this testing.

exterior assessment zones. Because the far field represents the furthest distance from the camera, it will have the fewest lines per foot, so this is a quick way to verify that the horizontal resolution is maintained across the entire assessment zone.

Quality of the live video image is just one aspect of the evaluation. Because it is unlikely that all alarms can be assessed using live video (think of multiple alarms, operator attention to other tasks when an alarm is initiated, or an adversary running very fast through a detection zone), a video recording and storage system is also needed. As with cameras, there are many choices to accomplish this, but what is important is that the recording and playback happens fast enough and with enough detail to determine the cause of the alarm. Speed of playback and display

is less important when the response will be after-the-fact review, as long as the image quality is sufficient to assess the alarm. The video test targets can be used to verify image quality for recorded images. It is likely that the recorded image will not have the same resolution (i.e., quality) as the live image; this will vary with the recording media and settings.

The test targets may also be used to test video surveillance systems. In this case, video image quality can be tested, although these systems depend on human operators to actually see a security event occurring in a live view, or assume that a delayed response using recording is all that is needed. If this approach will work for the facility, this test may be appropriate, but because humans are not good at detecting events, this will severely degrade assessment performance. In addition, many video surveillance systems use pan-tilt-zoom (PTZ) cameras and so may not be viewing an area of suspicious activity. This is why sensors are used to initiate reliable intrusion detection and are combined with fixed cameras, so the camera is always aimed at the proper location. Even new, fast PTZ cameras may not turn fast enough to catch a speedy adversary or nuisance source moving across a short distance or where part of the field-of-view is blocked. In general, low performance would be assigned to the assessment subsystem if resolution is low, only surveillance cameras are used, the cameras in use are all PTZ, and the subsystem depends on human sensing or live video assessment of events.

Video Assessment Subsystem

A video assessment subsystem allows security personnel to rapidly determine whether an intrusion has taken place at a remote location. In addition to allowing real-time remote observation of areas, the video assessment subsystem can record and store video of alarm areas and other significant event information. This permits retrieval of appropriate images, even under conditions of multiple simultaneous alarms or delayed security personnel attention. The video assessment subsystem is just one component of an intrusion detection system. There are numerous interactions among the video system, intrusion sensors, communications, the display system, and the operator that must be considered during the VA. Some examples include consistent display of sensor and video information, alarm and video image transmission times, delays in recording times, presentation of the information to the operator to minimize human error in assessment, and human interface controls for assessment and surveillance actions.

Because use of video is the best way to assess alarms, this chapter focuses on evaluation of the video assessment subsystem during a VA. Notes on the use of surveillance or human detection will also be included, however, particularly where these techniques compromise overall system effectiveness. The basic components of a video assessment subsystem are shown in Figure 6-2. The subsystem includes cameras at the remote sensor areas, display monitors at the local end, and various transmission, switching, and recording systems. Major components include cameras, lights, transmission switching, recording, storage, and controller equipment and monitors. Kreugle (1995), Cieszynski (2004), and Damjanovski (2005) have all written outstanding books discussing video subsystems and their component pieces in considerable depth. These books provide substantial detail to readers desiring more information on video technologies.

There are several exterior site characteristics that affect the video assessment subsystem, including the layout of cameras, lighting, weather conditions, and surface conditions such as flatness, reflectance, and drainage. Interior characteristics also include camera layout, lighting, and surfaces, as well as the placement of furniture or other objects in rooms, and protection of cameras and wiring. The assessment subsystem must provide the ability to assess all installed sensors by capturing an image before the alarm source leaves the sensor detection area and then transmitting this image to the display or recording location. Critical factors in obtaining the correct image of the alarm event depend on the sensor reaction time to its stimulus, how fast the source is moving, the size of the stimulus, the alarm sensor communication time, the alarm communication and display (AC&D) subsystem, and time to notify the video recorder to start recording the event. All of these parameters will affect the video recording of the alarm event depending on whether the recorder is recording in a post-alarm mode or a pre-alarm mode. If all of these factors are not

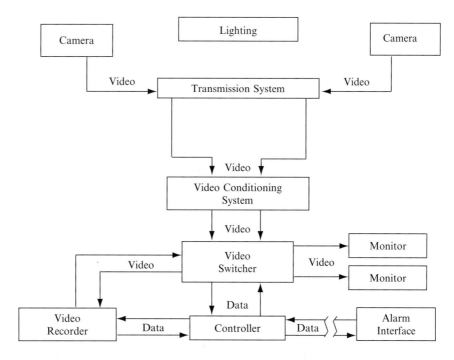

Figure 6-2 Block Diagram of Video Assessment Subsystem Components. The video assessment subsystem uses CCTV cameras to capture images of alarm sources in detection zones and then transmits those images to a location for review and storage.

properly accounted for, some recorded events may present the wrong set of images to the operator leading to an incorrect alarm assessment and indicating to the VA team that the assessment subsystem may have to be degraded.

Video Subsystem Equipment

This section describes the performance indicators that will assist the VA team in providing an estimate of probability of assessment. If the video assessment images do not meet protection objectives, it can be beneficial to evaluate the components of the subsystem in order to identify where deficiencies exist and to prioritize subsystem upgrades after the analysis. Each of the following components not only contributes to image quality but may also represent opportunities to defeat or bypass components of the

video assessment subsystem. Data collection sheets to record observations for the video assessment subsystem can be found in Appendix D.

Topics that will be addressed in this section include:

- Cameras and lenses
- Camera housings
- Camera mounting
- Lighting
- Signal transmission
- Recording and storage
- Monitors
- Other equipment
- Procedures

Cameras and Lenses
The camera and lens work together to create the video information that is used in alarm assessment. Because this is the

origination of the signal, proper camera and lens selection may be the most critical aspect to the assessment subsystem. The camera must provide sufficient video signal amplitude to drive a video monitor and should produce a full video signal at high- and low-light levels. The lens will determine how large an area the camera will view. An illustration of a full video signal is shown in Figure 6-3. Video waveform monitors, which are specialized oscilloscopes that can display video

frequencies, are used to examine the video signal and verify signal strength.

If a full video signal is not produced in the camera, the video image will be compressed into fewer shades of gray than normal and will result in low contrast, washed-out pictures. In addition, required details may not be distinguishable from the background. Many cameras do not maintain the darkest portions of the scene at the black reference level (see Figure 6-3) in daylight environments, which also

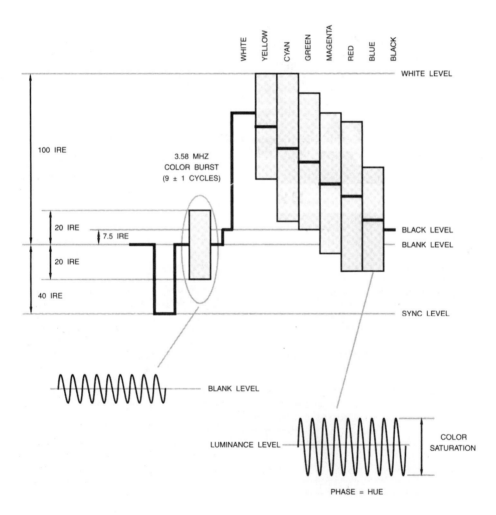

Figure 6-3 Full Video Waveform. Video signals are measured in IRE units and a camera should provide a full video signal from the reference black level at 7.5 IRE units to peak white at 100 IRE units, which equates to a 1-volt peak-to-peak signal. With a full video signal of 92.5 IRE units, the best video quality should produce multiple shades of gray.

produces lower contrast images. An example of a video waveform and the corresponding scene on a monitor is shown in Figure 6-4.

The choice of a black-and-white or a color camera (or any other type of camera for that matter) depends on the threat, level of video detail required, and reason for the need for color. Use of color cameras requires that the entire video infrastructure can process color video signals. Although the use of color can have advantages, there may be higher equipment costs and maintenance functions. The minimum resolution required at a specific site must also consider operator capabilities. Each person perceives images differently, and one way to counteract any negative effects of these variations is to specify a higher-than-necessary image resolution at every stage of the signal (camera to monitor). Factors that may also tend to encourage the use of higher resolution include poor lighting, complex scenes, low scene reflectance, and maintenance problems. These aspects are discussed in the appropriate sections that follow. Many of these details are most pertinent to exterior cameras and assessment sub-

systems, but the principles and concepts still apply in interior applications.

Just as with cameras, there are many different lenses available; the specific choice will depend on the operating environment and required performance. Where varying light sources are expected, for example exterior daylight and night lighting, auto irises are required. In applications where light is constant, perhaps interior rooms where lights are always on, manual irises can be used to reduce cost and maintenance. Automatic variable focal length or zoom lenses are frequently used in video surveillance systems using PTZ cameras, but these cameras will not provide effective assessment because they generally will not be pointed at the assessment zone when a sensor alarm occurs (if a sensor is used). An effective assessment zone cannot use an infinite number of focal lengths at the same time, so variable focal length lenses do not aid effective assessment. A PTZ camera with an automatic zoom lens would serve no security purpose because without the capability to re-point the camera as the zoom feature is used, the zoom area is very limited when assessing alarms. This is why assessment

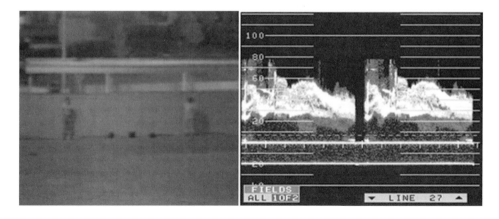

Figure 6-4 Comparison of Video Waveform and Monitor View of Image. Note the video signal level and the clarity of the scene on the monitor, which is an indication of the quality of the video signal. The video waveform is a good way to analyze video signals for deficiencies, and pictures can be used to document video evaluation results. The video test targets are visible against the far wall.

subsystems are severely degraded when PTZ cameras are the primary means of assessment; however, PTZ cameras can be used as backup assessment cameras in the event of a fixed camera failure. This would permit somewhat degraded temporary performance while the fixed camera is replaced. In this case, the camera should not be used for surveillance activities while it is being used for assessment backup. Clearly, the location of the PTZ camera must allow for assessment, and the lens focal length must be set to be comparable to that of the lens being substituted.

The most widely used lens is the magnetically operated automatic iris lens system. In most cases, the video signal amplitude is monitored, and a drive signal is created to maintain the amplitude at some predetermined adjustable level. As the video signal level decreases, the auto-iris lens is driven to increase the iris opening to gather more light. At some point, however, the iris is driven fully open, and a lower light level will result in a reduced amplitude video signal.

Some cameras are designed with an automatic gain control (AGC) circuit to maintain the video signal level as the light is reduced; however, the AGC circuit adds additional noise to the video signal. The resulting image at the lower light levels can also be compromised by the reduced contrast between black-and-white levels until the image becomes unusable. This effect is found in low-light-level operation, such as in a perimeter at night with artificial lighting. Cameras with AGC circuitry can extend the dynamic range of the camera slightly, although some additional noise may be observable on the video monitor. If this noise reduces image quality under low-light conditions, the probability of assessment will be affected. Alternately, the electronic shutter option for a camera can also be used. This camera feature uses a manual iris lens, and the camera electronics limit the light that collects on the camera imager, thus limit-

ing the light exposure level. These generally cannot compensate for full bright sunlight, so signal quality must be verified under this condition to determine performance.

The primary requirement of an exterior video assessment subsystem is to display the entire assessment zone, including the clear zone between the inner and outer fences for multiple fence perimeters. Camera and lens selection and positioning must ensure assessment of any visible cause of fence and clear zone sensor alarms regardless of the time of day. For these reasons, the following criteria must be verified for exterior cameras during the VA:

- The inner and outer fence spacing should be uniform in double fence systems.
- Minimum clear zone width must be appropriate for the speed of the defined threat (i.e., crawling slowly versus running upright).
- The type of surface between clear zone fences must be appropriate.
- Grading and maintenance of the clear zone should be performed.
- Area illumination level and uniformity must support resolution requirements.
- Camera angles relative to fences should be considered in the evaluation of assessment for exterior perimeters.
- There should be minimum clear zone obstructions in the camera field-of-view.
- Viewing heavy shadow and bright light areas simultaneously should be avoided.
- Viewing directly into sun at sunrise or sunset should be avoided.

Deviations from these criteria will generally reduce subsystem efficiency and increase overall system and maintenance cost by increasing equipment requirements to achieve acceptable system effectiveness.

Some of these criteria were discussed in Chapter 5; others are discussed in subsequent sections in this chapter.

Camera layouts for interior assessment follow the same principles and guidelines as for exterior cameras. Because of the shorter distances generally found in interior applications, resolution sufficient for classification or identification is relatively easy to achieve. Interior cameras will still use the same resolution limited field-of-view as exterior cameras; however, this distance will be much closer to the camera. Interior cameras generally use lenses up to approximately 16 mm for $1/_2$-inch or $1/_3$-inch format cameras. Lighting levels suitable for human comfort and safety (30- to-100 foot candles) will be adequate for most cameras. Many interior cameras are now equipped with manual iris lenses and electronic shuttered lighting control on the image device.

Camera Housings

Video cameras in an exterior environment require protection from temperature extremes and from precipitation; interior cameras must be protected from simple attacks that can reduce or eliminate the ability to assess alarms. Camera housings come in two types: integrated with the camera body or as a separate unit that holds the camera body. If cameras are not protected from weather or simple attacks, the probability of assessment will be degraded.

An integral environmental housing forms the outer shell of the camera. This camera housing is quite rigid and sturdy and can be pressurized with dry nitrogen and equipped with thermostatically controlled integral heaters to create a constant operating environment for the camera. A sun shade is often attached to overhang the lens and deflect light or precipitation from the camera faceplate. In high winds, the faceplate may not remain entirely free of precipitation, and some reduction in assessment can be expected.

Another option is to mount the camera inside a separate sheet-metal or fiberglass housing, which permits access to the camera by a hinged or removable lid. Separate housings must be large enough to contain the camera, lens, and cable connectors. Their chief advantage is the accessibility to the camera for adjustments, such as lens focusing. The housings cannot be pressurized, so some dirt and dust accumulation can be expected inside. They can be equipped with heaters, insulation, fans, defrosters, and faceplate washers and wipers, all of which can be controlled automatically, except for the washers and wipers, which must be remotely controlled from the assessment station. The washers and wipers have proven to be a considerable maintenance problem, and they are not recommended unless unusual environmental conditions exist. Washer reservoirs, which must be located at the camera, require more frequent access to the camera for maintenance. If properly adjusted and kept free of ice, the wipers can maintain adequate assessment in high-precipitation situations, whereas non-wipered camera faceplates may degrade assessment during these times. If these features are used, their effect on assessment subsystem reliability and performance should be verified. The conditions at each site would determine the need for these devices, and their added maintenance requirements could be a source of assessment subsystem degradation.

Camera Mounting

Cameras must be mounted so that they are stable, protected from simple attacks, provide unobstructed views of the assessment zone, and do not have blind spots. Exterior cameras should point roughly parallel to any fences. In multiple fence perimeters, cameras can be positioned at any point between the inner and outer fences, but there are some practical restrictions. The detection zone should be centered between the fences to minimize the effects of the fences on various sensors; therefore, the camera pole or tower should not be located in this area. If the camera is mounted above or too close to the inner fence (in fact, any fence), it will not see through the fence, which will reduce assessment capability. If outriggers are used on top of the fence, there is a similar effect, and this provides a place for an intruder to hide after crossing the detection zone. In this case, assessment would be difficult. Cameras located just inside the outer fence and slightly angled into the facility can see through much of the inner fence, thus eliminating hiding places along the inner fence. Even a slightly delayed image capture would still reveal an intruder at, or attempting to cross, the inner fence. Camera towers in these locations may be vulnerable to an attack or may provide an aid in bridging the detection zone, and this distance should be considered during the evaluation. Tamper protection should be installed on camera towers to detect bridging or equipment attacks, as appropriate for the defined threat.

Exterior camera mounting heights are typically 15 to 30 feet. A height of 26 feet is recommended for better assessment of a crawling intruder because of the better perspective looking down at the target. Low mounting heights are convenient for camera installation and maintenance, but the length or depth perspective of a crawling intruder is not as good as from a higher view; therefore, assessment performance may be degraded if low-mounted cameras make crawling intruders difficult to see. Exterior assessment cameras should be mounted on stable towers. Wooden poles are not recommended for use because they tend to twist, warp, and reposition the camera field-of-view as the pole cures and dries out over time. Solid poles provide a potential hiding spot or a possible heavy solid shadow area that may cross the perimeter sensor zone, making it difficult to see an intruder. Freestanding

triangular towers with cross-member supports are preferred both for their stability and the flexibility in location options. Because these towers are nearly transparent because of their lattice construction, they can be located within the assessment zone without providing a possible hiding place. The freestanding tower, as its name implies, has no guy wires for support. The tower is attached to a base buried in concrete several feet below ground level. The location of the tower is important in minimizing wind-induced tower vibration being coupled into the ground, which could cause nuisance alarms in some sensors and affect image quality. Examples of exterior camera mounting poles and towers are shown in Figure 6-5.

Interior cameras mounted at the corners of a room just below the ceiling usually provide the best assessment locations. Corners away from doors or windows are preferred to eliminate camera tampering from someone in the camera blind spot and out of the camera field-of-view. Because of the blind spot in the camera field-of-view (below the camera), wide-angle lenses should be used to provide full wall-to-wall (90 degree) camera coverage. By tilting the camera down, the ceiling lights that would adversely affect the camera signal can be avoided but a complete view of the area or equipment is still maintained. In typical interior applications, the assessment zone will contain items other than the asset being protected, which will affect the maximum usable zone length. When tall equipment or furniture is located in the room, a second camera may be required to observe the obstructed side; a good location may be the corner diagonally across from the first camera. Some facilities use tape or painted lines to mark places on the floor where furniture or other objects should not be placed because they will block camera views. This practice is not recommended because it provides an adversary with detailed information regarding

Figure 6-5 Examples of Exterior Camera Towers. The wooden poles in the picture on the left are starting to warp, which will change the camera field-of-view. They will also cast shadows into the zone at different times of day and night. The triaxial towers on the right are the recommended camera tower because they are transparent and very stable.

where cameras can't see and creates a hiding place for an intruder. Because some interior sensors use reflected energy, it is important that the camera field-of-view cover the entire detection area, so assessment capability is consistent for all alarms.

All cameras must be installed to ensure that no light sources are in their field-of-view. Direct light causes the auto-iris lens circuitry to reduce the lens aperture, thus darkening the image details. Possible sources include exterior or interior lights and objects or surfaces that reflect light. Illumination sources in the field-of-view that can blind cameras either directly or by the glare on the faceplate glass form the basis for degradation of assessment capabilities.

Exterior cameras should not view portions of the sky to prevent camera electronics from attempting to average the wide range of IR light content in the sky compared to the low visible light content of the ground. As much as possible, perimeter zones should have cameras facing away from the sun to minimize reflections on the housing faceplate glass at low sun angles, such as dawn or dusk. A perimeter section adjacent to a roadway presents problems from vehicle headlights and taillights, even when the roadway is a considerable distance from the assessment camera. Each of these aspects of camera performance is part of the evaluation and should be checked for all cameras at different times of day, but at a minimum, dawn/dusk, full daylight, and full dark.

Mounting a camera in an unprotected area could allow camera tampering. To detect camera tampering, the video line can be electronically supervised. Video presence detectors, which can monitor the video signal and produce an alarm if the video level increases or decreases by a preset amount, are commercially available. Some inexpensive video presence detectors detect only the presence of the sync signal. This capability may be helpful in detecting catastrophic camera or video line failure, but is of little use if the camera scene is obscured, perhaps by placing a lens cover or a piece of cardboard in front of the camera lens. In this event, the sync pulses are still present even though the camera view is blocked. If the detector is not looking for added video signals, white noise from any fiber optic signal conditioning transmitters located at camera towers could produce a signal that is mistaken for the sync pulse. If video loss detection is in use, the VA team must carefully assess the method of video loss detection and consider how effective the circuit is in detecting video tampering attempts.

Lighting

Artificial lighting allows exterior cameras to operate at their maximum performance at night and to ensure that no degradation of the video signal affects operator efficiency for interior cameras. Both exterior and interior lights should be installed above the camera, so they do not interfere with video quality. Lighting performance can be evaluated many ways, but the best approach is to actually measure the light-to-dark ratio across the camera field-of-view. A maximum light-to-dark ratio of no more than 6:1, which is the ratio of the highest light reading to the lowest reading, and an overall average of 1 foot-candle in the assessment zone is recommended. It is important that the entire camera field-of-view be included in the light-to-dark ratio average light calculation, because the camera is a light averaging device and

averages the light across the entire field-of-view, not only the assessment zone. This can be important in double fence exterior perimeters because the camera may see beyond the fences, even though the assessment zone is between the fences; thus, the camera field-of-view is likely to have a different light-to-dark ratio than the assessment zone. Light is measured using a light meter and by sampling light in a grid pattern across the area, for example every 3 to 10 feet across the length and depth of the area. Not every assessment zone is checked, but a sample of suspect zones should be measured to document system performance and to ensure that proper lighting is provided. These zones are selected by viewing video images on assessment monitors and evaluating those zones that appear too dark or too bright, or that contain many shadows.

As an alternative to actually measuring the light-to-dark ratio, video images displayed on monitors can be used. Bright and dark spots show up clearly on the monitor (or recorded images) and will affect image quality. An example of this is shown in Figure 6-6. Although this method does not give the actual light-to-dark ratio, it does show that this is a degradation factor that should be included in the analysis, and it may be an opportunity for upgrade. Other sources of scene degradation include the presence of shadows in assessment zones, either as a result of sunlight or artificial light at night. If this approach is used, pictures showing the bright and dark spots, or shadows, should be used to document the reason for subsystem degradation.

Night lighting should be continuous and present every night of the year. Some lighting systems use alarm-activated lighting. If this approach is used, assessment subsystem performance should be degraded significantly as a result of the notification of detection this gives to an adversary. This degradation should also account for the fact that sufficient light

Figure 6-6 Good and Bad Night Lighting. On the left is the monitor view of an exterior assessment zone with a measured light-to-dark ratio of 6:1. On the right is another zone whose light-to-dark ratio is 24:1. The dark and bright spots provide places where an intruder can hide and avoid discovery.

will not be present for the camera until an alarm occurs; therefore, the camera and lens will be set for low-light conditions (allowing high video noise content) but on an alarm the lights come on. At this point, the camera and lens must adjust to the increased light at the precise moment that the alarm occurs, thus degrading the initial images that contain the source of the alarm. In addition, many exterior lamp types require a considerable restrike time if power is interrupted. If the site contains critical assets, a backup source of immediate lighting will be required.

In exterior applications, lights should be placed inside the fence of a perimeter; if there are multiple fences, lights should be inside the innermost fence. They should be tilted up a little to cast as much light as possible into the perimeter, and far enough away from fences so that they do not provide a climbing or bridging aid to an adversary. Interior lighting is not usually a problem, as the light required for normal operations is usually sufficient for good video images. If interior lights

are turned off at night, video quality will obviously suffer. Sometimes, facilities choose to use low- or no-light cameras for these times of day. This is acceptable if the image quality still provides the level of detail needed to assess not only real intrusion alarms but also the anticipated nuisance alarm sources. If the visual image quality drops so that the test targets cannot be seen, subsystem performance should be degraded.

Another aspect of lighting that should be considered during the VA is surface reflectance. Once again, image quality is the final test of this parameter, but it can be useful to know where performance degradation occurs when considering any upgrades. Sometimes simple changes, such as slightly tilting a light or adding another light, when combined with ground reflectance can bring image quality up to desired performance. Too much reflectance from a floor or exterior surface will act as a mirror and reflect the light, thus causing video degradation by obscuring the video in this bright spot (see Figure 6-7). If there is too little reflectance, there

Figure 6-7 Examples of Reflectance. The picture on the left shows the reflectance off an exterior surface that creates a large bright spot that can hide adversaries dressed in white clothing. In the picture on right, the shiny interior floors blind the camera and make assessment at the far end very difficult. For exterior applications, surface reflectance should be a minimum of 30%. Interior surface reflectance should be 30% to 80%.

will not be enough light to meet minimal camera illumination requirements.

Signal Transmission

Because video assessment cameras are usually located at a significant distance from video monitors, communication links are required to carry the video signal between these points. The signal quality at the end of the transmission path should be as faithful a reproduction of the original signal as possible, but any technique for transmitting a video signal results in some signal degradation. Evaluation of the signal transmission method and its effect on image quality at monitors or recording and storage devices is part of the assessment subsystem performance estimate. The following information is provided as an aid in determining specific sources of signal degradation, which can be useful if any system upgrades are required, although not strictly required during a VA.

The performance required for video transmission is based on the frequency of the signal to be transmitted and the physical and/or electrical environment in which it will be used. Camera resolution dictates the bandwidth required. Different transmission techniques and their associated cabling can be tailored to provide almost any bandwidth. The transmission path should not degrade camera bandwidth to the extent that a high-resolution camera operates at a lower resolution; this is not cost or performance effective. If significant bandwidth degradation occurs, characterized by lower contrast and lack of detail within the image, assessment performance should be degraded. Any transmission line has resistive and reactive losses. These losses, primarily functions of the distributed capacitance and conductor resistance, are usually expressed in decibels (dB) per unit length. Signal attenuation increases with both the signal frequency and cable length and varies widely among the various cable types.

The most common method of video transmission uses copper cable, which has many forms. Coaxial cable is the most popular choice, although unshielded twisted pair, triaxial, and twin axial systems are sometimes used to meet specific needs. Video signals are normally transmitted from 75-ohm signal drivers that, for most efficient use, must be carried on a 75-ohm cable and terminated at a 75-ohm impedance. The most commonly used coaxial cable for video transmission is RG-59. Although this cable produces video signal losses, its small diameter, low cost, and flexibility make it popular. RG-59 cable can be used in lengths up to a few hundred feet, if necessary, without appreciable signal degradation or the necessity for signal conditioning equipment. Coaxial cable of smaller diameter, such as RG-179 or RG-187, should be used in the shortest lengths possible and only if bulkier cable is too large to fit, as in video switcher input and output panels. These miniature cables have about five times the high-frequency loss per unit length of RG-59 cable. Larger diameter copper cable, such as RG-11, is commonly used when the video signals are transmitted over several hundred feet. RG-11 has about 40% of the high-frequency loss per unit length as RG-59 cable. This type of cable comes with an insulating jacket suitable for direct burial if small animals do not present a chewing hazard to the insulating jacket. The single multiconductor RG-59 coaxial cable that is frequently used in camera control cables and includes power, video, remote camera control functions, and lens control functions is rapidly being supplanted by fiber optic installations.

Fiber optic cables use an optical path rather than an electrical path for the transmission of information. The conductor is a glass or plastic fiber, rather than copper. A converter is required at the transmitting end of the optical fiber to convert the electrical video signal into an optical signal. This conversion can be by a simple light-emitting diode (LED) or a high-intensity laser. The usable length of the transmission path is affected by the diameter of the fiber, fiber material, source intensity, signal bandwidth, and wavelength of the transmitted light. In the receiver, a photodiode converts the optical signal back into the electrical video signal present at the camera. Fiber optic transmission has several advantages over copper wire and has become the transmission medium of choice in new installations. The number of connectors, splices, and taps will reduce the effective length of the system because there are signal losses at each of these junctions. In addition, length of the cable and whether the mode of transmission is single or multimode will limit the bandwidth of the fiber. Review of installation details of fiber optic media may provide insights to the VA team into causes of any signal degradation.

Video signals may also be transmitted using RF or optical wireless transmission equipment. RF equipment is widely available for wider bandwidth transmission for security applications. There are some advantages to this medium through the use of spread-spectrum systems that are available in long- and short-haul transmission systems. The risk of having the signal intercepted or blocked by the adversary must be considered when evaluating RF transmission techniques. If the defined threat has the capability, RF transmission of video signals is relatively easy to observe, block, disrupt, or modify (Schiesel, 2005). Although technically plausible, and in many cases extremely cost effective, these systems are not widely used in high-security applications because of these simple interception and attack methods. It should be noted that encryption of the video signal may prevent interception or modification of the signal, but will not help if the signal is blocked.

Optical video transmission has many of the same characteristics as RF transmission techniques. The video signal is transmitted by amplitude modulation of an LED or laser; typically an audio or data channel is also provided. As in RF transmission systems, the chief advantage of optical video transmission is the ability to provide line-of-sight transmission across or among physical obstacles without the need for laying cable. This can be especially useful for temporary use in facility retrofit installations. Another advantage to optical transmission systems is their immunity to interference in high electromagnetic or electrostatic environments. Their maximum useful range may be only several hundred to a few thousand feet, but they can be cost effective in the right circumstances. The main disadvantage of optical video transmission systems is that operation may be hindered in fog, rain, or snow, depending on the density and the distance between the transmitter and the receiver.

It is likely that a facility will use combinations of transmission media across a site. During the VA, video signal degradation at the camera and monitoring ends of the transmission line should be compared, and if degradation that compromises the ability to assess alarms occurs, performance will be degraded. Degradation should be documented using photos of the images on video monitors for visibly bad images (see Figure 6-7) or using video waveforms for more subtle changes (see Figure 6-4).

Video Recording and Storage

A video recording system is used to provide a record of significant events for subsequent retrieval or archiving. The record may be kept permanently or may be kept only until alarm assessment is complete. There are a variety of recording devices and storage media available, each having characteristics that must be matched to the specific performance required of the assessment system. In the past, the most popular means of recording and storage used video tape recorders (VTRs). Today, digital video recorders (DVRs) are overtaking VTRs as the preferred storage

medium. A few systems still use only solid-state memory. Each of these methods has strengths and weaknesses for recording and storage when assessing alarms. Understanding these strengths and weaknesses assists the VA team in the evaluation of assessment subsystem performance.

The most important criterion for judging a recording device is its ability to reproduce the detail of the original image. This can be measured in horizontal lines of resolution using a resolution chart. Testing using this chart indicates that video tape recorders provide up to 400 lines of resolution. DVR resolution is reported as high as 500 lines, and solid-state devices can record up to 585 horizontal lines of resolution. These are the maximum possible values; this should be verified to determine whether the recorder resolution matches the resolution required by the assessment subsystem. If the evaluated resolution does not match the requirement, degradation of the recorders is appropriate. Goodenow (2005) described the difficulty the FBI has in using stored images of bank robberies. Oddly, this story only addresses cameras and not the recording media, which may be another factor in image quality. Many DVRs also use video image compression methods to preserve space on the storage disk and allow for storage of more information. There are various compression techniques that are used by DVR manufacturers, and they can cause degradation of the image detail within the recorded image. Degradation can be evaluated by comparing the camera video and stored video images. If the compression technique compromises the quality of the image so that alarm assessment takes longer or cannot be completed, the probability of assessment will be degraded. Note that most DVRs do not have any better resolution than the old VTRs, although some devices that use less or no compression can meet the 500-line resolution described previously. The attraction of using DVRs is their increased reliability, because, unlike VTRs, they have no moving mechanical parts that fail. To achieve these higher resolutions, more storage space is needed for each image, which may require additional storage devices or more DVR. These aspects of video storage are critical to the assessment subsystem evaluation and should be thoroughly evaluated and documented during the VA.

The second criterion for video recording is the speed of image capture from start to finish of the alarm event. VTRs may record in real-time, time-lapse, or alarm event recording modes. Real-time recording speed will capture the alarm events, but tape storage limits will require a new tape every few hours. The time-lapse and event recording modes have a delay of 0.5 up to 1.5 seconds before full video images can be recorded, allowing the possibility that the alarm source is not captured. DVRs can be set to record in the same modes as a VTR, but do not delay the recording in the time-lapse or alarm event modes (this is due to the use of electronic, not mechanical, mechanisms). Solid-state memory devices have no delay before recording an event, but do have severe storage limitations and therefore can only record a few individual images for any alarm event. The degradation of any of the recording devices using the speed of capture criterion depends on whether the recorder being used could miss an alarm event recording. For example, if the alarm source is a bird that flies through the video scene in 1 second, then a VTR in event recording mode that could take up to 1.5 seconds to record an image might miss this type of alarm event. Speed of capture is not usually an issue with DVRs or solid-state devices.

The third criterion is how the video recorder presents the recorded images to the display monitor. VTRs usually have only one output to display the alarm event and cannot record another event until the previous event playback has finished. To review an event, the tape must be rewound to the alarm event and then played, thus disabling the recording function of the tape recorder. This disadvantage is often resolved through the use of multiple VTRs, which can make alarm assessment even harder because multiple machines must be operated to review and record sensor alarms simultaneously, and this can confuse the operator. DVRs are more flexible and can present and record multiple events at the same time. Solid-state recorders are limited to one or two outputs that are capable of displaying events, but they also have the ability to record and play back simultaneously. Integration and display of alarm information are discussed in the next chapter, but if the display of alarm video is independent of the alarm communication and display subsystem or must be manually controlled by an operator, assessment effectiveness should be degraded. This is due to the length of time this process can take and the very real possibility of human error in selecting the proper image.

Once alarm recording and storage are established, the next criterion to consider is the number of images per alarm event that are captured and reviewed by the operator. In a real-time recording mode there are 30 frames per second of full video, which requires large storage capacity regardless of the medium. To reduce this capacity, only some frames are captured, using a programmable interval between frame capture. The interval between images is advantageous during review, as any movement in the recorded images will be emphasized during playback; however, this interval can have disadvantages if it is so long that the alarm source occurs between recorded frames. Evaluation of nuisance alarm sources, expected speeds of the adversary, and the interval between recorded images must be made to determine whether degradation of the recorder is necessary.

Another aspect of the number of images captured on an alarm is the time the operator will need to review all of the recorded images. For example, if a DVR has been programmed to record 10 seconds before an alarm and 20 seconds after an alarm, the operator will need 30 seconds to review all of the video. If the source of the alarm is not readily apparent, the operator may need to review the images a second time. At this point, 1 minute has passed, and the assessment still has not been made. This effect must be considered in the overall analysis of the whole security system and should be reflected in the estimate of probability of assessment.

The reliability of the recorders is the last criterion considered during evaluation of video recorders. VTRs have several moving parts, pulleys, and recording/playback heads that are all critical to recording and playing back the video images. The tape itself can be used only a certain number of times before it starts to degrade. A VTR requires more operational maintenance than either of the other types of recorders. DVRs (or network video recorders) are basically desktop computers and can take advantage of the increased reliability, lower costs, and easier maintenance of these devices. Although computer hard drives and cooling fans can fail, this is a rare event, and the reliability of these devices is quite high. Most computers now have redundant power supplies, hard drives with capabilities that minimize any failures, and network video recorders that are capable of storing alarm images in multiple locations to provide high reliability for recording and retrieving recorded images. Network video recorders or DVRs attached to networks are only as reliable as the network itself. If the network fails, alarm recording or playback can be compromised and alarm assessment performance would be degraded. Solid-state memory devices do not have critical moving parts associated with the recording or storage unit; therefore, they also have a high reliability.

At many facilities, video images are captured, stored, and saved for a specified period of time for use in after-the-fact review and investigation of security incidents. If this approach is used, the information captured and image quality of the stored images should be evaluated by the VA team. Often, the stored images are meant to be used to prosecute an offender, and each legal jurisdiction has different requirements for what information must be included. Various details including time and date stamps, the presence of other people in addition to the offender in the image, the ability to positively identify the alleged offender and any items they may have in their possession, a unique physical identifier contained within the image (that substantiates the location of the attack), and the percentage of the image that the offender occupies are examples of the legal requirements that must be met to admit video evidence into courts. In addition, the emergence of digital video recording is complicating legal prosecutions because the stored images can be easily altered. Many manufacturers incorporate watermarking or encryption of the data so that tampered images can be identified, and some of these protection schemes have survived legal challenges. Note that if this is an intended use of stored video, image quality, other information, secure storage of images, and maintaining the chain of custody will also be requirements for the video recording system. As with all elements of the PPS, these requirements must be met under all environmental, operational, and facility states to support legal prosecution, which will vary among jurisdictions. Current information on the status of digital video in legal proceedings can be monitored through the International Journal of Digital Evidence (www.ijde.org). Additional details concerning the use of recorded images are discussed in Chapter 10.

Monitors

Monitors are used to view video images and are available in a variety of sizes. The distance between the monitor and the viewer has a direct effect on the clarity of the picture as perceived by the viewer. The closer the operator is to the monitor, the smaller the screen can be; the farther away the operator is from the monitor, the larger the screen should be to maintain the operator's assessment effectiveness. Suggested distances and monitor sizes are shown in Table 6-1.

The operator must be able to distinguish between intruders and nuisance alarms on the monitor. These scenes can range from the closest to farthest view of the assessment zone, and the monitor should perform equally well under both extremes. The monitor can only reproduce an image up to its resolution limit and, as with all video components, must be matched to the resolution requirements. Using a high-resolution monitor with lower resolution cameras, recorders, or transmission systems will not help assessment performance.

Many video surveillance systems display multiple images on a single monitor. For example, 4, 9, or even 16 images are displayed at one time. This is a highly ineffective method of assessment or surveillance, and use of this sort of display approach would cause serious degradation in performance. Degradation occurs because when the multiple images are displayed on the monitor, they no longer take advantage of the full resolution across the whole monitor screen. Therefore, the resolution of a four-image display (2×2) only uses half the available resolution for the display. An example of this is shown in Figure 6-8. Details that may be perceived in a full monitor image may not be discernable in a four-image display. Clearly, the more images that are displayed, the worse this problem becomes. Another common feature that makes it difficult to assess alarms (or even support surveillance observations) is the use of automatic sequencing through all site cameras. This time period can be programmed but is on the order of 1 second per image. If this sequence is interrupted on an alarm by the automatic switching and display of assessment images to the operator, it could be difficult to differentiate the normal sequencing of images from alarm event images, even with additional aids such as audible tones or changing text colors. Certainly it would be difficult for the operator to detect any suspicious activity in real time, with many images scanning at such a fast rate, at a reduced resolution, and at some distance from the monitor. The inability to discern image details through the entire assessment zone, display of multiple images on monitors, sequential scanning, and distance from the monitor are all sources of P_{As} degradation.

Table 6-1 *Monitor Size/Distance Relationship.*

Monitor Size (Diagonal Measure in inches)	Distance from Monitor (ft)
9	3-7
12	4-9
13	4-10
14	4-12
17	4-13
19-21	4-15
25	7-17
26	8-18

For effective observation of images on the monitor, the operator should be close enough to quickly and comfortably assess alarms.

Figure 6-8 Change in Display Resolution with Multiple Images. On the left is the display of a single image using the full monitor resolution. On the right, four images are displayed on the same monitor, effectively reducing the horizontal resolution by 50%.

Other Equipment

Many analog video assessment subsystems also use some or all of the following equipment:

- Video conditioning
- Video switching
- Tamper protection
- Controllers
- Battery backup
- Lightning protection

Any nonfiber optic video cable will cause some video degradation through high-frequency attenuation, induced noise, and phase shifts. High-frequency attenuation reduces resolution, and phase shifting can cause image smear or ghosts resulting from impedance discontinuities along the cable or at splices and cable connections. Induced noise can be seen on the monitor as high-frequency or random snow or as power line noise (light and dark horizontal bars on the monitor). Both forms of noise can partially obscure the monitor image, effectively reducing subsystem resolution. To compensate for these degradations, signal conditioning must be performed at one or more points along the video transmission path. A brief explanation of this equipment and how it is used is described in this section. If signal degradation is noted during the evaluation, the probability of assessment will be lowered. During the VA, the evaluation team must determine whether the degradation and its cause is known to site maintenance personnel. If they are not aware of the signal condition or do not know how to fix it, the VA team must consider that the quality of repairs compromises accurate alarm assessment, and the probability of assessment should be reduced.

Video equalizers compensate for the high-frequency signal losses in long lengths of video copper cable. The amount of equalization needed depends on the cable selected and its length. Equalizers usually provide a gain adjustment to compensate for resistive losses in the cable and either one or more high-frequency adjustments. Equalization can be performed at either end of the transmission line. At the camera end, this technique is called pre-equalization and will selectively amplify higher frequencies.

This approach provides amplification before the signal amplitude is reduced by the cable run, which generally provides a higher quality signal at the receiver end. When used at the receiving end, the technique is called post-equalization. Post-equalization offers an easier adjustment, because this end of the cable is usually located where test equipment can be easily accessed, and the effects of equalization on signal quality can be easily determined. Post-equalization will also amplify any noise in the video signal. For exceptionally long cable runs, both pre- and post-equalization may be required.

A common problem in long video cable runs is that power line frequency signals are coupled into the video signal as a result of grounding problems, which induce power line frequencies into the video signal and can be seen on the video monitor as light and dark bars that propagate vertically through the video image. This effect is known as hum bars. These signals can be reduced or eliminated by using video isolation transformers that electrically isolate the video signal from a ground potential.

Most alarm assessment subsystems have more cameras than monitors because an alarm console operator cannot efficiently make an assessment of more than one zone at a time. Video switching equipment can be used to manage the large number of camera inputs and the smaller number of monitors and recorders. The best performance is found using automatic switchers that are programmed to present specific video for each sensor without operator intervention. Manual switching by the subsystem operator is possible, but it is another source of assessment subsystem degradation because of the human error that may occur in switching the correct video image and that during the time it takes to switch the video, the operator may miss the alarm source. The lowest performance is found in sequential switchers, where a human

operator is expected to detect the alarm condition in scanning video images. The short duration of these multiple images makes assessment very difficult. The chance that the operator would actually see significant movement in the image has been studied and has a very low probability of detection, particularly over a long time (Tickner and Simmonds, 1972; Tickner and Poulton, 1973).

Ancillary equipment located near the camera end of the assessment subsystem may require protection from tampering. The junction boxes containing power distribution, signal conditioning, lightning protection, and other video equipment should be protected with tamper alarms to warn of attacks on the camera circuitry. Typically, these camera junction boxes are located on or near the camera tower.

An older method of integrating the alarm communication and display subsystem with the video subsystem that is still found at some older facilities uses a video controller. This controller automates the various functions of assessment (video switching, recording, display, annotation) to seamlessly present the alarm assessment information to the operator and is their interface to the computer. In addition, the controller responds to operator commands to switch particular cameras to specific monitors. Many of these functions are now performed by the main alarm communication and display computer, complex matrix switcher controllers, or by network interface controllers. The VA team must look at the performance of the video assessment subsystem in providing the human operator with video of the alarm source and must verify that information is provided in a consistent, speedy, and accurate manner, under all conditions, before assigning the probability of assessment.

Some or all of the equipment in a video assessment subsystem must still operate when the main source of power is interrupted. The reliability of the main source of power and the requirement for continued, unrestricted operations determine the amount of emergency power capacity needed. It is important to evaluate which components do not have back-up power and what affect this has on the probability of assessment. For example, if exterior lights are not on back-up power, assessment of exterior alarms at night will not be possible. If only some interior lights have back-up power, video images should be evaluated under the reduced light to determine if sufficient lighting remains for assessment.

Lightning or other high-surge currents can readily damage input circuitry in wired video transmission equipment or to fiber optic transmitters and receivers. Subsystems using multiple cable distribution, such as camera sync distribution networks, are especially vulnerable to significant damage because of the large amount of equipment connected to these lines. Surge suppressors can effectively clamp the maximum voltage appearing on a conductor to safe levels. Several types of commercial surge protection devices are available and should be incorporated into the video assessment subsystem to manage these environmental conditions. Absence of surge protection in these environments would be another degradation factor.

Procedures

A number of procedural issues are part of a thorough VA of a facility. These include maintenance, testing, and training of facility personnel. The VA team should review the documented procedures at the facility and verify that they are used as written, that periodic maintenance and testing is performed for the video assessment subsystem, and that all maintenance personnel are properly trained to ensure required assessment performance. Each of these areas is discussed in this section at a high level. The variety of policies and procedures at facilities makes it difficult to cover this topic in depth.

Maintenance of the assessment subsystem is one of the most critical procedural aspects at a facility. Periodic maintenance is required to repair, replace, and adjust each component of the assessment subsystem to ensure proper operation under all environmental and operational states at the site. Optical focus of the camera lens is a major factor in initial video subsystem installation. The day-to-night illumination levels and energy spectrum changes that occur as a normal part of facility operation cause most of these problems. Cameras are shipped from the factory adjusted for certain light levels, which may not be the same as those found at the facility. It is critical that cameras are focused under the actual lighting in use at the facility as part of the initial installation, and focus should be maintained over the operational life of the camera. This is generally done at night from the actual camera location for exterior cameras because this represents the lowest light level. In a like manner, interior cameras should be focused under the lowest light level expected for their location. If this installation routine is not used, it is likely that video images will not be focused under all lighting and environmental conditions, and assessment performance should be degraded. Cameras in sealed environmental housings typically pose a serious restriction to this procedure and require additional procedural guidance to ensure proper focus. If video images appear to be out of focus, performance should be degraded, and the VA team may need to verify if cameras are focused under site lighting or if they are installed as shipped.

Diagnostic equipment should be designed into the central facility equipment racks to support subsystem maintenance. This equipment should include a video waveform monitor, a test signal generator, and dedicated video monitors. In addition, a selection of spare parts should be immediately available on-site as replacements for critical equipment, such as cameras, auto-iris lenses, surge protection devices, transmitters and receivers, and power supplies. Lamps in light fixtures, particularly for exterior use, should all be replaced at the same time to reduce operational impact and eliminate the need to continually replace single lamps. Adequate maintenance requires proper documentation of all video subsystem components in use. Vendor maintenance and operation manuals should be purchased as part of the equipment procurement. The VA team should verify that equipment documentation includes:

- Theory of operation
- Functional block diagrams
- Cabling diagrams
- Schematic diagrams
- Parts lists with manufacturers' and commercial equivalent part numbers

The use of incoming inspection and equipment burn-in before equipment installation limits early equipment failures and ensures that components operate as required. Maintenance problems are best resolved by a technically competent staff who understand the complexities and interrelationships of video hardware and software and their integration. Periodic maintenance updates may be provided by the vendor, and this documentation should be monitored and implemented as soon as possible. A maintenance laboratory equipped with test equipment will facilitate timely component adjustment and repair at the facility. Equipment documentation should be available at the facility and at a separate central document storage location. All equipment modifications made on-site should also be documented and stored at these two locations.

The maintenance log of all subsystem repairs and adjustments should be reviewed during the VA to verify that periodic maintenance is performed, that failed equipment is replaced quickly, and that subsystem performance is not degraded over time. Contingency plans should exist and be implemented so the subsystem continues to operate, even in a degraded mode, as a result of equipment failures. If no maintenance log exists, performance should be degraded because of the uncertain reliability of the subsystem. Maintenance trends can also be used to identify recurring problems and equipment failures and degrade assessment subsystem performance. Key degradation factors include long delays in maintenance and repair of failed components and recurring unidentified problems (such as camera failures during certain seasons or times of day that cannot be traced). All operational testing of subsystem components should be documented, so that the VA team can determine if the procedures are sufficient and in standard use.

Discussions with assessment subsystem operators and maintenance personnel may uncover system failure modes that escape notice during the short evaluation visit. These may include details such as when assessment images or system components do not provide quality images, times of the year when there are more nuisance alarms, and communication problems with responders. These conditions should be documented and, if possible, attributed to an installation, component, or design problem. Particular attention should be paid to whether this degraded condition can be easily observed by an outside adversary, thus revealing a possible vulnerability. The amount of assessment degradation is based on the frequency and severity of these conditions.

Any subsystem of this complexity should have a defined set of test procedures for verifying video signal and image quality and that after-maintenance or repair tests are conducted to confirm that devices are operating normally and have not been compromised by an insider. Test results should be reviewed to verify that maintenance personnel understand the procedures and have the know-how to perform them. Training of maintenance personnel should also be reviewed to establish that there is a training program, the technical competence of the staff, and that training is current and documented. Training can be through formal classes at the site or vendor, or on-the-job, but the VA team must be able to determine that the staff is capable of maintaining the video assessment subsystem to perform as required.

Estimating Performance

The performance measure that is provided to analysts as a result of the evaluation of the assessment subsystem is the P_{As}. This measure is a result of the combination of proper matching of video subsystem components with respect to resolution, proper installation and maintenance, appropriate capture speed of video images and automatic display of video images, and integration of sensor detection zones and camera fields-of-view. Some methods of alarm assessment are easier to quickly estimate than others. For example, alarm assessment by dispatching a patrol or guard is generally estimated as a low probability, unless there is data to support that the patrol arrives quickly enough to determine the cause of the alarm and collect more information about an actual intrusion. In a like manner, video surveillance systems have a low probability of alarm assessment because they rely on human detection of intrusions or other suspicious activity, the use of PTZ cameras (normally) that may not be aimed at the area of interest, and the display of multiple cameras on a single monitor, often scanning at a relatively rapid rate.

For a qualitative analysis, probability of assessment can only be high if all criteria listed below are rated as high. If any criterion is rated as medium, probability of assessment will be no better than medium, and if three to five criteria are medium or low, the probability of assessment will be low. If there are many ties

among criteria, the performance category should be used as the estimate of P_{As}. The guidance provided in Table 5-1 can be used to raise or lower estimates in each category. In addition, the probability of alarm assessment should be assigned a low rating if assessment depends on live video and medium if sensors and cameras are integrated using timely manual switching of recorded images by the operator. Video assessment criteria and key performance indicators for each include:

1. Proper matching of video components
   a. All video components must be matched for resolution. For example, an 800-line camera that displays video on a 400-line monitor will limit assessment resolution.
   b. No signal loss through transmission system
   c. Required resolution supported and maintained by recording or storage devices. If assessment is to be accomplished through the use of archival storage, the resolution must be sufficient for an operator to determine the source of the alarm.
   d. Use of fixed cameras, not PTZ, for primary assessment
2. Installation
   a. Camera mounting is stable with no movement or vibration
   b. Exterior cameras are installed on a steel lattice tower, not wooden poles
   c. Exterior cameras do not look into the horizon or the setting or rising sun
   d. Lights are above cameras (exterior and interior); lights or reflections do not blind cameras
   e. No blind spots in assessment zone; complete coverage of sensor detection zone
   f. No exposed power or signal wiring
   g. Camera housing is used and tamper protected

h. Video signal and power cables in tamper junction boxes (exterior) or alarm panels (interior)

3. Maintenance
   a. Periodic documented testing to verify component function and system resolution
   b. Maintain lighting, cameras, environmental controls (if used), transmission system, monitors, and recording and storage media
   c. Focusing of cameras under site lighting before installation
   d. Knowledge of installation and training of maintenance staff sufficient to support system
   e. Maintenance logs support a high degree of attention to system upkeep

4. Performance
   a. Assessment design that is appropriate for the threat (classification or identification resolution level)
   b. Correct operator identification of video test targets under all lighting and shadow conditions
   c. Image is captured showing alarm source with fast auto-playback to operator (this is tightly coupled to the response strategy, which is addressed more in Chapter 10)
   d. Use of pre- and post-alarm image capture as part of image display
   e. Amount and type of storage—sufficient capacity, resolution, and speed of acquisition and display
   f. Even lighting—acceptable light-to-dark ratio and average light level, no bright/dark spots, or dense shadows at different times of day

5. Subsystem integration
   a. Camera field-of-view of entire sensor detection volume
   b. Automatic switching of zone in alarm to display for operator assessment
   c. Multiple alarms can be acquired and stored for assessment
   d. Effective video loss detection
   e. Effective junction box and line supervision tamper notifications
   f. Effective subsystem status notifications of off-line or online conditions of equipment
   g. Human factors—consideration for the human interface to the video components for maintenance and operations

A quantitative analysis uses the same criteria described previously, but will assign a numerical value to each criterion and the overall probability of assessment. The major difference is that considerable data are used to support the quantitative estimate. The data may result from statistically valid performance tests at the site during the VA or by using benchmark data from long-term evaluations done in test environments, either by the site or a third party. In practical reality, a quantitative probability of assessment is expressed using three levels to numerically represent the probability of assessment. These are 0.25, 0.5, and 0.95. These approximations are all that is required, which will be explained in more detail in Chapter 7. The lowest value is used when video surveillance systems, guards in towers or dispatched patrols or other human observation are used as the primary method of alarm assessment. The 0.5 value is used when assessment depends on live video, there is a delayed response, it is effective only for a single alarm, or timing of alarm and video capture does not happen fast enough for an operator to see the alarm source. The highest value of 0.95 is used for highly effective and integrated video assessment subsystems that provide the required resolution under all environmental and operational states, and where there is an alternate method of alarm assessment during adverse weather when video cameras are not effective.

Summary

This chapter described the principles, techniques, and tools that are used during a VA to provide an estimate of the probability of alarm assessment (P_{As}). It is a basic principle of effective PPS evaluation that detection is not complete until an alarm is assessed, because assessment is the act of determining whether the alarm is due to an adversary intrusion or a nuisance source. Alarms may be assessed through human observation (patrols) or by using closed circuit television cameras for video assessment. The use of video assessment is the recommended approach. The primary factor to be considered is that the image contains sufficient detail so that an operator can quickly and accurately make this decision. Related issues include proper matching of video subsystem components with respect to resolution, proper installation and maintenance, appropriate speed of capture of video images and automatic display of video images, and integration of sensor detection zones and camera fields-of-view. P_{As} may be estimated qualitatively or quantitatively, as appropriate.

References

Arnold, E., Fatal Robbery: A crime lab backlog made the effort to enhance gas-station footage frustrating for police. *Riverside Press-Enterprise*, April 29, 2005, B1.

Cieszynski, J., *Closed Circuit Television*, 2nd ed., Oxford: Elsevier, 2004.

Damjanovski, V., *CCTV: Networking and Digital Technology*, 2nd ed., Burlington: Elsevier Butterworth-Heinemann, 2005.

Goodenow E., Fuzzy Robbery Photos Little Help, Police Say, *The Columbus Dispatch*, March 16, 2005, 8B, available at http://go.reachmail.net/rmgo.asp?tid =126162&eid=46239&sb_id=66946,669 46, April 20, 2005.

Kruegle, H., *CCTV Surveillance: Video Practices and Technology*, 1st ed., Newton: Butterworth-Heinemann, 1995.

Schiesel, S., Growth of Wireless Internet Opens New Path for Thieves, *New York Times,* March 19, 2005, p A1, available at http://www.nytimes.com/2005/03/ 19/technology/19wifi.html, April 20, 2005.

Tickner, A.H., and Simmonds D.C., et al. Monitoring 16 Television Screens Showing Little Movement, *Ergonomics*, 15(3), 1972, 279–291.

Tickner A.H., and Poulton, E.C., Monitoring up to 16 Synthetic Television Pictures Showing a Great Deal of Movement, *Ergonomics*, 16(4), 1973, 81–401.

7

Data Collection—Entry Control Subsystem

The entry control subsystem includes all the technologies, procedures, databases, and personnel that are used to monitor movement of people and materials into and out of a facility. An entry control subsystem contributes to a total PPS by allowing authorized personnel and material through normal access routes and by detecting and delaying unauthorized movement of personnel and material. Entry control elements may be found at a facility boundary or perimeter, such as personnel and vehicle portals, at building entry points, or at doors into rooms or other special areas within a building. In addition to checks for authorized personnel, certain prohibited items or other materials may also be of interest on entry or exit. Examples of prohibited items include drugs, weapons, or explosives; exiting materials of interest can include precious metals, manufactured product, or other enterprise assets (laptop computers, projectors, cell phones, etc.) subject to theft. The key concepts discussed in this chapter include:

- Objectives of the entry control subsystem and its relationship to PPS objectives
- Entry control subsystem components for personnel, contraband, and vehicles
- Evaluation of access controls
- Evaluation criteria used to estimate subsystem performance

The background information for this chapter can be found in Chapter 10 of the *Design* textbook. This topic is slightly out of order compared to the process flow shown in Figure 1-3 because a well-integrated PPS combines entry control subsystem functions into the alarm communication and display subsystem. Thus these two topics are covered in reverse order to achieve a more efficient information flow.

Throughout this discussion, a portal refers to an entrance to or exit from a specific area. The entrance or exit can exist in a variety of locations and for different purposes. Some portals are used to control entry into a facility; others are used to control entry to specific areas within that facility. This variation in usage often dictates different requirements for a specific portal application, for example controlling entry of people only, or also controlling entry or exit of prohibited materials. Each portal may contain one or many entry control devices, depending on protection objectives.

For evaluation purposes, entry control is defined as the physical equipment used to control the movement of people or material into an area. The term *access control* refers to the process of managing databases or other records, determining the parameters of authorized entry, such as whom or what will be granted access, when they may enter, and where access will occur. Access controls are an important part of the *entry control subsystem.* The terms are often used interchangeably in industry; however, there are advantages to differentiating between the two. Because the technical issues associated with the installation and use of entry control equipment are different than the administrative controls required to manage authorized access, they require separate consideration to achieve an effective and integrated subsystem.

Entry Control Subsystem Overview

The primary objective of controlling entry to facilities or areas is to ensure that only authorized persons are allowed to enter and to log these events for documentation purposes. The objective of searching personnel, vehicles, and packages before entry into these areas is to prevent the introduction of contraband materials that could be used to commit sabotage or to aid in the theft of valuable assets. The primary objective of exit control is to conduct searches of personnel, vehicles, and packages to ensure that assets are not removed without proper authorization. A secondary objective of entry and exit

control is to provide a means of accounting for personnel during and after an emergency.

These subsystem objectives must be achieved while considering the defined threat to the facility. Various entry control technologies and procedures have different strengths and weaknesses, and, as with other elements of the PPS, selection of the appropriate technologies depends on threat capability and motivation. For example, metal detectors are appropriate when the defined threat will be carrying metal objects, such as weapons or tools, but are not effective against explosives. In a like manner, use of explosives detection equipment at an entry point implies that the adversary is expected to be carrying explosives into a facility. If the defined threat does not have weapons, tools, or explosives, use of this equipment may not be effective in the overall PPS.

An adversary may use several methods to defeat an entry control point. These include bypass, physical attack, deceit, and technical attacks. Any or all of these methods may be used by the defined threat, and consideration of this is an important prerequisite to entry control subsystem evaluation. Bypass means that the adversary can overtly or covertly enter or exit by avoiding any entry controls (see Figure 7-1). Just as with sensors, entry or exit control points that are easy for an adversary to bypass will not be effective, for example when a security system has metal detection installed in a portal located in a fence line rather than at entrances to buildings. Because metallic items can easily be thrown over a fence, metal detection in this application cannot be considered effective.

Direct physical attack occurs when an adversary uses tools to force entry into a security area. Pry-bars can be used to force open doors and cutting tools can be used to defeat turnstiles. Another example of how physical attack can be attempted is to attack the control wires of the system. A door or turnstile is often

Figure 7-1 Exterior Perimeter Personnel Portal. The portal is easy to bypass because the fence sensor stops next to the portal and there is no detection of intrusions over the top of the turnstile.

controlled by a relay that switches power to the release mechanism. If the wires leading to the release mechanism can be accessed by an adversary, the door can be released by applying the proper voltage to the wires or in some cases simply shorting across them. The effectiveness of the portal must be measured by determining its resistance to this attack method. Hardening the release points and protecting electrical controls make the system more effective. An effective design will have all control wires installed on the secure side of the boundary and all access boxes protected by tamper monitoring switches.

Deceit involves an adversary attempting to convince a guard or employee to allow them to enter on false pretenses. An adversary may attempt to convince an employee to hold a door open because he is carrying an armload of material or because she left her badge at her desk and needs to reenter and retrieve it. Often, system effectiveness against deceit is not a factor of the physical design of the system but is determined by training and procedures. When evaluating the resistance of a system to deceit, the VA team

should examine the procedures against vouching (allowing another individual into a security area based on perceived authorization) and how well the workforce is trained in this policy.

Technical attacks typically take the form of using a forged credential or guessed personal identification number (PIN) to try to enter the area. Magnetic stripe encoders are easy to purchase and use. Forged badges are not difficult to produce and a system's effectiveness will be influenced by how well it is configured to prevent simple attempts at technical attacks. The use of both a badge and a PIN greatly complicates the adversary's task. The adversary must first encode a badge with information that matches an authorized individual's information and then must guess the correct PIN that is associated with that badge. A system that relies only on PINs *or* badges will not be very effective against this form of attack. Another technical attack is attempting to access the authorization database to insert false information. A system that does not protect the computers that maintain the access control database will not be effective against this attack.

One key to entry control evaluation is to consider the tools, weapons, and technical capability of the defined threat and verify that this threat can be detected as the facility is entered through entry points. Another key is to establish the nuisance alarm rate (NAR) for entry control technology. This is a particularly problematic area in the entry control subsystem, given the range of materials that can be detected that are not the objects of interest, and the need for a human to confirm that the alarm is due to the specific item of interest. A high NAR in entry and exit points will decrease overall PPS effectiveness and become a significant operational burden, particularly during high traffic periods such as shift changes.

There are many individual entry control technologies that are available and as many combinations of them that are used in a PPS. Some of the most common devices are described next, along with their strengths and weaknesses, how they should be combined for the best performance, and how access controls contribute to entry control subsystem effectiveness. In general, these devices are used to control personnel, contraband material, and vehicle entry or exit and include manual, machine-aided manual, and automated operations.

Manual systems use personnel to control entry to restricted areas based on possession of a credential. Intermittent personnel and package searches for contraband can also be performed. The major shortcomings of manual systems are:

- The ease with which the credential can be counterfeited
- The ease with which an individual's face can be made up to match an image taken from a stolen badge or from a remote storage image comparison system
- Inadequate searches by guards or operators for contraband
- Guard inattention after a period of time

Machine-aided manual entry control subsystems use one or more entry control elements to assist a guard or operator in deciding whether to allow or deny entry to or exit from a protected area. When this type of entry control subsystem is used, the final decision to allow or deny entry or exit is made by the human operator. Using additional entry control devices, such as contraband detectors or personnel identifiers, to enable a more informed decision for entry or exit requests enhances security by providing more information to the human operator before granting access. The final action taken, however, is still determined and initiated by the human, which is why machine-aided entry control retains some of the disadvantages of a manual system. Most machine-assisted designs use a card reader or PIN pad that allows the system to give a visual or other signal to an operator that indicates authorization for entry. For example, a card reader may display a photograph of the individual on a computer monitor so that a guard can compare the picture to the individual's face.

Automated entry control subsystems manage routine processing automatically; however, operators are required to continuously monitor information displays and interact with the systems in special circumstances, such as alarm assessment, user assistance, and duress alarms. The advantages of an automated subsystem are higher security through authentication of credentials and personnel, consistent performance, inability to make an exception (as a human can), logging of all transactions, and the ability to immediately suspend access rights if needed. The disadvantages include higher installation, maintenance and training costs, and increased installation times.

The entry control subsystem uses probability of detection (P_D) as its primary measure of effectiveness. Sometimes it is more useful to classify performance into classical error rates rather than classical probabilities. In the security industry, the terms *false accept rate* and *false reject rate* are also used to characterize entry control device performance. The false accept rate is the mathematical complement of P_D and is equal to $1 - P_D$. This is a key measurement of subsystem performance because it represents the probability of defeat of the device. The entry control subsystem can be broken into two major categories—personnel and vehicle control. Contraband material control, such as metal or explosives detection, is a subset of each of these categories. Data collection sheets useful in entry control subsystem evaluation can be found in Appendix D.

Personnel Control

Personnel identity verification refers to the process of confirming that the person requesting entry is actually the person they claim to be. The following three bases are used to verify the identity of an individual:

- Tokens or other items in the possession of the individual (such as a card, key, or credential)
- Private information known by the individual (such as a password or a PIN)
- Biometric features that measure some detail about the physical or behavioral nature of the individual (such as hand shape or iris pattern, or behavioral features such as signature or speech pattern)

There are strengths and weakness associated with any entry control subsystem developed around any one of these bases. The most secure systems use some combination of two or more methods to compensate for individual vulnerabilities. An example of a personnel portal is shown in Figure 7-2.

Figure 7-2 Typical Personnel Entry Portal. The portal uses a magnetic card and PIN combination to grant entry. Out of view at the far end is a larger gate that provides wider entry. Note that the portal extends from floor to ceiling, to avoid easy bypass. The section above the turnstiles is tamper-protected to detect intrusions into the electronic controls.

Tokens

The most common token used for entry control is the photo identification (ID) badge. It is difficult to quantify the effectiveness of a photo ID badge system because inspection of the badge is subjective, and these badges are relatively easy to counterfeit. In one series of evaluations we conducted, all 32 attempts to enter using fake or incorrect photo identification were successful.

Coded Credentials

A coded card contains machine-readable information and is used to rapidly read a person's claimed identity into an automated access control system. Many coded card technologies have been put into commercial use, including magnetic stripe, proximity, and integrated circuit or smartcard technology. When a person presents a card at a reader, they are claiming to be the authorized holder of that card. A coded badge, however, does not by itself positively identify an individual. It only serves as an additional means to substantiate the cardholder's authenticity and determine access authority. The effective use of a coded badge assumes that the user acts in accordance with a set of administrative procedures in which the badge is not lent to others, and lost or stolen badges are reported immediately (see Figure 7-3). It also assumes that administrative procedures for badge control exist and are followed, especially the termination of access rights for lost, stolen, and expired badges. The coded badge becomes ineffective if the user does not follow these rules or if the badge is stolen or duplicated without the user's knowledge. These drawbacks may be reduced by using other means of identity verification such as a PIN or biometric device, which are discussed later.

The most common type of coded credential is the magnetic stripe. Magnetic stripe encoding is identical to the technology widely used in commercial credit card systems. A strip of magnetic material located near one edge of the badge is encoded with badge data, and the data are read by moving the magnetic stripe badge through a slotted magnetic stripe reader. The advantages of the magnetic stripe badge are that they are inexpensive, can hold a moderate amount of information, and can be encoded on-site by security system administrators. The main disadvantage is that the standard magnetic stripe badge can be easily read and counterfeited with inexpensive equipment. More sophisticated magnetic techniques are adding to the complexity of counterfeiting coded badges, but these techniques are not yet in common use.

A proximity badge is one whose information can be read without the badge being physically placed into a reader. These badges are more difficult to alter or duplicate. Proximity badges and readers can operate over distances from a couple of centimeters to more that two meters. One of the main advantages of longer distances is hands-free operation, where the badge does not have to be removed from clothing and passed through a reader. This can be helpful in situations where personnel often push carts or carry large items or in areas where chemical or radiological contamination is of concern. The main disadvantage of longer distance technologies is that when two or more badges are within range of the reader, there is uncertainty about which badge was read when the door opens. This can allow easy entry to an unauthorized person, who appears to be wearing or carrying a legitimate badge. In most high-security applications, shorter range readers are chosen to provide the highest security effectiveness.

Smart-card technology may include both memory and processing capability. A smart card is the size of a standard bank credit card, with an integrated circuit embedded in the card. Metallic contacts on the surface of the card allow for com-

Figure 7-3 Personnel Door Vulnerabilities. Both doors are propped open, a common procedural violation for controlled doors. Note that in the photo on the left, the facility took the trouble to remove the exterior door hardware to make it harder for an intruder to attack the door. The photo on the right shows an interior door into a limited access area. This can be detected by a door-held-open alarm. (Photo on right provided by Joe St. Pierre, CPP.)

munication with a reading device in the case of contact smart cards. Contactless smart cards are also available that use a radio frequency (RF) interface to communicate with the card reader over short distances (1 to 2 centimeters). The main advantages of the smart card are its large memory, its high degree of resistance to forgery or compromise, and the potential for encryption algorithms to reside on the card. These advantages must be balanced with the relatively high cost of smart cards. When facility populations are large and the security level is not extremely high, the cost of smart cards is prohibitive. Issuing smart cards to a small population for use at a very high-security

facility or certain areas of a facility may be appropriate; however, engineering and integration of smart cards into a system are expensive. When a facility has extensive administrative concerns such as training, health care records, or property control, a smart card that combines one or all of these record-keeping functions with security could be cost effective.

Any type of coded credential can be decoded and duplicated if sufficient resources are devoted to the attempt. Therefore, the coded credential should not be the only means of identification for facilities requiring moderate or high security. In these facilities, personal identification (e.g., a photograph, a memorized ID number, or a biometric device) should be used in conjunction with a coded credential. The more these features are combined, the more effective the system. As security requirements for a given facility increase, the contribution of the coded credential to the overall security of the facility decreases. Thus, the resistance to decoding and counterfeiting of the coded credential alone is effective only in facilities with low to moderate security requirements or threats.

Private Information

Resistance to decoding or counterfeiting applies to systems using only coded credentials for entry control, or if a PIN or biometric template is included on the credential. Security increases dramatically when two or more methods of identity verification are used. A common method for upgrading security is the use of a memorized PIN in conjunction with the coded credential. This approach requires both a keypad for PIN identification and a reader for badge verification.

Storing the PIN in a central controller's memory (and potentially within the field panel's memory, rather than directly on the badge) is the most typical implementation of PINs and is reasonably secure and flexible. Recall the earlier point that any device can be decoded given sufficient resources. If a credential that includes a PIN can be decoded, both bases for access control have been defeated. If a PIN is stored in the central controller's memory, it is not related to the badge number in any way and can be easily changed without altering the badge. There are methods that allow for the PIN to be encrypted in the central controller and field panel memory that generally rely on a decryption key stored on the badge.

Another consideration in measuring subsystem effectiveness is the minimum length of the PIN relative to the number of personnel enrolled in the system. For example, if 1,000 persons are enrolled in

the entry control system and three digit pins are used, the successful guess of an enrolled PIN is a certainty. A general rule is that the number of possible PINs allowed by the PIN length should be at least ten times larger than the number of people enrolled. Other factors that enhance system performance are visual shielding to prevent someone from observing PINs when they are being entered and a system configuration that generates an alarm when multiple incorrect PINs are entered by a single user at a portal. During a VA, encoding and storage of the PIN must be considered when making an estimate of their effect on subsystem performance.

Whenever all access control records reside in the central database, the loss of either the central controller or communications between the controller and field hardware will cause entry control points to stop working. Most modern systems distribute the access control database to field hardware to prevent this failure. Typical system architectures have field panels that are smart controllers, which can monitor areas under their control for alarms and entry requests. These field panels can control up to 16 card reader and PIN pad combinations. These field panels include memory banks capable of holding the complete access control database for even large facilities. In this configuration, entry requests are handled at the field panel level, and the record of that transaction is passed to the central controller as time permits. This also means that if the central controller fails or communication between the controller and the field panels are lost, the entry control portals will continue to operate with the last downloaded version of the access control database. Another method of achieving this level of reliability is the use of dual redundant central controllers and redundant communication paths. Whenever the database is stored at the field panel, care must be taken to protect this hardware with tamper switches and installation at locations that are within the secure area.

Badge Control Equipment Components and Functions

The basic functions of badge control equipment are to verify the authenticity of credentials, to grant or deny access to credential users, and to keep a log of all accesses. In addition to performing these basic tasks, badge control equipment may also perform a variety of other functions, depending on the system design and options. Some of these functions are summarized in the following paragraphs.

The time-zone function of the central controller divides days of the week into several time zones, so that each zone can be defined by the system administrator. During enrollment, each credential is assigned an authorized time zone; thereafter, the specific credential can access the facility only during the authorized times. The multiple area authorization function, which allows a given credential to access specified entry points and bars it from accessing others, controls area entry for a given badge. The area authorization of the credential is assigned during enrollment. The antipassback function prevents a credential from being used for two or more successive entries or exits. This function prevents an employee from using a badge to gain entry to an area and then giving it to another employee to be used again. The antipassback function requires an area to have at least two credential readers. One or more readers are used for entry only, and one or more other readers are used for exit only. This arrangement enables the central controller to track all credentials in any given area at any given time.

The occupant listing function enables the central controller to maintain a current list of all occupants checked into a given area. In the event of an emergency evacuation, an occupant list can be printed or viewed to identify personnel who were in the controlled area just before evacuation. This allows security or safety personnel to verify that all individuals have cleared the area. In addition, guards can use this feature to verify that the area is empty before securing it for a nonoperational period, such as a holiday. As with the antipassback function, the occupant listing function requires separate entry and exit readers at every portal. During the VA, the following badge entry control factors will have an effect on personnel entry control performance:

1. The badge equipment should have tamper alarms and line supervision. These features will strengthen security, deter vandalism, and simplify maintenance. Tamper alarms associated with the system should be tested frequently.

2. The central controller should have uninterruptible power supply (UPS) backup or a backup file in permanent storage.

3. The system should be of modular construction. This allows easy replacement of defective or damaged parts, ensuring minimum downtime.

4. The system should allow for expansion to meet new requirements.

5. The system should satisfy the facility's security requirements. The VA team must bear in mind that badge-only entry systems are most useful in low security facilities. Systems with PIN options must be used for facilities with higher security requirements. For a moderate-to-high-security facility, a guard force, perimeter sensors, video assessment, and an integrated alarm communication and display subsystem should be used in conjunction with the entry control subsystem.

6. The facility should maintain a stock of spare parts. Reordering may cause lengthy and costly delays. An extended downtime could compromise

security or require additional guards for a period of time.

7. The reliability of coded credential devices must be considered. The most common complaints about the reliability of a card system, especially with swipe cards, are degradation from wear of the coded card itself and the card readers.

Biometrics

Several issues should be considered during the evaluation of a biometric personnel identity verification system. These system characteristics and definitions are discussed next and include:

- Verification error rates
- Counterfeiting
- Throughput rates
- System reliability
- User acceptance
- User compatibility
- Cost

Each entry control component, whether automated or manual, makes verification errors that affect the practicality and the security of the system. The primary errors are:

- False rejection: the erroneous conclusion that a presented identity is false when in fact it is valid. A false rejection is frequently referred to as a Type I error.
- False acceptance: the erroneous conclusion that a presented identity is valid when in fact it is false. A false acceptance is frequently referred to as a Type II error.

A Type I error is not a breach of security but may create an operational problem that demands an alternate entry solution. A breach of security, however, does occur in the case of a Type II error. Ideally, both Type I and Type II error rates should be zero, but in practice they are not. The acceptance tolerance affecting Type I and Type II errors, whether in a manual or automated system, must allow for variations in the equipment, the consistency of the personal attribute being measured, and the consistency with which the credential or personal attribute is presented for assessment. In general, as the acceptance tolerance is tightened, the chances of a false acceptance are decreased, but valid user rejections are more likely to occur. The choice of which threshold value to use is a tradeoff because there is no threshold setting where both error rates are zero. Low false acceptance error rates are associated with high security; low false rejection error rates are associated with user friendliness. In high-security applications, especially with few users, a relatively high false rejection error rate can be justified to provide a very low false acceptance probability. False rejection errors can cause unacceptable delays in high throughput applications, so a higher false acceptance rate may be justified in such applications.

Biometric devices are generally highly resistant to counterfeiting and can maintain adequate throughput if the appropriate device is selected. The reliability of biometric devices must also be considered. The operating environment (indoor versus outdoor, noise, dust, lighting) can have a significant impact on the performance of biometric systems. In addition, testing and field use show that for each biometric identity verifier, there is a small percentage of the user population, however cooperative, that has considerable difficulty in acquiring a successful verification. This difficulty sometimes arises from a physical impediment, such as very poor eyesight, a damaged hand, or a stuttering voice. Other times, the biometric presented is not of sufficient resolution or quality to be properly acquired (i.e., small or worn fingerprints). Occasionally, the reason for the difficulty is unknown. To accommodate these users, the entry control subsystem must provide an alternate entry or exit method. Alternate entry methods must be evaluated to confirm that they do not introduce vulnerabilities.

Automatic identity verification is based on the matching of a measurement of a biological feature (biometric) of an individual with an authenticated reference measurement of the same feature. Automatic identity verification offers potential advantages over manual verification in both performance and cost. Elements of performance for automatic identity verifiers are error rates and processing times for the various tasks being performed. Overall performance is a measure of how well a verifier meets the specific requirements of a particular application. Because requirements differ from one application to another, it is necessary to match the features of the verifier to the requirements of the application. The best verifier for one application may not be the best for another. Many commercially available systems perform automatic identity verification based on a variety of biometric features including eye, fingerprint, hand geometry, speaker verification, face recognition, signature dynamics, and other techniques. The European Community (2005) recently published a report on the promise and problems of using biometrics.

Biometric entry control equipment should incorporate controls that prevent unauthorized entry attempts. These controls include tamper-detection sensors, line security supervision, door monitor switches, authorization verification checking, personal identification number checking, personal identity verification, personnel tracking, and two-door portals. The use and effectiveness of these controls are part of the VA.

Locks

Locks are a basic element of security systems. Although they are often the least expensive means of adding security for small and lower security facilities, they have several drawbacks that make them less secure than automated electronic systems, especially for larger systems. The following list describes why automated entry control subsystems generally provide more effective security over locks:

1. The issue of a lost or stolen credential has less impact on the system than a lost or stolen key. If a credential is lost, it can easily be voided by deleting the data from the central controller. A lost or stolen key, on the other hand, requires re-keying the lock and issuing new keys.
2. Card-access systems simplify operations because entry can be controlled by location and time.
3. Key control often becomes unmanageable and less secure over time as keys are lost.
4. Temporary access can be granted using a badge that expires on a predetermined date, avoiding the need to issue and reclaim a key.

In addition, locks can be bypassed through simple technical attacks (see Figure 7-4) such as lock picking or cutting through the doors (which is discussed more in Chapter 9). For these reasons, locks alone do not contribute much to overall physical security, especially in facilities with moderate to high threats. Nonetheless, it is a good practice to use locks at all facilities. Additional information on locks and their effectiveness is provided in Chapter 9.

Material Control

Contraband is any material that is to be excluded from a protected area and includes weapons, explosives, and tools that may assist an individual in the theft of assets. Contraband detection is performed at entry control portals using

Figure 7-4 Vehicle Gate and Lock. This gate is not used often, and the lock is meant to prevent access, but it is hanging on the fence and not in the latch. Even if locked, it can easily be cut or bypassed by going over or under nearby fence sections.

metal detectors, explosive detectors, x-ray imagers, and manual searches. The use of these technologies is a function of the defined threat, specifically any weapons, tools, or materials they will carry into the site, or items they might remove. If the item entering or leaving the facility does not have characteristics that are detectable, material control via technology will not be effective. For example, weapons made of plastic or composites will not be detected using metal detectors. The ease of bypassing material inspection stations must also be evaluated. Material control must be performed on both personnel and packages.

Personnel Metal Detection

The most common means of detecting metallic contraband on personnel is the metal detector. Metallic contraband can be detected by both active and passive techniques. One passive system used for the detection of metal is a magnetometer. The magnetometer is a device that monitors the earth's magnetic field and detects changes to that field caused by the presence of ferromagnetic materials. This method detects only ferromagnetic materials (those that are attracted by a magnet). Materials such as copper, aluminum, and zinc are not detected. Because most firearms contain parts made of steel, most can be detected by a magnetometer. Although the term magnetometer is often used generically to refer to all metal detectors, this device differs significantly from active metal detectors.

Most active metal detectors currently in use in personnel contraband detection generate a time-varying magnetic field. The magnitude of the metal detector's response to metallic objects is determined by several factors:

- Conductivity of the metal
- Magnetic properties of the metal (relative permeability)
- Shape
- Size
- Orientation of the object within the magnetic field

Portal (i.e., walk through) metal detectors are widely used in security screening because of their speed of use, effectiveness at detecting standard firearms, and nonintrusiveness. During the VA, basic operating principles of the technology in use, detection and target speed, detector installation, maintenance and testing, access controls, and other procedures are all evaluated to determine the performance of the entry control subsystem.

One type of active metal detector generates a continuous, time-varying magnetic field within the archway. In the simplest case, a continuous-wave detector requires only two coils. The transmitter coil generates a magnetic field, while the receiver coil continuously monitors the transmitted signal. Metal placed between or close to the coils will disturb the signal that is coupled between the transmitter and receiver coils. Any disturbance to the signal between the coils is detected and analyzed. The processor compares the signal to a threshold value to determine whether an alarm condition exists, or it can compare the received signal to the transmitted signal to detect differences in the phase between the received signal and the transmitted signal. Detecting phase shift in terms of magnitude and the direction of the shift allows the detector to differentiate between types of metals.

Most metal detectors apply a pulsed magnetic field to identify items. An electromagnetic pulse generated by the transmitter coil produces eddy currents in conductive metal objects within the archway which, in turn, generate their own magnetic field. The receiver coil or coils can detect this rapidly decaying magnetic field during the time between the transmitted pulses. The magnitude and duration of the eddy currents and the associated magnetic field depend on the composition and geometry of the metal object. Coil design also has an effect on detector performance.

When implemented correctly, a portal metal detector can provide a high probability of detecting firearms and some types of incendiary or explosive devices

while maintaining an acceptable NAR. A carefully thought out procedure for weapons screening can enhance the P_D and lower the false alarm rate. The most important operational aspect is that personnel supervising metal detection ensure that people entering the portal maintain the proper speed. In most instances, metal detectors have user-selected programs to vary sensitivity and speed response and to permit operation in a variety of modes. A procedure that requires persons being screened to briefly stop within the arch can be helpful. Although stationary metal is not detected, the process of stopping and then starting ensures that the metal is moving at the proper speed during at least some of the time it is within the detector. In addition, there should be no way for entering or exiting personnel or prohibited items to avoid the detector.

During the VA, installation and use of metal detectors must be verified to ensure that the NAR is balanced with adequate sensitivity. The NAR, as applied to metal detectors, usually refers to alarms caused by noncritical metal objects such as calculators, loose change, keys, rivets on clothing, or alarms caused by an external event, such as portal proximity to metal structures or objects. Reduction of nuisance alarms in commercial metal detector equipment is accomplished in several ways. Electrical noise in the vicinity of the metal detector is addressed by filtering the AC power input and by processing spurious signals out of the received signal. Safety shoes can also be a source of nuisance alarms at some facilities. Nonmetallic safety shoes are now available and may provide one solution to this problem. An alternative would be to provide a change area so that safety shoes do not need to be worn through the metal detector. Nearby metal structures can affect the sensitivity of a metal detector, and whenever possible, it should be located at least 3 to 4 feet away from metal structures. Ferromagnetic structures, or materials with a relative permeability much greater than 1.0, can distort the transmitted field, thus disrupting the uniformity of the detection field. Nonferromagnetic metal structures can act as shields and reduce field strengths. Metal in the floor should also be considered when evaluating a metal detector system. An elevated ramp or aluminum shield may be necessary to offset the effect of metal structures in the floor. Stationary metal can also provide a path for electromagnetic noise. Proper grounding and isolation techniques are required to prevent metal structures from conducting noise from far-away sources to the metal detector and should be confirmed by the VA team. Installing multiple metal detectors in close proximity or operating a metal detector in conjunction with x-ray equipment may require special installation procedures. When metal detectors operate less than 20 feet apart, all detectors should be the same make and model. Evaluation of portal metal detectors should consider interference by other devices and degrade performance as appropriate.

Metal object characteristics such as size, shape, metal thickness, and metal mass are an important part of maintenance and testing of portal metal detectors. Proper operation of the metal detector requires consideration of the objects that are of interest during screening. This is facilitated through the use of test objects that simulate the characteristics of any prohibited items. The choice of test object depends on the function of the metal detector. Metal detectors used for handgun screening should use an appropriate standard object. A metal detector adjusted to detect a single type of gun will generally be vulnerable to other types. If standards for metal detector testing and adjustment are used, a set of at least three standards representative of the three general classes of handguns (ferromagnetic materials such as steel, nonferromagnetic materials such as aluminum, and one that is composed of both) should be used. The

VA team should review the maintenance and testing schedule used to ensure optimal metal detector performance for prohibited items.

When a portal metal detector is used to detect very small quantities of metal such as gold, detection may be very difficult. Hand-held metal detectors can detect very small quantities of metals and are better suited to the task of screening very small items; however, their effective use is highly dependent on operational procedures. Operational procedures should require that the entire body be screened, and when an alarm occurs in the vicinity of common items such as belt buckles, the item must be removed and the area underneath rescreened. Most hand-held metal detectors operate on the continuous-wave technique. The transmitter and receiver coils are co-located in a loop, rod, or paddle attached to the grip. As a result of their short operational range, it can be easy to miss even large objects if the detector does not pass over them. Hand-held metal detectors also can be considered intrusive because of the proximity of the detector to the person being screened, particularly when the screener and the person being screened are of opposite gender. For these reasons, the search procedure using a hand-held unit must be carefully designed and followed.

Secondary or manual searches using hand-held metal detectors are commonly used to discover alarm sources in the event of a portal alarm. Metallic items can be located quickly by the hand-held metal detector, minimizing the extent of hands-on search. The hand-held metal detector should be swept over the body at a distance of no more than 3 or 4 inches in the following pattern:

1. Starting from a shoulder, sweep down the front of the body to the ankle region, then to the other ankle and back up the opposite side of the body, ending with the opposite shoulder. If the detector's scanning

coil diameter (or length) is less than half the person's body width, the pattern must be modified to ensure adequate coverage.

2. The pattern used over the front of the body should be repeated over the back of the body.

3. Starting at one shoulder, sweep the detector coil over the outside of the arm to the bottom of the sleeve, then up the inside of the arm to the armpit. Sweep down the side of the body to the ankle, then up the inside of the leg and down the opposite leg and back up the other side of the leg. Repeat the sweep of the inside and outside of the arm opposite the side where the sweep began, ending at the shoulder. Particular attention should be paid to pockets.

4. Sweep the head area and ask that all headgear be removed for search.

5. Whenever an alarm occurs in the vicinity of common items such as belt buckles, the item must be removed and the area underneath must be rescreened.

Variations to this pattern exist, but each search should be a complete body search. Stopping the search after finding the probable cause of the portal detector alarm does not ensure that there are no other items on that person. Also, some medical surgical implants, such as knee and hip replacements, can cause portal metal detector alarms. A detector incorporating a variable intensity or pitched tone that provides some indication of the size of the metallic item being sensed can direct attention to specific locations. The VA team should observe hand-held searches to ensure that the entire body is covered and that each search follows the same pattern to prevent incomplete searches.

As with portal detectors, metal in the floor can be a problem with the hand-held metal detectors. If interference from floor material affects portal operation by caus-

ing nuisance alarms, this should be noted and used as a degradation factor in the performance evaluation of the component and subsystem.

Trace Detection Systems

Trace detection systems collect particle residue and vapors emanating from an individual and examine these for the presence of explosives and other chemicals. Collection methods include portals that move air over the person being inspected and collect that air in preconcentrator and swipe methods that bring a swab in direct contact with the person being inspected. These systems can detect a wide range of common explosives. An example of a trace explosives detector is shown in Figure 7-5.

During the evaluation, it is important to ensure that the equipment used can accommodate peak loads through the portal. Operating procedures should be adequate to differentiate between nuisance alarms and the presence of actual contraband. The systems used should be tested to demonstrate that they are effective against all compounds that the defined threat is expected to carry. The quantities expected should also be considered, as well as methods that the adversary might use to mask or seal the contraband to prevent detection. These systems also require periodic maintenance and testing to verify that they continue to perform as expected. These activities should be confirmed and documented during the VA.

Package Material Control

To prevent sabotage to vital equipment in some facilities, it is necessary to detect contraband contained in packages being transported into or out of certain areas. These packages can range in size from hand-carried items to large shipping containers. Techniques for searching packages must be used to detect the presence of contraband materials such as weapons,

Figure 7-5 Commercial Trace Explosives Detector. Sandia National Laboratories developed an explosives detection personnel portal with a unique sample collection and preconcentration system that Smiths Detection has commercialized in the IONSCAN SENTINEL II, which can also be configured to test drugs. (Photo courtesy of Cindy Schifano/Smiths Detection.)

explosives, or other unauthorized materials. Packages that cannot be searched effectively for prohibited items by one of the methods discussed next should be excluded from critical areas. This section discusses types of package searches, technology components, installation, maintenance and testing requirements, and safety issues.

There are three basic methods of package search:

- Physical or manual search
- Machine-aided manual search
- Automated detection search

Machine-aided manual search and automated detection search methods involve energy and energetic particle search techniques and are most commonly focused on explosives detection.

Physical or manual searches include not only package inspection, but also observation of personal behavior. A person behaving furtively or who is hesitant to subject themselves or their packages to inspection should be considered suspect. A package should not be accepted from a person for inspection unless they are also willing to submit to personnel screening. If an individual refuses to comply with procedures, or if a firearm, explosives, or other contraband are found, entry should be denied and the person should be escorted to a holding area for appropriate action. If material of a suspicious or unknown nature is found, entry should be delayed until responsible security personnel are satisfied that the material is benign.

Only packages that can be opened should be presented for physical inspection. The package or bag should be inspected to determine if contraband is concealed in the top, bottom, and sides of the package. Objects in packages should be inspected both manually and visually to verify that they are not explosives or other contraband. Electronic items should be operated if requested; however, the sole fact that an electronic device is operational should not be construed as proof that the device does not contain contraband. The inside of any radio, computer, calculator, or other electronic equipment should either be inspected or excluded from the secure area. Because many electronic devices are difficult to inspect internally, an active search may be necessary to completely screen these devices. If physical searches are used, the VA team should observe the frequency, completeness, and consistency of the search by trained personnel. Physical searches alone are not an effective means of material control, and would be rated as no better than a medium effectiveness for evaluation purposes. Better material control can be achieved through active detection techniques.

X-ray Imaging X-ray inspection systems, like those found in airports, constitute the major commercial package search systems for explosives detection in use today. These systems, or adaptations, are also found in other facilities such as correctional institutions, government agencies, and industrial facilities. Most commercial x-ray baggage inspection systems are designed for high throughput of handbags, briefcases, and baggage carried by airline passengers. An image of the contents of a package is obtained by various x-ray techniques. The image is dependent on the density and absorption or backscatter characteristics of articles within the package. Data are displayed directly or processed on a computer and displayed on a computer or standard television monitor. The image is viewed by a human operator, and detection is accomplished by visual pattern recognition. Verification of effective operator training in visual pattern recognition is an important aspect of the evaluation.

All hand-carried items, such as purses, briefcases, packages, lunch boxes, and overcoats, should be searched; any items that cannot be searched properly because of construction or contents should be excluded from protected areas. As a person proceeds through a contraband screening area, their hand-carried items should proceed separately and be inspected for contraband at the same time as the individual is screened. All delivered packages and bulk items should also be searched before being taken into protected areas.

For best performance, two people should operate an x-ray scanner. The first person should assist in orienting packages properly on the conveyer belt. This procedure can actually enhance security. Adversaries may know system vulnerabil-

ities and take advantage of them by carefully packing contraband and placing the package on the conveyor in an orientation that may not reveal the contraband. If an operator takes the package from the person being screened and places the package on the conveyor, potential adversaries cannot control the orientation. The second person should operate the x-ray scanner. The scanner operator should not be in position more than 30 minutes at a time because the ability to recognize contraband in the display image is compromised after that period of time. The two operators should switch positions approximately every 30 minutes or be assigned other duties for at least 15 minutes every hour.

Another method of searching packages is by analyzing the vapor emanating or extracted from the package. Commercially available hand-held detectors for personnel explosives vapor detection might be used in a package search for a relatively high vapor pressure explosive (dynamite). In fully automated search systems, a visual image is not produced, but alarms are generated based on direct computer processing and analysis of the acquired data. Explosive identification test kits are available from various vendors that may be useful in certain package search scenarios. The procedure uses a wipe test, where suspect material is transferred to a swab patch by wiping the package. The swab is then tested by applying chemicals such as aerosol sprays; a color reaction to the chemicals indicates the presence of nitrogen-based explosives. Different sprays are used for the specific identification of explosives including TNT, TDX, and PETN.

Evaluation Criteria for Contraband Detection

Performance indicators for contraband detection systems include the following important factors:

- High sensitivity
- High contrast and resolution on display (for x-ray devices)
- Adequate scanning rates
- High detection probability (≥ 0.9 desired for quantitative analysis)
- Low nuisance alarm rate (≤ 0.05 desired for quantitative analysis)
- Discrimination between targets and innocuous items
- Detection and discrimination of targets of various sizes, shapes, and materials
- Detection and discrimination of targets in any orientation and location within the package

During the VA, contraband detection equipment should be evaluated considering these factors, and performance degraded if there are deviations.

Asset Tracking

An additional material control function is the use of various technologies to aid in the tracking or recovery of assets that leave a facility. Tracking technologies, such as serial numbers, unique property number labels, and bar codes, are used at many large facilities to assign valuable equipment to specific employees, to record where the equipment is located, and to identify the make, model, and other information about the equipment. Examples of these assets include laptop computers, cell phones, company-owned electronics, and large pieces of capital equipment. Use of these technologies also aids in periodic inventories. Similar technologies are used to aid in both tracking and asset recovery in the event of a theft event. The technologies used include those already cited, as well as covert microdots, radio frequency identification (RFID) tags, and other electronic tags. The use of these technologies in recovery responses to asset loss must be aligned with the response strategy and

procedures in use at the facility, and the VA should verify that assets can be recovered using these technologies. Each type has strengths and weaknesses, and varying costs, from quite inexpensive (bar codes) to expensive (RFID tags). It is important to note that each technology also has a range of defeat methods, and these should be part of the evaluation of asset tracking effectiveness. Bar codes, property number labels, and microdots may be easily removed; serial numbers may be altered or damaged to be unreadable; and RFID tags exhibit all of the problems of any RF technology. These include ease of blocking or interfering with the specific item signal, or collisions from similar RF devices. Other technology tools include the use of tracking software on laptops that sends covert messages over the Internet if the laptop is stolen and proper passwords are not used to log on. During the VA, the use of any technology should be reviewed to verify that it is installed, maintained, and operated properly, and that there are documented procedures and training for all employees on property control. Documentation of successful recoveries of assets is another source of data on the effectiveness of these technologies. The recovery of assets is discussed more in Chapter 10.

Vehicle Control

Vehicle portals should subject all entering drivers and passengers to the same methods and techniques described in the section on Personnel Control. Vehicles themselves use the same three bases for entry control, that is, tokens, information, and unique characteristics. Examples of tokens are cardboard placards, stickers, RFID tags, bar codes, special license plates, and electronic tags. Vehicle information can use vehicle identification numbers (VINs) or serial numbers. Unique vehicle characteristics may include combinations of tokens and information, along with vehicle traits such as body style, color, weight, or model. For example, if the facility only buys Ford vehicles, any vehicles that are not Fords can be denied entry or, if a vehicle pass is assigned to a brown sedan, it should not be accepted for a yellow truck. Many of these techniques are susceptible to counterfeiting or theft and therefore do not contribute heavily to security, although they can be used to limit accidental entries. Vehicle searches are another method of verifying authorized vehicle entries.

Vehicles should be searched for unauthorized personnel, firearms, explosives, and incendiary devices before entering a controlled area. The search should include truck cabs, front and back seats of a car, engine compartment, undercarriage, and cargo area. If emergency vehicles and emergency response personnel are allowed into the facility without search, they should be escorted while on-site. Manual vehicle searches should be con-

ducted in a portal or monitoring station by trained security guards. The portal should include a method to detain the vehicle until personnel and vehicle searches are completed, such as vehicle gates or barriers (see Figure 7-6). All material, packages, and other cargo carried by any vehicle should be searched for firearms, explosives, and other contraband before entry into a controlled area. Screening of material and bulk items carried by vehicles can also be accomplished using the same hardware and procedures described earlier in the section Package Material Control, although this is less typical. This section describes searches and aids, hardware, installation considerations, and vehicle entry/exit control methods.

The three methods used to search vehicles for explosives and firearms include physical search by hand or canines, handheld explosives detectors, or automated full vehicle search. Physical examination

Figure 7-6 Vehicle Gate Controller. This picture shows the electronic controls used to operate a vehicle gate. The arrow points to the switch that operates the gate, which is in an unprotected enclosure and available for use by any adversary seeking entry. (Photo provided by Joe St. Pierre, CPP.)

by security personnel is slow and less effective against well-hidden or disguised explosives. The search should include the engine and driver compartments, the trunk, and undercarriage of the vehicle. The most effective method of undercarriage inspection is through the use of pit or ramp, over which the vehicle should park. A guard can then inspect the undercarriage. There should be a vehicle barrier in the up position in front of the pit or ramp area during the inspection. If the inspection reveals no contraband material, the barrier is dropped and the vehicle proceeds. If a pit or ramp is not possible, a small hand-dolly on which a mirror(s) or camera is attached can be used. The dolly is pushed under the vehicle, and the mirror permits security personnel to inspect the undercarriage directly and the camera can provide a video image to the operator. The dolly should be rolled back and forth, from front to back of the vehicle, from both sides of the vehicle, while security personnel observe the undercarriage in the mirror(s). Security personnel should inspect the undercarriage carefully. Because the undercarriage is the most difficult to inspect, it is a likely place for an adversary to conceal contraband. There are also drive-over camera inspection systems that provide a video image to a remote inspector.

Canines can be an effective method of searching vehicles. Well-trained dogs and handlers can provide a high P_D for either drugs or explosives. The dogs can be highly motivated and are very mobile and fast. Dogs are cost effective to implement but can be expensive to maintain. Both the dogs and their handlers require frequent retraining. Dogs usually work well only with one handler, and the pair should be considered a team. Other factors affecting dog performance are the dog's health and workload. Dogs can become irritable and do not perform well when overworked, especially in harsh environments.

The second approach is technology-assisted manual search. In this approach,

equipment such as hand-held gamma-backscatter scanners assist security personnel in performing a physical search. Hand-held gamma backscatter devices are anomaly detectors that indicate the presence of some material within the body of a vehicle that is unexpected. These devices can indicate that there is a package hidden in the fender or a tire but cannot determine what the material is.

The third method is full vehicle scans using thermal neutrons or x-rays to image or automatically detect explosives. There are several technologies for screening vehicles for explosives and other contraband. Most of these systems are quite large and may cost as much as $10 million. Techniques range from backscatter x-ray, to dual-energy x-ray, to neutron techniques. Backscatter x-ray has the potential for generating automated alarm on detection of low-z materials. Dual energy technology generates an alarm on detection of low-z materials in the correct range of x-ray absorption for explosives. Thermal neutron activation techniques cause an alarm on the detection of large areas of high nitrogen concentration in high nitrogen-to-hydrogen-ratio materials. Fast pulsed neutron techniques can further analyze areas of high nitrogen concentrations for nitrogen-to-carbon-ratios and nitrogen-to-oxygen-ratios. Because these systems are seldom seen in industrial facilities, they will not be described further. Neutron techniques are fairly effective, backscatter and dual energy techniques are somewhat less effective, and transmission imagers (both gamma and x-ray) are the least effective; however, they all are better than human searches.

Subsystem Integration Issues

The following section covers entry control subsystem components, general evaluation criteria, system software, control software, and operator training. The issues noted in this section pertain to higher security applications and may be more than is appropriate for small sites with low value assets. This determination is a function of defined threat, asset value, and the risk tolerance of the facility or enterprise.

Entry Control Subsystem Components

In general, automated entry control subsystems include the following components:

- Central control
- Guard station
- Communication network
- Portal(s)
- Enrollment station
- Bypass system

These components function to permit or deny facility access to personnel and to prevent the entry or exit of contraband material. The level of security depends on the sophistication of the portals, degree of tamper-proofing afforded by the communication system, and type of central control. Automated portals usually require a local controller or processor. If most of the system capability is located in the central controller, the amount of central control time dedicated to servicing each portal may be excessive. If a significant portion of system capability is located at the portal and most portal control decisions are made locally, however, expansion of the entry control subsystem will be enhanced because central control service time for each portal is minimal. Thus, additional portals can be incorporated into the system with little effect on overall system transaction time. This consideration is a part of the evaluation of entry control subsystem performance.

The functions performed by the portal controller can include the following:

- Personnel prompting
- Door status control

- Subsystem timing control and event sequencing
- Diagnostic checking of portal subsystems
- Processing required for other portal components
- Execution of a personnel identifier matching algorithm
- Data formatting for transmission to central control
- Command decoding and execution of commands generated by central control
- Encryption of data to be transferred to central control and deciphering of data transferred from central control

Central control consists of a processor or processors and associated peripheral equipment located within a secure area. If emergency power systems are used, they should also be within the secure area because both central control and the power system are vulnerable to attacks that could render the entire entry control subsystem inoperable. Such an attack would force the activation of a backup manual entry control subsystem. If there is no manual backup to the entry control subsystem, performance should be degraded.

Functions performed by the central processor depend on the system design. At one extreme, only minimal capability is designed into the portals. Consequently, data are transmitted to central control, and passive decisions are made by the central processor. At the other extreme, significant capability is designed into the portal system, sometimes referred to as distributed intelligence, and most passive decisions are made at the portal. In all cases, portal system status and alarm status signals are sent to the central processor from where they are transferred to the information display in the guard station. The central processor should also perform functional tests (e.g., transaction logging and alarm logging or state-of-health tests) to verify that each portal in the entry control system is functioning properly. Automated systems including an identity verifier use a stored reference file containing characteristic data (e.g., fingerprints, hand geometry, PIN) for authorized personnel. The individual seeking access is verified by a comparison with a previously recorded characteristic.

Conditions may occur that cause the subsystem to degrade or even shut down entirely. The system must degrade gradually, rather than catastrophically, when the operating environment no longer supports full operation. Two important factors that affect the overall security of a facility are general power outages and sabotage of the entry control subsystem power. In most cases, a power system's greatest vulnerability to sabotage is not from within the secured area, but along the transmission lines between the power-generating station and the secured area. Emergency power should be provided for personnel entry and exit during a power outage. The entry control subsystem should have sufficient emergency power to maintain required security at all times. One solution to this problem is the use of alternating current (AC) UPS. The security afforded by continuous power will, in some cases, justify the additional cost. Any battery storage system associated with an uninterruptible AC or DC power supply system requires periodic maintenance and inspections, and this should be verified during the VA. Standby diesel generators may also be used. The use of generators, however, produces an interruption in the service because it takes several minutes to start up and switch over to this type of emergency power. The vulnerability of the entry control subsystem during this time is an important degradation factor in the VA.

The display system provides guards with information from the central processor. Therefore, portal status consoles and portal communication-network alarm consoles comprise a part of the information display system. Continuous monitoring of the information display system should be performed by the guard force. A log of alarms and normal portal transactions should be provided as part of the display. A two-guard strategy protects against a single insider who, either intentionally or under duress, ignores a portal or communication network alarm. Where only one guard is assigned, a duplicate display should provide the same information to guard force personnel in another area. Information display is covered in more detail in the next chapter.

In the course of normal personnel transactions with portals, occasional situations arise that require assessment. Closed-circuit television cameras can provide visual coverage of the entire portal interior to aid in assessment, as described in the previous chapter. In addition, an audio communication link with each portal is necessary to allow guard communication with personnel having difficulty using a portal.

The major function of the enrollment center in an automated entry control subsystem is to create the reference files that are used for personnel screening and are transferred between the enrollment center and central control. The enrollment center contains identity verification terminals similar to those in the portal system. Other equipment normally used in automated systems (e.g., badge readers for coded credentials) may also be present. The enrollment center is a sensitive portion of the entry control subsystem and requires physical protection. It may also require guard supervision, depending on the level of security at the site and location of the enrollment center. Access to the area where badges are fabricated and encoded for automated systems should be restricted. The security aspects of the method for transferring the data to central control should be considered during the VA.

Portals must be designed to allow disabled personnel who cannot use normal entry facilities to enter and exit. This is called a manual or portal bypass. The location of a portal bypass depends on the entry-control strategy used at a particular facility. If large numbers of people are processed at an entry point, the need for a portal bypass in the same general area is justified. If smaller numbers of personnel are admitted at several entry points, a centrally located portal bypass may be more cost effective. For example, logical locations for a perimeter portal bypass might be at a vehicle access area where guards are normally present or at a central badge office.

The type and degree of modification for entry control subsystems required to accommodate the physically handicapped are mandated by state and federal standards. These specify pertinent dimensions, clearances, and design criteria for stairways, walks, ramps, handrails, doorways, and reach distances for controls. If it is not feasible to control entry of disabled personnel routinely, then a bypass portal, which will allow the passage of wheelchairs and other handicap equipment, can provide personnel verification devices located in accordance with appropriate specifications. Screening for weapons and explosives can be accomplished using hand-held detectors in the bypass portal. Care must be taken to ensure that the protection associated with the portal bypass equals or exceeds that of the portals. Because use of the portal bypass is infrequent, access per user may be more time consuming than through the portal. Personnel requiring bypass access must be suspected of being unauthorized or of carrying contraband material.

When evaluating the effect of a portal bypass, the VA team should determine if a second identity verifier, of a different type, is used for personnel verification. Procedures, such as calling the requester's immediate supervisor for verification of identity, could also be used and should be validated by the VA team. Manual search by guard equipped with a hand-held detector is suggested for bypass contraband detection and should be observed during the evaluation to verify completeness and consistency.

General Evaluation Criteria

Under typical loads, the subsystem's performance should not adversely impact security or user operations. The subsystem can be divided into two areas with regard to performance: online and off-line functions. Online functions should be treated as a higher priority by the system. Online functions include alarm annunciation, portal access requests, and alarm assessment and require an immediate response to the user. The time from the moment a sensor is activated to the moment it is audibly and visibly annunciated should be under two seconds. The time from the moment a sensor is activated to the moment a video recording of the alarm scene is initiated should be less than 1 second. Operator requests for the status of sensors or system components should be satisfied in less than 2 seconds, and there should be instant feedback that the command was initiated.

Off-line functions include generation of preformatted alarm history reports or ad hoc database queries that are not time-critical. These functions should not interfere with reporting of entry control alarms, which must have a higher priority in the integrated PPS. When operator report or query requests are made, the subsystem should immediately indicate how long the requested function will take, and provide the option to abort the function at any time. It is possible that some off-line functions may be provided on-line; however, these activities should not impact the timely reporting of alarms. If this priority scheme and feedback is not present, subsystem performance will be degraded because of the likelihood that some intrusion alarms will be missed during long report processing times.

There must be sufficient internal and external redundancy and fail-over mechanisms to preclude the loss of any single component from causing catastrophic failure of the subsystem. The exact implementation to achieve this will vary with the facility and depend on the subsystem structure and what is categorized as a catastrophic failure. As a general requirement, if failure of any single component results in significant vulnerability to the subsystem or the assets being protected, it must be made redundant or fault-tolerant. In cases where the failure can be caused by the adversary, the redundant components must be separated such that both cannot be compromised with a single local attack.

Maintenance support includes the necessary equipment for personnel to properly diagnose and repair system failures. The type of equipment required is highly site dependent and should be tailored to the specific communication approach, assessment devices, display devices, and processors. Maintenance procedures, training, menu-driven test programs, and self diagnostics should be provided as part of the maintenance support system. For frequently changing installations, a small functional duplicate of the operational system should be available to allow hardware or software to be modified and tested without disrupting the operational environment. The system should provide menu-driven tools that allow authorized personnel to make modifications to the operational system without losing detection and other significant capabilities.

An audit trail of all changes made to the stored data and system software must be maintained in as automated a fashion as possible. The audit trail includes the identification of the person making the change (both persons when two-person control is required), a description of the change made, and the date and time of the change. The audit trail data must be archived in nonvolatile storage. The system software should have at least five levels of system access authorization to control the following:

- Access to operator functions
- Read access to the database
- Read/write access to the database
- Read/write access to source code
- Read/write access to executable code

Each access authorization level should be protected by password or credential control. In normal operation, automated entry control subsystems provide a given level of security; however, component failure can decrease security to an unacceptable level. Failure of critical equipment may cause total system failure. Operational spares should be available to minimize repair time. An operational spare philosophy does not, however, totally eliminate the need for qualified technical personnel to maintain complex equipment. Efforts to minimize the impact of subsystem failure vary from strategies that limit the extent of the system failure to strategies that use guards to provide temporary protection during the failure interval. The VA team should verify that equipment or procedures are used that prevent adversary attacks from compromising the entry control subsystem.

Redundant communication lines to each portal in the system should be used if feasible. Active dual communication lines to each portal allow independent computer circuit checks. The presence of redundant communication lines will maintain expected performance of the entry control subsystem. If these lines are not redundant, degradation of the entry control subsystem is appropriate.

At a facility perimeter where high throughput is required, several portals will likely be used, and failure of a single portal would not cripple system operation. Similarly, an area that has several entrances, each controlled by a portal, may not be greatly affected if one portal fails. The same level of security would be maintained, although throughput would be reduced. Where a controlled access building or perimeter has only one entrance and traffic flow is low, a single portal to screen personnel would be the most cost-effective solution, but failure of that portal may have a significant impact. In this event, hand-held scanning devices (e.g., metal or explosives detectors) can be used to screen personnel for contraband. A photo ID badge check could also be used. If portal traffic is too high for one manual portal, two parallel manual portals may provide the necessary flow rate. Use of this procedure at a facility would maintain facility security and should be observed and verified by the VA team to establish performance. Central control must maintain constant surveillance of portal operations to detect a failure with minimum delay. In automated systems, this requires diagnostic tests of the portal. Furthermore, diagnostic checks should detect failure of a portal component before failure of the entire portal. These checks enable maximum use of remaining portal components, if a partial failure occurs, and also provide an alert of the problem for prompt repair.

When an alarm occurs as a result of an overt attempt to force entry or exit through a portal, a period of time elapses before an assessment can be made and a response force can arrive. During that time lapse, completion of the entry or exit attempt must be delayed. Proper construction of the portal provides the required delay. The time delay provided is a function of the following:

- Delay between initiation of the attack and activation of a sensor
- Assessment time required
- Guard response time
- Delay time afforded by the hardening of the perimeter of the area accessed by the portal

The first factor is essentially determined by portal design. The second and third factors depend heavily on the response procedures implemented at the facility. If guard response time is excessively long, the necessary portal harden-ing may be costly and impractical. The fourth factor is determined by the hardening of the fence or building perimeter. Hardening of the portal to provide lengthier delays than provided by the perimeter would not be cost effective; therefore, both must provide adequate delay to permit response.

Evaluation of the system software used to operate the entry control subsystem is another aspect of the VA. The operating system may be from any proven commercial source that is compatible with the overall PPS and that is the current supported version. A flexible operating system should be selected to accommodate future modifications. Databases, compilers, and other system software must also be current and supported. The software should be capable of producing both formatted and ad hoc reports of any data contained in the central database and the audit trail files. An integrated system database and reports structure provides the framework for storage, manipulation, and output of critical system data. Commercial database programs, if integrated with the security system software, will provide most, if not all, of the desired capabilities. The ability to create, query, modify, copy, and delete database items is also required. These functions should be accomplished in a manner that isolates the user from the underlying structure, and access to these functions should be limited. Whenever entry control processing encounters an error condition, a message should be printed to either a maintenance or console operator's log or display depending on the severity of the error. The system should be capable of handling a 50% increase in system capacity (sensors, cameras, and portals) and maintain the performance requirements without software or hardware modifications. This allows for expansion of system capacity without severe degradation of the system performance as the activity controlled and monitored by the system increases. The internal hardware elements should be rated at no less than 150% of the expected operating levels. These aspects of the system software and expansion capability should be considered during a VA; deviations will result in degraded performance estimates.

Access Controls

In addition to the system software, the access control software that commands the entry control subsystem hardware and maintains and manages the data and logic necessary for system operation must be evaluated as part of the VA. In general, the software must receive electronic information from the installed entry control devices, compare this information to data stored in a database, and generate unlock signals to the portal locking device when the data comparison results in a match. Failure to achieve a successful data match will not unlock the portal. In addition, this software should be capable of enforcing entry requirements and procedures used by a portal or sets of portals. These requirements may include the following:

- Where two-person rules are used, if a second authorized person does not enter an area within a specified time after the first authorized person entered, an alarm is generated. Also, if a single person remains in the area longer than a specified time after a person exits, an alarm is generated.
- Permits the entry of an escort(s) and a predetermined number of authorized visitors. Does not permit visitor entry unless visitors are immediately preceded by an authorized escort within predetermined time constraints. When exit is controlled, all visitors must immediately precede the escort or an alarm is caused.
- Permits the facility to determine the number of invalid entry attempts that are allowed before an alarm is generated.

- The software should accommodate a variable time-out (the length of time that a portal remains in access after an authorized entry is granted) for each portal.

In addition, the system operator and another authorized individual should be able to place any portal in access (deactivate alarms and unlock the portal) from the operator's console. When a portal is placed in access, the system should log the time of the event and the name of the person taking the action in the activity log, and provide constant notification that the portal is in access. If these functions are programmed into the entry control subsystem, the VA team must verify that they are working and observe operator initiation of these functions.

Facility enrollment procedures and operation should also be observed during the VA. The software should be capable of enrolling and removing records from at least one remote location. Enrollment of a potential entrant should require concurrence of two authorized persons, which requires a two-person control policy and procedure. The time, date, and portal parameters should be entered into the central database when an access is authorized. Authorized portals may be entered as individual numbers, names, or logical sets of portals, based on system design and operational needs. Each of these operations should be verified as part of the performance evaluation of the entry control subsystem. Deviations from these requirements will result in degradation of performance of the subsystem.

The access control software should automatically update individual portals or devices that control portals, with data from the central database to permit entry to authorized personnel when the portal or system is operating in a degraded mode. The software should record all successful and unsuccessful entry attempts in an audit trail file. This file should permit storage of entry attempts that may be immediately accessed by the system operator. Minimum data to be recorded include name of entrant, event time, event date, portal number or name, and badge number. The software should provide an alarm signal to central control when the preset number of invalid entry attempts has been exceeded from a single portal for a single entry event and for each subsequent invalid attempt from that portal, a tamper indication is received from the portal, or any other unacceptable condition is detected.

Operator Training

Handling user assistance requests can be burdensome and time consuming for security personnel. Training of system users in proper entry procedures is necessary to minimize both portal system alarms caused by improper operation and requests for assistance via the audio communication link. The incorporation of a duress alarm feature into an automated portal system may be advisable under certain circumstances. A duress feature can be in the form of a unique feature of the PIN, such as a special reserved first or last digit, code reversal, or an extra digit or two that must be added within a specific time period. Personnel must be properly trained in the use of duress codes and practice its use.

User training should be conducted in two stages: a preenrollment stage and an operational stage. A group presentation during the preenrollment stage acquaints users with the entry control subsystem, explains the need for it, and shows that it not only enhances facility security but also benefits the user. The presentation should also inform each user of their authorized access areas. This session could reduce inadvertent portal alarms caused by unauthorized entry attempts. The presentation should also describe the types of portals used at the facility and illustrate their use. An operational stage

exercise allows users to try the portal system before making an actual attempt to gain access. The best location for this exercise may be at the enrollment center where portal enrollment equipment is located. If feasible, a mock-up of the entry control system portal would facilitate training. The lack of user training procedures could result in degraded system performance because of the effect this can have on security personnel morale and confidence in the entry control subsystem.

Estimating Performance

After completion of tours, interviews, and testing, the VA team should document the entry control subsystem strengths and weaknesses. System observations and their effects on entry control effectiveness and overall system performance should be noted for use in analysis. This can be done qualitatively or quantitatively, using the following guidance. Remember that entry control is just one part of the VA and the analysis cannot be completed until similar information is collected about the other protection subsystems. In addition, it is recommended that the overall performance of each portal be estimated and provided to the analyst. Although each portal component can be estimated, in practical reality this is not required, particularly considering that portals can be easy to bypass. The key point in the analysis will be the balance that portal performance shows with other PPS elements.

If a qualitative analysis technique is used, observations and their effects should be recorded using indicators such as high, medium, or low to represent each component of the entry control subsystem including technology, people, and procedures. Five evaluation categories and associated criteria are used to help determine a qualitative score for P_D. The five categories and key criteria are:

1. Proper technology selection
   a. Correct devices for defined threat and operating environment
2. Installation
   a. NAR from surrounding environment is minimized
   b. Compliance with manufacturer's specifications or local electrical fire codes
   c. All vulnerable electronics are located in a secured area or tamper-protected enclosures
   d. Tamper alarms are included and monitored as separate alarm sources
   e. Portal devices are arranged to allow for efficient flow and sufficient time for an operator to complete screening
   f. Separation of unscreened and screened personnel is maintained in portal
   g. Bypass methods allowed for biometric devices, bypass balanced with other components of entry control subsystem
3. Maintenance
   a. Periodic testing to verify required operation using test standards
   b. Expansion capability
   c. Spares on hand
   d. Maintenance logs, timely repairs, or contingency plans
   e. Training of personnel in maintenance and operation
   f. Access control software and databases are current and procedures are followed
4. Performance against defined threats
   a. Bypass, deceit, technical and physical attack tactics, as appropriate, are prevented
   b. Procedures are in place and used, training is provided
   c. Logs all transactions
   d. When closed, portal is placed in a secure state
5. Integration with other PPS components

a. Hold person or vehicle in location on an entry or exit alarm
b. Immediate effective response to alarms
c. All alarms are reported to the alarm communication and display subsystem at all times
d. Authorized entries do not generate an alarm

Unless all categories are rated high, and this is supported by documentation, P_D will be no more than medium. If multiple categories are weak or deficient, entry control performance will be low. See Table 5-1 for additional guidance on resolving ties among categories. When the evaluation categories result in many similar estimates, the Performance category is the primary factor and should be used as the overall estimate.

Analysis using a quantitative technique will consider the same categories as shown here but will represent P_D as a mathematical probability. This estimate is much the same as the estimate provided for exterior and interior sensors described in Chapter 5.

Summary

This chapter described the entry control subsystem purpose, components, and evaluation. Entry control is used in both entry and exit of personnel and material and is supported by the use of access controls. Access controls include the procedures, databases, and parameters used to allow entry. The entry control subsystem can be broken down into two major categories—personnel and vehicles. Contraband detection is one aspect of each of these major categories. The methods of entry control were described, along with important indicators of performance. The estimate of performance of entry control portals is the probability of detection and is provided as an overall measure of portal performance, not for each device.

Reference

European Community, 2005, Biometrics at the Frontiers: Assessing the Impact on Society, available at ftp://ftp.jrc.es/pub/EURdoc/eur21585en.pdf, April 20, 2005.

8

Data Collection—Alarm Communication and Display Subsystem

Alarm communication and display (AC&D) is the PPS subsystem that transports sensor alarm and video information to a central location and presents the information to a human operator. The two critical elements of an AC&D subsystem are the speed of data transmission to specified locations and the meaningful presentation of that data. Most AC&D subsystems integrate the functions of detection (detect and assess a potential intrusion) and response (initiate either immediate or delayed response procedures) as well as other subsystems, such as radio communications and entry control. This chapter focuses on the intrusion detection functions of the AC&D subsystem and discusses integration of PPS components. The key concepts of this chapter include:

- The component pieces of the AC&D subsystem, their functions, and the data that are collected during the VA

- A description of the evaluation techniques used in the VA and how AC&D performance is estimated
- Information Handling. This system is a translator that processes raw sensor data into useful information. The methods used in the information handling subsystem are tightly coupled to the techniques used to display information.
- Control and Display. The control and display is the system used to communicate alarm information to an operator, including both user input and system output.
- Assessment. This system, usually video based, helps an operator determine the alarm source. For AC&D, this system is mostly concerned with the ergonomics of video equipment and the human-factors engineering of assessment system control.
- Off-Line Functions. The off-line subsystem covers the other noncritical

systems such as log file handling and printing.

- Access Control Functions. These functions detect unauthorized access attempts into the facility or the subsystem itself.

The background information for this chapter can be found in Chapter 9 of the *Design* textbook. Although an AC&D subsystem is a complex integration of people, procedures, and equipment, evaluation by the VA team can be reduced to a handful of performance indicators.

In an effective AC&D subsystem, intrusion detection alarms and associated information must always have priority over other security events such as routine access requests. These requests are less critical because a decision to grant user access to an area can be delayed for a few seconds without seriously annoying a user or, more important, not degrading overall system effectiveness. Intrusion detection alarms require immediate action to effectively protect assets, and thus a well-integrated AC&D subsystem must prioritize intrusion alarms and associated video information over other security events.

Alarm Communication and Display Overview

A block diagram of an AC&D subsystem is shown in Figure 8-1. Effective AC&D subsystems have the following characteristics:

- Robust
- Reliable
- Redundant
- Fast
- Secure
- Easy to use

Although the most visible components of an AC&D subsystem are the operator console and the central computers (which are most often installed in controlled locations), many of the less visible components are not. These transparent components are often the real workhorses of the system. For example, the field panels that perform the direct monitoring of exterior sensors are generally located in exterior locations. The robustness of the subsystem is an indication that the displays, operator controls, data collection, delivery and storage, output controls, and communications to other subsystems are

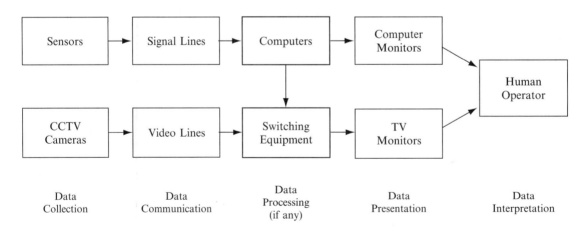

Figure 8-1 Integrated AC&D Subsystem Components. The AC&D subsystem is responsible for collecting and displaying information to a human operator quickly and reliably to make the operator an effective part of the overall PPS.

flexible enough to allow the AC&D subsystem to manage component elements without customization of their standard hardware or software, and to allow for at least some system expansion over time.

AC&D subsystems should be reliable and have a long mean time between failures (MTBF). A reliable subsystem requires less maintenance and is more trusted by operators and maintenance personnel. Other characteristics of a reliable AC&D subsystem are that alarm information is reliably communicated and displayed and that no information is lost. By their nature, electronic components cannot be 100% reliable. Components will eventually fail. Robust and highly reliable AC&D subsystems take this chance of failure into account and provide redundant or back-up capability for critical components. By maximizing the robustness, reliability, and redundancy of AC&D systems, the time that critical AC&D components are off-line for repair can be minimized.

Alarm information must be available to security personnel in a timely manner. The AC&D subsystem speed should be a small fraction of the overall alarm assessment and response times. These times vary from site to site, but the speed of data collection and presentation should be a negligible factor in calculating assessment or response times.

The AC&D subsystem is a major component in the overall PPS. Because the PPS helps protect the site's vital assets, it follows that the AC&D subsystem must be secure from attacks by adversaries. For example, procedures should limit who has access to AC&D displays and the system configuration, and only authorized persons should have access to AC&D information, components, and wiring. As part of this protection, AC&D communications should also be secured from access by attackers.

AC&D subsystems must be easy for an operator to use. While a multitude of sensors can provide much data, it must be displayed in a fashion that presents the most essential information to the operator on an alarm. In addition, operators must not be overwhelmed with data, so that they do not become the slower component in processing vital information. Their interactions with the system must be efficient, and they must be able to perform necessary operations quickly and easily. A subsystem that is easy to use reduces the amount of time the operator needs to quickly and accurately interpret the data presented and minimizes training and retraining time.

Each of these characteristics play a part in the overall effectiveness of an AC&D subsystem, but the single most important measure of AC&D effectiveness is how quickly integrated alarm data from sensors and video data from cameras and video storage devices are displayed to the operator. When an alarm event occurs, the AC&D subsystem must communicate to the operator where and when an alarm has occurred and what or who caused the alarm. In addition, the operator should, through training and AC&D subsystem prompts, know how to respond properly.

The difficulty of AC&D subsystem evaluation is due to the reliance on the response time of the operator. Measuring operator response is a difficult process. Electronic communications systems, on the other hand, are easier to measure. This dual nature of alarm communications and display subsystems makes measuring system effectiveness somewhat complicated. Communications systems can be understood, network topologies modeled, and system times measured. With humans, however, other aspects, such as ergonomics, human factors engineering, and physiology also have an effect and are much harder to quantify.

The overall performance measure of the AC&D subsystem is the probability of assessed detection, P_{AD}. The following sections discuss the various components of the AC&D subsystem, and performance measures that must be estimated by the

VA team. Data collection sheets are provided in Appendix D to aid in the characterization and testing of the AC&D subsystem at a site. In addition, Appendix E contains a list of specific criteria that can be used to help evaluate an AC&D subsystem. This table can also be used to compare various AC&D subsystems in preparation for procurement of new equipment. In this case, it can be useful to add a column on one side of the table showing the defined threat (or multiple columns if several threats are used) and three to five columns on the other side where evaluation scores, such as high, medium, and low, can be used to document how well the subsystems being considered meet the criteria.

Communication

The AC&D communications system moves data from collection points (sensor and tamper alarms, video, self-test signals) to a central repository (database, server) and then to a control room and display. The central repository may be colocated in the control room and may consist of multiple computers or displays. Alarm communication has several characteristics that compel the evaluation. These characteristics include the amount of alarm data and speed of delivery, and high system reliability. If a sensor activates, the alarm communication system must guarantee that accurate data are sent to the AC&D computers. Guaranteed message delivery means the communication system must be 100% reliable. Alarm reporting speeds are driven by the technology of the communications system, but the interpretation of those data is driven by human-factor considerations and interactions between the AC&D and assessment subsystems.

Effective integration of the AC&D and assessment subsystems requires that alarms be reported with no perceptible delay, generally on the order of a few milliseconds, which is a small fraction of the total assessment time. The best possible communication system would provide instant communications with 100% reliability. In reality, it is not possible to meet this standard. A good AC&D communication system design balances the cost of the system with its performance. Depending on the design, a range of protocols can be used to balance speed, reliability, and cost. To ensure that messages reach operators, redundant hardware is required to handle hardware failures, and the system must automatically route messages through the redundant hardware. In addition, the protocols used should detect and correct message errors and duplicate messages.

Just as with the video assessment subsystem, AC&D data transmission uses different transmission media to connect the component parts of the subsystem. Common media types used to move data from one physical spot to another are twisted pair or coaxial copper wire, fiber optic cable, and RF communications links; however, most current systems have come to rely on network communications. The advantages and disadvantages of each transmission type were discussed in Chapter 6. These wires are connected in a variety of configurations, including point-to-point, star, loops, bus, and rings, and then combined into hierarchies for large or complex systems. The quality of data and display of information can be affected by the transmission system, but during the AC&D evaluation the key point is to verify fast relay of integrated video and data.

Current systems use two levels of communications because smart sensors are not common in today's market. A smart sensor would be one that is capable of transmitting its status using high-level data communication, such as network Internet Protocol (IP). Most sensors available today still use relay contact closures to communicate status. For this reason the discussion of AC&D communications needs to be divided into two categories. The first category is the data flow between field panels and central computers, and the second level is the low-level communication between field panels and sensors. Another possible level is communication between multiple central computers that may or may not be at a higher level than field panel-to-computer communications. Because most of the measures to protect the communications between the computers is the same as for the communications between the field panels and the computers, these two levels are considered together.

High-Level Communications

To ensure that data are not degraded, the communication system uses various transmission protocols. In AC&D subsystems, errors induced by adversaries or attempts to spoof or disrupt communications must be detected. Error checking is an important feature of the communication system and is a type of line supervision. Low-level transmission protocols and associated hardware monitor the communication link to ensure that it is operating correctly and that data have not been altered during transmission. Communication systems can either be static or dynamic. Static systems always represent the secure condition by the same signal; during nonalarm states, the line supervision signal can be easily discovered and characterized by an adversary. Thus, a static system can be easily defeated by substituting a counterfeit signal. Dynamic systems, on the other hand, generate a continually changing signal to represent the secure condition and are more difficult to defeat. Most modern systems use data encryption to provide supervision and protection of data integrity.

Copper wire communications using any of the protocols have inherent characteristics that make them more susceptible to adversary intrusions and monitoring.

A fiber optic system is more self-protecting than equivalent copper wire systems. Regardless of whether communications use copper wire or fiber optic cables, if redundant communications paths are contained in one large cable or in a single conduit, any complete break in the cable will disable all the associated communications. To reduce the possibility of such a failure, security considerations require an independent physical path from each field panel to the central computers. Physical protection techniques, such as metal conduit and concrete should be used to prevent or delay physical access to the line. A communications line protected by metal conduit is most secure if the joints are securely welded, but only if these areas are inspected or tamper protected. For long distances, burial of the communication line is costly but will delay an attacker, allowing patrols time to observe unauthorized activities. Extra wires or fibers should be included in the cable when burying it to allow for either future expansion or individual line failure. It is recommended that either the conduit or the cable path be covered with concrete or asphalt and that manhole access to communication lines is prevented. If the entire area surrounding the cable path is paved, digging will be more difficult, and the exact location of the cable is more difficult to detect by an adversary. The recommended placement for communications lines is inside a secured area, which limits access to only those allowed inside the area.

Low-Level Communications

The most common means of protecting low-level (field panel to sensor) communications is the use of direct current (DC) supervision. DC supervision uses end-of-line resistors to maintain a constant current in the line. An alarm condition, such as a sensor alarm or a valid tamper alarm, is indicated by a specific current outside the normal (no alarm) range. DC supervision is relatively inexpensive and provides adequate protection against casual threats such as vandalism and accidental cutting of the cable. Multilevel DC monitoring is used to monitor communication lines for tampering attempts by cutting or shorting the alarm lines.

Information Handling

The communication system moves alarm and video data from remote locations to a central location. This central location is usually a collection of computers but in simpler systems can be a single computer. The central computers process the alarm data into useful information. These processing functions make up the information handling system. The information handling system provides functions to reflect the real-time security state of intrusion sensors, the system, and the facility. Alarm handling functions, such as assessment or sensor access status, are also performed. Alarm data are organized and categorized by geographic location, priority, or other common characteristics. The information handling system may then use alarm analysis techniques to prioritize information for display. Finally, information handling can trigger control actions such as video routing and recording commands.

All information handling is implemented as a software model of the AC&D subsystem. The software model describes all aspects of the AC&D subsystem and provides a mechanism to store information on the state of the overall PPS. System states record information on the operational status of all system components, keep track of which components or consoles are in control, and store information on operator status. In other words, they store all relevant system information. The sensor state stores information about sensors. Some of this information includes:

- Sensor name (a descriptive name for the sensor)
- Sensor location (the geographic location of the sensor)
- Sensor type (a description of the sensor type)
- Sensor history (summaries of the sensor activation history)
- Maintenance data (information on the maintenance history of the sensor)
- Other data as needed for alarm analysis

The most important data stored in the sensor state are the current alarm status of the sensor. The sensor state reflects the real-time status of every sensor attached to the AC&D system. It is critical that the information handling system models all sensors completely and that the model accurately reflects actual conditions around the site.

The raw data that drive information handling relate to the sensor alarm state. Each sensor reports its state (secure, alarm, tamper, access, or failed) so that individual alarm points are captured. Information handling then combines and categorizes these data. Most sensors are combined into groups; therefore, individual sensor data are best used when they are combined with data from other sensors. In many ways, a group of sensors can be thought of as a "super sensor" that is an aggregate of all its component sensors. Sensors are also grouped geographically. Sensors closely related in space are usually handled as a single entity. For example, it makes sense to group sensors that are in the same room or to group complementary sensors protecting a single perimeter sector. Geographic sensor groupings are also easier to display to operators. Even when sensors are grouped, the system must provide the capability to present the status of individual sensors.

Prioritization is a method used to assign relative importance values to various sensors or groups. Generally, sensors closest to the asset are given a higher priority than those farther away. This is an example of a simple static prioritization scheme. In addition to prioritizing by proximity to the assets, priorities can also be set dynamically. Dynamic priorities are usually set on groups of sensors. For example, if more than one constituent sensor in a group is active, that group may be assigned a higher priority than other sensors or groups. Sensor or group priorities are used to direct operators to those events that are most important. There are many different prioritization schemes that can be used, but the system must use one that makes the operator most productive to be evaluated as effective. Alarm information is commonly displayed based on priority and time of arrival. Those events with the highest priority and occurring most recently are displayed first. It is also possible to group and prioritize sensor information based on likely activation sequences.

Given the location of sensors and the likely path taken by an adversary, it is possible to construct timing sequences of likely attack paths. If sensors placed in those paths activate at times predicted by the timing sequence, the probability of intrusion is greater. The information handling system can analyze alarm data and sensor activations that match the sequence analysis may be displayed with higher priority. Alarm handling is the sequence of operations that the information handling system performs to process sensor alarm data. Several operations are involved: acknowledgement, assessment, and access.

Acknowledgement is an operator action. The user may acknowledge alarms explicitly through direct action or in conjunction with another operator action. An acknowledgment tells the alarm handling system that the operator has seen the alarm. Unacknowledged alarm points usually flash and sound audible alarms to the user. Acknowledged alarms can cause the information handling system to dis-play real-time video or further assessment actions. The information handling system then keeps track of the acknowledged state of sensors.

Assessment is another operator function, which is the process of determining the cause of an alarm. When operators request assessment video, the information handling system controls video switching equipment and video storage equipment and then displays the appropriate video for the specified request. The operator then enters data concerning the assessment into the system log files, generally through the use of a keyboard or mouse.

Sensor access is an optional operator command function. An accessed sensor is one for which the system will mask intrusion alarms; however, tamper alarms will be reported and displayed to the operator. The information handling system may continue to track sensor status, but that status is not reported. Requested accesses are controlled by the information handling system. Some systems require two or more operators to concur with access requests, and in robust AC&D subsystems, the information handling system enforces this two-or-more-person rule. Fully integrated AC&D and entry control systems allow for sensors or groups of sensors to be placed in access by authorized individuals from an entry control point. This feature allows an authorized user to enter a secured area without causing alarms and without calling a console operator to allow access. This is not only a convenience to the user, but also relieves the console operator from the distracting chore of placing multiple locations into access, allowing him/her to focus on the more important function of monitoring alarms. This feature also allows the user to place the sensors back into a secure state when exiting the area.

Control and Display

The control and display interfaces of the AC&D subsystem present information to an operator and enable the entry of commands that affect operation of the subsystem and its components. The ultimate goal of the subsystem is to promote the rapid evaluation of alarms. Questions that must be addressed in the evaluation of the operator's console include:

- What information should be presented to the operator?
- How should information be presented?
- How does the operator communicate with the system?
- How should the equipment be arranged at the operator's workstation?

An effective control and display system presents information to an operator rapidly in a straightforward manner and responds quickly to operator commands. The display subsystem, however, should not overwhelm operators with detail— displays should show only necessary information, and control functions should be limited to those that make sense in the context of the current display.

The control and display system must be evaluated with the human operator in mind; therefore, operation under conditions not directly related to the AC&D subsystem must be observed during evaluations. Meeting standard personnel occupancy conditions relative to temperature, humidity, noise, and general comfort factors provides an environment that enhances an operator's effectiveness and reduces frustration and fatigue. For example, adjustable lighting allows an illumination level that makes viewing computer monitors more comfortable for individual operators. The console design should facilitate the exchange of information between the system and the operator, such as alarm reports, status indications, and commands.

A good human interface improves the mechanics of issuing commands and of deciphering the information presented. Thus, the amount of data displayed should be limited to only that required by the operator. Data should be presented in a manner that makes their relationship obvious. On the other hand, the techniques for transferring information from human to machine should limit the opportunity to make errors without compromising system efficiency.

As a result of these factors, the console evaluation must consider the following details:

- What the operator must be able to see—people, equipment, displays, and controls
- What the operator must be able to hear—other operators, communications equipment, and warning indicators
- What the operator must be able to reach and manipulate—hand controls and communications equipment

The space around the operator consists of zones of varying accessibility and visibility. All primary displays should be approximately perpendicular to the operator's line-of-sight and should be easily visible from a normal working position. Indicators and operator inputs should be prioritized, and the most important ones placed in the primary interface area, as illustrated in Figure 8-2. Displays in this primary interface area do not require extreme eye or head movement from the operator's line-of-sight. Placing the principal items to be viewed within a 30-degree viewing cone will avoid such extreme movement. Frequently used operational displays should be located in the secondary area. Eye movement, but not head movement, from the normal line-of-sight is all that is required to view these displays. Infrequently used support displays, such as backup systems and power indicators, may be placed beyond the secondary area.

Because the operator's attention is not always directed to the display panel, audible signals are effective for alerting the operator to a significant change of status.

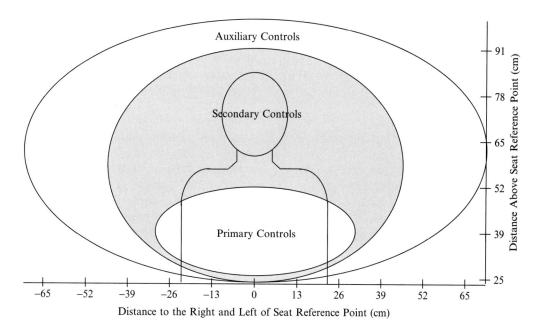

Figure 8-2 Placement of Displays and Equipment. Operator control is easier and more effective when the most important displays and controls are placed in the primary interface area and at the proper angles for comfort and ease of use. This keeps them in direct view of the operator.

Audible alarm characteristics, such as pitch and volume, can be used to separate classes of alarms, for example, security, safety, or maintenance. Care should be taken when using audible signals to keep the types and number of signals to a very small number. Signals must be unique and be distinguishable in the rich audible environments commonly found in AC&D control rooms.

Displays are generally placed in the center of the console. Controls are located on, below, or around the displays and must be readily identifiable. This identification is accomplished by clear labeling, color-coding, well-spaced grouping, and coding by shape. Labels should be large enough to be clearly identifiable. Locating a control near the appropriate display minimizes searching and eye movement. Touch panels that place controls directly on the display can eliminate the need for many other control devices, but do require significant maintenance.

Consoles should provide a visual signal in conjunction with any audible signals. A visual signal, such as a flashing light or blinking message, should be used to identify the significant information. Colored lights or indicators display the status of alarms more clearly. For example, traffic light colors (red, yellow, and green) are easily recognizable as indicators for alarm/action, caution/abnormal, and proceed/normal, respectively.

Support equipment should be located in relation to its importance and frequency of use. Communications equipment such as microphones, telephones, CCTV monitors, and controls must be given the console space necessary for their functions. Equipment that is not necessary for display and control functions should not be located in the operator's immediate workspace. Locating computers and automatic control circuitry (i.e., CCTV switching equipment and communication electronics other than microphones and controls) in a separate room offers several advantages:

- More space is available for maintenance personnel.
- Operator activities are not interrupted by maintenance.
- Distracting noises, such as fans, are reduced.
- The equipment can be secured from unauthorized tampering.
- Equipment environmental requirements can differ from those of the operators, and this is more easily accommodated.

When more than one person operates the console, it is necessary to consider the interrelationships among the operators and equipment. Essential equipment should be duplicated for each operator, but operators should have common access to secondary or infrequently used equipment.

Well-designed graphical user interfaces (GUI) provide a capability for enhanced display of security alarm information. Conversely, a poorly designed interface can quickly overwhelm an operator. A good graphical display has a limited number of features. Current GUIs provide a wealth of features for displaying information, but an effective display limits the ways information is presented and places constraints on which operations are allowed.

On a modern display monitor, the GUI will use a window as the primary method of displaying information. A window can be any size up to and including the entire display screen, and multiple windows can be generated at any one time, but may not be visible at all times. A window can contain text, graphics, or controls and multiple windows of various sizes allow maximum flexibility when displaying information. A good alarm display, however, should limit the size and number of windows. The number of windows presented at any one time may be a distraction to the operator, rather than enhancing their capabilities for reviewing alarm

information. A general guideline for these GUIs is that no more than three windows are visible at any one time. One of these windows should be the full size of the screen and contain an overview of the system status. A smaller window containing subordinate information can be displayed as needed. Subordinate windows should never be larger than half of the screen. A third window may be displayed that contains menus or other operational controls. Limits on the number and size of windows allow operators to quickly find important information. Windows should not have to be resized or moved to view information. Each window should be easy to access for visibility and the interactions necessary to obtain additional details related to the original information. These interactions use menus within each window or from the master window.

A menu is a list of available commands. When a command is selected, a function is performed. Menus are usually displayed along the top of a window and can be nested, where selecting an item causes a subordinate menu to be displayed with additional items. Menus provide a clear and concise method of organizing system commands. Some points to consider during the VA are:

- A menu structure should not be too large or over nested.
- A good menu should have no more than nine items and should not be nested more than three levels. Users tend to get lost in deeply nested menus.
- Limiting the number of items in a menu reduces the time required to find a particular item.
- Limiting the number of nested levels makes a menu structure easier to use.
- Complicated menu structures are intimidating to new users, and experienced operators find them annoying.

Although menus can display system commands in an easy-to-use structure, common commands should not be placed in menus but should be available as separate buttons. A button simulates the action of a push-button switch and operators push buttons to initiate system action. Buttons are usually activated by depressing a mouse button or key on the keyboard. These evaluation points should be considered:

- Only the most important commands should be placed on buttons.
- Only those commands that are valid in the current context should be available.
- Buttons can be very flexible. Sensor or map icons can be made to act as buttons.
- Buttons can be grouped into button bars. A button bar organizes buttons into a single area on the screen for ease of access.
- Buttons can be context sensitive, although changing a context button should be done in a consistent manner. Button flexibility must not be overdone.
- Visible buttons should be limited to a maximum of nine.
- Buttons should have good descriptive text labels that indicate their function.

The primary advantage of GUIs is the capability to display maps or graphics of the secured area. Maps allow the user to quickly relate a sensor alarm to its location. Several map sources are possible and all fall into one of two groups—scanned copies of paper media or electronically created graphics. Either group provides a useful graphic for alarm annunciation. Of all the possible graphics sources, the best is a stylized sketch based on a topographic map or other hard copy map. True maps usually have too much detail for effective use in security applications. Effective displays require small-scale maps of about 1:5,000. A sketch based on a larger scale map can be created

and eliminate unnecessary detail, while providing the necessary scale. Any maps provided on a display should be interactive. In other words, the system should represent sensors on the map and provide mechanisms for the operator to display and control those sensors by performing operations on the graphic.

To support an interactive map, sensors or sensor groups should be displayed on the graphic. When estimating operator performance, the following points should be considered:

- All sensor graphics or icons should use the same graphic, be the same size, and use consistent colors for similar sensors.
- When feasible, the sensors should be displayed together as a single icon. This type of display can reduce screen clutter.
- No map should contain more than 50 sensor or group icons, although the total number of sensors displayed can vary based on the complexity of the map graphic.
- A sensor icon should represent the status of the associated sensor, and sensor states should be displayed using unique colors and shapes.

Grouped sensor icons should indicate the state of the worst-case sensor associated with the group. For example, if any sensor in the group is in alarm, the group icon should indicate an alarm. An intrusion alarm may be the worst-case sensor state, but other primary sensor states are possible, including secure, tamper alarm, and access. Secondary states include maintenance, uninstalled, and under test. All states should be displayed to reflect current security system status.

Graphically displaying information on a map does not eliminate the need for textual display of information. Dedicated areas of the display should be provided for descriptions of sensors. A good system will also provide some type of online or quick help. Also, text should be limited to vital information only; details can be placed in subordinate windows.

Although color can be an effective aid in highlighting important information, it should be used sparingly. A user should not be dependent on colors to operate a system (note that about 10% of the population has some form of color blindness). These points should be evaluated:

- The number of colors should be kept to seven or fewer. Every additional color visible on the screen adds to the perceived complexity of the display.
- Menus, buttons, and backgrounds should be in consistent shades of color, with gray being a common color choice.
- Maps should be black and white or use low-saturation colors.
- The primary colors should be reserved to indicate sensor status: red for alarms, yellow for access, and green for secure status.

The overriding evaluation principle for the AC&D subsystem must be operator first. Operators must always be in command of the system. To achieve this goal, these criteria must be met:

- Minimize the number of actions required to perform any command. An operator should only need to click the mouse once or twice or depress a single key for any major operation.
- Only valid operations, based on context, should be available. For example, the operator should not be able to access a sensor if it is already accessed.
- The system should use prompts to guide the operator through complex operations. A context-based command selection (as in the preceding bullet) could be used to direct operator actions without removing their control.

- Display systems should never override an operation in progress. If the user is assessing an alarm, the system must never replace the current assessment information to notify of a new alarm, but should signal the operator with an audio signal and master icon indicating new alarms are present. The initial assessment should continue, and a nonintrusive notification of the new event should occur inside the current window accompanied by an audible signal. The operator can then choose to abort the current operation at his discretion. This principle applies in all situations.
- Systems should not annoy the operator. Avoid using loud, continuous alarms or bright, flashing displays.

The primary purpose of any AC&D subsystem is to enhance site security. This is accomplished by making operators more efficient and effective in their duties, thus providing the best protection for the cost of subsystem implementation. An easy-to-use system is much more likely to succeed than an unnecessarily complex one. During the evaluation, verify that there is a simple user interface that limits the total number of maps, sensors per map, buttons, menus, dialog boxes, and colors. In addition, the console should be kept free of unnecessary paper or other clutter (see Figure 8-3).

Presentation of assessment video only requires two windows or two monitors— one to present live information from the camera covering the sensor and the second to present the recorded information of the alarm event. Because there may be multiple alarms, however, it is suggested that four monitors or windows be used in an automated AC&D subsystem. This will allow operators to view video images quickly and comfortably; more than eight monitors may create a confusing environment for the operator. One primary monitor will display live video coverage of the

Figure 8-3 Console Layout and Clutter. Note the spacing and layout of the console and displays, the operator's position to the side of the main control keyboard, and the tarp that is used to block the sun. Close examination of the top monitor on the far left shows that the monitor is using a 3 × 3 multiplexed display of surveillance cameras. This AC&D subsystem contributes little to overall system effectiveness.

highest priority alarm, while a second monitor displays the alarm video that was automatically recorded when the alarm occurred. If two or more alarms are awaiting assessment, a third monitor displays alarm video for the next highest priority alarm. The fourth monitor is available for manual video selection by the operator. It is presentation of integrated video, graphical, and textual information that makes a good AC&D system. If an operator can select the wrong video or alarm information by mistake, the system is not fully integrated and performance should be degraded.

The operator communicates with the control and display system through the use of one or more input devices. Such input devices include, but are not limited to:

- A typewriter keyboard
- A function keyboard
- A touch screen

- A mouse
- A track ball

One or more appropriate input devices should be selected based on the intended operation and the operator should be proficient in its use. The input command structure should be natural and easy to use and protected against input errors.

Offline Systems

This section describes several simple components that perform noncritical functions for the AC&D subsystem. These components are noncritical because they are not required for the AC&D subsystem to perform its primary function of displaying and controlling alarms and system status, but they are critical for configuration and maintenance of an AC&D system, which is another aspect of performance.

An event logging system is used to record all events that happen on the AC&D subsystem. An event is any sensor change, operator command, or operator assessment. Events are also generated by system failures. All events are saved on the system for later review, and each event is tagged with the current date and time to expedite this review. A logging system is useful for supporting system maintenance. Maintenance personnel can review historical logs of sensor activations and analysis of the log data can disclose sensors that are out of alignment, or expose sensors that have long-term problems. The logging system may also be used to assess operator performance. When all operator commands and actions are logged on the system, analysis of the event logs can reveal how well specific operators are handling AC&D operation. If event logs are kept on the AC&D subsystem, the VA team should review these for signs of system and operator effectiveness, and possible degradation considerations. Event logs can also be used after the fact to reconstruct the events leading up to an adversary intrusion, and may be used with supporting alarm video for any legal actions against intruders.

Many systems keep event data in a relational database. The use of a database allows one console to view log information, while maintenance, training, or supervisory functions are also running. Modern systems may also connect to other corporate databases, such as personnel rosters, to pull information into the security system. Presence of these interconnections should be checked as part of the VA, and access and configuration controls should be in place to prevent unauthorized access to these databases. Lack of these controls would be a major degradation factor in the VA.

A supervisor's console may be used by an AC&D subsystem for retrieval of previously stored data. This console provides a means of retrieving system event logs and generating reports without disrupting operational security. Supervisory consoles allow authorized users to configure the AC&D subsystem, review and analyze event data, and act as back-up display consoles. Adding extra consoles allows supervisors and maintenance personnel to perform their functions without interrupting the primary AC&D operators. If these consoles are used, they must be protected both physically and by software access controls just as the primary AC&D consoles are protected, or there will be a degradation of system performance.

Older AC&D subsystems use a printer for each system event. This event printer provides a hard-copy backup of the event log. Also, operators can make use of the hard-copy events to generate shift reports or review previously assessed alarms. With modern computer hardware and redundant storage systems, the event printer may be unnecessary. Many facilities, however, are comfortable with the event printer and keep them for printing specific events or time periods, for example, as part of an audit. Presence of an event printer does not degrade performance, unless it is the only method of presenting system status.

Evaluation Techniques

The primary performance measure for an AC&D subsystem is the probability of assessed detection (P_{AD}). It is a basic principle of an effective PPS that detection is not complete until an alarm has been assessed, and this is why P_{AD} is used as the performance measure for the AC&D subsystem. Factors that contribute to this include time for alarm receipt, time to assess the alarm, ease of system use and control by the operator, and operator workload. The formula used for probability of assessed detection is:

$$P_{AD} = P_D * P_{As}$$

where P_D is the estimated probability of detection after evaluation of the sensor subsystem (or human sensing) and P_{As} is the estimated probability of alarm assessment after evaluation of this subsystem. This formula can be used qualitatively or quantitatively; the key is to verify that both sensors and assessment work together to protect assets. The VA team establishes performance of the intrusion sensing and alarm assessment subsystems individually and then evaluates the AC&D subsystem to show how all subsystems work as an integrated system. For example, if there are effective sensors but PT video surveillance cameras are used for alarm assessment, P_{AD} would be very low because of the low probability of assessment. Because P_{AD} is the product of sensor and alarm assessment performance, if one term is low this will have a significant effect on the overall value of P_{AD}. There is one major advantage to establishing performance of the sensor and alarm assessment subsystems individually. The VA team can easily identify the weaker subsystem and target this functional area for upgrade if the baseline analysis shows that the PPS does not meet the protection objectives.

The AC&D subsystem can be evaluated quickly through observation and a few simple evaluation tests. If sensors and video are not well integrated, the AC&D subsystem may not perform very well but can still be evaluated to determine how much it contributes to system effectiveness. It is expected that the AC&D and alarm assessment VA team members will work closely together to provide performance estimates (this may be the same person on some teams).

As with other aspects of PPS evaluation, begin the AC&D evaluation with a good understanding of the threat. Questions such as: Do outsiders have technical knowledge? Do outsiders have any access to the AC&D subsystem or its components? Help establish the evaluation objectives. Remember, insiders drive AC&D performance more than outsiders do. Start the evaluation by watching the operator

for a few minutes. Observe the process for operators to log in or out of the system and note whether or not passwords are required, if each operator has his/her own password, or if passwords are shared or common.

Also observe operator and system activity. For example, are alarms constantly reported to the system? Is the operator also talking on the radio? How many operators are there? Do they split responsibility? How? What kind of message traffic is occurring (status messages, alarm messages, access granted, and failed messages)? Estimate how many messages there are in a period of time (a few minutes or an hour) and whether the operators pay attention to them. Should they be paying attention? Review alarm logs and interview personnel to determine the number of nuisance alarms. Observe the AC&D subsystem itself and talk to operators about procedures. Many sites will place a sensor in access after a few alarms, which may not be apparent from the alarm logs. If sensors are in access, ask why and how long they have been this way. Determine whether there any sensors in the maintenance state that are connected to the system. The nuisance alarm rate may appear acceptable because failing sensors are turned off, and this is a major source of performance degradation.

Measure the average time for the system to receive an alarm and the time it takes the operator to assess the cause of the alarm. The total is assessment time. This number should be fairly low (2 to 10 seconds). Also check assessment time for multiple alarms and multiple locations, if possible. If the assessment time is long, note the conditions that cause this. For example, is this because the recorded alarm event is long (15 to 30 seconds)? In ineffective systems, time for alarm receipt (30 seconds or more is possible) can considerably exceed the time for the operator to assess alarms. In addition, if the sensor and entry control subsystems are interconnected, alarms should be generated and timed during peak entry control activity. If sensors report more slowly during these times, AC&D performance should be degraded. Ask operators if there are many occurrences of multiple alarms and their causes. Also ask if there have been times where they knew a sensor caused an alarm because it was not maintained or repaired promptly. How are alarms acknowledged? What actions (how many) does the operator take after assessing alarms? Are alarms displayed that are not acknowledged for long periods? How does live video get switched to assessment monitors—manually by the operator or alarm activated? Does the system override previous operator actions to present new information? Does the operator display recorded video manually? Note where video monitors are relative to the operator and how many monitors are used. Are assessment zones displayed in a consistent manner, so that each zone occupies about 70% of the monitor and in roughly the same position on the monitor? Are video images scanned or multiplexed? Is video information presented quickly? How easy is it to switch to the next alarm? Are alarms prioritized? How? Do door alarms or entry requests have a higher priority than perimeter alarms or interior sensors? Answers to these questions provide the basic data that are used to estimate the performance of the AC&D subsystem by applying the principles described under the subsystem component descriptions previously.

If possible, communications should be interrupted at some key alarm communication points (such as a field distribution box) to determine how the overall system and the operator respond. If the entry control and sensor subsystems are integrated, ask for a node map of the system and verify that access points into the network (router closets, termination points, entry and exit points to the building) are protected at multiple levels, such as room and junction box. If the network can be accessed from points other than the AC&D subsystem location, system performance should be degraded.

Establish whether there are any critical points that can be used to prevent system operation. Are AC&D components tamper protected? Verify how signals get to the AC&D subsystem by checking junction box locations and transmission media. Determine which, if any, communications protocols are used to handle message traffic. Does the operator access all AC&D functions through one keyboard?

Because the AC&D subsystem is fairly complex, the evaluation is best conducted by separating the individual functional components. These components include:

1. Operator workload
2. Displays (input/output and ergonomics)
3. Video system integration
4. Maintenance
5. Communications systems for moving sensor data to a display
6. Processing systems (computers)
7. Other functions (such as entry control)
8. Physical infrastructure (power, environmental, cabling, etc.)
9. System administration

Poorly integrated AC&D subsystems impact overall system effectiveness in three ways. First, they cause the degradation of P_D and P_{As} because of the multiplication of these two factors. Second, they affect operator performance by making control of the subsystem complex, uncomfortable, and hard to use. Finally, they will increase response time because it can take much longer to acquire and assess alarms. Generally, components 1 through 3 above degrade operator performance; components 4 through 7 degrade P_D, and components 8 and 9 provide insider attack opportunities. Figure 8-4 shows a typical AC&D subsystem at a large industrial facility.

Operator Workload

To evaluate operator performance, spend time in the room where the AC&D

Figure 8-4 Modern AC&D Subsystem Control Room. Note the multiple monitors and operators required to monitor security status at the facility. The four smaller video monitors to the right and left of each operator are too high and too far away to be used comfortably. The four large computer monitors directly in front of and above the operators display text and graphical information about security status across the site. The sensors that are present are not integrated with video, and the operator must manually switch video to monitors to investigate suspicious events.

subsystem is located, preferably with just the system operators. Return at different times of day and night to watch what the operators do. Note the general state of the room: Is it clean and well organized? If not, this may be an indication that security is not a priority or not taken seriously. Are operators dedicated to the AC&D subsystem, or do they have other duties? Are these other duties occupying much of their time? If so, the operators will be distracted from their primary tasks of monitoring system status and making assessments. Do alarms and video arrive in a timely manner? Based on judgments of these operations, degrade calculated P_{AD} by as much as 10% (or more if conditions are very bad).

Displays

When evaluating the effectiveness of alarm and video displays, consider the following indicators:

- Do operators know how to use the AC&D subsystem?
- Can operators explain how the system works?
- Do operators know the current system status?
- Can they show observers the system status?
- Is the system easy to operate?
- Could a VA team member operate it given what he/she observes?

Degrade calculated P_{AD} by as much as 10% if the evaluation indicates a poor display system.

Video System Integration

This is really consideration of alarm assessment. As noted in the last chapter, manual or delayed assessment or surveillance cameras all result in low to very low alarm assessment capability. This part of the evaluation requires the collaboration of the video assessment expert and the AC&D expert to estimate. The following indicators apply only to systems where sensors and fixed video cameras are integrated to provide timely assessment:

- Does the system display only live video?
- Is the video system easy to use?
- Is the video system well integrated with alarm handling?
- How is video recorded, stored, and displayed for assessment?

If the AC&D subsystem does not have a good video storage system or if it is not used for assessment, degrade the calculated P_{AD} by about 20%. For live video systems or video surveillance, the operator must be dedicated to the AC&D console, and have no other duties. Performance degradation will then depend on the layout of sensors and assessment cameras. If the layout prevents the operator from quickly and accurately assessing multiple alarms, degrade P_{AD} by an additional 20%.

Network Issues

Because the high-level communications on modern systems use networked IP protocols, there is a great temptation to place alarm communication traffic on existing wide area networks. This can result in considerable cost savings; however, great care must be taken when considering whether or not to use this approach. While firewalls and other means, such as encryption, can protect alarm communication from intrusion there is still considerable concern regarding denial-of-use attacks. An adversary need not hack into the alarm communication link or AC&D software to disrupt alarm communications; they need only disrupt the network. Worms or viruses that crash the network prevent all communications on that network (Acohido, 2005). For this reason, it is best to use a closed network for alarm communications protecting high-consequence targets. Closed networks require an air gap between them and the outside world. It is essential that there be no connection to the Internet to keep the alarm network safe. Care must also be taken to adequately protect the AC&D network if there are any connections to other local or wide-area nets, especially when those networks allow connections to the Internet.

Another consideration concerning networks is who maintains it. Again, the temptation will be great to save money by having the same information technology (IT) personnel who maintain other nets to perform alarm communications network maintenance. This may be the best solution, but for systems protecting high-consequence assets this decision needs to be carefully analyzed. Do IT personnel have appropriate clearances? Are they required to respond to network outages within a time frame that does not compromise security across the site? Or is it more appropriate for on-site security personnel to be trained to maintain the system?

Evaluation of the AC&D subsystem network, particularly whether it is closed or attached to other systems, will provide information on hacking attacks on the system. Notes should be made on the presence of network security software and whether it is integrated into AC&D subsystem operation. If network performance equipment is attached to the AC&D subsystem, reviewing the performance logs will indicate any network problems, such as limited network availability or degraded performance at certain times of the day. Maintenance logs of network failures should also be reviewed to verify the timely repair of failures and reliability of the overall network.

Other Evaluation Aspects

As with the other subsystems, the procedures for using, repairing, testing, and certifying the AC&D subsystem should be documented and verified as to their use. Installation of all equipment, including all exterior and interior alarm panels, and central repository and console equipment, should be evaluated to ensure proper installation (see Figure 8-5). Exterior equipment should have appropriate conditioning equipment on power and data lines to preclude environmental effects from electromagnetic interference or power line surges. Maintenance schedules should be reviewed to determine who responds and how quickly repairs are made. A critical point to consider is whether maintenance personnel are scrutinized by technically knowledgeable personnel when performing maintenance, particularly if this work is outsourced. Validation tests should be performed after repair of communication components, such as field junction boxes, network routers, and switchers, to verify that the components have not been modified to allow undetected entry.

Estimating Performance

There are three major considerations of AC&D subsystem effectiveness: technology performance and integration, operator effectiveness, and display layout and

Figure 8-5 Maintenance of AC&D Subsystem. This is a view of the area behind the equipment panels of the alarm communication and display subsystem. This indicates a lack of attention to system maintenance, makes system repair difficult due to the inability to quickly identify signal wires, and exposes the system to easy attacks by insiders.

ergonomics. In addition, AC&D subsystem performance is a function of correct installation, maintenance, testing, and operator training. The key performance measure is the P_{AD}, which must be high to have an effective AC&D subsystem. Use of surveillance or delayed review of videotape or other stored images will result in lower performance, which is only acceptable for low-value assets or low threats.

Qualitative performance estimates can be made by considering the following performance categories and criteria:

1. Technology Integration
   a. Time to receive, display, and assess an alarm is short
   b. Alarms are assessed using recorded video, does not depend on live video
   c. Stored images have appropriate resolution
   d. Limited number of video monitors and displayed images use full screen (no scanning or multiple camera displays on monitors)
   e. Automatic switching of sensor in alarm and associated video to monitor
   f. Ability to queue and display multiple alarms for assessment, based on priority scheme
   g. Configuration and access controls are used for different levels of operators
   h. Databases are secure
2. Operator Workload
   a. The system operator is dedicated to monitoring the security system status and alarms and not printing badges, manning radios, writing reports, or other tasks that distract them
   b. Operator workload is the same day and night
   c. If multiple operators, they understand their responsibilities and perform them effectively
   d. Operators are trained and knowledgeable about use of system

e. System controls allow placing sensors in access to reduce nuisance alarms
3. Display Layout and Ergonomics
   a. System is easy to use
   b. Operator controls are located in appropriate locations and accessible
   c. Audible tone on alarm, flashing display to emphasize alarm text/location
   d. System is controlled through a single keyboard or other input device (mouse, touch screen, etc.)
   e. Video information is displayed uniformly from zone to zone
   f. Control room environment is conducive to performing alarm assessment and other tasks
4. Installation
   a. All components are installed properly and in accordance with applicable codes
   b. Components do not degrade signals or operator performance
5. Maintenance
   a. All components maintained properly and repairs are promptly completed
   b. Subsystem is tested periodically and results are documented
   c. Support equipment stored in a separate room with limited access
   d. Personnel are trained in proper maintenance procedures

For the overall AC&D subsystem to be rated high, performance in each category must be high. The most important aspect of the system is the automatic display of recorded video of sensor zones in alarm, at a sufficient quality that the alarm can be assessed. The use of video surveillance, manual switching of video, or sequential scanning systems, with multiple cameras displayed on individual monitors, will result in low performance of the AC&D subsystem.

A quantitative evaluation concentrates on establishing the P_{AD} for the system. This is supported by either on-site tests or through the use of benchmark data from other locations or documented research. The preceding criteria are used to degrade the initial P_{AD} calculation using evaluation and timing tests to establish AC&D subsystem performance.

Summary

This chapter described the AC&D subsystem of the PPS. Because this subsystem is the central monitoring point for all security status information across the site, it is a complex integration of people, procedures, and equipment. Despite this, a handful of evaluation criteria can be used to estimate system performance. The primary measure of the AC&D subsystem is the ability of an operator to quickly and accurately assess alarms. This requires the integration of sensor and video signals; fast, reliable transmission and display of this information; and an effective operator. Delays in, or degradation of, any of these functions will severely limit the effectiveness of the AC&D subsystem. Technical components, along with operator workload and display ergonomics, must all work together to ensure timely assessment of alarms, initiation of the proper response to alarms, complete knowledge of facility and PPS security status, and creation of event logs. Performance estimates of subsystem effectiveness start by calculating the product of probability of detection and probability of assessment to give the probability of assessed detection. The probability of assessed detection is then degraded using other AC&D-specific indicators to estimate the performance of the subsystem.

Reference

Acohido, B., March 21, 2005, Cyberattacks on Corporate Networks Rising, Surveys Show, USA Today, p. 6B, available at http://www.usatoday.com/tech/news/2005-03-20-it-attack-usat_x.htm, April 20, 2005.

9
Data Collection—Delay Subsystem

As described in Chapter 2, the second function of an effective PPS is delay, which slows down the adversary and allows time for the desired assessment and response. This delay is only effective if it follows detection. Increases in adversary task time are accomplished by introducing impediments along all possible adversary paths to provide sufficient delay for any suitable response. The key concepts of this chapter include:

- Review of basic delay concepts
- Description of common barrier types and characteristics
- Estimating delay times for analysis

The background information for this chapter can be found in Chapter 9 of the *Design* textbook. In general, estimates of delay times are made using literature searches, actual testing, or approximations made using data from literature or tests. The delay time of any barrier depends on adversary tools and the barrier material.

Adversaries have the option of using tactics of force, stealth, deceit, or combinations of these tactics during an attack. Delay evaluation during a VA is primarily directed toward adversary tactics of force or stealth; the entry control subsystem addresses deceit. Data collection sheets for use in barrier evaluation are provided in Appendix D.

Delay Overview

With the exception of a few barriers provided by natural elements such as rugged coastlines, high cliffs, mountaintops, and vast distances, delay must be provided by barriers that are carefully planned and positioned in the path of the adversary. Most security barriers at industrial facilities are designed to deter or defeat sporadic acts of vandalism, inadvertent entry, or casual thievery. For more motivated or capable threats, however, fences, buildings, doors, and locks present little deterrence or delay.

The amount of delay provided depends on the nature of the barrier and the tools used to breach the barrier. Detection and barrier subsystems must be co-located so that the barrier is encountered immediately after the sensor. This delays the adversary at the point of an alarm, increases the probability of accurate assessment, and allows for an effective response. Barrier effectiveness is supported through the use of the principle of balance, which ensures that each aspect of a specific barrier configuration is of equal strength. For example, an adversary is not likely to cut a hole through a metal door if the surrounding wall is made of sheet rock, which is easily penetrated by kicking or hitting with a hammer or even a fist. In some instances it may be preferable to have weak points in the barrier system and supplement them with rapid response. The intent of such a weak link is to channel or funnel the adversary into a path that appears less time consuming. In reality, the system is still balanced through the use of timely response and limited physical barriers that hold the adversary at defined locations.

It can be difficult to ensure that barriers are in effect under different facility states (gates and doors must periodically be open or unlocked), and this is an important aspect of delay evaluation. Quite often compensatory measures will be used when a physical delay barrier is inoperative or ineffective. An example is to station a security officer at the entrance of a facility during business hours when the front door is unlocked. These variations must be identified and evaluated during a VA.

The concept of barrier penetration versus defeat requires additional explanation. A barrier is normally considered as penetrated when an adversary reaches a point 3 feet beyond the barrier. Other criteria may be used, but it is important to establish the penetration criteria before beginning the delay subsystem evaluation. A vehicle barrier is penetrated (1) when the ramming vehicle has passed through or over the barrier and is still functioning, (2) when a second vehicle has been driven through the breached vehicle barrier, or (3) when the vehicle barrier has been removed, bridged, or defeated in such a manner that a functioning vehicle has passed through, over, or under the barrier. A vehicle is any apparatus that is capable of moving people or equipment via direct or remote control to the asset area. Obvious examples of vehicles include cars and trucks; not so obvious examples include motorcycles, all-terrain vehicles, airplanes, helicopters, hang gliders, parachutes, boats, submarines, bulldozers, backhoes, and bicycles. Quite often useful vehicles are already present within the facility. If the adversary can quickly hotwire (or obtain a duplicate key for) a large truck already inside the facility, they have a powerful tool at their disposal, which they did not have to bring to the site.

In contrast, defeat is a much broader term that implies that the barrier is no longer effective in delaying the adversary. This distinction is important because it is often easier to defeat a barrier via stealth or other means than it is to penetrate it. As an example, a door that has been unlocked by an insider has been defeated, even though it has not yet been penetrated. In the case of a portal vehicle barrier, overpowering an unarmed guard and pushing the button that lowers the barrier results in at least temporary defeat of the barrier. This tactic may be much quicker than trying to ram or penetrate the barrier in a more traditional attack. In all cases, the delay expert and the analyst must consider ways the defined threat might defeat a barrier, which could be quicker than penetration via brute force.

A close examination of the large variety of attack tactics and tools an adversary can use to penetrate a given facility will likely indicate that existing barriers do not ensure that adversary delay time will always be sufficient for the system. Most conventional barriers such as distance, fences, locks, doors, and windows provide short penetration delay against forcible (and perhaps stealthy) attack methods that use readily available hand or power tools. Against thick, reinforced concrete walls and other equally impressive-looking barriers, explosives become an effective, rapid, and more likely method of penetration by a determined adversary. An example of this is the use of vehicle bombs. In addition, recall that security guards are not an effective delay unless they are located in protected positions and are equipped as well as the adversary (i.e., armed adversary and unarmed guards).

On the positive side, a barrier system can be configured or enhanced to provide effective delay times. For instance, the presence of multiple barriers of different types along all possible adversary paths complicates the adversary's progress by requiring him to be equipped with a number of different attack tools and skills. Co-locating barriers with sensors will also aid in accurate assessment of and response to threats.

There are a variety of active or passive barriers that can be used to provide delay, and many are present in the normal course of building construction. Depending on the threat tools and adversary capabilities, these barriers will have different delay times. Location of the barrier also plays an important role in the delay time and effectiveness of a barrier. A thick concrete wall on the exterior of a building may be susceptible to rapid breaching with explosives. The same wall, when incorporated into an interior underground vault, however, may provide substantial delay, as the adversaries may not be able to use large quantities of explosive without collapsing the entire structure around them. The use of multiple barriers of different types along all possible adversary paths complicates the adversary's progress by requiring him/her to be equipped with a number of different attack tools and skills. The vari-

ous categories of barriers are described in the following sections, along with important notes for consideration in estimating delay times for each barrier.

One of the most important evaluation concepts of a VA is that delay times are a strong function of the defined threat and skill. Stealth, cunning, and surprise can be valuable assets to any adversary. The VA team should not only look at the physical delay elements present in a PPS, but will look at their condition and integration with the rest of the PPS. The team must consider unique ways that an adversary most likely would exploit weaknesses in the PPS. One of the often overlooked aspects of a VA is how the adversary can use existing tools and materials within the facility to achieve their goals. Some simple examples include the use of on-site vehicles as noted previously; maintenance and construction tools for penetration, such as cutting torches, large wrenches, and forklifts; and fuels, such as gasoline, diesel, or propane to create diversionary events. The presence of very large construction equipment at the facility or in close proximity presents a significant vulnerability to any site. Bulldozers and large front-end loaders are capable of pushing over or through almost any commercial barrier or building. These large machines often do not require keys, or if they do they are universal to all equipment made by a particular manufacturer. If the adversary's goal is sabotage and destruction of assets, the presence of useful tools, fuels, and other material within the facility can have a substantial impact on overall task times and probabilities of success.

As stated previously, delay is effective only if it follows detection; however, detection can take different forms. The most obvious form of detection is through the use of electronic sensor systems that relay information back to a monitoring station. When dealing with truly massive delay barriers, such as 15 feet of heavily reinforced concrete or underground bunkers, it may be acceptable to use human observation as the one and only sensor system. Security patrols conducting scheduled or random inspections may be capable of detecting manual entry attempts with sufficient time to interrupt and neutralize adversaries. In the case of explosive or high power thermal attacks, which could yield much shorter delay times, security personnel would be alerted by the sounds of explosives being detonated or by large quantities of smoke created by thermal tools. In either case, the goal is to ensure that any response has ample time to prevent adversary success.

The one exception to delay only being effective after detection is when barriers are used to significantly increase the difficulty of a task, thereby forcing an adversary to change or abandon their tactics. For example, many monuments or critical facilities use concrete-filled steel posts or jersey barriers to prevent vehicle entries to a site. This may force the adversary to abandon the vehicle and continue the attack on foot, or possibly use a second vehicle. Of course, barrier effectiveness varies with the size, weight, and speed of the vehicle. In addition, these barriers are often used to establish a stand-off distance for vehicle bombs. This strategy can be effective, for a defined vehicle and amount of explosives, but if larger vehicles or quantities are used, the effectiveness will be reduced. In this case, the barriers do not provide effective delay but are used to increase attack difficulties and limit adversary attack scenarios. This will not work for determined adversaries, however, and still exposes the asset to successful attacks if detection does not occur.

Perimeter Barriers

Perimeter barriers are part of the outermost protective layer of a PPS and function to exclude unauthorized personnel from an area. Barriers such as fences and gates may not significantly delay determined adversaries; however, properly designed and positioned barriers can delay personnel and vehicles long enough for other elements of the PPS to be effective, that is, to detect intrusions, assess alarms, and respond. The most common type of perimeter barrier is chain-link fencing with gates of comparable materials. Most existing industrial perimeter barrier systems may be penetrated quite rapidly with simple tools or breached by climbing. There are many methods of stopping or significantly delaying vehicle penetrations into a protected area. Providing significant delay for a determined adversary crossing a perimeter barrier on foot, however, is a much more difficult problem and may require considerable hardware and land area, particularly when there is no immediate response.

Fences

Fences installed around a site can be classified as boundary, temporary, or security installations and are constructed using a variety of materials. A boundary fence is often used to define the outermost limit or border of a facility. Signs are placed on the fence, usually at 50- to 100-foot intervals, to establish ownership and to warn casual transients of possible dangers within the perimeters. A typical boundary fence is 4- to 8-feet high and is constructed of standard chain link fabric. Other boundary fences are made of posts on which strands of barbed wire are installed. This type of fence is often referred to as a cattle fence and is used only to define a boundary. A boundary fence should not be considered a physical barrier of any consequence, for any adversary.

Temporary fences are installed to prevent entry to individual areas and are used to enclose construction or storage facilities adjacent to a security area. The construction materials used in these fences range from 7-foot high, 4 × 4-inch wood posts with 10-gauge mesh (6 × 6 inch) to 8-foot high, 2.375-inch outside diameter steel posts set in concrete with 11-gauge chain-link mesh, bracing, and 45-degree extension arms with three strands of barbed wire. Personnel penetration times for a temporary fence range from 3 to 18 seconds when gloves, bolt cutters, or pipes are used as an aid.

Security fences usually consist of galvanized steel posts and fabric, and 45-degree extension arms angled outward with three strands of barbed wire or coiled concertina wire. Security fences are not usually less than 8-feet high and are braced, as necessary, at all corners, gate openings, or structurally weak points. The fabric is usually clamped to a bottom rail or cable. Top and bottom rails are used to help support the fabric, as well as to add to the overall bracing of the fence. These rails, together with all other bracing, are located on the inside of the fabric. All vertical posts are set in cylindrical concrete anchor footings. In addition to line posts, much heavier corner or terminal posts are used in perimeter fence construction. Although chain-link fences may serve as a deterrent to casual intruders, they have little effect on minimally equipped and motivated adversaries. Intrusion times for typical security fences from a variety of tests show that chain-link fences do not delay adversaries for more than a few tenths of a minute.

Placing rolls of barbed tape on or near standard fences can moderately enhance their capability to delay intruders. Attaching one roll of barbed tape to the outriggers of an existing perimeter security fence is a cost-effective addition that requires an intruder to bring additional aids or bulky equipment to climb over the fence. Barbed tape coils can be tied to the chain-link fabric and the existing barbed wire by means of stainless steel wire ties. Reversing the outriggers to point from outside to inside when installing barbed tapes as a fence topping eliminates the handgrip used by outsiders in climbing over the fence. If the top rail on a barbed tape-topped fence is eliminated, the fence fabric becomes loose and flexible and, consequently, is much harder to climb.

Other enhancement possibilities include the placement of barbed tape either horizontally on the ground or against the chain-link fabric. When the rolls are stacked vertically, the bottom row should be staked to the ground with anchors (metal tent pins). The barbed tapes can be placed on either side of the chain-link fabric, but they are usually placed on the inside of an outside perimeter fence and on the outside of an inner (double) fence. This prevents accidental injury to the casual passerby, both outside and inside a site or facility. When rolls of barbed tape are placed horizontally, they must be staked to the ground. Even when perimeter fences are enhanced with numerous rolls of barbed tape, cutting, climbing, and crawling attacks are still possible using simple breaching tools. In addition, the presence of barbed tape rolls on fences or on the ground will severely limit alarm assessment, and this effect must be considered during the VA.

Modern anti-climb fence material consists of 6- to 8-gauge welded wire fabric with center to center spacing of $1/_2$ inch or less. The large wire diameter and close spacing are a good deterrent to untrained or ill-equipped adversaries; however, they provide minimal additional delay to a well-trained and equipped adversary. No matter how large the wire size, or how close the wire spacing, a ladder can always be used to quickly breach a fence. Even stout fences are susceptible to being knocked over by large vehicles. An example of anti-climb fence material is shown in Figure 9-1.

Manual fence penetration methods vary and include breaching aids such as gloves, hand tools, ladders, bridging materials, and explosives. Stepladders and other bridging methods can be used to bypass fence disturbance sensors and may not leave evidence of entry or exit. Bypass of perimeters may also be accomplished through the use of structures,

Figure 9-1 Anti-Climb Fence Fabric. The material combines small openings and large-gauge hardened wire to increase hand tool cutting times. The material is somewhat slippery for unskilled climbing attempts. Even the best fences can be defeated in a matter of seconds with a ladder or similar unsophisticated equipment.

trees, or other climbing aids located close to the perimeter fences, as discussed in Chapters 5 and 7. Explosives will likely generate an alarm, but cutting a fence with hand tools may not be noticed for some time.

In summary, perimeter fences should be constructed of commercially available fence materials in good condition and properly installed. The fence should be located such that it provides the greatest synergistic benefit for the adjacent detection and assessment systems. Fences that are broken, severely rusted, unattached, or in any other obvious state of disrepair will be unlikely to show any signs of breaching and would contribute to lower delay time estimates.

Gates

Gates establish specific points of entrance and exit to an area defined by fences and walls, usually in personnel or vehicle portals. They function to limit or prohibit the free flow of pedestrian or vehicular traffic and establish a controlled traffic pattern. Gates may be manned or unmanned, and automatic or manually operated. Gate barriers contiguous with the perimeter fences should be equal in effectiveness to the fences so as to function as equivalent barriers. Gates often require additional hardening features because, as a consequence of their weak hardware and the fact that vehicle driveways are generally aimed directly toward them, they are easy to defeat.

Chain-Link Gates

Chain-link fabric gates are used in virtually all industrial and government facilities. The usual height of perimeter gates is 8 feet plus an additional 1 foot for the barbed wire outriggers. Pedestrian gates are normally 3 to 6 feet in width with their supporting hardware designed to accommodate the weight of the frame, fabric, and locking mechanism. Vehicle gates vary in width from 8 feet to a virtually unlimited size; however, most that are more than 15-feet wide require overhead guy cables or rollers to support their weight. Consequently, vehicle gates must have larger, stronger, and more durable hinges and frames. If the hinges are not appropriate for these heavier gates, barrier performance estimates should be lowered.

Common gates are swing and sliding types. Variations of each include double- and single-leaf swing gates, overhead supported or cantilevered sliding gates, one-way sliding gates, and bi-parting gates. Any of these may be used as either pedestrian or vehicle gates, the only difference being their width and hardware requirements. The site plan will usually dictate which type of gate should be used.

Standard pedestrian and vehicle chain-link gates afford about the same penetration resistance as fences. Barbed tape on top of a gate or fence presents a psychological barrier to the casual intruder but offers little or no deterrence to a more determined adversary with prior knowledge and proper equipment for scaling or breaching the barrier. The methods and times required to scale or penetrate gates are identical to those for standard fences. The orientation of vehicle gates and driveways could reduce the probability of their being breached by vehicles. Driveways constructed with multiple turns on each side of the gateway, with the smallest turning radius consistent with the maximum length of any vehicle using the gate, will reduce the approach and departure speed of vehicles. One vehicle penetration test at approximately 18.5 mph, however, indicated that a light truck could readily breach a conventional double-leaf swing gate. Swing gates can be forced open by slowly moving a vehicle up to the gate and then quickly accelerating. This penetration potential can be reduced by placing a hazardous obstacle inside the gate so that entering vehicles must make a sharp turn to avoid the obstacle. Denying rapid vehicle access forces the adversary to physically carry any tools or breaching aids to the personnel barriers or to consume time in attempting to move the vehicle through the barrier. If the adversary is prevented from using a vehicle to penetrate a secured area, the adversary is forced to move more slowly on foot inside the area and may be left with no rapid means of escape. Additional information on the use of gates and barriers designed to stop vehicles is included in the section Vehicle Barriers.

If multiple hardened gates at the perimeter are installed, additional delay can be achieved. These gates must be interlocked, requiring one gate to be closed and locked before the other can be released and opened. The area between the gates provides a holding area to allow sufficient time to determine whether contraband materials or unauthorized personnel are attempting entry or exit, as described in Chapter 7.

Turnstiles

Turnstile (rotational) gates are designed exclusively for control of pedestrian traffic. They are manufactured in two heights, low and full. Low, waist-high turnstiles (nominally 36-inches high) are used to handle crowds, count attendees, and collect admissions. To ensure complete control, these turnstiles must be constantly attended, and they afford little or no barrier constraints. The full-height turnstile, which completely surrounds a user as he/she passes through the gate, provides better security control, but is still vulnerable to some attacks, as noted in the previous chapter. For delay evaluation, only full-height turnstiles are discussed in this section because of the ease of bypass of low turnstiles with no tools. These turnstiles are made of steel three-arm security gates with rotating bars interleaved with fixed bars spaced to prevent passage.

Appropriately hardened and protected turnstiles can be used for pedestrian traffic control and as barriers for perimeter (or building) entry control systems.

Test results show that turnstile gates can be forcibly penetrated and entry accomplished within 1 minute by forcing or cutting. Surreptitious entry by disassembly or defeat of the ratchet mechanism requires 2 to 6 minutes. These times include time to enter, exit, and remove any evidence of penetration. For increased penetration delay, turnstiles should be upgraded by protecting the ratchet mechanism and the electric outlet box and by reinforcing the turnstile bar arms. The ratchet mechanism and electric outlet box can be protected with armor plate covers that are welded on, or assembled with nonremovable bolts. Hollow bar arms should be upgraded by the insertion of tool-resistant steel bars or composite materials to resist cutting, and all bolts should be replaced with welds. In security applications, all turnstiles should be designed with gate arms set for double closure of the entry passage so that either one arm on each array or three bars on the interleaved side must be cut. This increases penetration time by a factor of two.

Commercial turnstiles are easily penetrated by a variety of tools. Tests have shown that the penetration time for commercial turnstiles ranges from 20 to 90 seconds. Upgrades to increase the turnstile penetration time include the following mechanical and structural revisions:

- Redesigning and relocating the operation mechanism to an inaccessible position
- Increasing the number of rotating arms from 42 to 72
- Installing plastic inside 36 arms (two opposing sets) to resist cutting by thermal tools
- Installing silicon carbide chips in the other 36 arms to resist cutting with power and hydraulic tools

- Designing and installing a mechanism to position the turnstile so that two sets of arms are between the attacker and entry into the secured area

These improvements also require changes to other parts of the turnstile. Modifications include a new center post to support the 72 arms, new top and bottom bearings and bearing plates, additional fixed arms, and relocation of some support posts. The increase in the number of arms and the installation of a positioning device will force an attacker to cut two to four arms instead of only one. This improvement, along with hardening the plastic and metal fillers in arms, will increase the penetration time of the upgraded turnstile over the commercial turnstile significantly.

Gates should be evaluated with regard to their physical condition, as well as how they are integrated into the overall PPS. Important questions to consider during the VA include: Are the gates locked during nonoperational hours? When the gates are open, are they staffed or unattended? Do the gates have sensors and video assessment capability? The answers to these questions and the appropriate locations of delay elements are a large part of the delay subsystem evaluation.

Vehicle Barriers

Vehicle barriers must be capable of stopping a defined threat vehicle at a specific distance away from a secured area, regardless of attack location. The stopping capabilities of stationary and movable barriers must be balanced so that no weak section is present in the subsystem. Two-way protection with barriers may be necessary in some situations, such as preventing a threat vehicle from entering and leaving a secured area.

Ground vehicles can be used by adversaries to penetrate most perimeter barriers.

For a vehicle to be stopped, the vehicle's kinetic energy (which is proportional to the square of its velocity and directly proportional to its weight) must be dissipated. A car, light or heavy trucks, buses, or heavy equipment can crash though most fences, and a vehicle equipped with a beamlike hoisting device could be used to lift intruders and equipment over fence arrays. To determine the effectiveness of vehicle barriers, they should be evaluated by considering the following two factors:

- The threat vehicle that the barrier system is intended to stop (which includes weight of vehicle, impact velocity, and physical characteristics).
- Site-specific considerations such as terrain, road layout in and around the secured area, buildings and parking lot layout, climate conditions, and the traffic patterns around the area.

To provide full penetration resistance, barriers must fit the particular situation and be installed properly. Barriers that are difficult to remove should be installed in areas where they cannot be monitored continuously. For example, deeply buried, concrete-filled pipes can be constructed so that they will be difficult to defeat, thereby reducing the need for surveillance of the area, whereas cable barriers can be defeated easily with hand-carried cutting tools. These barriers should be located only within areas that are well patrolled or use sensors. Another factor in the selection and placement of a vehicle barrier is the height at which it will impact the vehicle. The optimum height for any barrier depends on its construction and the anticipated threat vehicle. Testing has determined that a height of 30 inches works best for most vehicles.

Most commercially available security vehicle barriers are tested and rated according to standards defined by the United States Department of State (SD-STD-02.01). The ratings include the weight of the vehicle and the speed at which it hits the barrier. Previous versions of the standard also included the distance the vehicle traveled after impacting the barrier. Commercially available safety vehicle barriers are tested against very different standards that tend to emphasize the importance of reducing passenger injury, ease of barrier repair, and limiting damage to the vehicle. Quite often safety vehicle barriers are not suitable for use as security vehicle barriers.

Most current vehicle barriers are designed to stop vehicles through one or a combination of the following methods:

1. Vehicle Arrestor: Absorbs virtually all of a vehicle's kinetic energy and applies a low-to-moderate resistive force to gradually stop a vehicle in a relatively long distance. Examples are weights that are dragged by a vehicle and accumulate with distance traveled or piles of loose sand.
2. Crash Cushion: Absorbs a large portion of a vehicle's kinetic energy and provides a stiff resistive force to stop a vehicle in a reasonable distance. Examples are liquid-filled plastic containers and arrays of empty steel barrels that are backed by strong supports.
3. Inertia Device: Exchanges momentum and kinetic energy with a vehicle during impact. This device provides a stiff resistive force to stop a vehicle in a reasonable distance. Examples are relatively small concrete shapes and sand-filled barrels that are not anchored.
4. Rigid Device: Provides very high resistive force to stop vehicles in very short distances. The vehicle dissipates almost all of its own kinetic energy as it deforms during impact. Examples include massive concrete shapes and steel structures that are well anchored.

Both safety and security concerns are normally considered when determining which barrier type should be used and evaluation should consider security effectiveness of vehicle barriers.

Vehicle barriers can be separated into two categories, stationary and movable. Depending on the requirements and constraints, some barriers are compatible with either application. A stationary barrier is one that is not normally moved to allow passage of authorized vehicles. Examples of stationary barriers include cables and posts, concrete shapes, trenches or berms, guardrails, and walls. Moveable barriers can include cables, crash beams, posts, hydraulic wedges, filled drums, nets, and large vehicles. Use of the proper device depends on the amount of traffic and the frequency of moving the barrier. At facilities where there is heavy traffic flow, hydraulically activated wedges may be the best option; when traffic flow is light and the barrier is moved infrequently, filled drums or concrete shapes can be effective.

Vehicles can be used to enter facilities in a number of ways. Light vehicles can breach most fences and some vehicle barriers by simply ramming the barrier at high speed. In most cases, no significant delay or injuries are incurred. Using a light vehicle to breach a concrete median or wedge barrier will cause major vehicle damage and seriously injure the passengers. An adversary could also use a vehicle as a battering ram to open a hole in the barrier and then drive a second vehicle through, either after moving the first vehicle out of the way or using the first vehicle as a ramp to drive a second vehicle over the top. Vehicles can be designed or be modified to provide a bridge or ramp for a second vehicle to penetrate the most carefully designed barrier system. Motorcycles can be driven through or over many simple vehicle barriers. In addition, a motorcycle can be used with a ramp to quickly bypass many vehicle barriers; however, unless the ramp is quite complex this is only a one-way tool. Another tactic used to gain entry to a facility is by disguise (i.e., deceit). This can be accomplished by using delivery trucks, emergency vehicles, and contractor equipment. Depending on the defined threat, each of these tactics should be considered during the VA, and appropriate estimates of delay times against these attacks should be made.

Preventing vehicle penetration into a facility is important, as a vehicle can also be used to haul equipment for use in entering a building or other structure. A motorcycle can carry a rider and enough explosives to breach most existing walls or vaults and can be used to haul all but heavy tools, such as large generators or air compressors. Any functioning vehicle can also be used for retreat. When driven over rough terrain, a modified four-wheel-drive vehicle or motorcycle could possibly outrun and outmaneuver most standard response vehicles.

Heavy construction equipment and large vehicles can also be used to breach many vehicle barriers. Bulldozers, backhoe loaders, road graders, and other large-construction equipment can often be found near or within a facility. These vehicles can be used to move concrete barriers out of the way or push over cable-reinforced fence systems. Revetments, massive reinforced stem walls, or steel structures embedded in concrete footings are required if these large vehicles are part of the identified threat. Even then, the vehicle will likely be able to gain access to the site, but if the barrier is properly designed and installed, the vehicle will be delayed long enough for response forces to interrupt and neutralize the adversaries. Examples of massive vehicle barriers are shown in Figures 9-2 and 9-3.

In summary, vehicle barriers should be evaluated to ensure that they are capable of stopping the threat vehicle (consider both vehicle weight and velocity) within the specified distance. Both fixed and movable barriers should be evaluated to determine the delay time required to defeat the barrier by means other than ramming with a vehicle. Quite often

Figure 9-2 Massive Concrete Vehicle Barrier. These barriers are used to prevent large vehicle attacks into a facility, but require careful integration with response tactics to ensure that the barrier does not interfere with response actions. In addition, note the shadows cast by the wall, which can make video assessment in these locations difficult at different times of day. (Photo courtesy of Don Utz/Kontek Industries.)

Figure 9-3 Fixed Decorative Concrete Vehicle Barrier. This barrier is similar to the barrier in Figure 9-2, but with a more aesthetically pleasing outward appearance. The picture shows the barrier in the process of installation at the site. The barriers are terrain following and do not need any excavated foundations. (Photo courtesy of Don Utz/Kontek Industries.)

simple attack methods can render both movable and fixed vehicle barriers useless in a matter of seconds.

Buildings

Perimeter barriers are the first layer of delay at many large industrial or government sites; however, many sites do not use perimeter barriers, thus buildings become the first delay layer in these systems. Buildings normally include walls, floors, and roofs, as well as doors and windows, and these elements are often overlooked when evaluating delay elements in a PPS. In addition, grilles and utility ports provide a means of entry into a building that can bypass sensors and formidable delays. Identification of buildings containing critical assets and the presence of these bypasses are an important part of a VA. This section describes the key characteristics of these delay barriers and how they are evaluated in the VA.

Walls

Walls of buildings, vaults, and other structures are usually considered to be more resistant to penetration and less desirable as targets for forcible entry than doors, windows, vents, and other conventional wall openings. Most existing walls, however, can be breached in short periods of time if adequate tools are used, and they may be the optimum path for forcible entry. Explosives are especially effective in producing holes large enough for both personnel and tools to enter. Combinations of tools, such as power and hand tools or explosives and power tools, are often required to penetrate walls. Determination of delay times for facility walls should start by VA team review of the defined threat tools, as well as consideration of which tools are available on-site. Once this has been established, estimates of delay times should be made

after considering these tools, barrier materials, and credible entry paths.

Reinforced concrete walls are commonly used in structures related to the storage and protection of critical assets. Because of their structural reputation and rugged appearance, concrete walls are almost universally believed to be formidable barriers. Testing has shown, however, that standard reinforced concrete walls are vulnerable to rapid penetration when appropriate tools and methods are used. Concrete walls are designed to support structural loads and, except for vault walls, are not normally designed specifically to block or delay penetration. In conventional construction, strength and thickness of concrete and size and spacing of reinforcing materials are based on structural requirements. Four-inch thick reinforced concrete walls are common but are not considered to be structural or load bearing. They are used as curtain walls to enclose the space between load-bearing structures such as columns. Concrete walls 6 inches or less in thickness are vulnerable to penetration with hand tools and small amounts of explosives. There are a large number of possible combinations of concrete thicknesses and strengths and sizes and spacing of reinforcing bars (rebars). For penetration evaluation, interpolating or extrapolating the desired data from wall cross sections that have already been tested and analyzed is often necessary.

Expanded metal-concrete walls are often used in the construction of bank vaults. Expanded metal-concrete construction is not the same as standard reinforced concrete. In a typical wall, vertical layers of $5/_{16}$-inch thick, 3.64-lb/ft^2 expanded metal reinforcement panels are placed perpendicular to the wall face at $2 1/_{2}$- to 3-inch centers. Rebars are strung through the expanded metal openings at 16-inch centers vertically and 6-inch centers horizontally and welded to the expanded metal to form a rigid structure. Then the concrete is poured around the reinforcement and vibrated. Using hand tools to cut the reinforcing material of an expanded metal-concrete wall requires a longer period than cutting the reinforcing material of a standard wall.

Concrete block walls are used in the construction of small buildings and offices. Standard concrete block walls are easily penetrated with hand tools, power tools, or explosives. The strength and corresponding penetration times against power and hand tools are enhanced significantly by filling the hollow cores with concrete and reinforcing material. Various combinations of block walls backed with other structural materials, and reinforcements have been evaluated as to their effectiveness against penetration by hand and power tools and times range from a few minutes to tens of minutes, depending on the specific tools used. Both concrete block and thin concrete walls can be readily breached by vehicles. In addition to delay testing, numerous news reports of errant vehicles crashing into and through block walls and timber frame construction are available. Large vehicles such as dump trucks, concrete trucks, and the like have the potential to penetrate 6- to 8-inch reinforced concrete walls.

Precast concrete tee sections are commonly used in building construction for walls, roofs, and floors. The outer edge of the flange where the tees join is 2 inches thick. The stem of the tee is reinforced with number 3 rebar and pre-tensioning steel, but the flange is only reinforced with 12-gauge woven-wire fabric. Number 4 rebars, which are used to join sections, are cast into the flanges at an angle and are widely spaced. From a barrier standpoint, the precast tee is similar to a thin concrete wall with woven-wire fabric and can be quickly penetrated with hand tools. In addition to precast tee sections, modern construction often uses a steel I-beam superstructure, which is clad with precast concrete wall panels. The wall panels are commonly 4 to 6 inches thick and are reinforced with 12-gauge woven wire fabric and number 3 or 4 rebar.

Because the walls are not load bearing, the amount of steel reinforcement is minimal. Penetration times for such walls range from 1 to 2 minutes for explosive attacks.

Wood frame walls are normally covered with gypsum-based sheetrock for fire protection. Sheetrock walls provide virtually no delay and can be defeated by kicking or demolition with small hand tools.

Although not in use anymore, walls made out of asbestos are still found in older buildings. These walls are made of asbestos fiber and Portland cement. Corrugated asbestos was available in thickness ranging from $^1/_8$ inch to $^3/_8$ inch. Corrugated asbestos walls cannot be considered as significant barriers. The mean time to penetrate a corrugated asbestos wall with hand tools is less than 1 minute.

In summary, walls should be evaluated against the defined threat to estimate delay times. Walls that are directly accessible to ramming by a vehicle should be evaluated against these threats, if applicable. Because walls are not usually monitored using sensors, they should be examined to determine if they can be covertly breached by an adversary without detection.

Floors and Roofs

Roofs and floors function as climatic barriers, provide working surfaces, and to some degree function as protective barriers; however, their use as protection against penetration by determined adversaries is generally ignored during most VAs. Penetration equipment includes hand, power, and thermal tools and explosives, used alone or in combination. Construction methods and materials used for roofs and floors are similar. The basic materials vary slightly in total thickness, type and quantity of steel reinforcement, and the concrete strength required to carry loads. In general, floors offer more resistance to penetration than roofs because floors are protected by the main structure and are designed to accommodate heavier loads than roofs.

One common roof type is constructed with prefabricated, prestressed concrete tee beams, lightweight concrete, rigid insulation, and a three-ply, coal tar pitch, built-up roofing membrane with gravel. This type of construction is vulnerable to penetration by hand and power tools, with penetration times on the order of a few minutes. The most vulnerable areas for penetration are the flange area of the tee beams and the joints if they can be found and attacked by the adversary. Roof construction should be inspected during the VA and flange locations should be identified. A similar roof is constructed using a ribbed metal subdeck, standard reinforced concrete, rigid insulation, and a three-ply, coal tar pitch, built-up roofing membrane with gravel. This roof provides substantial resistance to penetration when only hand tools are used.

Metal roofs are also used in many buildings. One type is constructed with a metal roof deck, rigid insulation, and a three-ply, coal tar pitch, built-up roofing membrane with gravel and is used on light structures. This roof is vulnerable to penetration by hand and power tools in a few minutes. A variation of this is construction using 24-gauge corrugated metal with $1\,^1/_2$ inches of fiberglass insulation and a wire fabric. This roof is used on most metal buildings and has very little resistance to forced penetration using hand tools.

In modern construction, reinforced synthetic rubber roofing membrane often replaces the three-ply coal tar pitch, built-up roofing membrane mentioned previously. Synthetic rubber roofing and built-up coal tar roofing provide similar delay times when attacked with hand, power, or explosive tools.

Roofs using reinforced concrete beams, a concrete slab for the main roof deck, rigid insulation, and a built-up roofing membrane are used on some multistoried facilities and offer better resistance to penetration than most other roofs. The main deck may be 6 or more inches deep with multiple layers of reinforcing steel, making it similar in construction to a wall. This type of roof is fairly resistant to hand and thermal tools.

The last roof type discussed consists primarily of wood materials and contains a wood sheathing, rigid insulation, and a built-up roofing membrane. It is inexpensive and commonly used in many small structures, although its use is discouraged by most fire codes. Penetration by hand tools is possible in a few minutes or less.

Because of the similarity in design and construction of roofs and floors, no additional detailed information on floor construction is provided. In general, floor fabrication includes an increase in size and strength of structural members to carry the increased loads that are required. This additional strength provides floors with greater penetration resistance than most roofs. Some finishing materials used to cover floors (e.g., asphalt floor covering) contribute little to penetration resistance. Floors constructed below ground or on grade would require tunneling or the removal of considerable debris to achieve penetration.

Roofs and floors should be inspected for physical construction, condition, and ease of access. As it is often impossible to determine roof and floor construction simply by looking at them, the delay expert must be sure to obtain appropriate construction drawings of the surfaces being evaluated to make delay time estimates.

Doors

In all structures, the value of a barrier subsystem is ultimately determined by its weakest link. This section describes the various doors used in typical industrial facilities and applies the criterion of balanced design that is necessary to the effectiveness of a barrier array (see Figure 9-4). Doors are classified as standard industrial doors (including personnel, attack, bullet resistant, and vehicle doors), vault doors, and turnstiles. Penetration delay time through static structures can be increased through the use of thicker and/or composite materials. Because of their functional requirements and associated hardware, however, doors impose structural restrictions and are, in many cases, one of the weakest links in a structure. For example, many buildings with heavy concrete walls provide pedestrian access through commercial hollow steel doors. The barrier value of the basic structure is relatively high, but this is compromised by the use of ordinary doors, frames, and hinges that can be quickly penetrated. Consequently, for barrier purposes, the principle of balanced design requires that doors with associated frames, hinges, bolts, and locking mechanisms be strengthened to afford the same penetration delay as provided by the floors, walls, and ceilings of the parent structure. Conversely, if the door assembly cannot be enhanced, it may not be cost effective to upgrade the building structure.

Personnel Doors

Personnel doors vary in type, style, and class, but most common exterior doors are $1\,^3/_4$-inches thick with 16- or 18-gauge (0.060- or 0.048-inch) steel surface sheets. Construction is usually hollow-core or composite with or without glass or louvers. A composite door core consists of a noncombustible, sound-deadening material, usually polyurethane foam or slab. Light-gauge vertical reinforcement channels are sometimes used inside hollow-core doors to add strength and rigidity to the door assembly. Penetration time through either standard hollow-core or composite doors is essentially the same. Steel pedestrian doors are found throughout government and private industry in single or double configurations and use a wide variety of locking devices. Exterior doors usually swing outward, regardless of their functional design, and have their closing devices attached internally. Hinges are mortised with either removable or nonremovable pins. Additional doors are provided for emergency exits, as required by fire and life safety codes. The requirements for panic-bar devices on all emergency exits make the door only a one-way barrier. This requirement

Figure 9-4 Unbalanced Delay. The turnstile and fence are easily penetrated by a vehicle, making the use of the heavy vehicle gate barrier less effective.

provides a number of exit paths to outside attackers after a building has been breached.

Standard industrial doors are vulnerable to a number of attack modes. An attack that uses explosives is a noisy mode of entry and produces obvious evidence of penetration. The explosives used can range from a small commercial charge, such as those used for quick entry by firemen, to potent charges. The use of a thermal cutting tool offers an alternate entry method that may not initiate a door alarm that senses only door movement. Explosives and thermal cutting tools are characteristic of high threats and would be expected at high-security facilities with critical assets. Other attack modes include simple attacks against panic bars, locks, hinge pins and louvers, windows, and mesh in doors (see Figure 9-5). Panic bars can be defeated using a drill and a hook, and exposed hinge

pins are also vulnerable to cutting or prying attacks. Many key locks can be picked. Lock picking time varies with the type and physical condition of the lock but averages about 1 minute for a skilled intruder. A pipe or strap wrench used on key-in-knob locks reduces penetration time to tenths of a minute. A pry bar inserted between the door and frame is equally successful. These methods do have some limitations. Picking tools are effective only if a keyway is available; a pipe wrench is effective only if locking hardware is exposed. Many doors need no entrance capability at all (e.g., emergency exits) and, therefore, can be fully flush-mounted with no external hardware. If keyways are required, there are several high-security locks on the market that require relatively long pick times, but these locks must be paired with doors of equal strength to be most effective. A fire axe, sledgehammer, or crowbar is an effective

Figure 9-5 Ineffective Door Delay. This door leads to a storeroom for a valuable asset. Note the poor lock and loose hasp on the relatively good door. (The chain is there to keep the lock on the door.) The vent in the door also makes this entry point weaker than other parts of the door. The facility went to the trouble of installing an anti-pry strip over the joint between the two doors, but because the doors are loose, this is not effective.

means of penetrating louvers, windows, or mesh on doors. A large crawl-through hole can be made in plate, tempered, or wired glass in 15 seconds or less.

Attack- and Bullet-Resistant Doors

Many door manufacturers, through contact with security engineers and consultants, have recognized the need for high-security attack and bullet-resistant doors and have modified or added to their product lines accordingly. These doors incorporate the types of modifications or upgrades mentioned in the previous section and offer the added benefit of balance; that is, the frame, door, hinges, locks, and so forth are all designed to deny a particular threat or meet a specification or standard. A brief listing of ballistic- and attack-resistance standards are shown in Table 9-1. The standards cover a wide range of threats and attack methods that may not be applicable for all facilities.

Bullet-resistant doors are available in a variety of sizes and styles, but most fall into one of two categories: opaque or transparent. Opaque doors are normally constructed of steel or aluminum armor plate and, occasionally, thicker plates of mild steel. The bullet-resistant plates are either on the face of the door and frame or part of the core of the door and frame. Full-length hinges or hinges with self-engaging lock pins are often used in combination with one or more high-security locks and deadbolts. The doorframes are usually constructed of steel or aluminum sections and are filled with either metal or plastic to ensure ballistic and physical integrity.

When considering the use of attack- or bullet-resistant doors, emphasis must be placed on the type of door being purchased and the threat the door is intended to protect against. An attack-resistant door with a single-cylinder lock is little protection against most threats. Choosing multiple and different locks and deadbolts is a more logical choice for this type of door. A bullet-resistant door should provide protection through all door components. The lock area, frame, and sill plate should be armored to protect against the same level of threat as the door itself. Grouting or overlapping steel plates should also be specified for the frame-to-wall gap. Many of the features incorporated into bullet-resistant doors will resist attack; however, the glazing systems of some transparent bullet-resistant doors are still vulnerable to tool attacks.

Readers should be aware that the terms *bullet resistant* and *attack resistant* are not synonymous. Although the door industry has responded favorably to requirements for more robust products, a door should be considered bullet or attack resistant only if it has been tested and certified by an independent testing agency, such as Underwriters Laboratories (UL), H.P. White Laboratories, or the U.S. Department of State. Even when a door is tested and certified by an independent entity, the delay expert must be sure that the test procedures and specified threat used for testing correlate with the defined threat. As an example, a door rated to withstand small-caliber handgun attacks may fail catastrophically when attacked with a high-power hunting rifle. Similarly, a door tested and rated to

Table 9-1 *Attack- and Bullet-Resistant Door Standards.*

UL – 752	Bullet-Resistant Standard Small Arms to High-Powered Rifle
NIJ – STD 0108.00	Ballistic-Resistant Material Standards
NIJ – STD 0306.00	Physical Security of Door Assemblies and Components
UL – 608	Standards for Burglary-Resistant Vault Doors

The use of these doors depends on the defined threat tools, capability, and motivation.

stop adversaries using hand tools for 30 minutes may provide only 30 seconds of delay against explosive attack.

The VA team should look at the delay provided by the door itself, but also consider how the door is attached to the structure around it. This is especially important during facility upgrades when new high-security doors are used to replace existing industrial doors. Improper installation of high-security or bullet-resistant doors can significantly reduce their delay time.

Vehicle Doors

Many of the foregoing considerations of pedestrian doors also pertain to vehicle access doors. These considerations are especially true where the construction of the door is essentially identical and the main difference is size. A vehicle door-way is one of the largest structural openings that must be protected. Corrugated roll-up and hollow-steel panel doors are found throughout industrial and government buildings. Standard industrial doors are available in swinging, sliding, rolling, telescoping, folding, and parting designs. They are used primarily to minimize the effects of weather, noise, and pollutants or to provide privacy. Many vehicle access doors seriously degrade the barrier value of a substantial structure because they are not balanced with the delay of the structure. Penetration of vehicle doors can be accomplished by cutting, ramming with a vehicle, or explosives. Quite often, vehicle doors do not have any physical locks to keep them closed. Instead they rely on the actuation mechanism to hold the door in the desired position. As a result, it may be easy for an insider to simply push a control button and open the door. Once inside the structure, an adversary could also open a vehicle door to allow additional intruder entry or rapid egress from the target building.

Although there are usually fewer vehicle doors than pedestrian doors within a facility, most vehicle doorways may be easily penetrated in a very short time by ramming the door with a vehicle. Design limits imposed by the door's function and its hardware make it an inherently weak link in a barrier system, as well as making it difficult to barricade. The corrugated steel roll-up door shown in Figure 9-6 is widely used. This type of door affords little resistance to forcible entry. Specifications only require a stiffness that is sufficient to withstand a wind pressure of 2 pounds per square inch (psi).

High-energy vehicle impact can be prevented by imposing controls on vehicle approach speeds. Long, straight approaches can be avoided in favor of right-angle turns or sharp curves. Vehicles can be parked in the driveway in front of existing doors, or retractable locking bollards can be used to protect the door from vehicle ramming.

Vault Doors

Vault doors are usually classified according to the thickness of solid steel in the door. Security vault doors are classified as 1, 3, 4, 5R, 6R, 9R, and 10R, with 10R representing the greatest thickness (9 $\frac{1}{2}$ inches). Class 5 vault doors, which conform to Federal Specification Door, Vault, Security AA-D-600B, dated March 26, 1969, and revised June 13, 1973, theoretically afford the following security protection:

- 30 minutes against surreptitious entry
- 10 minutes against forced entry
- 20 hours against lock manipulation
- 20 hours against radiological techniques

Testing performed in accordance with specification AA-D-600B limits a two-person attack team to the use of hand tools and devices that cannot be (1) more than 20 inches long when disassembled or folded, (2) carried in a case that exceeds 1.5 cubic feet in volume and 9 inches in thickness, and (3) in excess of

Figure 9-6 Standard Roll-Up Vehicle Door. This door is commonly used in shipping and receiving areas, warehouses, or other areas where vehicle access is required. These doors are relatively easy to penetrate using small hand or power tools.

25 pounds, excluding the case. Further, no explosives or thermal devices are permitted, which considering present day threats, leaves this door potentially vulnerable to rapid penetration by either method. Tests performed on Class 5 vault doors indicate that penetration through the door can be accomplished with power tools, thermal tools, or explosive devices in 1 to 5 minutes. Other types of heavier vault doors may be suitable for selected security purposes and may offer significant penetration resistance for defined threats, but they are also much more expensive.

In general, the locking mechanisms used for vault doors are combination locks coupled to engage bolts; they are tested to withstand 20 hours of lock manipulation. The typical Class 5 locking mechanism, however, is vulnerable to forced penetration by hand tools, thermal tools, hand-held power tools, and explosives. Tests have shown that lock defeat is possible in 2 to 5 minutes. Other locking mechanisms are available with additional features such as automatic dead bolts that are activated by drilling or by thermal or explosives penetration attempts, time locks, wedge-locking bars, and locking thresholds.

When evaluating doors for delay purposes, the total door installation, including fittings, locks, and hardware, must be considered. The situation, orientation, and function of the doorway are also important factors. For example, doorways can be designed with multiple doors to form airlocks that control vehicle and personnel entry. Multiple doors will increase penetration time because each door in the series must be attacked, with tools lifted through the opening in the previous door and used in the confined space between the doors. By using combinations of doors that are constructed of different materials, penetration time can be increased. For example, a double swing door located adjacent to and inside a roll-up door would complicate penetration by requiring the repetitive use of hand, power, and thermal tools.

Windows, Grilles, and Utility Ports

Windows provide only minimal penetration delay to adversaries. Windows should follow the principle of balance so that they will not be the weak link in a barrier system. In addition to doors and windows, industrial facilities have many unattended structural openings, such as ventilating ducts, utility tunnels, and service openings, that can be used as intrusion paths by adversaries. Few existing structural openings would delay a determined adversary for very long, especially if the openings are designed to provide easy access for maintenance. These openings can function as a concealed pathway and, therefore, should be protected using sensors and barriers when they are large enough to allow undetected entry by a crawling adversary.

A utility port includes all types of unattended framed openings other than doors and windows. They include ducts, air shafts, tunnels, crawl spaces, sewers, drains, water inlets, areaways, conveyer openings, trap doors, skylights, roof access hatches, filter banks, diffusers, louvers and registers, attics and false ceilings, dumb waiters, elevator shafts, pass-throughs, chimneys, rafter walkways, coal and ash chutes, roof vents, manholes, cupolas, equipment penthouses, and exhaust fans. These openings often contain grilles installed for safety and ornamental reasons that also function as insect and rodent barriers, but provide little security. This section describes window frames, glazing materials, and protective coverings, as well as grilles and utility ports.

Windows

Window frames and sashes are classified as fixed or operable, casement, awning, sliding, or other applications. The size of the glazed opening varies according to the sash dimensions and configuration. These two elements of the frame may be the most vulnerable parts of a window, especially when laminated security- or armor-type glazing material is used. The strength and weight of the frame material of a window varies widely with the class of window and manufacturer. Some manufacturers fabricate a security sash; however, this term can be misleading as the frame material is not hardened. When windows are installed in doors, the metal strips separating the glass can be weak, and several special window frames are manufactured that contain concealed materials that resist cutting tools. The frames and sashes are made of stainless steel, steel, aluminum, and wood, with aluminum and steel most common. If a window is operable, the locking mechanism may constitute a weak link, and, if forced, this window can be opened.

The position and operation of the locking mechanism of a window vary with type and manufacturer. The locking mechanism should be located so that it is not readily accessible from the exterior. Frame attachment to the structure may be improved by the use of additional or heavier fasteners or by welding the frame fin, but these techniques may not affect the delay time through the window unless additional upgrades are made to the glazing materials and/or protective coverings.

Glass, plastics, and composites of the two are the most commonly used types of glazing materials. Glass glazing materials include standard, tempered, wire, and laminated glass. These types of glass provide a barrier to the elements but will not provide significant delay times. Standard glass materials are highly frangible. Penetration by hand tools generally requires less than 20 seconds. Where a higher level of penetration resistance is required, thick security glass can be used. In addition, standard glazing materials can be upgraded with a protective grille of expanded steel mesh or other forms of metal grilles.

Tempered glass is formed by the reheating and sudden cooling of a base glass.

Although tempering greatly increases the mechanical strength and thermal stress characteristics of the glass, it can still be easily broken with moderate force. It can be quickly shattered into gravel-sized pieces by hand tools, and complete penetration can be accomplished in much less than a minute. Wire glass is used primarily in fire doors and fire windows as required by fire codes; most types of wire glass are UL listed for this purpose. The $1/4$-inch thick material is fabricated with diamond, square, or hexagonal wire patterns; the minimum size is No. 85 ASW gauge. Penetration of wire glass can be achieved by hand tools in less than 30 seconds.

Laminated glass is manufactured for safety and security; however, not all types of laminated glass are recommended by the manufacturers for use in security areas. Laminated glass is composed of two or more panes of annealed float, sheet, or plate glass bonded to a layer or layers of plastic, which range in thickness from 0.050 to 0.090 inches. The thickness of the layers ranges from $9/32$ to $13/16$ inch, depending on the manufacturer. Safety glass that is $1/4$-inch thick can be quickly penetrated using hand tools, and $9/16$-inch thick security glass can be penetrated with a sledgehammer and fire axe to produce a crawl-through hole. Safety and security glass is not transparent armor; it is simply more resistant than standard glass to forcible penetration.

Transparent plastics (acrylics and polycarbonates) can be used as substitutes for most glass; however, some are combustible and their use is restricted by fire codes. Acrylic plastics up to 1-inch thick can be easily and quickly broken with hand tools. Surprisingly, however, both acrylics and polycarbonates are highly resistant to thermal tool penetration attacks. The impact resistance of polycarbonates, on the other hand, approaches the same performance level as that of bullet-resistant glass. Tests show that $1/2$-inch thick Lexan resists hand tool attacks

for up to 2 minutes. Thermal tool attacks require more time to penetrate, and combustion and toxic gases also result, which may limit the usefulness of these attacks. Glass/polycarbonate composite glazing ranging from $7/16$-inch to $11/16$-inch thick is composed of a tough core layer of polycarbonate laminated between two outer layers of glass. In tests using common hand tools on three aluminum framed panels of $7/16$-inch, $9/16$-inch, and $11/16$-inch glass/polycarbonate composite, respectively, all panels were penetrated when sledgehammers and fire axes were used.

In new construction, windows in facilities with critical assets should either be eliminated or have a maximum one-way dimension of 5 inches or less. Such narrow windows have been used in the prison industry for many years. Even if the glazing material is broken by an adversary, the resulting opening is too narrow for human passage.

One improvement to windows is to reduce inside occupants' day and nighttime visibility to the potential adversary, particularly in a guard tower or guardhouse. Because of the large amount of light entering or used in a guard tower or guardhouse, windows are usually transparent both ways. If the amount of light inside a tower can be reduced, daily routines are much harder to observe from the outside. One solution is to install reflective sunscreen materials on the inner surface of windows. These materials use a reflective coating (silver, copper, bronze) to reduce the amount of light and heat entering through windows. As a consequence, a large percentage (50% to 90%) of light striking a window is reflected and much less enters through the glass. Use of these materials will not add to the penetration times, but will make it harder for an adversary to observe security procedures and operations.

Plastic films, usually consisting of 4- to 10-millimeter Mylar, and an adhesive may be applied to the surfaces of glass windows to reduce the hazards from flying glass shards. Mylar films do not significantly increase the delay time for glass windows but may reduce personnel injuries from flying glass. Films are most effective against single events, such as a thrown rock or a Molotov cocktail. If the glazing is exposed to an explosive event the entire film covered glass panel may be thrown into the interior of the building with sufficient force to injure or kill nearby personnel. This phenomenon may be limited by the use of safety bars located inside the window opening to catch the glass and film debris.

Grilles and Utility Ports

Electrical, mechanical, and service passageways are potential bypasses of the PPS that must be considered during the VA of the delay subsystem. Most tunnels used to link buildings are not protected.

Entry may be controlled only by lift-off covers or manholes, which are not equipped with locking devices or interior barriers. Pipe chases are used inside buildings and are often quite congested; however, they still allow space for maintenance work. Some facilities have interconnecting vertical and horizontal chase systems, which could provide adversary paths. Pipe sleeves and cable trays are usually only large enough to permit pipes and cables to pass through a wall or floor. Equipment penthouses, air supply fans, exhaust fans, gravity ventilators, in addition to sewers for storm and sanitary drainage, and manholes for electrical power and telephone cables may also provide adversary paths (see Figure 9-7). In addition, most buildings include ducts used for heating, ventilating, and air conditioning (HVAC) systems, and these may be entry or exit paths for some adversaries. If the defined threat includes

Figure 9-7 Steam Tunnel Port. If this is an entry path for the defined threat, it should be protected with a sensor, and additional delay may be required.

motivated and appropriately equipped adversaries, these aspects of building structures must be considered as part of the VA.

Grilles are often used at the ends of utility ports and chases for aesthetic reasons and/or to keep out rodents and debris. In most industrial settings grates are not locked in place and can be easily removed with hand tools. To balance delay, it is important to make sure all grates and utility ports provide consistent delay with the other elements of the subsystem during the VA.

Windows, Grilles, and Utility Ports Summary

Standard windows and utility ports constitute potential weak links in a barrier system and may require enhancement to provide significant delay. Windows without enhancement have little penetration delay time because most windows can be penetrated with hand tools in less than 30 seconds. Utility ports may have lift-off covers that are not even equipped with locking devices or interior barriers. Both windows and utility ports require enhancement to provide significant delay. Tunnels, manholes, roof and wall openings, and ductwork must be enhanced by installing interior barriers or a series of barriers. The degree of improvement in windows should be dictated by the balanced design concept. With the proper selection of enhancements (protective coverings, grilles, mesh), different glazing material, or methods of frame attachment, the delay time of windows may approach the delay time of doors or even walls for some threats. Once the appropriate delay has been attained for windows, grilles, and utility ports, they must include sensors and video assessment capabilities in the area. This is especially important for utility ports, as they are often in concealed locations, which allows extended work time for an adversary if no means of remote detection is present.

Other Barriers

There are a number of specialized delay elements that are used in high-security systems, where more capable and determined adversaries are expected. These include armor, vaults, earth and overburden, underground facilities, airborne attack barriers, tie-downs and restraints, and nonlethal weapons. Each of these elements is described only briefly next. For sites where the defined threat requires the use of these delay elements, it is assumed that knowledgeable experts are part of the VA team, and they will provide the appropriate estimates of performance.

Armor

Armor can be broadly defined as any material used to protect personnel, equipment, or structures from high-velocity projectiles. Although armor is commonly thought of as a heavy steel plate, many materials used in the construction industry, such as concrete, stone, brick, or cinder block, provide appreciable resistance to projectile penetration. Gravel and sand have been used for many years as a convenient, effective, and economical means of defeating projectiles. In many instances, minor modifications or the addition of complementary materials will greatly enhance the defensive characteristics of a structure. The protection of security personnel in gatehouses and guard posts may be an important security element at critical facilities, and hardening these structures against projectiles by the use of appropriate armor can enhance their survival. For the purposes of this textbook, armor is classified simply as either heavy or lightweight. Heavy armor is considered only briefly for the sake of completeness. Emphasis is placed on the uses of lightweight armor because of its wider application to fixed-site facilities and its adaptability. Lightweight armor is subdivided into opaque and transparent structural armor, and body armor.

Heavy armor generally refers to massive steel castings or plates, 1-inch thick or greater, which are intended to resist penetration by modern missiles and artillery. Although commonly found in military combatant ships and tanks, steel of this thickness is seldom used for fixed-site protection.

During the last few decades, considerable effort has been devoted to improving lightweight armor. Many of the improvements have been made possible as a result of advances in material technology and development of a basic understanding of the mechanics of armor penetration. To determine the type of lightweight structural armor needed for a given facility, establishment of the required level of protection is the essential first step. Grouping small arms into classes based on their penetrating capability or level of threat is helpful. For example, the National Institute of Justice Standard 0101.04 designates six levels of ballistic protection for police body armor. The protection levels range from .22 caliber long rifle rounds up to and including .30 caliber armor-piercing bullets impacting at 2,850 ft/sec. or less. Similar protection levels for structural armor should be defined for evaluation use. In choosing a protection level, two factors must be considered: the worst-case, most probable threat and the cost of armor to protect against this threat.

Once a protection level is established, the next step is to evaluate the installed components and verify their performance to the required level. Installing a single layer of material, which in itself provides all the needed protection, is rarely a cost-effective solution. Rather, all the materials used in the structure should be evaluated in terms of their function as armor so that these materials will provide the best level of protection possible.

Opaque structural armor includes materials such as concrete, steel, ceramic, fiberglass, Kevlar-phenolic, and aluminum. Depending on the thickness of the materials used, they may stop a variety of small-caliber handgun rounds. Engineered combinations of these materials are capable of stopping high-power rifle rounds if the barrier is of sufficient thickness. In addition to the rated protection capability of opaque armor, multi-hit protection should be considered. Most test standards include a multi-hit test protocol, which should be evaluated considering the defined threat.

Transparent structural armor consists of a highly specialized, limited class of materials. For many years, it was common practice to merely increase the thickness of ordinary glass to increase its protection capability. This caused problems of distortion and loss of transparency. The invention of laminated, prestressed (safety) glass was the beginning of a new era for bullet-resistant transparent composites. Concurrent with this development, transparent plastics, such as Lucite and Lexan, became popular because of their impact resistance. Unfortunately, Lucite and Lexan are susceptible to scratching, chemical etching, and crazing if they are used as outer surfaces exposed to normal exterior environments. Most transparent armors marketed today take the form of a composite glazing that uses the transparent plastics as inner layers with external layers of float glass or safety glass. These composites provide good protection against handgun attacks with very little distortion or loss of transparency. Even with the use of plastic laminates, transparent armor capable of protecting against .30- and .50-caliber armor piercing rounds are quite thick and quickly become translucent or opaque when they are hit with multiple projectiles.

Body armor has been used by law enforcement agencies for many years. To be useful, the armor must be lightweight (preferably not more than 8 to 10 pounds), comfortable, and nonrestrictive to body movements. Modern protective apparel that meets these requirements can provide personnel with full-torso protection against handgun and small-grenade attack. Protection against higher energy rifle fire and artillery projectile fragments, however, demands a considerable increase in weight, and, as would be expected, the heavier armor is more restrictive to movement. Most modern body armor is made from either Kevlar or Spectra. Rigid inserts made of steel or ceramic laminates are normally used in the chest area to provide protection from rifle fire. Even with the use of appropriately rated body armor and inserts, response force personnel can be incapacitated by the blunt force trauma inflicted by high-power rifles. As an example, a .357 magnum handgun produces approximately 680 foot-pounds of energy at muzzle velocity. A 7-mm (.283 cal.) Remington Magnum hunting rifle produces approximately 3,000 foot-pounds of energy at muzzle velocity. These energy levels are sufficient to crack ribs and collapse lungs even if the bullet does not penetrate the armor. Extensive information on the protection performance of body armor is available from the National Institute of Justice website at www.oip.usdoj.gov/nij/.

Recent changes in federal firearms legislation have once again made it legal for most individuals to purchase, own, and use armor-piercing, incendiary, and tracer ammunition. Such ammunition is advertised in national catalogs for both .30-cal. and .50-cal. rifles. This should be considered when defining the threat for a facility and establishing delay times for any body armor in use at the facility.

Vaults

An above-ground vault is composed of four basic structural elements: floor, walls, roof, and door(s). Some vaults require ventilation ducts, which must be considered as potential entry paths for adversaries. The door, the largest opening in the vault, should provide the same delay time as the other major elements. Testing of some doors shows penetration times of a few minutes using hand or thermal tools. The openings in a vault (vault door, ventilation ducts, conduit runs, etc.) may be weak points in an otherwise hardened structure; however, these openings are necessary for entry and utility purposes. They should be considered in the overall penetration resistance of the vault.

The location of a vault within a building could be a factor in determining its penetration resistance, for example, placement on an exterior wall versus completely within the building. An exterior wall location may provide an adversary with a stealthy penetration path or permit the use of explosives on the wall or roof in the same manner as an exterior building wall. In this case, the adversary penetrates the building exterior and vault wall in a single attack. When the vault is located deeper within the building, the adversary may be reluctant to use explosives or is limited in the amount that can be detonated without causing a structural failure from the resulting overpressure and shrapnel. As a result, the adversary must breach the building exterior and the vault in separate attacks, a much better delay design.

There are three general types of commercial modular vaults currently produced in the United States, including precast, high-strength concrete, precast concrete with steel backing, and composite or laminated panels. The high-strength designs include steel rebar, steel fibers, and graded sizes of crushed granite or limestone to obtain the typical 14,000 to 20,000 psi compressive strengths; thickness ranges from 3 to 11 inches. Precast concrete with steel backing is a reinforced concrete panel with a steel sheet attached to the surface of the panel. The panels are usually thinner and lighter than the all-concrete panels used for comparable protection. Composite panels use a combination of wood, steel mesh, and steel backing sheets, and are encapsulated into a laminated panel 40% lighter than equivalent concrete panels. Their nominal thickness ranges from $2\,^5/_8$ inches to $11\,^1/_2$ inches. Delay times for modular vaults are based on testing with hand tools and limited thermal tools. Because of the limited tool set, the advertised delay times for modular vaults range from 15 minutes to 2 hours. In reality, however, a dedicated adversary team with the proper power and thermal tools, or explosives, can breach a 12-inch modular vault in just a few minutes.

A popular misconception is that commercial vaults are impenetrable; however, as shown in the preceding discussion, this is not true. Almost all vaults are constructed with insurance industry loss ratios in mind. Historically, items of significant value are rarely lost or stolen when stored in a commercial vault, either of fixed or modular construction. This low-loss ratio keeps insurance premiums to a reasonable level and commercial vaults are constructed in accordance with the market driven cost/benefit relationship. This practice is certainly acceptable and makes perfect sense when the items being stored are replaceable, such as gold, diamonds, money, and similar assets. When it comes to the storage of certain high-consequence assets, such as nuclear materials, biological, or chemical agents, however, replacement is not the issue. Theft and unintended use of such materials have the potential to injure or kill thousands of people. As a result, high-consequence loss materials are usually stored in specifically designed vaults and bunkers intended to preclude entry by even the most determined and well-equipped adversaries.

Earth and Overburden

High-security facilities that require protection against high-level threats often use earth cover and overburden to provide delay against well-equipped adversaries. A well-compacted, deep, earth overburden (in excess of 20 feet) will provide an effective time-consuming barrier against most penetration methods. Assuming an average earth depth of 20 feet, the following times would be required

to penetrate to the roof by three methods of attack:

1. Manually—a large number of people would require several hours to reach the roof
2. Mechanically—a large back-hoe equipped with a 1-cubic-yard bucket would require approximately 40 minutes
3. Explosively—a crew of people would require approximately a half hour to remove the earth remaining after the detonation

Penetration rates for an earth overburden are dependent on the physical characteristics of the soil and the depth necessary to gain access to the underlying structure. The physical characteristics of soil are type (structure), texture (size of soil particles), density (porosity of both dry and wet soil), and cohesiveness (shear strength as an adjunct of friction). These natural characteristics may be adjusted to produce optimum resistance to penetration by mixing soil types and textures that provide the best cohesive characteristics and compaction and hence produce the maximum density. If the toughest and heaviest soil is used as an overburden, varying the depth will be sufficient to produce the delay time required for a particular defined threat and attack mode. An engineered overburden consisting of natural soils reinforced with concrete slabs, wire rope, riprap, and chain-link fabric can effectively double delay times.

Underground Facilities

Underground facilities provide an excellent means of enhancing PPS effectiveness against theft or sabotage of hazardous materials or other critical assets, and costs for construction and operations could be reduced. Underground facilities normally fall into one of three categories:

- Cut and cover, which is the most economical form of construction. The soil from the construction site is removed to make room for the facility and is then bermed on top of the completed building.
- Complete burial, where a large amount of soil is removed from the site to allow construction of the facility, with the final grade comparable to the surrounding landscape.
- Tunneling, boring, or blasting into solid rock to create an opening within the confines of a mountain or ridge. Because of the tremendous overburden involved, tunneled facilities are some of the most secure and survivable structures on earth.

Many design tradeoffs take place in the development process of an underground facility, even a very small facility. One important tradeoff is the balance between a facility's daily operations and its physical security.

Overburden is a major part of any underground facility, and the depth and type of material are important. Overburden is used as a barrier against forced entry attacks, a mitigator against explosive attacks and vehicle bombs, and as a moderator of temperatures within the facility. A combination of rock rubble and earth could also be used. Other materials used in combination could provide additional protection.

Personnel and vehicle entryways are another security and operational concern. Evaluation criteria for these areas include minimization of the number of entryways, elimination of line-of-sight paths, installation of vehicle barriers and inspection portals before below ground entrances, installation of intrusion detectors and assessment cameras before and inside entryways, and designing collapsible entryways to limit explosive attacks. Door entrances should use an offset sally port configuration, and construction should be at least as formidable as the surrounding concrete structure. Interlocking composite

doors are a good solution for high-security entrances. Facility utilities could be protected by being almost totally contained within the underground facility. These characteristics should be evaluated during a VA of underground facilities.

Airborne-Attack Barriers

Since the attacks of 9/11, airborne intrusion deterrents have become an important part of the threat capability at some facilities. The variety of options available to determined adversaries in the use of airborne modes of penetration presents special problems in providing significant delay times or effective deterrents. At present, there are few cost-effective barriers or deterrents to airborne intrusion in use at facilities other than those provided by the natural environment, such as power lines, poles, etc. Helicopters and small fixed-wing and short-takeoff-and-landing aircraft pose a significant threat of intrusion by adversaries at some high-security facilities such as prisons, power plants, and government installations. All types of airborne vehicles can be considered intrusion threats when used in conjunction with other vehicles.

Airborne threat vehicles are classified as powered, nonpowered, intrusion, and intrusion/escape. Each type has features that may be either advantageous or not to the adversary, and the selection will be the one that best satisfies the attack scenario, for example, a fast escape vehicle such as a helicopter, rather than a spectacular, but slow, hot-air balloon. The use of some types of airborne threats can be partially dismissed, such as intrusion and escape by hot-air balloon, glider, or parachute. Deterrents against helicopters, a more likely threat, are usually effective against other types of aircraft. If the defined threat includes the use of airborne vehicles, delay estimates should reflect the delays that remain after bypass of exterior barriers. Airborne vehicles may be detected through the use of radars, acoustics, and human observation. The VA team should ensure that the site has clear, unambiguous, plans and procedures for dealing with an airborne assault if this is part of the defined threat.

Waterborne-Attack Barriers

Waterborne attacks should be evaluated whenever an asset is located within a site bounded at any point by water. Obvious targets include cooling systems for nuclear power plants, and ships at military facilities and commercial ports. Waterborne attacks are complicated by the fact that the attack may come from either the water surface or underwater. The delay expert should review the types of water barriers and sensors that are present to protect assets and the paths that lead to them. If the target is physically in the water, detection and delay must also be in the water, before the asset, to be effective. If the target is on shore, it may be possible to erect land-based barriers in the path of attack. Installation of simple buoys is valuable in delineating the protected area and determining an intruder's intent. Because many, if not all, waterways are open to the public, it is imperative to have a clear line of demarcation with appropriate warning signals. As with airborne attacks, the facility should have clear, unambiguous, plans and procedures for dealing with waterborne intrusions. Air-cushioned boats (hovercraft) are capable of traversing water and flat land at fairly high rates of speed without ever having to stop at the shoreline and they present a unique and potentially formidable threat to any near-shore facility.

Tie-Downs and Restraints

The use of tie-downs and security restraints can be a cost-effective addition to delay in any PPS. Tie-downs and restraints are used synonymously to refer to any means of securing assets at the point of storage or within a transportation vehicle. Tie-downs can take many forms ranging from simple steel angle covers to sophisticated containers that house an impressive array of cut-resistant materials and dispensable delay materials (see Dispensable Materials and Deployable Barriers). The use of restraints is usually reserved for protection of critical assets and is cost-effective, as the restraints are normally small and fairly simple. Even large tie-downs may be cost effective compared with other delay options. The use of tie-downs in close proximity to the asset can also limit the attack mode of the adversary and reduce the possibility of damage to a theft target. Tie-downs are one of the few delay elements that can help to minimize the efforts of an insider. By tying critical assets down, the chances of a simple grab and run by an insider are significantly reduced. Examples of tie-downs or restraints include shipping containers, chains, shelf covers, cages, nets, and locks.

Shipping and storage containers are usually not thought of as part of an access delay system, but they can add modest amounts of delay. This delay normally comes in the form of increased task time for removing a bulky container, such as a 55-gallon drum, or taking additional time to remove the desired asset from the container. By combining storage containers with simple tie-downs (or by fastening the container to the floor) delay time can be increased by a few tens of seconds. Simple restraints can take the form of chain tie-downs, shelving covers, bird cages, steel nets, and steel cages. These devices allow reasonable access to stored material by authorized personnel, but add an additional barrier to an adversary's path. One example of a simple restraint is shown in Figure 9-8.

Locks are usually considered an integral part of any PPS. When it comes to the use of padlocks on simple restraints, however, the cost often outweighs the potential benefits. In this case it may be more cost effective to use fine threaded bolts (in

Figure 9-8 Simple Shelf Restraint. Delay is added by installing expanded steel doors over the outside of the shelves. Although there is some operational impact, this system reduces the ability of a thief to quickly grab a valuable asset and escape.

significant quantities) in place of padlocks. By shrouding the bolt heads, the use of ratchets and box end wrenches can be eliminated, increasing adversary task time. More sophisticated restraints or those requiring control over access to an asset can use shrouded high-security padlocks.

Nonlethal Weapons

Nonlethal technologies have been evolving over the last two decades to address response gaps in the use-of-force continuum for both civilian and military law enforcement. Nonlethal weapons are defined as weapons that are explicitly designed and primarily used to incapacitate personnel or material, while minimizing fatalities, permanent injury to personnel, and undesired damage to property and the environment. This definition allows a broad array of technologies to be considered for nonlethal application. Nonlethal weapons include pepper spray, stun and bean bag guns, tasers, thermal heating devices, lasers, and very loud noise generators. By their nature, nonlethal technologies often exhibit a wider range of effects and less certainty in effectiveness as compared to their lethal counterparts. Successful nonlethal technologies must ultimately provide enhanced responses for security personnel. This implies technologies that provide reliable and significant effects at ranges sufficient to transition to greater force if necessary. Repeatable, significant, and demonstrated effectiveness for use in a specific application scenario is the key to evaluation of these devices. Security personnel will be reluctant to use nonlethal weapons if there is uncertainty in the effects of their use or if the lack of a consistent effect exposes them to additional risk. Current nonlethal weapons are typically used from close contact to tens of meters from potential adversaries. Any technologies used should be adaptable across a range of security operations, provide significant benefit in a variety of nonlethal application scenarios, and include complete training in their proper use and deployment. Although it is a low risk, any nonlethal technology has the potential to cause death or permanent injury under some conditions, and this must be part of the decision to use them.

Nonlethal weapons applications often involve deterring or subduing crowds, or individuals within crowds. Motivation of these adversaries is variable, but generally these threats are poorly armed and have limited capability to avoid incapacitating effects. Contrast this with the threats against high-security systems where access delay technologies are often installed. These threats are highly motivated with significant training, sophisticated weapons, and breaching tools and substantial knowledge of the security system design and operation. As a result, nonlethal weapons are not generally used at these facilities. Many nonlethal weapons have reduced effectiveness against persons using stimulant drugs such as crack cocaine and methamphetamines.

Dispensable Materials and Deployable Barriers

Activated dispensable materials (dispensables) are generally used to augment other barriers to delay or disrupt adversaries. These dispensables can be used to physically impede an adversary or to physiologically interfere with an adversary's sensory inputs, such as obscured vision, olfactory irritants, and impaired hearing. Examples of dispensables include sticky foam, rigid foam, aqueous foam, visual obscurants, and a variety of irritant and inflammatory chemicals. For access delay applications, the deployment of these materials is designed to be nonlethal. Some dispensables come with a high penalty in terms of cleanup and safety risk and must incorporate a high-reliability command and control activation system. The use of activated dispensable delay technologies can significantly increase overall access delay when used in conjunction with substantial passive barriers in high-security systems. Deployable barriers are objects such as entanglements and barbed steel bands that can be used alone or in combination with other dispensable materials to provide a synergistic delay effect.

Dispensables can be broken into two broad classes based on their function: entombing and blocking materials, and sensory interfering materials. Entombing and blocking materials include rigid foam, sticky foam, and rubble (i.e., rock and gravel and other materials such as sticky spray and slippery materials that can significantly increase the physical burden required to accomplish a task). These materials may be dispensed directly on the asset to be protected or they may be used to block access to it. The materials are effective because they physically impede the adversary. They also effectively obscure the location of the asset and anything else that may be entombed in them. Use of these agents requires thoughtful consideration of cleanup, toxicology, safety, command and control, and waste issues. The effectiveness of the foams can be increased significantly through the use of tie-downs, chains, cables, and deployable barriers.

Sensory interfering materials include obscurants such as cold chemical smoke, pyrotechnic smoke, glycol/water and mineral oil fogs, and aqueous foam. Sensory irritants and inflammatory agents, such as the riot control agents Ortho-Chlorobenzylidene Malononitrile (CS) and Oleoresin Capsicum (OC), are also included in this class of dispensables. Obscurants are effective because they reduce an adversary's vision. This requires additional time by the adversary to decide what he/she must do to succeed. Obscurants also force the adversary to be more cautious so as not to accidentally injure him/herself. Finally, additional time is consumed troubleshooting equipment problems that arise on the scene and improvising solutions. The delay effectiveness of visual obscurants also depends on the task to be performed; their effectiveness increases as the level of eye-hand coordination required to perform the task increases.

Sensory irritants and inflammatory agents can be used with the obscurants and, in some cases, mixed and dispensed simultaneously. Irritants are effective because they force the adversary into protective clothing and breathing equipment. This increases the heat stress on the adversary and makes working more difficult. The choice of agents is probably restricted to CS and OC. The effect of these agents on humans is either temporary incapacitation or physical encumbrance, depending on whether or not personal protective gear is worn. The desired effect is temporary incapacitation. If the adversary comes prepared and is dressed in protective gear, he/she is still encumbered, and work output will be significantly reduced as a result of heat exhaustion. The materials described here are effective in small doses and have large safety margins.

Dispensable materials are commonly evaluated through the use of delay enhancement factors. These factors are simple numeric multipliers that can be applied to a task done with and without the dispensable material. As an example, an obscurant may be assigned an enhancement factor of 1.5. This means that a simple activity such as unbolting a tie-down fixture, which takes 48 seconds in the clear, would take approximately 72 seconds in an obscured environment. Depending on the dispensable material used and the complexity of the task, delay enhancement factors can range from 1.1 to 6. It is unlikely these materials will be used in most industrial facilities, but if they are present, they should be evaluated for delay times by the VA team.

General Delay Subsystem Evaluation Factors

The following list summarizes the steps required for a good delay subsystem evaluation. Depending on the threat, asset, and type of facility, all or a subset of these steps may be used.

- Define the barrier in detail: wall, roof, door, composition, thickness, location, passive, active, etc.
- Define the adversary team in detail: number, skill, motivation, physical

attributes, tactics, protective gear; body armor, etc.
- Adversary transportation if part of threat. Vehicle size and attributes; trucks, heavy equipment, train, plane, helicopter, etc.
- Define the attack mode: deceit, stealth, force, overt, covert, insider
- Define the possible tool set: type, weight, size, power source, run time, carry or roll, etc. List all known tools and small arms that could be used. What tools if any, are needed to actually reach the target?
- How will adversary penetrate or bypass barriers: crawl through, walk through, see through, etc.
- Define the physical conditions surrounding the barrier: level terrain, hillside, underground, confined space, interior, exterior, size of work area, etc.
- Define the adversary's objective: theft (How heavy is the target? How big? Can it be made smaller?), sabotage, vandalism, publicity, etc.
- Brainstorm/formulate attack scenarios.
- Estimate/predict attack results, including adversary consequences such as collateral building damage or collapse, asset damage, wiring, lights, water, gases, quantify the probability of success (high, low, medium). Interior/exterior explosive overpressure versus distance, shrapnel, debris, smoke, etc.
- Determine which tasks could potentially be done simultaneously or which must be done sequentially.
- Select one or two credible attacks based on the preceding two steps. Which attacks have a reasonable probability of success with the least delay time?
- Step through the selected attacks and assign times to each step/task. Determine if there is applicable rate data that can be applied, extrapolated, or interpolated to the barrier in

question. If not, then testing or expert judgment is required.

- Apply plus or minus factors depending on the complexity of the tasks, endurance, unintended damage, overkill, protective force intervention, tool changes, fatigue, heat, body armor, etc.
- Total up the numbers and factors to arrive at a delay value.
- Have VA team review and concur.
- Consider novel attack method; determine if approach is truly feasible. If so, repeat process.
- Consider worst case scenarios, evolving threats, failing gracefully (the addition of one or two adversaries or new threat guidance should not cause the entire protection system to fail catastrophically).
- Look at the big picture. How many fences are there? Barriers? Distances between them? Type of barriers. Can they be attacked simultaneously? Concurrently? Protected fighting points (for both sides), blast protection areas.

Additional guidance on the evaluation of barrier delays is available through the U.S. DOE (2000).

Estimating Performance

Analysis of barriers depends on three major categories of performance criteria. These include:

1. Delay is a function of tool-set, adversary skill and knowledge, barrier location, and environmental conditions. The first two items are defined by the defined threat, and the last two are facility dependent. Compare barrier material to defined threat tools, make estimate of delay using guidance already described.
2. Detection before delay: If delay is present with no or limited detection, it is not effective.

3. Integration
   a. Alarm assessment aided by barrier delays
   b. Response personnel in protected locations
   c. Multiple barriers, balanced protection
   d. Consider operating environment

For qualitative estimates, establish a time definition for each category (high, medium, low), for example:

- Low: less than 3 minutes
- Medium: 3 to 10 minutes
- High: greater than 10 minutes

Note that this technique still requires some idea of the actual time a given adversary will take to penetrate a barrier using specific tools. To aid in this estimate, some nominal delay times are provided in Appendix F. Note that these are not real delay times, but rather relative values considering the tools and tactics listed. These values can be used as starting point for qualitative analyses.

Quantitative delay data ideally come from site-specific testing of the barriers in question by groups equipped as the defined threat. Unfortunately this is a very time-consuming process with correspondingly high costs. In lieu of actual testing, the VA team may rely on historical test data of similar systems or use data from demolition companies or safety estimates to approximate delay times for some tools and attacks.

Summary

This chapter described the access delay subsystem, its principles, components, and evaluation criteria. Consideration of the defined threat tools and capabilities, as well as barrier material, was repeatedly emphasized. Access delay is provided by both passive and active barriers. Passive delays include fences, gates, vehicle barriers, walls, floors, roofs, doors, windows, grilles, utility ports, and other elements. Active delays include nonlethal weapons, dispensable materials, and deployable barriers. Effective delay is always preceded by detection; without detection, barrier delay time is zero. Delay time estimates are made for each threat and barrier along adversary paths and are used in system analysis. Qualitative estimates use relative delay times, and quantitative estimates are established through testing or literature searches.

Reference

U.S. Department of Energy, 2000, Barrier Inspection, available at http://www.oa. doe.gov/guidedocs/0009pssig/sec5.pdf, April 25, 2005.

10

Data Collection—Response Subsystem

Response is the third and final function of a PPS that is evaluated during a VA. There are many ways to respond to a security event; the appropriate response depends on the defined threat, the value of the asset, the other risk management alternatives used at the facility, the risk tolerance of the enterprise, and legal considerations. Because of this range of possibilities, this discussion is limited to the major types of responses, the implications and effectiveness of these responses, and the primary evaluation criteria for each type. Response at a facility plays a large role in the VA of a PPS and may drive overall system effectiveness to quite a low value, even when effective detection and delay are present.

The key concepts discussed in this chapter include:

- An overview of the response function, including strategies
- Relationship between response performance measures and strategies

- Security communication and its contribution to system effectiveness
- Description of the performance measures used to evaluate response at a site

The background information for this chapter can be found in Chapter 12 of the *Design* textbook. At any given site, one or more response strategies may be in use, and this will affect data collection activities accordingly. It is assumed that for high-security sites, with an immediate, armed response, the VA team includes at least one team member skilled in response tactics and procedures to conduct the evaluation. In addition to the response strategy, security communication is a critical part of any response function, and must be considered during the VA.

Response Overview

Response at a site is a complex subject, but there are some basic principles and concepts that can be considered during an evaluation. The key information collected during the VA relates to two important and interrelated factors. The first is the time it takes for the desired response to be placed into effect; the second is the effectiveness of that response. These aspects of response are facilitated by reliable communication among the responders and with others. The time to respond is related to whether there is an immediate response, located either on-site or off-site. During the initial design and implementation of a PPS, each facility decides if the purpose of response is to react after a successful attack or to stop the adversary from completing a successful attack. This decision should be based on the PPS protection objectives—the defined threat and consequence of loss of the asset. The misalignment of response and protection objectives at a facility cause serious degradation of PPS effectiveness. For example, if the facility contains critical assets and the defined threat is even moderately motivated, the presence of an immediate response is required in an effective PPS.

Response can be broadly categorized as delayed or immediate. Delayed response refers to any after-the-event reaction, where preventing a successful attack is less important than initiating asset recovery or incident review procedures, or where evacuation of the facility is the response to an attack. Examples of delayed responses include review of surveillance tapes after an asset has been lost or damaged, incident investigation, asset tracking and recovery, criminal prosecution, or combinations of these procedures. Immediate response refers to the timely deployment of personnel to an intrusion to prevent undesirable events from occurring or to the immediate implementation of a mitigation procedure, such as evacuation, after a successful attack, to limit the effects of undesirable events. Immediate deployment of personnel is typically found at facilities with either on-site security guards or those with agreements with off-site groups, such as private security companies, local law enforcement, or military troops (in some locations), to respond when needed. These personnel are not always members of the security staff; this will be discussed further in the Immediate Response section. Generally speaking, if there is no immediate response to security events, there is a basic assumption that the asset can be lost and that this risk is acceptable. This may be acceptable when the asset value is low, the threat is not very capable or motivated, the frequency of the event (the probability of attack) is low, the asset is protected using another risk management alternative (i.e., insurance) rather than physical protection, or liability concerns limit the use of an immediate response. For critical assets, however, lack of an immediate response to a malevolent intrusion increases the risk of asset loss and therefore must be carefully considered during the VA.

The two measures of an immediate response are the time for arrival and neutralization effectiveness. The time it takes to arrive is used to establish interruption; neutralization is a measure of response success, given arrival. Interruption is a measure of the detection, delay, communication, and response functions of the PPS and is represented by the probability of interruption (P_I). Neutralization measures response force numbers, training, tactics, and use of any weapons or equipment and is represented by the probability of neutralization (P_N). The use of these two terms to measure overall PPS effectiveness was described in Chapter 1; additional information about how these measures are used is provided in Chapter 11. In addition, the VA team must estimate the probability of communication (P_C), which is essential for an effective immediate response.

Interruption refers to arrival of response personnel at a location that will prevent the adversary from progressing in their attack. Interruption may be accomplished with one person or multiple personnel, depending on the threat. For example, arrival of one person at a location may be sufficient to scare away teenage vandals, but more motivated threats may require more capable response personnel. For low to medium threats, interruption alone may be an effective response, but for more capable medium to high threats, neutralization of the adversary may become necessary. Interruption depends on reliable, accurate, and fast alarm reporting and assessment, as well as dependable communication and effective deployment to the proper location. These are all elements of the PPS.

Neutralization refers to any confrontation between the adversary and responders, and is defined as defeat of the adversary. Some threats may require more than just response presence in order to be defeated, and neutralization is used to measure this aspect of response effectiveness. Effectiveness elements include response tactics, procedures such as use of force and after-detainment actions, training, number of personnel who respond to the alarm, and the equipment they carry. Neutralization, then, is more a measure of training and capability. Neutralization may use the entire force continuum including presence (interruption), verbal commands, physical restraint, intermediate force weapons such as batons and pepper spray, or deadly force (at some high-security locations). The techniques used depend on the defined threat, but the response force must be at least equal to the adversary in terms of equipment, weapons, and number to successfully neutralize the adversary.

Communication among all responders during an attack is required to maintain contact, share information, and coordinate tactics or procedures. Generally, this is accomplished through the use of hand-held radios, but other methods, such as land-based and cellular telephones, pagers, and duress alarms are also used. The method of communication

in use at a facility is part of the evaluation of response at a site and is discussed later in the Response Communications section.

In combination with response capability and performance, the response strategy must also be considered. The basic response strategies used include deterrence, denial, containment, and recovery. There must be an alignment of response strategy with the threat and asset value, or system effectiveness will be degraded. Data collection sheets that can be used during the response subsystem evaluation are provided in Appendix D.

Response Strategies

There are several general response strategies that can be used at any given facility; some high-security sites with multiple critical assets use more than one strategy. Because the response strategy plays a major role in how a facility is evaluated during a VA, a brief discussion of each strategy, examples of when they are used, and the key principles of each follow. It should be noted that the analysis does not differentiate between on-site responders who are direct employees or contractors. The time to arrive and effectiveness after arrival are the key evaluation criteria, not the employment relationship with the facility. It may be true that some responses are aided or hindered by the employment status of the responders, but this effect is captured in the performance estimates.

Deterrence
One common response strategy when on-site security personnel are present is deterrence. This approach is used to discourage some low-level threats from attacking a site by presenting the appearance of very tight security, thereby suggesting that an attack would not be successful. This strategy is used at almost all private and government sites. For this

strategy to be effective, security personnel must be visible and appear to be capable. They must be consistently responsive to all real or potential intrusions. Any patrols must be truly random (unpredictable in their route and time) and response to an incident or intrusion should be timely and effective (i.e., if the threat is well armed, the response should not be an unarmed patrol without a duress alarm).

Because this strategy relies on the adversary's perception that they are not likely to succeed, this approach will work only against less capable or motivated threats. For example, vandals may be discouraged from spray painting graffiti on buildings if they believe they will be observed and caught, but more motivated and skilled criminals may not be deterred from a theft attack. To illustrate this point, consider shoplifting. Each year, millions of dollars are spent to implement security technology and services designed to deter and prevent shoplifting, yet each year retail outlets continue to report significant losses to shoplifters (Jack L. Hayes International, 2003). Although it is agreed that never being attacked is a desirable state, the shoplifting example shows that deterrence alone cannot be relied on to protect assets. Where deterrence is the only or primary response function, assets should have low consequence of loss, and be covered by other risk management alternatives such as insurance.

In truth, deterrence is not really a protection strategy, but is rather an anticipated result of implementation of security measures at a facility. This can be an effective approach, but the absence of attack does not prove PPS effectiveness. Deterrence cannot be discounted, but it is risky to assume that this means that the PPS will be effective if an adversary is not deterred (i.e., they attack anyway). Any well-designed PPS will have some deterrence value, but more important, it will also protect assets against more motivated

and capable threats who are willing to take more risk to achieve their objectives. For example, an armed intruder might not be deterred by the presence of unarmed contract security guards (Meeks, 2005).

Denial

For some critical assets or production facilities, such as hazardous chemical, biological, and nuclear materials or toxic waste, where release of these materials into the environment through sabotage would cause many injuries, deaths, or contamination, a denial strategy is required. Denial refers to the protection of material by preventing adversary access to areas where materials are stored or to vital equipment used to process the material. For a successful sabotage event to occur, the adversary only has to complete the attack on the material and cause the release; capture of the adversary after a successful release does not prevent the consequence of the attack. While many sites use safety monitoring and controls to mitigate release of material, these controls and equipment may also be targets of the attack. At facilities where hazardous material is present, a denial strategy may be the optimal response, particularly for capable and determined adversaries.

For a denial strategy to be effective, an immediate and effective response force is required. This means that there must be a sufficient number of on- or off-site personnel who are equipped as well as the defined threat and can prevent successful sabotage. These responders are often armed, highly trained, and organized into tactical teams.

Containment

A containment strategy is generally used when the adversary goal is theft of an asset. Containment means that the adversary is not allowed to leave the site with the asset; that is, they are contained on-site and the theft attempt is not successful. This strategy is usually reserved for sites with high-value or high-consequence assets, such as large banks, museums with valuable collections, precious gem or metal repositories, or hazardous material storage locations. Prisons also use a containment strategy, but they are attempting to prevent inmates from leaving the facility, not the theft of assets.

As with denial, the most effective containment strategy will provide sufficient numbers of properly equipped personnel to prevent an adversary from successfully leaving a facility with the asset. This approach has an advantage over a denial strategy in that containment for a theft scenario (not a prison escape) can allow more time for the response, as the adversary must get to the asset, acquire it, and then leave the site. A containment strategy allows the response force to wait at strategic positions around the site boundary to prevent adversary escape, whereas a denial strategy requires the response force to successfully prevent completion of the sabotage attack by the adversary. Containment does not eliminate adversary possession of the asset; it prevents them from leaving with the asset.

Recovery

In the event that deterrence or containment strategies fail, a backup approach is recovery of the stolen asset. Of course, this is not an effective approach for denial targets, as protection failure results in release of hazardous material. For other assets, the difference between a recovery strategy and a delayed response is not distinct. In most recovery strategies, the recovery is immediate (i.e., hot pursuit of the adversary as they speed away in their car). For some sites, there is an acceptance that assets may be lost for a period of time, and recovery of assets at some point in the future is the primary response. Recovery responses include investigation, tracking of assets, and fol-

low-up using criminal prosecution. Note that in this context, recovery refers to asset recovery, not recovery of facility operations after a natural disaster, accident, or sabotage event.

An effective recovery response assumes that the facility is prepared to lose the asset, temporarily or permanently, and that this loss will not compromise their business goals. As an example, if a thief successfully steals a proprietary formula for a new product, then makes copies and sells them, recovery of the original paper copy will not protect the enterprise from loss of the formula. In this case, the response is effective only if the formula is recovered before the information is shared with others. As noted in Chapter 7, Asset Tracking, several technologies can be used to aid in recovery responses. It is worth repeating that this implies that the facility can lose the asset for some period of time; if not, this is a vulnerability that will result in higher risk. For some high-value assets, a recovery plan is required as a never-to-be-exercised plan B. Requirements may stipulate that an effective containment strategy be in place to protect assets, but there may still be a need for a backup "what if" plan. In some cases, this requirement exists primarily to define and exercise agreements with local law enforcement agencies. Using this basic understanding of response strategies, the various response methods can now be discussed.

Delayed Response

In general, delayed response includes a spectrum of activities that are used to identify the individual responsible for the theft or sabotage of assets. Use of this type of response assumes that the asset can be lost, either permanently or temporarily. If, on the other hand, the asset meets criteria that make it too valuable to lose (as a result of consequence analysis), the VA team should note the discrepancy between protection objectives and system implementation and collect the data that documents this mismatch in expectations. Delayed responses include review of recorded video surveillance information, initiation of an investigation into asset loss or damage, attempts to recover the asset, and criminal prosecution. It is likely that some combination of these approaches will be used in a delayed response and evaluation of the equipment, procedures, and people used to support the recovery of the asset or criminal prosecution will be required.

Equipment

If the delayed response uses stored video images, there are a number of technical considerations that will be important to effective use of this information. In reality, this will come down to the effectiveness of the video capture system, which was described in some detail in Chapter 6. As discussed in that chapter, surveillance systems may not capture the person or other information of interest, particularly if a PTZ camera is not pointing at the affected area. If capture and storage of integrated sensor and video data are used, these images may be used to identify, apprehend, and prosecute the adversary, if they meet specific legal requirements. In this case, the evaluation criteria will default to the performance criteria used for the alarm assessment subsystem, including resolution, lighting, transmission of video data, and quality of the stored image. The information that must be captured to be legally admissible will vary with the jurisdiction; this will be discussed further in the next section on Procedures. In any case, the VA team should review the intended use of video equipment and inspect the equipment to ensure that it is appropriate, installed correctly, and functioning properly.

Many companies also use overt and covert methods to mark assets so they can be readily identified if stolen. Technology such as microdots, bar codes, RF tags, and other devices are commonly used to facilitate recovery operations. Note that some devices are easily removed, so their effectiveness may be limited. In this case, performance of the tracking devices would be degraded, as noted in Chapter 7. If these devices are in use, application equipment used to apply the device should be inspected to ensure it is in working order, and working spare reading equipment should be available, as they will likely be loaned to law enforcement personnel for use in the investigation.

It may be that employees played a part in the theft. If this is the case, any access control records, employee timekeeping records, and so forth may also be useful in an investigation. An inspection of any systems used to compile this information should be conducted to verify its existence and credibility.

Procedures

Procedural aspects of delayed response evaluation include those described in the chapter on alarm assessment, as well as a few others concerned with the handling and protection of the video images. For each jurisdiction, different criteria apply to the admissibility of stored video information. In general, these address issues such as percent of the image occupied by the suspect, the ability to definitively establish the location of the event, time and date stamp, and an image that shows the suspect in possession of an identifiable asset or using a weapon to assault an individual. To ensure that any captured video images can be used to successfully prosecute, it is suggested that attorneys and local law enforcement be consulted to determine the appropriate criteria for the jurisdiction. In addition, procedures should exist that describe how site personnel protect the stored media until turned over to law enforcement or other investigators. The chain of custody could be an issue during prosecution and stored media should be protected appropriately. In addition, other requirements may be imposed on digital versus analog storage techniques. Analog video tape has been successfully used in criminal prosecution of offenders; however, the jury is literally still out on the use of digital images. This is primarily due to the ease of altering digital images, using readily available commercial software. Many manufacturers incorporate watermarking or encryption so that tampered images can be identified, and some of these protection schemes have survived legal challenges. Once again, these constraints should be verified with local authorities. The degree of compliance with these evidence constraints, the documentation of procedures for meeting these constraints, and the ability of responsible personnel to properly follow established procedures should all be a part of the VA evaluation.

Recovery procedures should include ready access to property identification numbers, tags, or codes, which can be quickly provided to law enforcement. These lists should include details such as make and model, serial numbers, unique identifiers, and the locations of any covert devices on the asset. The existence and availability of these lists and the level of available information provided for important assets should be verified during a VA.

People

As with other aspects of the PPS, people play a large role in overall system effectiveness. This is particularly true in response, as most responses require the intervention of people. If investigation is a major aspect of the response, the credentials and qualifications of the investigators should be verified by the VA team. Generally, investigators are former members of law enforcement, who have considerable experience in conducting investigations. Background

checks should be conducted on investigators and use of this procedure should be confirmed by the VA team. The VA team should also review investigative procedures and ensure that documentation meets corporate and legal requirements, and that all cases are handled using proper administrative procedures, such as assigning case numbers, keeping accurate records, and that privacy rights and liability concerns are addressed during the investigation. In addition, case records should be stored in a secure environment and information should not be shared with anyone who is not part of the investigation.

Staff involved in investigations should receive periodic refresher training on legal updates, corporate policies and procedures, limitations to their investigative authority, and liability and privacy issues. The VA team should verify that all training requirements are current and in compliance with enterprise and legal requirements, and that investigators appropriately protect all case files.

Immediate Response

There are several varieties of immediate response, and in some cases, they blend to form a continuous strategy. Much like the use of force, they may escalate from vocal command to intermediate force to deadly force; response may begin as an effort to deter adversary actions, and if that fails, may progress to an effort to keep adversaries away from the asset. If that fails, the strategy may expand into an effort to prevent adversaries from getting away with the asset. If the response is unable to keep the adversaries from getting away, it may be possible for the response to chase the adversary and attempt to recover the asset. And if all else fails, the strategy may shift to a delayed response strategy and focus on recovering from a successful theft.

Many large industrial or government sites have an immediate on-site security presence. These personnel are often part of the security organization, but at some sites they are part of the safety or medical organizations. Although the best responses to security events would be expected to use trained security personnel, other types of response are possible that would aid in security incidents. Any personnel who are immediately dispatched in response to a potential security event or actual intrusion should be evaluated for their effectiveness. Measures of effectiveness include response time (a measure of interruption capability), or tactics, equipment readiness, and training (measures of neutralization capability, given interruption). Measures that will be used in the VA depend on the defined threat and the corresponding response strategy. In addition, when estimating response time the VA team must also define arrival. For example, the response time can end with the arrival of the first responder, with a number equal to the defined threat, or something else. Once this time interval is defined, it should be used for all response time estimates. Several immediate response techniques are described in the following sections. They include sounding evacuation or shelter alarms to the surrounding community, observe and report, dispatch of unarmed on-site security guards, response by local law enforcement, and response by armed security personnel.

General Warning Alarms

In many instances, the cost of providing a response capable of neutralizing a likely adversary is prohibitive and a risk management decision is made not to incorporate an immediate on-site response. General warning alarms are typically used at facilities such as dams, hazardous or toxic material processing plants, refineries, and prisons. In these cases, the response is not to protect the asset and interrupt or neutralize the adversary, but rather to warn people in the surrounding area that an

undesired event has occurred and limit the consequences of the attack. Strictly speaking, this is protection of off-site assets (i.e., residents of the surrounding community) and is meant to reduce injuries to these residents; protection of the on-site assets is not the primary goal of these response systems. These responses are substantially the same as the response to natural disasters, which is entirely acceptable and one method of mitigating consequences of a successful malevolent attack.

Because it does not require much time to activate warning alarms and may not take long to act (think fire drills), the system response time required may be short. As such, this type of response is best when detection happens quickly enough to allow as much time as possible for the evacuation or shelter. As long as detection (including assessment) happens while there is still enough time for the surrounding community to respond to the alarm, this response can be effective. In addition, a high nuisance alarm rate will have an adverse impact on system effectiveness. If there are routine nuisance alarms, but no timely detection and assessment, the system will not be effective—imagine the disruption to a community where nuisance alarms happen regularly. If the town is evacuated every time there is a nuisance alarm, residents would ultimately lose confidence in the system and eventually not respond as desired. It is assumed that the local population understands the procedure to use and will follow it to remain safe. On the other hand, it is possible to test segments of the population to determine the effectiveness of the response procedure, and it may be a responsibility of the facility to periodically test the response to such alarms. If so, logs and results of these tests should be included in the VA review.

Observe-and-Report

This technique is used most often at facilities where unarmed on-site security guards are available, but there is no desire to have them interact with adversaries. The general idea is to have guards detect and assess alarms, then ask for assistance from local law enforcement. In some areas, as a result of high levels of nuisance alarms, local law enforcement may not respond unless unlawful activity has been confirmed by a person, either through live observation or alarm assessment (Stacom, 2005). After local law enforcement has been notified, the guards continue to track the attackers but do not engage them. They may record adversary acts, observe the attack from a distance (to serve as witnesses later), and collect as much supporting information as they can to aid in identification, apprehension, and prosecution of the attackers. This can be a risky approach because the mere presence of security guards could be justification for a victim to claim that they expected the guard to intervene, which could lead to a legal liability. If this response strategy is used, careful review of the procedures used and compliance with local legal requirements are of prime importance to prevent these unintended consequences.

The time for law enforcement to respond will determine overall response effectiveness. If law enforcement arrives in time to see the attack and apprehend the adversary before the attack has been completed, the response would be effective. If not, the response may be degraded, depending on the definition of acceptable response. This type of response by local law enforcement should be established beforehand between the site and law enforcement and formally documented. Details such as the location law enforcement should respond to, how on-site personnel will assist, nominal time to respond, and what other law enforcement activities have priority should be described. It is recommended that periodic practice exercises be conducted between the facility and local law enforcement to ensure an orderly and reliable response to events. The VA team should

review agreements and any records of successful responses by law enforcement and use this to judge response effectiveness. If there is no formal agreement, no practice exercises have been conducted, or records indicate that law enforcement cannot respond in time, response effectiveness would be degraded. Because law enforcement must serve many roles in the community, it is likely that the effectiveness of this type of response will be degraded to allow for this potential conflict. Note that this discussion assumes that local law enforcement is called only on a valid intrusion; more often they respond to nuisance alarms because the facility PPS does not provide timely and accurate alarm assessment, which further degrades response effectiveness. Since the attacks on 9/11, many industrial sites rely completely on local law enforcement for response, which makes their practiced interaction even more critical.

Dispatch of Unarmed Security Personnel

A similar response to observe-and-report is the immediate deployment of unarmed on-site security guards, but in this case they will attempt to interrupt and possibly neutralize the adversary. This response is effective if the responders have the advantage, either because of numbers or equipment, including non-lethal weapons. If the adversary has the advantage, however, the responders may be unable to fully interrupt or successfully neutralize the attack.

The time it takes these responders to arrive depends on the distance they are from the desired location, the speed of detection and assessment, and their deployment to the correct location. In addition to these aspects, evaluation should consider how the responders are trained to work together and to follow procedures on use of force and detainment. If the responders are given any equipment, such as handcuffs, pepper spray, batons, or other intermediate force weapons, there should be an initial training class and periodic refresher training on the use of these weapons. These classes should rigorously cover the proper use of force against intruders. Training on how to approach suspects or disturbed individuals and request their cooperation, and how to escalate engagements within the force continuum should also be included. Training records and documentation should be examined during the VA to verify compliance with all policies and procedures.

Other procedures include notification lists with all contact information, use of security incident reporting procedures and forms, how security incidents and responses are tracked, and any after action reviews or closeouts that are used. If procedures are not documented, guard training is not appropriate for their equipment, and current records on guard training are not maintained, response effectiveness will be degraded.

Dispatch of Armed Security Personnel

At some high-security sites, the use of armed on- or off-site responders is required. Armed response can be provided by a dedicated on-site group, local law enforcement, or in some cases, military personnel. As with unarmed responders, the response time depends on timely detection, distance from the deployed location, and deployment to the correct location. When armed response is used, it is assumed that responders understand the rules of engagement and use of force, and that they are authorized to use deadly force, if needed. Training records, as well as periodic recertification in weapons proficiency, should be verified during the VA. Any practical exercises performed by the responders as part of their training should also be reviewed to verify that required response times can be

met and that practice in tactical response takes place on a periodic basis. Limited Scope Performance Tests (LSPTs) can be performed to determine whether training is correctly executed in the field. These tests take a small slice of a response condition and test it in controlled and safe circumstances. LSPTs should be developed before testing and should contain clear objectives, measures, and performance criteria to be useful.

Clearly, an armed response is the highest level of response a site can implement. Armed responders are generally considered able to neutralize the adversary using deadly force under appropriate and well-defined conditions. For sites where these responses are used, the VA team must evaluate the probability of both interruption and neutralization to aid in overall system effectiveness.

In addition to the type of response and use of interruption and neutralization to measure the effectiveness of the response function, it is also necessary for the VA team to evaluate response communication before, during, and after an adversary attack. This part of the evaluation will result in an estimate of the probability of communication.

Response Communications

Security communications consist of the people, procedures, and technology used to share information among members of the response force during both normal and response operations. During normal operations, security communications may be required for conducting entry control, visitor escort, patrols, and other security functions (for an on-site security group). During response to an attack, communications are essential for organizing responders, directing them to the scene of the emergency, and successfully interrupting or neutralizing the adversary. Accurate and reliable communication is required for both interruption and neutralization.

The overall performance measure used is probability of communication (P_C), which is a measure of confidence that information will flow through the system, starting with alarm reporting and ending with deployment and engagement with the adversary. For a delayed response using video surveillance or assessment, P_C depends on the transmission system used to capture and store alarm and video information for later review. If the delayed response results from the manual discovery of missing items, P_C is not a useful measure, because it is assumed that discovery initiates the appropriate response, although this is not always the case. (We have been to many sites where we have been told assets are missing, but no one thought it meant anything so it wasn't reported.)

The two levels of security communications for an immediate response include alerting responders that the facility is under attack, and sharing attack details and tactical information among responders. Communications are a vital part of any PPS; the proper performance of many other security elements depends on communications. The assumption that clear and timely communications will exist during a security event can have significant and costly ramifications if this assumption proves incorrect. The VA team must carefully evaluate the effects of losing communications during a security response.

For an effective response to an attack, communication must be timely and reliable. In addition, the communications network may need to be resistant to eavesdropping, deception, and jamming. The most common system for maintaining effective control and coordination of the response force at a site is through the use of radios. In most cases, the radio systems used for response force communications are conventional, narrow-band frequency modulation (FM), clear-voice radio systems. Clear voice means that no attempt has been made to encode or scramble voice transmissions. Conventional FM radio systems have several advantages including simplicity, ease of operation, efficiency, and low cost.

Radio Communication System

In a conventional radio system, a fixed frequency or set of frequencies is shared with other users. If proper transmission procedures are followed and strict communication discipline observed, routine daily business can be conducted efficiently. The maximum range for reliable communication between two radios is limited, depending on the power of the transmitter, but generally 1 to 3 miles. More powerful transmitters and better receivers can be used that will extend this range to over 10 miles. Depending on the site location, configuration, and building construction, however, these systems may still experience loss of signal at some locations across the site. Other radio communication systems can be used that incorporate encryption and frequency hopping; however, these systems are expensive and complex, and not typically found at most facilities.

Conventional clear-voice radio systems have some serious disadvantages. Anyone possessing a conventional receiver, tuned to the proper frequency, can easily monitor transmissions as long as they are within range. Even if the frequency is unknown, scanners can automatically search and determine the frequency. There should be facility radio communication policies and procedures that dictate what information is revealed during routine operations and an attempt to minimize transmission of information that could be used by an adversary. Radio communications should be limited to only those transmissions that are absolutely necessary. More critical information can be communicated using more secure methods such as telephones and intercoms. Information an adversary might try to collect could include the size of the security force and their weapons, predictability of patrol routines and response procedures, locations of assets and how they are protected, the dedication of response personnel to protecting the facility, names of the response force members and where they are posted (information that can be used to assist in an attack), and the types of communication technologies used and their weaknesses.

When evaluating a communications network for a fixed-site facility, the VA team must consider the ability of the defined threat for eavesdropping, deception, and radio jamming. Although this is not a threat capability at most facilities, it is possible at high-security sites. Eavesdropping is unauthorized monitoring of information carried over a radio network. Deception is the transmission of misleading messages within the security communications network by an adversary that either confuse or deceive security personnel. Jamming consists of an adversary's attempts to prevent radio communications either through physical destruction of communications equipment or through intentional transmission of a disruptive radio signal on the security radio net. Jamming is considered the highest threat to security communications and is also the most difficult to protect against.

RF systems are most vulnerable to jamming because the adversary can jam the channel from a remote location. They can obtain the system operating frequencies either by monitoring transmissions or by obtaining readily available frequency documentation. Jamming may then begin by tuning a transmitter to the proper frequency. If the jamming signal is of sufficient power, it could mask the true signal to such an extent that effective communication becomes severely degraded or destroyed. Jamming should be considered a realistic threat because of the ease with which it can be accomplished and its degradation of the P_C. If jamming is a capa-

bility of the defined threat, standard operating procedures should be developed and practiced to adjust to this possibility.

Developing a high degree of communication resistance to eavesdropping, deception, and jamming is difficult but not impossible. Low cost- and operational-impact techniques that are used to protect radio communications include minimizing dependence on radios, maximizing the survivability of the radio network, and practicing jamming exercises against a simulated attack. Minimizing dependence on radio communications reduces an adversary's effectiveness not only in eavesdropping on the radio network but also in the deception and jamming of it. Some ways to reduce this dependence are to use an automated alarm communication and display system, send communications over alternate links, and preplan response procedures. The survivability of the radio network is characterized by its ability to continue to function during jamming and deception. There are several methods of maximizing the survivability of the radio network against jamming. These methods include the use of codes, identification of radio dead spots (locations where radio signals are blocked), jamming recognition training, practice in anti-jamming procedures, and proper maintenance of radio equipment. Periodic training exercises instill radio procedures as second nature in response personnel and help maintain their proficiency during security responses. Because of the inherent confusion and stress during a response, the use of unfamiliar procedures by security personnel would degrade the P_C. Even simple procedures, such as switching to a backup radio channel, are ineffective unless they have been rehearsed several times by all responders. The possible loss of radio communications requires that alternate communications options are available. Some alternate communications means to consider are telephones, intercoms, cell phones, and pagers.

In addition to standard operation, many radio manufacturers offer hand-held radios equipped with a duress button that sends an emergency signal to a central monitoring point, normally the alarm communication and display subsystem location. Duress is an operational alarm condition that the communication network must be capable of handling if duress alarms are part of the response subsystem. After notification of the duress alarm, critical communications should switch to another predetermined channel to deny the adversary any additional knowledge about response force actions. This capability is most valuable if users can press the button without endangering themselves or others. For this reason, most hand-held radios include a simple switch that can be covertly activated by the user or at a sudden change in radio orientation, such as from vertical to horizontal. The latter type of activation is subject to a certain nuisance alarm rate because there are many innocent activities that can cause these changes. This is a good example of the need for strict adherence to radio use procedures.

During a VA, a series of radio coverage tests must be conducted to characterize the effectiveness of the radio network at the facility. To conduct these tests, points are selected across the site, and tests are performed at each point to and from several fixed locations. Test points inside and outside of buildings should be included. The percentage of correct transmissions for each test is the measure of transmission success. If dead spots are found in critical areas, P_C should be degraded. Additional guidance on radio and duress communication testing are available from DOE (2005).

Radio Maintenance

A security force without enough functioning radios for its communications needs will be unable to maintain a high P_C. A sufficient supply of radios, antennas,

and batteries should exist at a facility to allow a radio for each on-duty responder. This planning ensures that the current shift will always have enough working radios and charged batteries to cover the shift. Regular maintenance should be performed on both vehicle and base-stationed radios, as well as for hand-held radios. The maintenance schedule should include calibration of radios and conditioning of batteries, and this schedule should be verified by the VA team. Responders should inspect their radios at the beginning and end of each shift and promptly report any deficiencies; sufficient spare radios should be available so that these defective radios can be replaced immediately and not compromise communication capability. For reliable radio communications, each responder should keep external radio connections clean, routinely inspect radios to ensure that there are no broken components, secure antenna connections, and protect the radio from severe weather or physical damage.

Battery analyzers should be used to determine whether the radio battery is acceptable for use. These analyzers cycle a battery through charge, discharge, and recharge under controlled conditions to determine whether the battery is acceptable for use. Batteries that do not meet manufacturers' specifications should be discarded and replaced. Batteries are removed from the radios for testing (and replaced with known good ones so that the radios are not out of service during the testing period).

A critical factor in communication is the interoperability of radios among response groups. A tragic example of this was the incompatibility between fire and police radios on 9/11 (Dwyer and Flynn, 2005). For high-security sites, where different groups of responders are expected to provide support, this issue is part of the evaluation and testing that is used to estimate communication probability. During the VA, radio maintenance and operating procedures, spares on hand, and interoperability of radios if multiple groups will respond should be confirmed and evaluated. Deficiencies in any area will result in a lower estimate of P_C.

Operational Issues

Incident management is a large part of any effective security (or other abnormal event) response. Many facilities have a set procedure for managing not only the immediate response to a security event, but also how and what information is released to the public, notification to corporate headquarters, and initiation of any restoration activities that may be required. These systems generally have a specified command center and designated personnel who staff the center during an event. If an incident command center is in use in a facility, its effect on overall response effectiveness should be evaluated. The performance measures of the system will still be arrival time, P_I, P_N, and P_C, but the incident management structure should not prevent effective response. The command center should have access to all the same communication links used by responders, and should use a predetermined chain of command, which could vary depending on the incident type. For example, the security manager might be in charge during a security incident, and a public relations person could be in charge during a facility accident. If incident management adds delays in dispatch, neutralization, or communication, response effectiveness should be degraded.

Estimating Performance

One simple but effective response analysis tool is the response storyboard. Basically, this is a series of snapshots in time showing where responders and intruders are located. This is illustrated in Figure 10-1. The tool works by starting a response test

and noting the location of each group (or each person in each group, if multiple responders and adversaries are expected) at periodic intervals. The interval can vary depending on the expected length of the attack. This is most useful for immediate on-site responses. These storyboards have been used to document the effects of incomplete procedures, lack of training or coordination, confusion over site layout, and inadequately equipped response personnel.

The actual performance measures and estimates used for analysis depend on the response strategy and the presence of an immediate response. For delayed responses, it is sufficient to ensure that there is timely and accurate detection, and that legally admissible and usable video information is captured as evidence. This requires a fully functional communication system, limited in this case to integrated sensing and video assessment, and transmission of this information to a storage location. This can be approximated using P_{AD}, as described in Chapter 8.

For an immediate response, response time, neutralization capability, and P_C are the key performance measures of the subsystem. In qualitative evaluation, response time is estimated as high if there is interruption while the adversary is still on-site, medium if enough information has been collected that the adversary can be apprehended and prosecuted after the fact (observe-and-report), or low if the adversary successfully completes a theft or sabotage attack. The latter two will result in loss of the asset. These qualitative labels and definitions are used so there is consistency in performance estimates for the different PPS functions. For example, a high P_D and high delay time are indicators of good performance. In a like manner, a high response time estimate using these definitions also supports good performance (which is somewhat counterintuitive!). These definitions can be changed so that response time labels refer to the actual

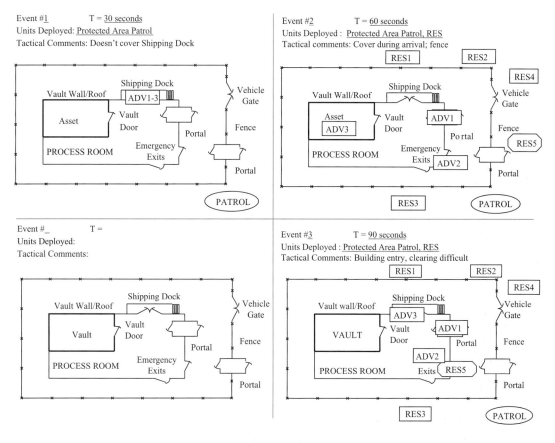

Figure 10-1 Response Storyboard. This technique shows the position of responders and adversaries at periodic intervals during an attack. It can be used to document an actual response, an exercise, or a walk-through of certain attack scenarios, which can show deficiencies in procedures, communication, or other aspects of response.

amount of time it takes to respond, much the same as delay times. In this case, a high response time means that it will take a relatively long time to respond, which may be an indication of bad performance. The choice of labels and definitions is left to the VA team but should be defined in advance and consistently applied throughout the analysis. If neutralization is also a response capability, interruption must first be rated as high, and response effectiveness will depend on evaluation of the responders to stop a successful attack. This capability can be evaluated using high, medium, and low levels, where neutralization is always effective, usually

effective, or rarely effective, respectively. Other descriptors can be used as desired, but successful neutralization requires a high P_I.

Response subsystem performance categories and criteria include:

1. Response Strategy (denial, containment, recovery)
   a. Must align with PPS objectives (defined threat and consequence of loss of asset)
   b. Procedures followed and practiced
   c. Training in use of force and detainment procedures

2. Estimate Response Time, including alarm receipt, assessment, dispatch, and deployment
   a. High—interruption while adversary is still on-site
   b. Medium—enough information has been collected that adversary can be apprehended and prosecuted
   c. Low—adversary has successfully completed theft or sabotage attack
3. Estimate Probability of Communication
   a. During all facility states and under normal, abnormal, and attack conditions
   b. Alternate means of communication if radios are not operating through jamming, damage, or failure
   c. No dead spots
   d. Radios are maintained properly
   e. Each responder has own radio
   f. Proper training and practice of procedures
4. Estimate Probability of Neutralization
   a. Responders have the advantage in numbers, equipment, or other areas
   b. Responders have trained together and work as a coordinated team
   c. Incident reports show effective neutralization

For estimates of each measure to be high, all criteria in the category must be high, and there must be alignment in response strategy and PPS objectives. If not, estimates will be no better than medium. Each category will be low if any criteria are low.

In a quantitative analysis, the response force time is measured under various response conditions and facility states, for each asset, and this information is provided to the analyst. P_N can be estimated by comparison of the response force numbers and capability to the adversary's numbers and capabilities or through the use of computer simulation tools. In addition, estimates can be made by reviewing actual or simulated table-top exercise results, and the results of any actual intrusion events. Figure 10-2 shows a rough estimator that can be used as a starting point for P_N when computer simulations are not used. P_I will be calculated during the analysis, using the response force time and other PPS performance measures.

If computer simulations are used, all PPS performance measures are input to the simulation, then response force locations, weapons, and other capabilities are described and the simulation is run. P_N is estimated by the number of simulations won out of the total. In addition, these tools provide additional data, such as how many attackers and responders are wounded or still alive at various points in the engagement, how ammunition was used, and how much time has elapsed. For computer simulations, a neutralization simulation expert will be required on the VA team, who provides the following capabilities:

- Determine the scope of any simulation analysis
- Identify events that cannot be accurately modeled in any simulations and the impact of this limitation on determination of response force effectiveness
- Identify the key objective of any simulations (e.g., determine if the security force can successfully defeat the adversaries with an 80% probability)
- Identify administrative controls used to attempt to overcome limitations in the simulation
- Oversee the conduct of the analysis to ensure adherence to established protocols
- Facilitate discussions among the participants concerning the validity and outcome of each simulation based on the accuracy of the model, rules of engagement, operator actions, win/

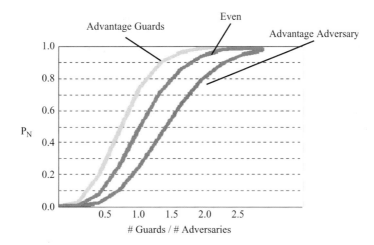

Figure 10-2 Rough Neutralization Estimate. For a very rough calculation of P_N, this chart can be used. The adversary could have the advantage by being armed versus an unarmed response, superior numbers, or better tactics. The example shows data based on high threats, but the ratio can be used as a starting point for neutralization against any threat.

loss criteria, operator problems, system problems, etc
- Monitor final run validity and outcome

Estimates for probability of communication generally start at 0.95 if all performance criteria are met, and test results support this. Tests should be performed that verify communication across the entire site, under all facility states, and for all asset locations. These results can be summarized by an overall value, but different attack scenarios may show that there are weaknesses in communication and P_C should be adjusted to reflect this.

Summary

This chapter described the evaluation of the response subsystem at a facility during a VA. The key information collected during the VA relates to two important and interrelated factors: the time it takes for the desired response to arrive at the proper location and the effectiveness of that response. These aspects of response are facilitated by reliable communication among the responders and with others. In addition, it is important to understand the response strategy in use at the facility. Response may use one of several strategies, including deterrence, denial, containment, and recovery. At some large facilities with multiple distributed targets, combinations of these may be used. A related matter is whether there is an immediate or delayed response. The performance measures used in response evaluation include response time, probability of neutralization, and probability of communication. For delayed responses, the probability of assessed detection may serve as the best measure of response effectiveness.

References

Dwyer, J., and Flynn, K., *102 Minutes: The Untold Story of the Fight to Survive Inside the Twin Towers*, New York: Henry Holt and Company, 2005.

Jack L. Hayes International, 2003, Fifteenth (15th) Annual Retail Theft Survey, available at http://securitysolutions.

com/news/security_shoplifting_employee_theft/, April 26, 2005.

Meeks, B.N., March 9, 2005, Are 'rent-a-cops' threatening security? Experts: guards are ill-trained, ill-equipped to handle threats, MSNBC, available at http://www.msnbc.msn.com/id/70929 09, April 28, 2005.

Stacom, D., Police Propose Fines for False Alarms, *Hartford Courant* (Connecticut), March 16, 2005, B4.

U.S. DOE, Radio/Duress Communication Tests, available at http://www.oa.doe. gov/guidedocs/0009pssig/AppC.pdf, April 29, 2005.

11

Analysis

At this point, all the appropriate data have been collected and analysis of the PPS can begin. There are two basic techniques for analysis—compliance-based and performance-based. Depending on the specific site, protection objectives, the importance of security in the overall enterprise, and the project scope, either method or a combination of both will be the appropriate choice.

The key concepts discussed in this chapter include:

- An overview of the two major analysis techniques
- A description of the six-step analysis process for performance-based evaluation
- Sample qualitative and quantitative analysis to demonstrate how the process is applied

The background information for this chapter can be found in Chapter 14 of the *Design* textbook. In addition, it is assumed that for quantitative analysis, the reader has access to the EASI model (or equivalent) and computer models or data to support neutralization probabilities.

As noted in Chapter 1, the measure of overall PPS effectiveness is described as system effectiveness and is expressed as a probability, P_E. P_E is determined using two terms: the probability of interruption (P_I) and the probability of neutralization (P_N). Performance-based analysis techniques use adversary paths, which assume that a sequence of adversary actions is required to complete an attack on an asset. The path may start and end outside the facility (outsider threat, theft goal), it may start outside and end inside the facility (outsider, sabotage), or it may start inside and end inside or outside (insider, sabotage, or theft). It is important to note that P_E varies with the threat. As the threat capability increases, performance of individual security elements or the system as a whole can decrease.

P_I is the cumulative probability of detection at the critical detection point (CDP) along a specific path. The CDP is defined as the point on the path where path delay just exceeds response force arrival time. The CDP is found by starting at the end of the path, and adding up path delays until this value just exceeds response force time. P_N is a measure of the likelihood that the response force will be successful in overpowering or defeating the adversary given interruption.

Analysis Overview

There are two basic analysis approaches used in a VA—compliance- or performance-based. Compliance-based approaches depend on conformance to specified policies or regulations; the metric for this analysis is the presence of specified equipment and procedures. Performance-based approaches, on the other hand, evaluate how each element of the PPS operates and what it contributes to overall system effectiveness. As discussed in Chapter 2, the use of compliance (or feature-based) systems is only effective against low threats, when assets have a low consequence of loss, or when cost-benefit analyses have been performed that show that physical protection measures are not the most cost-effective risk management alternative. A compliance-based analysis is easier to perform because the measure of system effectiveness is presence of prescribed PPS equipment, procedures, and people. The analysis consists of a review of facility conformance to the compliance requirements, the use of checklists to document presence or absence of components, and a deficiency report that notes where the facility is out of compliance. The VA report summarizes these findings and the facility makes improvements according to enterprise policy. Because the premise of this text is that overall system effectiveness is the goal of a VA, and that dollars spent on PPS elements result in improved protection while also complying

with requirements, the remainder of this chapter addresses performance-based analysis.

Although qualitative and quantitative analysis techniques are discussed separately, both approaches are used in a performance-based analysis; the unique aspect to quantitative analysis is the use of numerical measures for PPS components. The analysis process and techniques are summarized in Figure 11-1. There is always a qualitative aspect to even a quantitative analysis, but by using quantitative performance measures for PPS elements, particularly hardware, much of the subjectivity of compliance-based and qualitative analysis approaches can be removed. A quantitative approach is not applicable to every facility, but certainly is for critical or unique assets, and since the attacks of 9/11, there is greater interest in applying this approach to critical infrastructures, national security assets, and homeland security.

When conducting either a qualitative or quantitative performance-based analysis, the same six-step process is used.

1. Create an adversary sequence diagram (ASD) for all asset locations.
2. Conduct a path analysis, which provides P_I.
3. Perform a scenario analysis.
4. Complete a neutralization analysis, if appropriate, which provides P_N.
5. Determine system effectiveness, P_E.
6. If system effectiveness (or risk) is not acceptable, develop and analyze upgrades.

As described in the *Design* textbook and the previous Chapter 10, interruption is defined as arrival of responders at a deployed location to halt adversary progress. Interruption may lead to neutralization. Neutralization is defined as the defeat of the adversaries by responders in a face-to-face engagement. These probabilities are treated as independent

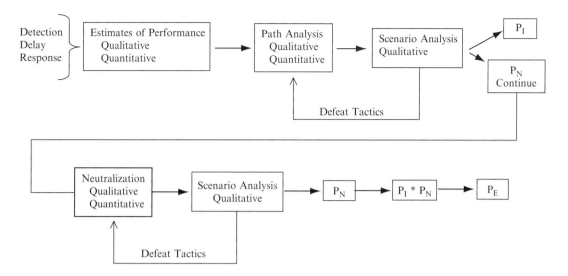

Figure 11-1 Analysis Process Overview. Both qualitative and quantitative techniques are used in performance-based analysis. Numerical component performance estimates are used to support the quantitative analysis of overall system effectiveness. This removes much of the subjectivity from the analysis, which makes it easier to justify the analysis results to management and allows for comparisons of multiple sites using the same protection objectives.

variables when the defined threat selects a path that exploits vulnerabilities in the PPS and is willing to engage with responders. In this case, P_E is calculated by the formula:

$$P_E = P_I * P_N$$

Some adversaries may not be violent and will give up when confronted by any immediate response; therefore, P_N is not a factor. In other cases, there is no immediate response, so P_N may not be a useful measure of system effectiveness. Under these conditions, P_E is equal to P_I. If desired, a facility may also choose to evaluate the PPS using risk as a metric, although this method is more commonly used in risk assessment, and not in vulnerability assessment. The risk equation was described in some detail in Chapter 1.

Qualitative analysis is based on the application of the first principles of physical security to verify the effectiveness of

installed protection elements (equipment, people, and procedures). These principles were described in the *Design* textbook, and a few of the most critical ones are reviewed next. The calculated P_E is a result of proper implementation of these security principles. For the system to perform effectively, it must incorporate the following security principles:

- Detect an adversary attack while there is still enough time to respond as desired (timely detection). Detection elements are best early on the path (before the CDP), and delay is best later (after the CDP or at the asset). If initial detection occurs at the asset, the PPS is fundamentally flawed.
- Provide a timely and accurate assessment of alarms to separate valid intrusions from nuisance alarms. The frequency of nuisance alarms should be low to maintain high system

effectiveness. The best alarm assessment technique is through the use rapid and automatic display of stored video images showing sensor alarm sources.

- Communicate alarm information to a response force in a timely manner, or record all required information for after-the-event response.
- Establish performance measures for each PPS function—detection, delay, and response—for each defined threat category or level. Estimates must be made considering all facility states, such as bad weather, operational conditions, and emergencies.
- Ensure detection occurs before delay. Detection is not complete without assessment, and delay before detection does not contribute to overall system effectiveness.
- Delay the adversary long enough to allow time for alarm recording and storage or for immediate response in time to interrupt the adversary.
- Use protection-in-depth (multiple layers). Protection-in-depth allows more opportunities to defeat the adversary, requires more planning and capability by the adversary, and avoids single point failures. (An example of a single-point-failure is the presence of only one layer, with an exploitable weakness.) In essence, if there is one weakness in a layer, the layer is vulnerable and will require an upgrade.
- Ensure balanced protection. Balanced protection verifies that all paths to assets have approximately the same P_I. Balance should be maintained within each layer and under all facility states. If balance is not supported, system effectiveness will be reduced.
- Engage and neutralize the adversaries, using force if appropriate.
- Conduct path and scenario analyses, and use analysis tools to predict system effectiveness, using interruption

alone, or in combination with neutralization, as the overall performance measure. There are many paths into a facility and the most vulnerable path is the one with the lowest P_I. Therefore, analysis characterizes the overall effectiveness of the system in detecting, delaying, interrupting, and neutralizing an adversary along all credible paths.

A quantitative analysis also applies these principles but uses numerical estimates, such as probabilities and delay or response times, to represent their application. This approach is more objective, but it is not mathmetically rigorous. Characterizing technology by testing to statistical standards, however, is still the best technique to objectively assess security elements and systems. The testing process allows data to be collected by considering attack techniques (e.g., walking, crawling, bypass, spoofing) and the effects of weather, installation, operation, and maintenance on the device. Testing provides insight into the best performance expected from a given device for a given threat and serves as the basis for application of degradation factors that are used in VA analysis.

Analysis Tools

There are a number of tools that can be used to support the performance-based analysis of a PPS. Some are software-based, and others are simple paper-and-pencil approaches. One simple path analysis computer tool was provided with the *Design* textbook (available at http://books.elsevier.com/companions/ 0750673672). Many large enterprises have proprietary software tools that aid in collecting and documenting VA information and automate the analysis process. The key to using analysis tools is to understand that they are only tools—the analysis still depends on the appropriate interpretation of data by the VA team. It is not sufficient to purchase or develop a software tool and then defer to the tool for results. It is imperative that knowledgeable people interpret tool results and draw the proper conclusions. If analysis were as easy as entering data into a software tool, anyone could do it, which is hardly a strong argument for the expertise of security experts. In addition to complex (and often very expensive) commercial software tools for security data collection and analysis, simple table-top models are also used to capture and represent aspects of physical security at a facility. One example is the storyboards described in the previous chapter; another is reusable sandboxes, where a small, scale model mock-up of the facility is made and response force actions are simulated using toy soldiers to represent defenders and adversaries. Investigative tools that are used to support analysis include timeline analysis (the sequence of actions that have been described by witnesses or supported by evidence can be related and substantiated) or investigative management software that allows for incident information to be entered into a system and shared by investigators. Another simple tool that can be used to support analysis is an ASD, which is a functional representation of a facility and asset locations, and is an aid in path analysis. Any or all of these tools can be used in an analysis. The choice is often a matter of enterprise policy or proficiency in specific tools. The next section describes the six steps of the analysis process and how these steps result in an estimate of system effectiveness.

Analysis Process

This section describes the performance-based analysis process at a high level. This section is followed by examples using qualitative or quantitative techniques. The *Design* textbook provides additional descriptive detail that may be reviewed to introduce this approach.

Adversary Sequence Diagrams and Path Analysis

An ASD is a functional representation of the PPS at a facility that is used to describe the specific protection elements that are present. It illustrates the paths that adversaries can follow to accomplish sabotage or theft goals. Because a path analysis determines whether a system has sufficient detection and delay to result in interruption, it is conducted first. The path analysis uses estimated performance measures, based on the defined threat tools and tactics, to predict weaknesses in the PPS along all credible adversary paths into the facility. This step is facilitated through the use of an ASD of the facility to be analyzed.

For a specific PPS and a specific threat, the most vulnerable path (the path with the lowest P_I) can be determined. Using P_I as the measure of path vulnerability, multiple paths can be compared and an estimate of overall PPS vulnerability can be made. The analyst may either construct the ASD manually using pencil and paper, or it can be created electronically using software tools.

There are three basic steps in creating an ASD for a specific site.

1. Describing the facility by separating it into adjacent physical areas
2. Defining protection layers and path elements between the adjacent areas
3. Recording detection and delay values for each path element

These steps and the process of drawing an ASD were described in Chapter 14 of the *Design* textbook; readers who are unfamiliar with this approach may find it useful to review this process before continuing this section.

The ASD represents adjacent areas of a facility using concentric rectangles and area names that correspond to the site. It models a PPS by identifying protection layers between adjacent areas. The first layer is always off-site (i.e., off facility grounds), and the last layer is always the asset. Each protection layer consists of a number of path elements (PE), which are the basic building blocks of a PPS. Table 11-1 shows the standard symbols that are used to represent path elements at facilities. These are the symbols used in modeling software developed and used at Sandia National Laboratories. There is nothing sacred about them, however, and if other symbols are more meaningful during an analysis, they can be used, but they must be applied consistently. For example, personnel doors should always use the same symbol, and vehicle doors should use a separate, but consistent, symbol. A key point to developing ASDs is that one ASD must be created for each asset (target location), unless the assets are co-located. At complex facilities, several critical assets may need protection, and ASDs should be developed for each unique location. It is expected that some parts of the ASD can be reused for multiple assets, but as the path gets closer to the asset, there may be differences in protection. This is related to the presence of multiple layers of protection at a facility;

if there is only one layer, the ASDs will look the same.

Once the ASD is created, the analyst assigns detection and assessment probabilities, delay times for PPS elements under different facility states, and any additional notes for each path element. The values recorded are the estimates provided by the VA team subject matter experts (SMEs) as a result of their evaluation. These estimates include P_C and the response force time, when there is an immediate response. This is the initial step in path analysis. Both entry and exit path segments can be modeled. The entry path segment is from off-site to the asset, and the exit path segment is from the asset back off-site. A given path element may be traversed once, either on entry or exit, or it may be traversed twice, on entry and in the opposite direction on exit. The adversary attempts to sequentially defeat at least one element in each protection layer while traversing a path through the facility to the target. The ASD represents all adversary paths to an asset; paths that are not credible are identified in scenario analysis (see next section). Although only some paths are credible for specific threats, representing the entire PPS on the ASD is recommended. This provides good system documentation, allows for faster

Table 11-1 *Path Element Symbols Used in ASDs.*

Path Elements		Asset Locations
EMP Emergency Portal	DUC Duct	BPL Bulk Process Line
GAT Gateway	EMX Emergency Exit	CGE Cage
ISO Isolation Zone	FEN Fenceline	FLV Floor Vault
MAT Material Portal	HEL Helicopter Flight Path	GNL Generic Location
DOR Personnel Doorway	OVP Overpass	IPL Item Process Line
SHD Shipping/Receiving Door	PER Personnel Portal	OPN Open Location
SUR Surface	SHP Shipping/Receiving Portal	TNK Storage Tank
VHD Vehicle Doorway	TUN Tunnel	
WND Window	VEH Vehicle Portal	

Each path element has associated detection and delay components. SUR is used to model walls, floors, and ceilings; DOR is used to describe personnel doors. One SUR or DOR is required for each different type of wall, roof, floor, or door in a layer. A generic target location (GNL) can be used to describe asset locations that are not represented in the existing list.

replication of analysis in the event that threats increase and facilitates sensitivity analysis (how well the system performs against higher or lower threats). This simple functional view also provides additional insights about credible adversary paths, which could be missed if some path elements are omitted.

For sabotage analysis, only entry paths are evaluated, and we assume the path elements will be traversed in only one direction because a successful act of sabotage requires proximity to the asset only long enough to cause damage. It does not require adversary exit from the facility to be successful. For theft analysis, the path elements are traversed twice—on entry and on exit from the facility. When only entry paths are considered, the total number of paths is the product of the number of protection elements in each layer. When both entry and exit paths are evaluated, the total number of paths is the square of the number of entry paths.

The path analysis is used to provide an overall view of the robustness of the PPS—whether the system has many weak paths, or only a few. By studying the potential adversary paths and the estimates of path element performance, the analyst can quickly determine how effective the PPS is and where vulnerabilities exist. For example, if there is no detection along a path until the asset, this is quickly revealed. Path analysis also identifies the CDP for multiple adversary paths. This information provides insights into common weak points along paths that need additional detection or delay to support the desired response. During path analysis, the assumption is that interruption and neutralization will occur at the CDP, although the actual response strategy depends on the asset. For example, if the asset is a sabotage target using a denial strategy, the response must occur no later than at the asset; theft targets can use a containment strategy. When a facility has multiple distributed assets that are targets of different adversary attack goals (sabotage and theft), response must be carefully planned to support both protection goals. This is described further in the next section. The key objective of path analysis is to evaluate the PPS at a facility at a high level and determine how well protected all assets are at all times.

Reviewing the ASD during path analysis can also reveal whether the PPS is balanced. For each protection layer, the detection and delay provided by path elements should be balanced. Examining overall detection and delay values can quickly show unbalanced elements or layers that will be preferred in adversary paths. Verifying balance across protection layers will also assist if upgrades are required. If a layer is already balanced, upgrades must be applied to each protection element to maintain balance. If a layer is not balanced, upgrades should be applied so that they bring the layer into balance.

It is likely that there will be at least two ASDs for each target—one each for the day/night or open/closed facility states. Depending on other facility states, more ASDs may be required. Examples of other facility states that deserve consideration include employee shift changes, guard force shift changes, fire or other emergencies, power failures, bad weather, and sensors in access during operational times. This process is not as onerous as it sounds; once an ASD for a specific asset is drawn, successive views need only capture the changes from one facility state to the next. Analysis is often expedited by making several copies of the initial ASD, and then modifying only those path elements that change. Once these differences are understood, it is a simple matter to describe them in a short paragraph in the VA report. Analysis of the facility states should emphasize additional path vulnerabilities at these times.

Scenario Analysis

Analysis of the ASD will identify the paths with the lowest P_I, which is the starting point for scenario development and analysis. A scenario analysis is conducted to determine whether the system has vulnerabilities that could be exploited by adversaries using varying tactics, resulting in lower effectiveness of the PPS. Some facilities use scenario analysis as a substitute for a defined threat, where they postulate attacks, then decide what equipment or capability is required to be successful. This is another option, but it can lead to some gaps in analysis. Analyzing the PPS using defined threats and then generating scenarios by looking at weak paths is the preferred approach to ensure that credible paths are not missed. Using the scenario, a task-by-task or layer-by-layer description is developed. This description should be detailed enough to provide a scenario timeline and enough information that performance estimates for sensing, assessment, communication, delays, and response can be made.

At this point the analyst reduces all the possible paths to those that are most credible. Paths can be removed from the final mix as a result of a number of tactical issues. For example, a path that appears very weak (low P_I) using element performance measures may not really be credible because there are a large number of responders on the other side of the door with the shortest delay. Or, the adversary may use one entry door over another because it is located in an isolated corner of the facility, even though both doors have the same delay. In reality, an adversary would select the door that gave them the greatest chance of successful entry, assuming a similar delay time. Of course, some paths will be eliminated because the adversary does not have the equipment or other capability to attack some protection elements (i.e., thick walls and only hand tools), and this is another source of path removal.

Once the path analysis is complete, scenario analysis begins. These steps should be followed to conduct a scenario analysis:

- Develop attacks and tactics designed to exploit weak paths. Consider attacks during different facility states using the defined threat and capability.
- Modify performance estimates for path elements using these tactics or under these states.
- Document the assumptions used and the results of the scenario analysis.

A scenario analysis is aided by the creation of adversary task timelines and the associated performance of any path elements along the path. An example of a theft scenario timeline is shown in Table 11-2. Scenario analysis considers specific tactics along the path, as well as attacks on the PPS itself or on the response force. These tactics include stealth, force, and deceit, and they may be used individually or combined during a scenario. For example, suppose the VA team determines that adversaries could easily jam radio communications at the facility. Evaluation tests indicate that an additional five minutes, on average, is required by responders to communicate using alternate means during jamming attacks. This time would be added to the response time used in the path analysis to evaluate how P_I changes. Other attacks on the system might include interference with alarm transmission, disabling the alarm monitoring center, or shining bright lights into cameras. Examples of attacks on responders might include overt or covert attacks on patrols, diversions, or ambush during deployment. Other aspects of scenario analysis include consideration of what on-site tools or other equipment might be used by the adversary to aid in the attack. For example, forklifts, explosives, cutting torches, ladders, or power tools might be available at the facility. In this case, the adversary would not need to bring this equipment, and the scenario analysis would add procuring these items to the adversary tasks that must be completed for success.

Table 11-2 *Example of Adversary Task Timeline.*

Task	Task Time (sec)	Cum. Task Time	Notations
Approach facility	N/A	0	Adversaries attack at night
Enter facility	80	80	Cut three fences including sensor fence. Engage any responders.
Traverse exterior area	10	90	Run across area to exterior door
Breach building	120	210	Breach two personnel doors with explosives.
Traverse interior (entry)	10	220	Move to asset
Acquire asset	60	280	Load asset onto cart (already at facility)
Traverse interior (exit)	10	290	Move asset in cart
Exit building	10	300	Doors open from entry
Traverse exterior area	10	310	Run to fences
Exit facility	10	320	Fences cut on entry
Leave vicinity	N/A	320	Leave area

The tasks to be accomplished by the adversary and the amount of time it will take to accomplish the task are listed to define the scenario. The example shows the use of quantitative measures, but qualitative measures may also be used.

In addition to the adversary task times, immediate response times must also be determined. The response time depends on the specifics of attack timing and response procedures, but a general notion of how many responders will be responding to the area and at what intervals is an effective first step in response time estimates. The time for alarm assessment information to be relayed to responders is included in the response time. Also, the ability of responders to engage from various locations, such as initial positions, while in transit, and at their deployed positions should be considered. For the example shown in Table 11-2, assume response is by a guard patrol and local law enforcement. The patrol responds in 3 minutes (180 seconds) to exterior locations and 8 minutes (480 seconds) to the inside of buildings. Local law enforcement takes 20 minutes (1,200 seconds) to respond. After the scenario is defined and the adversary task timeline is created, performance estimates of path elements are made for the path. An example is shown in Table 11-3.

Using the task timeline in Table 11-2, and the preceding response times, it can be seen that even if sensing and assessment occur immediately on the adversary's initial penetration of the perimeter, the patrol cannot respond to the alarm and interrupt the adversary, as it will take the adversary 80 seconds to complete this task, and the guards take 180 seconds to respond to exterior locations. The patrol might interrupt at the exterior wall, but there are only 30 seconds to spare (210 minus 180 seconds). If the patrol is delayed for any reason, or the adversary completes the breaching task faster, successful interruption might still not be possible. This is another analysis consideration. Note that if initial detection occurs while the adversary is traversing the interior, the patrol is still not fast enough to interrupt (480 seconds versus 320). Local law enforcement will not be able to respond until well after the adversary has left the site (1,200 seconds versus 320), even if there is detection at the perimeter. Similar analysis can occur for other adversary scenarios.

If one adversary tactic is to eliminate responders, scenarios are developed in which the attack begins by assaulting

Table 11-3 *Performance Estimates for Adversary Scenario.*

Task	P_D	P_{As}	P_{AD}*	P_I
Approach facility				
Enter facility				
Traverse exterior area				
Breach building				
Traverse interior (entry)				
Acquire asset				
Traverse interior (exit)				
Exit building				
Traverse exterior area				
Exit facility				
Leave vicinity				

*P_{AD} is the calculated value of ($P_D * P_{As}$) further degraded by AC&D subsystem performance

Detection and assessment values are added to each adversary task that reflect the current facility state along the path. The P_I can be estimated for each task or for the entire path. P_I must also consider the delay and response times for the path, but estimates for each task provide insights into the robustness of each layer and the overall system.

them. Because P_I calculates the likelihood of arrival of the response force and confrontation with the adversary is ensured in this case, the P_E is equal to the probability that the response force wins this confrontation (which is P_N). It is important for the analyst to work closely with the VA team response SME during this stage of the analysis, so that the most credible paths of attack and realistic tactics are considered. As a result of this analysis, modifications are made to the path model that show changes in performance values that reflect these more realistic attacks. This stage of the analysis broadens the path analysis to consider attacks on PPS devices or the response force, in addition to direct attacks on the asset.

Scenario analysis also considers response to attacks on multiple distributed assets at a facility. As noted previously, if the facility has assets that are both theft and sabotage targets, the response to attacks must be carefully considered. During the early stages of an attack, it may not be apparent which asset is the attack target. In these cases, the response team may have to wait until this is clear, or there must be enough responders to implement both denial and containment strategies. During scenario analysis, these attacks and their responses can be considered, and the ability to protect all assets under varying attacks can be evaluated. This is a good example of the use of response storyboards, which can be used to show the inadequacy of response to multiple simultaneous attacks or different individual attacks, including theft and sabotage. In addition, scenario analysis may also consider the neutralization effectiveness of an immediate response at various points along the adversary path, not just the CDP. In this case, it is assumed that interruption has occurred, and the goal is for the facility to understand how many responders can get to a specific point on the path and their effectiveness after arrival at this point. This analysis provides additional insight into system vulnerabilities and potential improvements to the overall PPS, especially response tactics.

At most facilities, only one threat team is considered; however, at some high-security facilities, it is likely that the adversary will split into many teams, each with a separate task. One team will likely still be dedicated to attacking the asset. A table of scenario tasks and task times could be completed for each team, but it is more straightforward to complete a timeline for the asset attack team only, with the effects of other teams rolled up into sensing or assessment values or decreased response effectiveness. It is unlikely that force scenarios such as this will be used during the VA of an industrial facility, however, much of the U.S.'s critical infrastructure is operated by private industry and this type of analysis is becoming more common.

As in path analysis, an important aspect of scenario analysis is consideration of different operating states at the facility or near the asset. There are usually at least two facility states—open and closed. For example, a door may be left open during daytime operation, but locked at night. A good analysis will include scenarios predicting performance under both conditions. For facilities that operate 24/7, there may still be differences among shifts, and these should be analyzed to verify that protection is balanced across all shifts. In addition to open and closed differences, there may be other predictable operating states at a facility including safety emergencies, maintenance activities, bad weather (particularly for exterior PPS components), and power failures. Each of these states can represent a new set of vulnerabilities for the asset, the PPS, or security guards.

As a part of scenario analysis, an effort is made to identify the worst-case attacks. Although analyses are not limited to these situations, they are useful because they define adversary attacks that test the limits of PPS effectiveness. Worst-case scenarios are generally used in neutralization analysis, as they predict the lowest response effectiveness. Although it is important to determine worst-case scenarios, other less severe but more credible scenarios are also created and evaluated.

These scenarios are then used in path analysis to calculate P_I, and also to estimate P_N, which is the other term needed to establish P_E.

Estimate Neutralization

After weak paths and suitable attack scenarios have been determined, a neutralization analysis can be performed. This part of the analysis is performed only at facilities where there is an immediate response resulting in a face-to-face confrontation with adversaries. Neutralization analysis provides information about how effective the response will be under different attack scenarios and is a measure of response force capability, proficiency, training, and tactics. This analysis assumes that interruption has occurred. If the defined threat for an asset or facility includes adversaries who will use force to prevent the response force from interrupting or neutralizing, analysis should consider the likely outcome of that engagement. This analysis can use qualitative or qualitative techniques, as described in Chapter 10. At many high-security facilities, computer simulations are used to quantitatively predict the probability of neutralizing violent adversaries after interrupting them. For other facilities, past records of successful responses to security incidents can be used to estimate P_N or the results of tabletop exercises can also be used. In a qualitative analysis, the side that has the advantage—in numbers, weapons, skill, tactics, or other areas—can be determined and assigned a high, medium, or low likelihood.

Other Analysis

In addition to the analysis tools described previously, other tools are useful when analyzing the PPS at a facility. These include blast effects modeling and response storyboards. Many sites are specifically concerned about the threat of vehicle bombs or other explosive devices at critical locations at a facility. In these cases, it can be useful to provide some analysis of the effects of such a device on these structures. A number of commercially available blast effects modeling tools are available to support this part of an analysis. Some are not extremely robust, but they do allow for a simple approximation of blast damage to buildings using standard construction. Inputs generally are simple and include the footprint of the building, building construction, size and location of the explosive charge, and surrounding terrain. The output is a graphic showing an approximation of blast damage. These images and supporting assumptions can be included in the final VA report as an option within the Analysis section.

Another useful tool, particularly during scenario analysis, is the response storyboard. An example of a response storyboard was shown in Figure 10-1. Creation of a response storyboard allows the analyst and tactical experts to get a sense of how long it will take for the response force to fully engage with the adversary and what tactics are appropriate at different stages of the attack and response. The response storyboard is often used to facilitate neutralization analysis and scenario development. It also can provide insights into tactical modifications that can make the response force more effective.

Calculate System Effectiveness

At this point, PPS effectiveness can be calculated using the qualitative or quantitative techniques described previously. Either way, system effectiveness can be represented using only P_I (as in the case of a delayed response using review of video and investigation, when mere presence of an immediate response will chase an adversary away, or when an adversary

will surrender if interrupted), or through the use of both P_I and P_N (at sites where an immediate response will engage with the adversary). If only P_I is used, analysis consists of path analysis and limited scenario development to support the estimate of system effectiveness (see Figure 11-1). When both interruption and neutralization are used, system effectiveness is the product of P_I and P_N, as described earlier in this chapter. In a quantitative analysis, the two terms are multiplied to establish system effectiveness. In a qualitative analysis, the two terms are combined to represent the overall state of system effectiveness. Just as in a mathematical multiplication, if one term is low, the other term will be decreased to that amount, even if it is very high. For example, if P_I is high and P_N is low, P_E will be low. In general, P_E can be no higher than the lower of the two values, and this is a good guideline for qualitative analysis. (For readers who doubt this, just use a few mathematical examples to demonstrate this effect. For example, the product of 0.9×0.2 is 0.18. Even if we round this up to the nearest tenth, it is still the lower of the two numbers. Try as many combinations as it takes to be convinced.) P_E is calculated for each threat category, as it is expected that the same system will have varying performance for different threats.

Upgrade Analysis

If the baseline analysis of the PPS shows that the system does not meet its protection objectives, and therefore it is vulnerable, the VA team can suggest upgrades that will address vulnerabilities. Usually, these upgrades are not specific technical recommendations, but are functional improvements that can be achieved by increasing performance at certain locations. For example, the team might suggest that an improved P_D at a certain point or that additional delay at an asset will increase P_E. In these cases, the analysis assumes an improved functional performance without identifying the specific sensor or barrier device, although the evaluation team believes this is an achievable goal. The upgrade options generally consider the interaction of detection, delay, and response features, as well as operational effects, life cycle performance-cost tradeoffs, single-point failures, reliability, quality, and maintenance of the security system.

The analysis is then repeated using these performance increases to estimate the overall increase in the ability of the system to meet its objectives. These results (which become new system requirements for upgrade designs) can be provided to security system designers who will determine which specific equipment or other upgrades will provide the required performance. These specific design details are generally addressed in a follow-on activity to the VA, often captured in a conceptual design project or phase. Once the analysis is completed, it is important to present both the baseline and upgrade analyses to establish the need for improvements and show the return on investment in upgrades. These aspects of the VA are discussed in Chapter 12.

The upgrade analysis is also the appropriate time to consider and evaluate the effectiveness of contingency plans and equipment. Contingency plans are used for various reasons, including when PPS equipment is under repair or when the impacts (cost, schedule, operations, acceptability) of PPS equipment required to meet protection objectives are deemed to be too great. For example, if a facility cannot afford to meet the protection objectives for all threats at all times, temporary procedures or portable equipment could be implemented during high-alert periods. Whenever contingency plans are part of security protection plans under elevated threat conditions, they should be evaluated using performance estimates and analysis tools to ensure that they will perform as required.

Qualitative Analysis

Because the analysis process can be conducted qualitatively or quantitatively, each approach is demonstrated in the next two sections. The reader should note that analysis can be quite complex; it is not the intent of this chapter to exhaustively cover analysis, but rather to introduce the key concepts used in performance-based evaluation. As such, the following examples take a limited approach to analysis and the use of analysis tools. True expertise in these methods can come only from training in the use of specific tools and analysis techniques, and practice in their application.

Facility Overview

For the qualitative example, a six-story commercial office building that could be located in any medium to large city will be used. The first floor has a front lobby, a conference room used by building tenants, a small cafeteria, and a shipping and receiving dock at the back of the building (see Figure 11-2). The building is open from 7 AM to 7 PM, Monday through Friday. A passenger elevator provides access to upper floors, and there is a freight elevator at the shipping and receiving dock. There is a fire stairwell at each end of the building that exits to the outside. Building tenants are allowed access during nonoperational hours by a security guard in the front lobby, who checks their identification and correlates this to an access list before admittance.

Tenants include several private small businesses, the Federal government, and a regional office of BIG Company, which develops new materials and formulations. The Federal agencies, located on the fifth floor, include the local FBI and an IRS office. The third floor is occupied exclusively by BIG Company. The other businesses are scattered on the other floors. BIG Company is the target of attack and

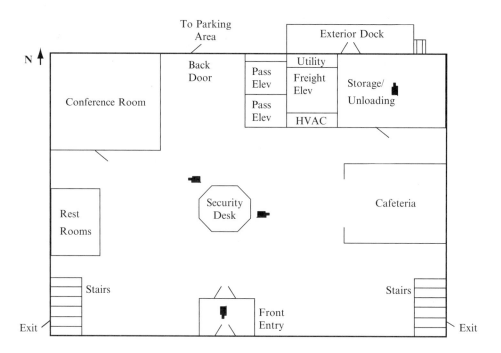

Figure 11-2 First Floor Plan of Office Building. This is the lowest floor of the building and provides common entry for all employees, visitors, and delivery personnel. Note the placement of security devices. Windows are not shown, but there are many on each floor.

analysis in the example and the third floor plan is shown in Figure 11-3.

There are approximately 200 employees working in the building, 40 of whom work for BIG Company. The exterior building walls are made from 14-inch slab concrete, and there are many windows on each floor. Exterior emergency exit doors are standard metal hollow-core doors with crash bars. These doors do not allow access into the building from outside and the exterior door hardware has been removed. The main building entry uses a set of two glass double doors. Interior doors are standard hollow-core wood personnel doors. There is a back entrance that is a standard metal hollow-core door. The building has a utility chase near the elevator shaft that carries communication and data lines and a heating, ventilation, and air conditioning (HVAC) system in the building that spreads out to each floor.

Building security includes unarmed security guards stationed in the front lobby to greet and aid visitors, as well as some security equipment. Visitors are allowed unescorted entry to the building during operational hours. Sensors are present on some doors in the facility. Fire alarms sound when the emergency exits are used. During open hours, interior sensors located throughout the building are placed in access; outside these hours, all sensors are fully operational. There are 30 surveillance cameras used in the building, but not in the emergency stairwells. The shipping dock has a surveillance camera and no sensors. The freight elevator is protected by locking the exit door to the loading dock. The elevator controls can be operated by anyone.

All cameras are pan-tilt-zoom (PTZ) color analog dome cameras. Lighting is standard fluorescent; at night only a few lights on each floor are on. There is a monitoring station in the lobby that displays surveillance video using an automatic sequential scanner on four 9-inch monitors. Video information is recorded

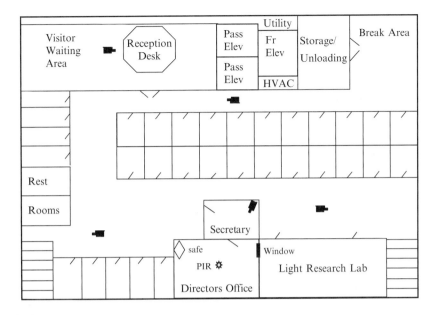

Figure 11-3 Third Floor Plan of Office Building. This is the floor that houses BIG Company and the site of the theft asset. There are additional security devices used on this floor that are not part of the general building security system.

on videotapes at the rate of one frame every 30 seconds per camera. Tapes are kept for 1 week, and then reused. Security system controls and panels are located on each floor in equipment closets using standard locks. There are two guards on duty during operational hours and one during off hours. At night, the security guard on duty sits in the first floor lobby at the security/reception desk. He is required to patrol the building once per hour and checks in at two guard tour locations on all but the third floor during the patrol. It takes him approximately 20 minutes to complete this patrol. The response strategies used include observe-and-report and delayed tape review. On a valid intrusion, verified manually by a guard who is dispatched to the alarm location, local police are called. There is no agreement in place covering police response time, and these calls are answered based on police dispatch prioritization. The security guards do not try to confront any intruders, but are instructed to cooperate if they do. Using the guid-

ance provided in Chapter 10, where high response time means there is interruption while the adversary is still on-site, medium shows the ability to successfully apprehend and prosecute adversaries after-the-fact, and low indicates that the response cannot prevent a successful attack, guard response time at the building is estimated to be low during the day and at night. Police response time is also estimated to be low for any threat.

In addition to the building security system, BIG Company has installed extra security elements on their floor. These include the use of a proximity card reader that allows the elevators to stop on the third floor, a receptionist in the entry lobby to the third floor in front of the elevator, BMS sensors on all office doors, five PTZ surveillance cameras that report to a monitoring station at the receptionists desk, and a PIR sensor in the office of the Research Director. The Director's office also contains a safe that has the most recent formula for BIG Company's latest product, which will revolutionize the industry. This formula is the target of the attack. The safe has $1/_4$-inch steel sides with a $1/_2$-inch steel door, and provides 10 minutes of delay (medium) to hand or power tool attacks. A 360-degree PIR sensor covers the room and safe. BIG company's security equipment reports remotely using the Internet to a central monitoring station 2,000 miles away at corporate headquarters. On an alarm, the central station calls the guard in the building lobby to investigate. The guard verifies alarms by going to the third floor and searching for anomalies. When he is done, he returns to the lobby desk, calls central control, and reports what he found. If he discovers an intrusion, he also calls the local police, who usually respond within 1 hour, depending on the time of day and volume of calls.

The ASD for this facility is shown in Figure 11-4. Table 11-4 shows the description of each path element on the ASD, related notes, and the estimate of performance for each element. Note that there may be complex paths into or out of a facility, which may be difficult to depict on an ASD. In most cases, these paths can be described and modeled as a single path element for analysis. For example, in this facility it is possible for an adversary to get to the roof, enter the equipment penthouse, gain access to the elevator shaft, descend the shaft, and force open the door at the third floor. This path could be modeled as a single path element (TUN), with the detection, assessment, and delay contributions of each portion of the path rolled up into a single value for the simplified element.

BIG Company has defined its most credible threat as three unarmed attackers, with hand and power tools, some additional equipment such as tape and gloves, and possible passive insider assistance. One person on the team is profi-

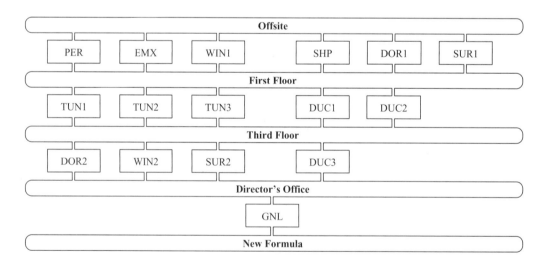

Figure 11-4 ASD for the Office Building. This ASD is specifically for the asset on the third floor. Assets on other floors would share the layers up to the third floor, and then substitute the specific protection elements and performance for these floors. Note that the ASD includes all protection elements, although only certain elements are applicable to the defined threat. It is more proactive and efficient to identify all the existing protection elements at one time, and then consider them as appropriate in succeeding evaluations, for example when the threat increases.

Table 11-4 *Path Elements and Descriptions.*

Path Element	Description	Notes	Performance Estimate
PER	Front Entry—two sets of double doors	The entrance doors are locked at night, and open during the day. The doors do not have sensors. Surveillance cameras cover the entrance and the lobby area.	P_D day/night = L P_{As} day/night = L P_{AD} day/night = L Delay = L
EMX	Emergency Exits	There are two emergency exits, one on each end of the building. Building exits have panic bar door opening alarms, but no security alarms. External door hardware has been removed.	P_D day/night = H for opening, L for cutting P_{As} day/night = L P_{AD} day/night = L Delay = L
WIN1	First Floor Windows	All building windows are fixed, tempered glass. There are no glass break detectors in the building.	P_D day = H P_D night = L P_{As} day/night = L P_{AD} day/night = L Delay = L
SHP	Loading Dock Door	The loading dock doors to the exterior of the building are normally locked, but are opened for receipt of materials and shipments. These doors have a BMS that is active at night and a surveillance camera. The door between the loading dock and the first floor of the building is left unlocked.	P_D day = L P_D night = H for opening, L for cutting P_{As} day/night = L P_{AD} day/night = L Delay = L
DOR1	Back Entrance	There is a back entrance to the building. The door is unlocked during normal working hours, but locked with a BMS active at night. The door is a standard hollow metal personnel type.	P_D day = L P_D night = H for opening, L for cutting P_{As} day/night = L P_{AD} day/night = L Delay = L
SUR1	Building Surface	The building is steel frame with precast concrete panel walls.	P_D = L, all times Delay = H
TUN1	Passenger Elevators	Elevators are kept at the first floor at night. They have a proximity card reader to control access to the third floor.	P_D day = L P_D night = H P_{As} day/night = L P_{AD} day/night = L Delay = L
TUN2	Freight Elevator	The freight elevator is located off the loading dock. It is generally kept on the first floor, but it can be operated by anyone who enters.	P_D day = L P_D night = H P_{As} day/night = L P_{AD} day/night = L Delay = L
TUN3	Stairwells	There are two stairwells, one at each end of the building that access each floor and exit to the exterior of the building. There are no sensors on the interior doors or in the stairwell, and only the exterior exit doors are locked.	P_D day = L P_D night = H P_{As} day/night = L P_{AD} day/night = L Delay = L

Continued

Table 11-4—*Cont'd*

Path Element	Description	Notes	Performance Estimate
DUC1	HVAC Ductwork	The building HVAC ducting runs through a chase from the penthouse on the roof to the plenum space on the first floor. The duct to the third floor is 48 inches on a side.	P_D day/night = L P_{As} day/night = L P_{AD} day/night = L Delay = L
DUC2	Utility Chase	There is also a utility chase running the entire height of the building. It interconnects to a horizontal service corridor providing service to each floor. This corridor runs alongside the outer wall or above the ceiling on each floor.	P_D day/night = L P_{As} day/night = L P_{AD} day/night = L Delay = L
DOR2	Office Door	The door to the director's office is a standard wood door with a cipher lock. It has a BMS sensor. A surveillance camera in the secretary's office is aimed at this door.	P_D day = L P_D night = H for opening, L for cutting P_{As} day = M P_{As} night = L P_{AD} day/night = L Delay = L
WIN2	Office Window to Hall	There is a window between the Director's office and the laboratory that lets the Director observe lab activity. It is a 4 × 4-foot window of tempered glass.	P_D day/night = M P_{As} day/night = L P_{AD} day/night = L Delay = L
SUR2	Office Wall	The office walls are standard steel stud with sheet rock covering.	P_D day = M P_D night = L P_{As} day/night = L P_{AD} day/night = L Delay = L
DUC3	Plenum Space Above Ceiling	The space above the false ceiling is used as a plenum for HVAC return. The entire office area shares a common overhead space.	P_D day/night = L P_{As} day/night = L P_{AD} day/night = L Delay = L
GNL	Safe in Office	The new formula is kept in a two-drawer document safe. There is a PIR sensor in the room that is in access during the day.	P_D day/night = L P_{As} day/night = L P_{AD} day/night = L Delay = H

These are the path elements that an adversary must penetrate for a successful attack. The far right column provides performance estimates for the various PPS components. During the day, P_C between the two on-duty guards is estimated as medium as a result of the loss of radio signals in elevators and a few other internal areas on each floor. At night, there is only one guard and his/her communication with BIG Company's central monitoring station and the police is via land telephone line. This P_C is high. Guard response time is estimated as low at all times.

cient at penetrating safes, one person acts as the helper, and the third person keeps track of the security guard. The adversary team is prepared to use moderate force to restrain the guard if needed. Considerable information about security-related activities has been gathered by the adversary team. They know when the building doors are locked or unlocked, when the lobby desk is staffed, and under what circumstances it is not staffed. They have observed the routines of the night guard and the arrival of shipments at the shipping dock. They have toured the building during the day and visited all floors (including BIG Company's) to determine the basic layout of the building. By causing alarms on the emergency exit doors during the day and at night, they know how long the on-site guard takes to respond. They have observed BIG Company personnel with proximity card badges, and successfully exited the elevator on the third floor by riding up with some of them. The team also knows that most employees of BIG Company take their lunch breaks between 12 and 1 PM.

Path Analysis

The initial evaluation of paths at the facility indicates a number of weaknesses, both during the day and at night. Review of the performance estimates in Table 11-4 supports this determination. In keeping with the security principles outlined previously and the general evaluation process, the detection, delay, and response performance at this facility is considered. To begin, note that during the day, detection (including intrusion sensing and assessment) is low. This is a combination of sensors being in access, limited alarm assessment capability, and devices that are easy to defeat (such as the proximity card operated elevator). The building is open to the public and anyone can easily enter the first floor. At this point, an adversary may use the stairwells, the elevators, the plenum, or utility chase to access the third floor. Using the guidance provided in Chapter 9 (low, less than 3 minutes; medium, 3 to 10 minutes; and high, greater than 10 minutes), with the exception of the outer building wall, delays in this facility are all low at all times. All doors are easy to penetrate with simple

hand tools, although this may not even be necessary for a daytime attack. The video cameras are not fixed, or associated with sensors, so P_{As} is low. There are some low-level attacks that may have a higher P_{As} during the day, but these would not be expected by the defined threat, which is a fairly motivated and capable group, and outnumbers the security guards. The alarm communication and display (AC&D) subsystem is not well integrated and requires manual manipulation by the guards to display areas of interest. The response is limited and an adversary could easily get to the safe during the day with little chance of detection; even if the adversary were detected at the safe, there would still be enough time to remove the formula and escape before the police arrive.

In some situations, personnel or guards might be able to assess fire door alarms, but this will take a few minutes even during the day, and a reasonably capable adversary can leave the area quickly enough to escape notice. Some attacks, for example, breaking through windows or walls, would be expected to be observed by people in the area, which will help if the adversary actually attacks this way. Unless employees pay close attention and actively intervene, anyone can get off the elevator at the third floor when an authorized person swipes their card. The receptionist is not expected to pose a credible barrier to the defined threat.

During the nighttime, or closed, state, the chance of detection is better for some attacks. For example, note that all doors with a BMS will have a high P_D if the doors are opened, but not if they are cut through for entry. Cutting through doors is well within the capability of this threat group. Alarm assessment is still low for night operation and is degraded from daytime performance by the lack of uniform lighting. Because there is only one guard, the existing adversary advantage in numbers is increased. Guard response time is estimated as medium, using the guidance defined in Chapter 10, where medium is assigned for an observe-and-report strategy. Police response time is estimated to be low, with little chance of arrival in time to prevent a successful attack.

Scenario Analysis

Many good scenarios can be developed to attack the safe. This discussion is limited to one daytime and one nighttime attack. Because it is a little easier, the daytime scenario is described first. Assume that the adversaries have found out that the Director will be out on travel for a few days—perhaps an insider told them (knowingly or not). Further, they know that when the Director travels, the secretary takes a longer lunch break—up to 2 hours, but never less than 1.5 hours. The path they will use is shown in Figure 11-5. It starts with entering the back door onto the first floor (DOR1), waiting until they see the secretary leave the building, then going to the southwest stairwell (TUN3)

and ascending to the third floor. Because this is daytime, and they are entering the back door at lunchtime, even the low P_D and low P_{AS} attributed to casual observation by the guard or surveillance cameras are reduced to zero. They put on maintenance overalls in the stairwell (where P_D will remain low, as someone might see them, in which case they will break off the attack), and enter the main office area of BIG Company, where they proceed to the Director's office. His door is closed (DOR2), but the BMS (and PIR sensor inside) are in access so they will not send an alarm. The PTZ camera dome in the secretary's office is covered with a paper cone that is taped in place, so it cannot transmit a useful image. One intruder stands out in the hall by the row of cubicles watching the doors to the waiting area and the halls and keeps an eye out for anyone who might notice the attack. If anyone heads toward the Director's office, he distracts them by asking for help with a maintenance order, as the secretary is not around. If this happens, he pushes

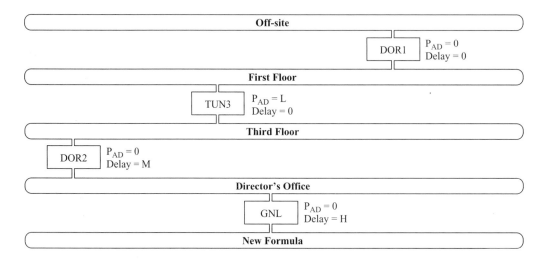

Figure 11-5 Daytime Attack Scenario Path. Performance of the PPS was already fairly low, but the intruders blind the camera, and pry the office door open rather than trying to defeat the lock. This eliminates any chance of video surveillance catching the attack and has the added benefit of blocking any recording of the attack. By prying the door open instead of cutting, the delay time increases to medium.

redial on a cell phone he has in his pocket and alerts the others. The other two attackers defeat the Director's office door by prying it open. They enter the office and close the door, so that it looks normal to a casual observer. They break into the safe (GNL) using hand tools, which is estimated as a medium delay. Once the safe is open, it will take another few minutes to locate the document, then one adversary makes a copy using the copier in the secretary's office, and the other scans the document using a small portable scanner; these steps are assigned a medium task time. When they are done, they put the document back, close the safe, and pull the office door closed. It is slightly damaged and may go unnoticed for a while. They leave the same way they entered (TUN3 and DOR1).

Evaluation of this path and scenario results in a slightly lower performance than the initial path analysis, using P_I as the measure of system effectiveness. The P_{AD} decreases to 0 because the installed sensors are in access, and there are no barriers to public entry into the building or stairwells. The riskiest part of the attack is that an employee of BIG Company might observe the adversary team but will likely assume this is a routine maintenance activity. If not, and the employee questions the lookout in the hall, he/she will explain that they are there to repair something (maybe in the utility chase, or the plenum). If that does not work and the employee says he/she will call security, the lookout sends the cell phone signal to the others, and the adversaries simply leave and plan to try and attack another day, which results in a high (although temporary) P_N. This supports the low P_{AD} estimate for human alarm assessment by employees. With a low P_{AD}, delay is not very relevant, but the adversaries can quickly defeat barriers and delays are short, especially given the response time of the guards.

Because the guards are unarmed and outnumbered by the adversaries, even if both guards responded during the theft attack, P_N is estimated to be low, which gives a low P_E for both interruption and neutralization (a low P_I multiplied by a low P_N can be no higher than a low P_E), even though facility guards are not expected to confront adversaries. Note the ease of attack and that the tools and capabilities used were easily procured items, such as overalls, hand/power tools, tape, rope, and gloves. P_N could be estimated to be high, if local police were alerted and responded before the attackers leave the site, but this is unlikely unless the intruders are unknowingly detected early in the attack.

The night scenario is a little more difficult and its ASD is shown in Figure 11-6. First, the intruders wait for the guard to start his routine patrol, defeat the locks on the front doors (PER), enter the southwest stairwell on the first floor (TUN3), move to the third floor, exit the stairwell, move down the hall to the area next to the Director's office, climb up into the overhead plenum space (DUC3), remove a ceiling panel in the Director's office, mask the PIR sensor from above (while watching the self-test light to see if an alarm is generated), drill the safe (GNL) for entry, remove the secret formula file, and exit via the Director's office door (DOR2, activating the BMS sensor), down the stairwell (TUN3), and out the emergency exit (EMX, while the guard is still on patrol). Exiting the door creates an alarm, but this is too late to aid the guard in detecting or assessing the attack. The entire attack takes a period of time that falls into the high time category (more than 10 minutes).

In this scenario, P_{AD} is still low, because of bypass of the BMS on the door and PTZ camera, and spoofing of the PIR sensor in the office. The PTZ camera does operate under very low light at night, but even if useful, will not provide images to the guard until the intruders are leaving through the office door. The delay time for attacking the safe is reasonable but is not useful given the lack of detection. In

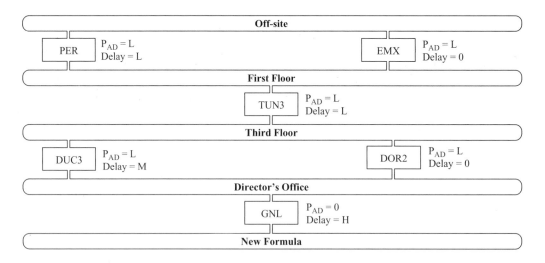

Figure 11-6 Nighttime Attack Scenario and Path. Note that this path uses different entry and exit paths. The path elements on the left are used on entry; those on the right for exit. TUN3 is a common element for both paths.

addition, the guard does not actually patrol the third floor and so is unlikely to discover the attack until he/she returns to the console on the first floor and receives notification of an alarm at the Director's office door from BIG Company's central monitoring station. At this point, the guard will go to the third floor to investigate. All of this takes time, and the intruders are making their way down the stairwell and out of the building.

Other credible scenarios include spoofing alarm assessment by continually triggering alarms at the emergency doors, an office door, or at the loading dock. The latter is a particularly good choice, as the door can be rattled from the outside, causing an alarm; but even using the surveillance camera, guards won't see the alarm source. Because night lighting is so low, it may be possible to blend in with the background and not be noticed on the closed-circuit television (CCTV) surveillance monitor. This would take a fairly high level of pre-attack intelligence to exploit, but it is possible. It is also possible to capture the guard, disable the guard using the rope and tape, complete the attack, and escape before anyone would know that

anything is wrong. In this case, the adversary might cause an alarm and lie in wait for the guard to come to assess the cause of the alarm, and then overpower the guard. The adversary could also exploit the night guard tour schedule in other ways, even if there were detection, because the response time of the guard from the top floor may be all the adversary needs to complete the task. For example, the intruders could forcibly break through the front doors after the guard leaves on his/her tour, and reduce their entry time for the attack. The reader is encouraged to consider other attack scenarios and practice changing performance estimates as needed to reflect the effect on the PPS.

Upgrade Analysis

Because both scenarios show a low overall system performance, the VA team considers some functional improvements to improve system effectiveness. The current system does not provide reliable detection or adequate delay, especially given the response time of the primary response force, the local police. To improve the P_I at night, both detection and delay elements are added to the PPS. In addition, the police response time was improved to high, which represents a good chance of interrupting the adversary. Although how the specific improvements are achieved is outside the scope of the VA, some examples are provided to illustrate improved system effectiveness. PPS improvements include adding sensors to some doors and areas, replacing PTZ cameras with fixed cameras, leaving enough lights on at night, and negotiating an agreement with local police. A new automatic AC&D subsystem using fast digital video recording and playback with sufficient resolution under day and night conditions is implemented, and delay is added at strategic locations, particularly in and around the Director's office. Daytime improvements are somewhat more difficult to achieve and focus on upgrades to the third floor. These changes might include better detection through sensors and visitor controls. The delays added in and around the Director's office will also be effective under daytime conditions. The guard response and patrol procedures were improved because of the ability to immediately assess building alarms using the new AC&D subsystem. This eliminated the need for the guard to patrol at night and reduced the guard's exposure to physical attack. Because guards can reliably assess alarms,

the police are now willing to respond more quickly because they know there is an intruder in the building when they are called. As a result of these improvements, the on-site guards can reliably assess alarms, notify police, observe-and-report, and use high-quality images to provide the police legally admissible information about any intruders. These changes improve BIG Company's security but also overall building security. These upgrades and their new performance estimates are summarized in Table 11-5.

These changes increase P_{AD} to high under most day attacks, and medium under some complex but still credible attacks, using the same defined threat. The earlier detection, additional delay, and faster response change P_I to high, and P_N to medium, because the opportunity still exists for the intruders to escape, although they are expected to surrender if confronted by local police. This results in an overall P_E of at least medium, but the high P_I is expected to discourage attacks by all but the most highly motivated threats.

Quantitative Analysis

A more rigorous method of analysis uses quantitative estimates of PPS component performance. This technique is generally

Table 11-5 *Functional Upgrades to Office Building.*

Description	Performance Estimates
All Exterior Doors and Interior Stairwell Doors, First and Third Floor Areas	P_D day/night = H (areas and opening or cutting doors) P_{As} day/night = H P_{AD} day/night = H
Directors Office Area (walls and safe)	P_D day/night = H P_{As} day/night = H P_{AD} day/night = H Delay = H
Response Time	Day/Night—Guards = M Day/night—Police = H

The earlier and more reliable detection, improved assessment, and strategically placed delays increased P_I to high. Both the guard and police response have improved under both day and night facility states.

used only at facilities that protect very valuable assets, and where there is an immediate response. Facilities such as military bases, commercial power plants (particularly nuclear, but other types as well), government agencies, and some critical infrastructures are good examples of these locations.

Facility Description

It is the year 2010. The Hartley Transportation Hub (Hartley Hub) is located in a medium-size city in the southwestern United States. The surrounding terrain is mostly flat and there is occasional heavy snow, rain, wind, and fog. The outside temperature varies from 20° F to 100° F. The Hub contains an airport, a rail cargo center, a trucking center, an air cargo terminal, and a secure cargo area. Also located at the Hartley Hub is a police substation. The Secure Cargo Area (SCA) is open every weekday from 5 AM until midnight; it is closed on weekends. The facility is meant to be a temporary storage location for various high value or critical assets, such as prototype microelectronics, precious metals or gems, drugs seized as evidence, or money being taken out of circulation. Hazardous materials in transit are stored in a special controlled room. The SCA is protected by the PPS shown in Figure 11-7; the legend for this figure is provided in Table 11-6.

During normal operating hours, the security force at the SCA consists of three armed security officers who are stationed at the front entrance. One officer operates the AC&D subsystem, another is stationed inside the personnel entry, and the third officer works the vehicle entry portal. When the facility is closed, there are two officers on duty (one operating the AC&D subsystem and the other on patrol). Anyone entering the SCA must pass through a personnel portal. Entering personnel first go to a badge exchange window (staffed by the guard who operates the AC&D system) where they exchange a plastic laminated identity badge for a facility access badge that includes a magnetic stripe and a picture. After the badge exchange, personnel pass through a metal detector and then an explosives detector. A security officer stands by the wall between the two detectors to verify that all persons pass through both detectors. The metal detector is always on. The explosives detector is used on a random basis or when there are hazardous agents stored in the controlled room. After passing through the two detectors, people exit through a set of double doors into the protected area of the facility.

The AC&D subsystem includes two video display monitors, one for exterior cameras and the other for interior cameras. Lights on this display indicate when a sensor is activated or a camera is in use. A computer monitor provides a graphic display of the site, with icons representing sensors and cameras. All cameras are fixed and are manually controlled by the operator. An audible alarm is sounded on a sensor alarm and the operator can enter a code to silence the alarm. Video information is recorded on tape at the rate of one frame every 5 seconds. Interior doors cannot be locked or unlocked by the operator, but sensors can be placed into secure, access, or maintenance modes.

All entering vehicles are searched in the vehicle portal. This portal consists of automatic sliding gates built into the inner and outer fences surrounding the SCA and is staffed by a security guard who conducts a manual search of the vehicle. Once the vehicle has entered the portal, the driver exits the portal through the open outer gate and enters the SCA through the personnel portal. The officer controlling the AC&D subsystem closes the outer gate, thereby "trapping" the vehicle in the portal, until it is cleared to enter. Once the vehicle is searched, the inner gate is opened and the driver, who has cleared the personnel portal, rejoins the vehicle. All vehicles admitted through

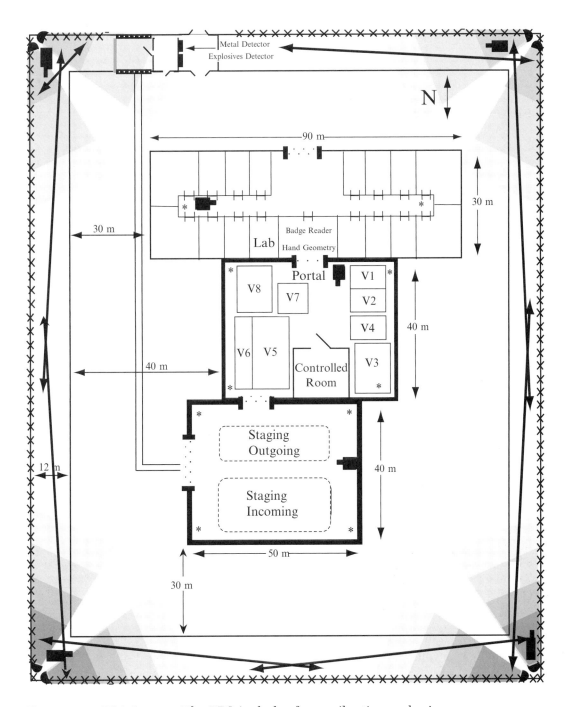

Figure 11-7 SCA Layout. The PPS includes fence vibration and microwave sensors on the perimeter, along with fixed CCTV cameras and lights. The interior areas have fixed cameras and microwave sensors. The drawing is not to scale.

Table 11-6 *SCA Layout Legend.*

PPS Element	Description	ASD Icon
	2 m chain-link fence mesh with outriggers (4 mm × 50 mm-mesh)	ISO
x x 〉	Fence vibration sensor	ISO
←——→	Exterior microwave sensors	ISO
	Fixed CCTV cameras	ISO, SUR1, SUR2
	Exterior light and lighting contour	ISO
••••••	Rolling vehicle gates	VEH
	Personnel portals	PER1, PER2
	Paved road from vehicle gate to staging area	SCA property, distance across layer
*	Interior microwave sensors	SUR2, SCA building
Vehicle Door	1.6-mm thick standard steel roll-up door, with balanced magnetic switch and grid mesh	VHD
Personnel doors	1.6-mm thick standard steel personnel door, with balanced magnetic switch and grid mesh. There are two doors, made of the same material, so the same ASD symbol is used.	DOR1
	15-cm thick reinforced concrete wall	SUR1
	30-cm thick reinforced concrete wall	SUR2
V#	Vinyl coated 3 mm × 50 mm-mesh cage enclosure	CGE
Controlled Room Wall	Standard sheet rock/wood stud wall	SUR3

The table describes locations and PPS elements used at the SCA. It also references the appropriate icon on the site ASD.

the portal must have an entry sticker on their front windshields. If the entering vehicle is picking up or delivering assets for storage, the officer assigned to the portal gets in the vehicle with the driver to go to the staging area. During this time no other vehicles can enter or leave the SCA.

The Staging Area of the SCA is accessed through a standard roll-up door that is large enough for a vehicle to pull through (see Figure 11-7 and Table 11-6). The officer and driver exit the vehicle and facility personnel unload the cargo, place the material in the incoming staging section, and complete the required paperwork. During operating hours, the roll-up door is open and unlocked and the BMS on the door is placed in access, preventing it from detecting any entry. When unloading is complete, the officer and driver

reenter the vehicle, drive back to the vehicle portal, wait for the inner gate to be opened, and park the vehicle in the trap. At this time, the officer exits the vehicle, the inner gate is closed, the outer gate is opened, and the driver and vehicle are free to leave the facility. The process is reversed for the removal of material from the facility and repeated for each vehicle moving cargo in or out of the facility, one at a time.

The Cargo Storage Building at the SCA includes the Office Area, the Storage Area, and the Staging Area. The Office Area is an administrative building where various facility personnel have offices and administrative work is done. There is also a small laboratory for maintenance, storage, and repair of small facility equipment. Located inside the Storage Area are a number of cages for stored assets and a controlled room, which holds hazardous materials in transit.

Stored assets are kept in a storage area that is composed of a series of steel mesh storage cages of varying size. The storage area may be accessed through one of two entry doors. One door is located right off the staging area. The other door is located between the office area and storage area. This door is equipped with electronic locks that are opened through the use of a magnetic stripe badge reader and a hand geometry unit. No stored assets are allowed through this door (all stored material must enter through the staging area). The controlled room is accessed via the storage area and holds environmental chambers for the storage of hazardous assets. The chambers can regulate temperature, humidity, and pressure to store these samples appropriately.

There are approximately 60 employees at the SCA. This workforce includes a Facility Manager, a Security Manager, an Operations Manager, engineers and technicians, material handlers, clerks, secretaries, custodians, and security officers. Various subcontractors are also allowed into the facility at times to do maintenance or emergency repair work on heating, cooling, plumbing systems, computers, forklifts, copy machines, etc.

The primary response force for the SCA is the local police. The local police are also responsible for protecting the airport, other facilities at Hartley Hub, and patrolling other areas of the city. As a result, their response time to an attack on the SCA is 20 minutes. When alerted by the dispatcher that the SCA is under attack, all eight police officers on patrol in the city return to the substation. The first four police officers to reach the substation become the response force to the SCA; the others are released back to normal patrol. These four officers collect their gear, review tactics and procedures, and then go to the SCA as a group. Once at the SCA, they contact the local SCA security officer

in charge and deploy according to a set procedure.

The primary function of the SCA security guards during an attack is to assess all alarms, and contact local law enforcement when intrusions are verified. There is an agreement in place between the Hartley Hub and local police that ensures that police will respond within 20 minutes to valid intrusions, if other higher priority events are not occurring at the Hub or in the community. The local police and SCA guards have had one practice drill together in the last 2 years. While they wait for the police to arrive, SCA guards use an observe-and-report strategy. The security guard operating the AC&D subsystem opens the vehicle gates for the police when they arrive, and passes along current information about the attack. The guards have .38 caliber revolvers and are authorized to use their weapons only when they or someone else is in imminent danger of attack by an intruder. They have no additional weapons. Each guard carries a hand-held six watt clear-voice radio with a duress alarm. Backup communication at the facility and to the police is accomplished through the use of land and cellular telephones. The security guards use authentication and communication codes when operating radios.

The ASD for this facility is shown in Figure 11-8. Performance estimates for the installed security elements are shown in Table 11-7. The defined threat used for the analysis is a small group of three to five criminals, who plan to steal one of the stored assets from the storage cages. They have a large truck, automatic weapons, hand and power tools, and are experienced at using all of their equipment. They are prepared to use force against the facility security guards and the local police to evade capture.

The SCA ASD shows layers starting at off-site, onto the SCA property, and then the exterior walls of the cargo storage building (the combined office, storage, and staging areas). The next layer is the

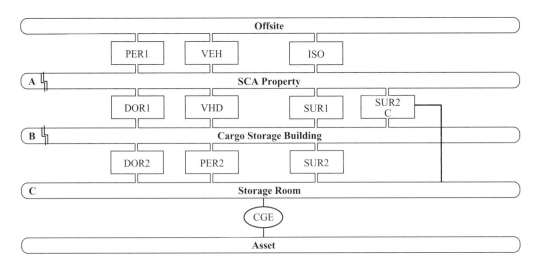

Figure 11-8 ASD for SCA Facility. This facility uses a double fence perimeter, including a clear zone with two lines of detection, and cameras and lights for alarm assessment. Personnel and vehicle portals are located on the perimeter, and another personnel portal controls access between the cargo storage building and the storage area.

storage room, which shares a common wall with the cargo storage building (SUR2, the 30-cm thick reinforced concrete wall). This common wall is the reason there is a jump from outside the building into the storage area—attacking this wall at the right location provides immediate access to the storage room and bypasses path elements in layer B. The small jagged lines at the left edge of layers A and B represent a vehicle path across these layers. This technique is used to show which layers can be traversed using vehicles or helicopters. At the SCA, a vehicle can be driven through the exterior perimeter, across the open space to the building, and through the roll-up door (even if closed) to breach all the path elements up to the storage room. The enclosure around the asset (CGE, which are storage cages V1-8 and associated detection or delay) is described as part of the CGE icon. There is no detection at the asset, only delay. Interior sensors are associated with path elements (DOR1, DOR2, PER2, and SUR2) between the cargo storage building and the storage room, as they would give an alarm if someone came through any of these elements.

In this facility, there are multiple target locations—the storage room and the controlled room that contain potentially hazardous biological samples. This is not meant to be an extremely credible attack scenario, but is used to illustrate how the ASD will change for multiple target locations. If the asset to be attacked is in the controlled room, the ASD shown in Figure 11-9 would represent the additional layer of protection that is available. In this case, the only path elements that are added are the delay for the controlled room wall (SUR3), and for accessing the environmental chambers (CGE); there is no detection in the controlled room. The sheet rock wall has a minimal delay to even simple tools, perhaps 10 to 15 seconds, and the chambers are not locked and easily opened (a few seconds of delay).

Path Analysis

An EASI analysis for the best interruption possible at the site is shown in Figure 11-10. This path uses performance estimates for a night attack on the closed facility, when all interior sensors are

Table 11-7 *Data for Physical Protection System Components at the SCA.*

Threat:	Three to five outsiders, large vehicle (truck), carrying hand and power tools, large handguns or automatic weapons, highly motivated, competent, possible passive insider assistance (information only)
Travel times:	Running, approximately 4 meters/second
Doors in personnel portal:	12-second delay per door
15-cm, reinforced concrete:	8-minute delay
30-cm, reinforced concrete:	30-minute delay
Climb fence:	10-second delay (climbing)
Tilt/vibration fence sensor:	0.1 probability of detection, open/closed
Microwave exterior detection system:	0.2 probability of detection, open/closed
CCTV cameras:	Fixed, black-and-white, 600 horizontal lines resolution
Alarm assessment:	0.25 probability of assessment, all times
Assessment time:	Manual (guard): 5-8 minutes
	Video: 60-90 seconds
Lighting:	Exterior: high pressure sodium
	Exterior light-to-dark ratio: 24:1 (night)
	Interior—fluorescent
	Interior light-to-dark ratio:
	Day: 3:1
	Night: 12:1
	Scene reflectance:
	Exterior: 30%
	Interior: 40%
1.6-mm doors (one door into vault area and one outside door into staging area):	1-minute delay
ID check (ID badge exchange):	0.9 probability of detection
Metal detector (ME):	0.9 probability of detection
Explosives detector (EX):	0.1 probability of detection
ID, ME, and EX time:	5-second delay for each
Combined badge reader/hand geometry unit:	0.85 probability of detection
Badge reader/hand geometry delay time:	8-second delay
Officer at post:	0.2 probability of detection
Officer at post:	30-second delay
BMS on building doors:	0.99 probability of detection
Interior microwave sensors:	0.9 probability of detection when on (off during normal daytime operations)
Time to steal asset:	2-minutes (including time to penetrate enclosure)
Time to sabotage assets in controlled room:	50 seconds
Average response time:	SCA: 3.8 minutes
	Local police: 20 minutes
Standard deviation on all times:	30% of mean
Probability of guard communication (P_C):	0.95

The defined threat is described in the first box of the second column, and all performance estimates are based on their tools and capabilities. Note that many of the PPS components have the same performance under open or closed states, although there may be different reasons for this.

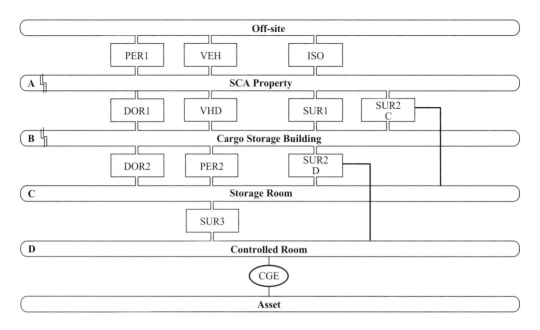

Figure 11-9 ASD for Controlled Room. This diagram shows paths to the hazardous assets stored in the Controlled Room, which adds another protection layer.

active; however, note the low performance estimates for PPS elements along the path, even including the interior sensors. These estimates are low because there are many bypass paths into the facility—over the vehicle portal, over the fence sensor (installed on the outer fence, a major vulnerability)—and the perimeter microwave detection pattern has many entry areas with no coverage. In addition, there is no real video assessment capability for sensor alarms, during the day or at night. During the day, the bypasses just noted exist, and the interior sensors are in access, there are too few exterior cameras to maintain resolution or complete coverage, and the interior cameras have blind spots under them. At night, the exterior and interior lighting is not very good, resolution is limited, and interior cameras do not match up well with sensor zones, particularly in the storage room, where there are many hiding places between the storage vault cages. During bad weather, such as fog, heavy snow, or rainfall, camera resolution is completely degraded, and P_{As} decreases to zero. The AC&D subsystem is slow and manually operated but does record images, although the recording rate could miss some running attacks. The response time from the local police is fairly long compared to the system delays (20 minutes or 1,200 seconds versus 352 seconds total along the path), resulting in a P_I = 0. Only two of the on-site guards are really able to respond during the day, and only one at night (one must wait at the gate for the police to arrive to let them in and brief them on status), so the advantage in numbers goes to the adversary. Interruption by on-site guards is higher (0.2, analysis not shown, changed response time to 228 seconds ± 68 seconds), but there is a question of effectiveness of the guards in neutralizing this adversary group, given their superior numbers and motivation (discussed further under Estimate Neutralization). Note that using the police response time, the CDP is outside the outer fence, which is why further path analysis was not conducted. The overall path analysis shows that the system is not very effective and there are several vulnerabilities.

	D22	▼		fx	=+EASI2.XLSIO21			

	A	B	C	D	E	F	G
1							
2			*Estimate of*	Probability of			
3			*Adversary*	Guard		Response Force Time (in Seconds)	
4			*Sequence*	Communication		Mean	Standard Deviation
5			*Interruption*	0.95		1200	360
6							
7						Delays (in Seconds):	
8		Task	Description	P(AD)	Location	Mean:	Standard Deviation
9		1	Cross perimeter	0.1	B	10	3
10		2	Run to Roll-up Door	0	B	12	3.6
11		3	Penetrate Roll-up Door	0.25	B	90	27
12		4	Run to Storage Vault	0.2	B	10	3
13		5	Steal Asset	0	B	120	36
14		6	Exit to outside	0.2	B	10	3
15		7	Cross perimeter	0.1	B	10	3
16		8					
17		9					
18		10					
19		11					
20		12					
21							
22			Probability of Interruption:	0.001644639			
23							

Figure 11-10 EASI Analysis of Night Path. This attack encounters active interior sensors and so is the best performance expected under all facility states or weather. The attack scenario used intruders on foot. The path starts at ISO, crosses to VHD, through DOR2, and then progresses to CGE where assets are stored. The exit path reverses the same path (DOR2, VHD, cross to ISO, exit). Analysis was performed using the local police, the primary response force. Because performance is so low, additional paths were not analyzed.

Before continuing this discussion, a discrepancy in model nomenclature must be addressed. In the *Design* textbook, EASI was described as using the probability of detection (P_D), but in truth this is really assessed detection (P_{AD}). This is an artifact of software model evolution and different path analysis tools. Because EASI is a simple single-path tool, the P_{AD} calculation is manual; more complex multi-path computer models take P_D and P_{As} estimates and calculate P_{AD} within the tool. This is also a good time to note that because assessed detection is the measure of the detection function, even in a quantitative analysis where there is good sensing (a P_D of 0.9) and excellent assessment (a P_{As} of 0.95), the overall P_{AD} will be the product of the two terms or 0.85. This is a good example of the error of depending

on software and the need for a human analyst to interpret results. In fact, the overall system performance is better than this, but because we know that we will never achieve a P_D or P_{As} of 1.0, the mathematical product limits the performance to an artificially low number. In reality, if sensing and alarm assessment were this good under all weather and facility states, P_{AD} would be estimated as 0.95. This performance also assumes the use of a fast and effective AC&D subsystem, which would not result in any additional P_{AD} degradation as a result of component delays or operator inefficiencies. This is a minor but noteworthy point that emphasizes the need for both qualitative and quantitative techniques in a VA. Even so, 0.85 is the same as rounding to 0.9, which is still very good performance.

A few notes on the analysis and performance estimates are provided to aid the reader in following the path analysis. The high P_D of the door BMS (0.99) and interior microwave sensors (0.9) are degraded by the low P_{As} of the system (0.25). The low P_{As} is primarily driven by the lack of a sufficient number of cameras to give full sensor and area coverage; the slow display and review of the recorded video by the AC&D subsystem further degrade P_{AD}. Delays assume the running rates shown in Table 11-7 or penetration of barrier materials using the data found in Appendix F.

Calculation of P_{AD} for the ISO path element may not be intuitively obvious and is reviewed to demonstrate how sensors may be combined into an overall estimate. The ISO icon represents the double fences, clear zone, sensors, and alarm assessment capability of the exterior perimeter. This zone uses a fence sensor on the outer fence, which is estimated as a P_D of 0.1 during the open or closed facility states (this is the best performance expected from this device; bad weather will only reduce performance, as noted previously). The microwave sensors have an estimated P_D of 0.2 during these same states. This means that the probability of passing undetected past each sensor is 0.9 and 0.8, respectively (subtract P_D from 1.0 to get nondetection probability). As explained in the *Design* textbook, the EASI model uses the probability of nondetection in calculations, and this calculation is incorporated into the model for each P_D entered into a cell. To calculate the combined P_D of the two sensors, we multiply the nondetection probabilities and subtract from 1.0 to get P_D. This number is then multiplied by the estimated P_{As} (0.25) to arrive at the P_{AD}, which is the value entered for the adversary task of crossing the perimeter. This calculation gives:

$$(0.9 \times 0.8) = 0.7 \text{ (probability of nondetection)}$$

Then $(1.0–0.7) = 0.3$ (P_D) and $(0.3 \times 0.25) = 0.07$ (P_{AD}), which is rounded to 0.1 for simplicity.

This is one technique used to represent overall detection at locations where multiple sensors must be combined to facilitate path analysis. The assumption in this case is that these are independent variables, which may not always be the case and makes the analysis a somewhat conservative overall estimate of P_I. Also, note that the column representing delay with respect to detection is always B, or beginning. This is another conservative technique used in this particular analysis because overall performance is obviously very low, and the minor changes in delay will have little effect on P_I for this path. (This is discussed in the *Design* textbook, but recall that delay may be at the beginning (B), middle (M), or end (E) of detection.) The reader is encouraged to try different combinations of this value to observe the effect of this change on this particular calculation and to consider use of this variable to better estimate P_I for different combinations of sensors and barriers in general.

Scenario Analysis

Given the low performance of the facility PPS during the initial path analysis, scenario analysis may not provide much additional insight, but some points can be highlighted. For example, consider a daytime attack where three adversaries use a large truck to crash the perimeter (ISO, perhaps from the side that leads right to the roll-up door. This is the fastest path, but crashing the perimeter is relatively easy from any side), drive across the exterior area, and into the Staging Area through the open roll-up door (VHD). Then they stop at the personnel entry door (DOR2) into the Storage Room, run through it (it is unlocked all the time), go to the storage cages (CGE), penetrate the cage and steal the asset, and leave in the truck, which is still usable, along the same path. The analysis is shown in Figure 11-11. This path and scenario are particularly good because they highlight the vulnerability of both the roll-up and personnel doors on this path, especially during the day.

In this scenario, notice that after the initial vehicle penetration of the perimeter, the P_{AD} for the remaining adversary tasks is increased to 0.95 because it is expected that during the daytime, someone will notice a vehicle barreling through the fences and doors, and personnel in the staging area and storage area will eventually see the intruders. Probability estimates are rarely 1.0 because of the possibility of failure or some other attack tactic, but 0.95 is nearly 1.0. The delay times for this scenario are quite short, even for a vehicle moving relatively slowly (e.g., 35 to 40 mph). The terrain around the SCA is relatively flat, so the vehicle could get up to a reasonable speed, crash the fence, and keep going with little damage. Given this scenario and police response, P_I is still 0.0; using response by SCA guards, P_I decreases to 0.16, not much of a change. This may seem like a useless analysis; however, it does emphasize that even increasing detection to the best it can be will not increase P_I for either response group.

Next, consider another nighttime attack scenario that starts with three attackers who climb over the fences (ISO, bypassing fence and microwave sensors), then cut a hole in the roll-up door (VHD, bypassing the BMS), enter through the personnel door (DOR1), and attack as before, then leave the same way. This scenario analysis is shown in Figure 11-12. P_I for the police is still 0.0, the same as for the initial night attack path analysis shown in Figure 11-10. The SCA guards also have a P_I of 0.0, a decrease resulting from the lack of detection, even considering their relatively fast response (compared to the police). This analysis

		D22	▼	f_x =+EASI2.XLS!O21				
	A	B	C	D	E	F	G	
1								
2			*Estimate of*	Probability of				
3			*Adversary*	Guard		Response Force Time (in Seconds)		
4			*Sequence*	Communication		Mean	Standard Deviation	
5			*Interruption*	0.95		1200	360	
6								
7						Delays (in Seconds):		
8		Task	Description	P(AD)	Location	Mean:	Standard Deviation	
9		1	Drive through Perimeter	0.1	B	1	0.3	
10		2	Drive to Roll-up Door	0.95	B	4	1.2	
11		3	Drive Through Staging Area	0.95	B	0	0	
12		4	Run to Storage Vault	0.95	B	10	3	
13		5	Steal Asset	0.95	B	120	36	
14		6	Exit to Vehicle	0.95	B	10	3	
15		7	Exit through Perimeter	0.95	B	10	3	
16		8						
17		9						
18		10						
19		11						
20		12						
21								
22			Probability of Interruption:	0.001823862				

Figure 11-11 Day Attack Scenario Analysis. During the day, interior sensors are in access, but the use of a vehicle to crash the perimeter makes these sensors ineffective even if on, due to the speed of the attack versus response time.

| D22 | ▾ | fx | =+EASI2.XLSIO21 | | | |

	A	B	C	D	E	F	G
1							
2			*Estimate of*	Probability of			
3			*Adversary*	Guard		Response Force Time (in Seconds)	
4			*Sequence*	Communication		Mean	Standard Deviation
5			*Interruption*	0.95		1200	360
6							
7						Delays (in Seconds):	
8		Task	Description	P(AD)	Location	Mean:	Standard Deviation
9		1	Cross perimeter	0	B	10	3
10		2	Run to Roll-up Door	0	B	12	3.6
11		3	Penetrate Roll-up Door	0	B	90	27
12		4	Run to Storage Vault	0.2	B	10	3
13		5	Steal Asset	0	B	120	36
14		6	Exit to outside	0	B	10	3
15		7	Cross perimeter	0	B	10	3
16		8					
17		9					
18		10					
19		11					
20		12					
21							
22			Probability of Interruption:	0.00035237			

Figure 11-12 Night Scenario Analysis. This attack path is similar to the one shown in Figure 11-10, but the intruders avoid detection along the entire path because of the gaps in sensor detection, low assessment capability, and a slow AC&D subsystem. Although there is clearly not enough delay on the path, this scenario shows how little the sensor and video subsystems contribute to P_I, given their vulnerabilities.

only underscores how the individual vulnerabilities in sensors and video combine to limit overall performance, even against a threat that does not use a vehicle to enter. These analyses should demonstrate the need for timely detection, adequate delay, and immediate response to ensure a reasonable P_I, over many paths and under varying attack tactics.

As noted previously, sabotage attacks are possible because of the type of materials stored in the controlled room, but none of these paths will be analyzed. It should be apparent that the same attack scenarios used for theft could be used for a successful sabotage attack and, because successful sabotage does not require that the adversary gets away, these attacks are faster. Other scenarios that might be considered are attacks during SCA Family Day when many unfamiliar faces can enter the facility, a time when the com-

pany Board of Directors (or other VIPs) visits, when adversaries masquerade as maintenance personnel, by insiders, or during a power failure or fire (diversionary or real).

Estimate Neutralization

Predictions of P_N used a computer simulation tool and the same scenarios described earlier to determine the effectiveness of the SCA guards and local law enforcement. Although P_I is low for both groups of responders, neutralization was still estimated using the scenarios described previously, and some others. For these simulations, it is assumed that interruption has occurred. By simulating these face-to-face encounters, additional insights as to response effectiveness are gathered, and opportunities for upgrade can be explored. In addition, each scenario was simulated using adversary groups of three or five members to determine any differences in neutralization using the largest and smallest number of attackers. For the simulation, the local police were given 9-mm semiautomatic pistols and pump action shotguns, which are their standard weapons. The threat was defined to have better weapons (9-mm semiautomatic pistols and an AK-47) than both response groups in some scenarios, and these scenarios were analyzed using superior weapons, for each adversary group size.

Using the simulation program, P_N of the SCA guards during the day and at night was estimated to be 0.1 for a group of five adversaries, assuming equal weapons. Simulations of the on-site guards against a group of three equally equipped adversaries gave a P_N of 0.2 during the day and 0.1 at night. This was explained by the fact that one guard always stays at the front gate, and the adversary team is expected to deploy one of their three members to observe the guard and arrival by local police, thereby allowing some small chance of neutralization given the even numbers (three attackers, three security guards) during the day. In addition, the security guards do not get a lot of training, only qualify on weapons once each year, and are limited as to when they can use their weapons, all of which adds to their inability to fight effectively. The local police were somewhat better at neutralization against three adversaries with equal weapons ($P_N = 0.5$ at all times), but not as effective against a group of five attackers using equal weapons ($P_N = 0.3$). Against a group of five adversaries with better weapons, P_N for the police dropped to 0.1. These neutralization estimates were highly dependent on the attack scenario and represent the best performance that was obtained. For example, one simulation of police against five adversaries used the following scenario: After defeating the perimeter, the adversaries split into two groups—a group of two who will attack the asset and a second group of three, who will deploy near the main entry gate into the SCA and await the police. If the police arrive before the other team escapes with the asset, the second team will open fire on the police officers, using the AK-47 to effectively stop their response. At least five simulations were performed for each scenario, and eight were performed for the police versus five better equipped attackers. These results are summarized in Table 11-8.

Baseline System Effectiveness

Applying the formula

$$P_E = P_I * P_N$$

gives 0.0×0.5, or 0.0 as the overall baseline P_E for the local police. The SCA guards give a slightly better result, 0.35×0.1 or 0.03, but this is still basically 0.0. Note that this used the best P_I achievable, and the best P_N against the lower number of attackers. Any other combination results in lower performance, although this is not useful when considering that using either local police or on-site guards resulted in an ineffective PPS. These results underscore the need for reliable interruption (i.e., arrival of responders) to neutralize effectively. As a result, the analysis shows that functional upgrades are needed to improve performance against the defined threat.

Upgrade Analysis

A number of upgrades must be made to improve the overall P_E at the SCA. Improvements to all three functional aspects of the PPS—detection, delay, and response—are considered. As in the qualitative example, some specific changes are provided to show how it might be done (using readily available technology

Table 11-8 *Results of Neutralization Simulations.*

Adversary Number/Weapons Response Group	3/Equal Weapons	5/Equal Weapons	5/Superior Weapons
SCA Guards	Day: 0.2 Night: 0.1	Day: 0.1 Night: 0.1	N/A N/A
Police	Day: 0.5 Night: 0.5	Day: 0.3 Night: 0.3	Day/Night: 0.1

The complexities of the simulations will not be addressed, but these are the summarized results. Because of the low performance of the SCA guards against five equally equipped attackers, no simulations against better equipped adversaries were conducted.

and some procedural improvements), despite the fact that this should not be a part of the VA. Some simple sensor changes at the perimeter, such as moving the fence sensor from the outer fence to the inner fence and adding more microwave sensors to provide contiguous detection in the perimeter (and over the personnel entry portal) will improve P_D. Alarm assessment can be improved by adding lights, moving them to the inside of the inner fence, adding exterior and interior cameras, and addressing assessment of sensors in the exterior zones on either side of the perimeter portal. There should be at least two fixed exterior cameras in each leg of the perimeter; interior cameras must be added to eliminate existing blind spots and to give complete sensor detection zone coverage for intrusion and tamper alarm assessments. The AC&D subsystem should be automated and should display multiple recorded video images to the operator well within 1 second. By adding some delay outside the roll-up door using moveable concrete posts or pop-up barriers, this attack path can be strengthened against vehicle attacks. Delay against vehicles can be added to the perimeter through the use of aircraft cable on the inner fence; interior delays have been added to the personnel door leading into the storage area and at the cages. Improvements in police response time include identifying a specific group of four responders who carry their

equipment in vehicles, and then respond right to the SCA, not the substation. This will reduce response time to 15 minutes. These changes have the same P_{AD} of 0.95 as before for a vehicle attack, but now enough delay has been added to increase P_I to a much more reasonable number. Note that delay has been doubled at the storage cages. (If delay were doubled once again at this location, P_I would increase to 0.9.) Improved operating procedures in the Staging Area will also help, for example, keeping the roll-up door closed when vehicles are not dropping off or picking up cargo and closing and locking the personnel door into the storage area would make some attacks harder. Using the same vehicle attack scenario of Figure 11-11, the new day path analysis is shown in Figure 11-13.

These upgrades result in a P_I of 0.7 for the local police; although the analysis is not shown, the SCA guards have a P_I of 0.9. Note that the increase in detection at the perimeter was not as effective as the increase in delays and decrease in response time for a vehicle attack. Using these same performance measures for an attack by adversaries on foot (as in Figure 11-10) gives a P_I of 0.7 (rounded up from 0.66, see Figure 11-14), which indicates balance along these paths for different adversary attacks. Addition of delay at the perimeter has also made it impossible for the adversary to continue the attack using the vehicle; this means that they will be on

	D22	▼	fx	=+EASI2.XLSIO21			
	A	B	C	D	E	F	G

	Estimate of	Probability of				
	Adversary	Guard		Response Force Time (in Seconds)		
	Sequence	Communication		Mean	Standard Deviation	
	Interruption	0.95		600	180	

Task	Description	P(AD)	Location	Delays (in Seconds): Mean:	Standard Deviation
1	Drive through Perimeter	0.95	B	60	18
2	Run to Roll-up Door	0.95	B	12	3.6
3	Run Through Staging Area	0.95	B	120	36
4	Run to Storage Vault	0.95	B	120	36
5	Steal Asset	0.95	B	240	72
6	Run to Perimeter	0.95	B	120	36
7	Exit through Perimeter	0.95	B	60	18
8	Enter Second Vehicle	0.95	B	10	3
9					
10					
11					
12					

Probability of Interruption:	0.712857123

Figure 11-13 Upgraded Day Attack Scenario Analysis. P_I for the police has improved to 0.7. Specific devices are not identified until the design stage that follows the VA.

	D22	▼	fx	=+EASI2.XLSIO21			
	A	B	C	D	E	F	G

	Estimate of	Probability of				
	Adversary	Guard		Response Force Time (in Seconds)		
	Sequence	Communication		Mean	Standard Deviation	
	Interruption	0.95		600	180	

Task	Description	P(AD)	Location	Delays (in Seconds): Mean:	Standard Deviation
1	Cross perimeter	0.95	B	30	9
2	Run to Roll-up Door	0	B	12	3.6
3	Penetrate Roll-up Door	0.95	B	120	36
4	Run to Storage Vault	0.95	B	120	36
5	Steal Asset	0.95	B	240	72
6	Exit to outside	0.95	B	120	36
7	Cross perimeter	0.95	B	60	18
8	Enter Second Vehicle	0.95	B	10	3
9					
10					
11					
12					

Probability of Interruption:	0.668385861

Figure 11-14 SCA Upgrade Analysis for a Foot Attack. The additional detection and delay improvements result in a very balanced system for multiple attack tactics, which is a highly desirable outcome. Note that there is no detection while adversaries run to the roll-up door, because this is a nighttime attack and there is a low likelihood the guard on patrol will see the intruders.

foot for the rest of the attack, which adds delay to their tasks. The task "Run through Staging Area" also has considerable delay. This is not due to the distance, but to the addition of delay at the personnel door into the storage area. In the same manner, running to the perimeter now takes 120 seconds, because the adversaries have to carry the asset to and across the perimeter, which also takes longer. Because the crash vehicle is disabled, the attackers need a second vehicle to make their escape, which requires that they either add another member to the team or have one fewer person to help during the attack. Note that after the perimeter is breached, these attack scenarios are the same because of the loss of the attack vehicle. The delay time for adversaries on foot is only 30 seconds, but the vehicle delay is 60 seconds because the adversaries in the vehicle need some time to recover from the crash, and then exit the vehicle with their equipment and finish crossing the perimeter. Consideration of alternate attack scenarios may show better system performance using these new performance estimates.

Improvements to both guard and police effectiveness in neutralization will increase P_N to 0.5 and 0.8 against equal adversaries, respectively, resulting in a P_E of 0.6 for the local police (0.5 for guards). These improvements might include giving SCA guards better weapons and having them train with local police more often. The response tactics of the local police can also be improved to reduce the chance of an ambush. Although these results may not appear to be very good, consider that the system started at zero P_E and has now improved to 0.6. Not a bad result for a few simple changes—adding some sensors, cameras, delay barriers, moving other devices to get better performance, and improving response time. The biggest expense will be the upgrade to a better AC&D subsystem, but this system should be operational for a significant period of time (5 to 10 years, possibly more if a good procurement specification is written).

Readers are cautioned not to interpret upgrade analysis as a simple process of filling in high performance estimates and completing the analysis. As noted previously, these functional performance improvements must be considered to be achievable by the VA team. The SCA uses a considerable amount of equipment and has an immediate response capability, and performance was improved by eliminating holes in sensor detection, improving the AC&D subsystem to give faster and more accurate alarm assessment, addition of delay (mostly at or near the target), and reducing response time. These are all reasonable improvements that upgrade the existing system. Use of performance estimates that are not achievable using existing technology or procedural changes (like a faster response) is not recommended and would not contribute to a useful analysis. As a related note, when quantitative performance data are used, the estimates should not be a result of simply looking up tested performance values of individual devices and using them in the path analysis model. Generally speaking, the tested values represent ideal or maximum performance and do not reflect effects of facility states on performance. As repeatedly emphasized throughout Chapters 5–10, the selection, installation, maintenance, and integration of PPS components as they exist at the facility have a major impact on performance estimates. This is why the VA team must actually visit the facility—to determine how much ideal performance should be degraded based on actual operation at the facility. Simply using the tested values in analysis does not require a trip to the facility and will likely lead to higher system effectiveness predictions than justified. At the same time, any preliminary work on facility ASDs and performance estimates that can be accomplished before the VA team's arrival on-site can be a time-saving procedure. This often happens in repeat facility VAs, where the ASD and performance estimates already exist, or when the VA team has received sufficient documentation that allows them to start drawing the ASD. In either case, the starting ASD can be modified as the team completes their evaluation activities.

Summary

This chapter described how to analyze PPS effectiveness after all appropriate data are collected. Two basic techniques can be used, compliance- and performance-based. Compliance-based approaches depend on conformance to policies and use checklists to document deficiencies of the protection system. They depend on presence, not effectiveness, of installed PPS elements. Performance-based approaches evaluate system effectiveness, while complying with regulations or policy at the same time. Performance-based approaches are recommended and they were the main topic of discussion in the chapter. Performance may be predicted using qualitative or quantitative techniques, and the primary difference is the use of numerical performance estimates for security elements, particularly hardware, but also the response force. This approach removes subjectivity from the analysis and provides a rational basis for assumptions and upgrade recommendations. A simple six-step process was described, starting with drawing an ASD and path analysis, followed by scenario analysis, and then calculating neutralization, if appropriate. Then overall system effectiveness is estimated, and an upgrade analysis is performed if the system does not effectively meet protection objectives. Examples of a qualitative and quantitative analysis were discussed to introduce the process and communicate some basic concepts.

12
Reporting and Using Results

After analysis of site data is complete, the VA team must report results in a manner that is useful to the managers at the facility and the enterprise. The goal of the report is to provide accurate, unbiased information that clearly defines the current effectiveness of the PPS, along with potential solutions if the current system is not effective. The VA informs facility management of the state of the PPS and supports upgrade decisions. Final reports and briefings are generally used to document this information and serve as a reference for any follow-on activities. In general, the VA report is then used in successive projects that address the identified vulnerabilities and improve the PPS at the facility. If upgrades are implemented, the VA report provides performance requirements to the upgrade design team. This team then selects the specific PPS components that will meet these requirements.

The key concepts discussed in this chapter include:

- Methods of reporting VA results
- Recommended content and format of written reports
- Using the VA in upgrade designs
- Project closeout activities

There is no comparable information on this topic in the *Design* textbook. This chapter reviews various methods and types of reporting, how VA results are used to support any follow-on work to address identified vulnerabilities, and project management techniques for ending the project in an ordered and effective manner.

Overview

The VA report provides a permanent record of VA team observations, their effects on baseline system performance, and potential improvements that can be made to increase PPS effectiveness if the baseline does not meet the protection

295

objectives. Reporting can be formal or informal, verbal or written, and may take the form of a short overview, or a longer more detailed document. The choice of reporting form and content is an aspect of the project agreement and generally follows the conventions of the enterprise or facility being evaluated. Regardless of how reporting is presented and documented, certain content must be included to make the report understandable and useful to the facility.

As described in Chapter 2, a VA may be a discrete project (with a set start and end point) or part of a larger project that is meant to improve security at a site. Generally, a VA does not end in a detailed design for security upgrades, but rather presents the baseline and upgrade analysis that describe current and improved system effectiveness. As a result, the VA team and the team that designs the upgraded PPS should be different groups. There are advantages to separating the VA team from the team of technical experts who will design upgrades, most notably the independence of the two groups. As a general rule, it is better to have one group evaluate and a separate group design upgrades to ensure independence in both stages. In addition, the VA team may not have the technical depth required to fully define all the equipment specifications, installation, maintenance, testing, and integration details that a good design requires. These details are covered in design stages that usually start with a conceptual design, proceed to a preliminary design, and end in a final design that will be implemented. The primary difference among the design stages is the level of detail that is included, which is an iterative process that requires discussion between the design team and facility personnel to agree on the best approach. The amount of time the design stages will take depends on the amount and types of upgrades required. For example, procedural changes are faster and easier to define and implement than the addition of many hardware components. These stages can be separated by formal reviews or progress more seamlessly from conceptual to final design.

After the VA project is complete, which is defined as delivery of all reports, completion of other administrative and financial project milestones and deliverables, and archiving of all project data and reports, the VA project can be closed. This process may not be followed if the VA project is the preliminary step in a larger project to improve security protection at the facility. Before the VA team is relieved of further project responsibility, there are some recommended procedures that will document the project and capture any improvements that can be applied to future projects. This is generally done through a short meeting with the entire VA team, but it can be accomplished through other means as well.

Each of these aspects of completing a VA is described in the following sections. Because of the wide variety of approaches used by different enterprises, these details vary for each specific site, but in general, these concepts form the framework for the end stages of the VA.

Reporting Results

The two most common methods used to present VA results include briefings and reports. Briefings alone may be acceptable if the evaluation is relatively simple, the site is small, the project scope is somewhat limited, and management is familiar with the VA process. In such cases, a high-level executive summary may be completed by the VA team and provided before their departure from the site. As noted in Chapter 3, the type and format of any reports on the VA are described in the master project agreement. It is strongly recommended that all VAs be documented in some kind of final report, even if these are only used to archive the data and analysis for future security evaluations.

Briefings and reports may be informal or informal and include varying amounts of detail depending on the project agreement and the analysis approach used. Informal briefings generally use slides or discussion to review the VA and recommendations, with no additional documentation provided to the facility. This type of reporting is used predominantly at small facilities where actions to address the VA findings are optional for facility management or where the VA is used to quickly establish the general state of security at a facility for comparison to other facilities and prioritization of any follow-on work. More formal briefings, which are generally longer and more detailed, are generally used at facilities where facility or enterprise managers are expected to take some action in response to the findings, or where a regulatory agency has primary oversight responsibility for implementation of upgrades. In this case, the formal briefing is often followed by a final written report that is delivered soon after the VA is completed.

Written reports may take several forms, ranging from short executive summaries up through lengthy, detailed reports that document all aspects of the VA. Many written reports are preceded by a briefing at the facility at the conclusion of the VA, and the report is used to formalize the VA activity and to serve as reference for any upgrades. The specific details included in the report will vary with the type of facility, its assets, and the project agreement. Report format is described in more detail in the next section of the chapter.

Developing effective briefings and reports requires presentation of information in an organized, easily understood fashion that supports informed decision making by facility or enterprise managers. Briefings should be structured to provide an overview of the VA project goals and protection objectives, a summary of the data collected, the conclusions of the analysis, and recommendations for

upgrades or next steps. VA reports generally elaborate on the information provided in the briefing by providing specific details of team activities, a detailed description of the methodology used, all the data that was collected, and analysis results and recommendations. The final report is then archived, along with supporting computer files and other data, to facilitate future VAs at the site. The next sections provide some recommendations on the information and format of successful briefings and reports.

Briefings

Briefings may be formal or informal, depending on the site, assets, and project agreement. For example, if the team is composed of employees of the enterprise, there may be different reporting methods used than if an outside contractor is used. In general, any briefing should describe an overview of the VA project goals and protection objectives, the target audience, the methodology used when conducting the VA, a summary of the data collected, the conclusions of the analysis, and recommendations for upgrades or next steps, at the appropriate level. Appendix G shows a sample presentation template that captures this flow and supports the case for effectiveness of the current system or the need for upgrades. The amount of time for the briefing will vary with the detail presented and whether it will be followed by a written report.

Report Content and Format

The following are suggested major headings for a VA report and notes on the content that should be included. Although not applicable to every VA, this structure ensures that vital information has not been inadvertently omitted. The entire VA team should assist with report preparation, which will reduce the amount of time needed to create the report and facilitate VA team agreement on the results. Inclusion of any appendices depends on the VA scope and analysis tools used, as well as the desired formality of the report. Longer and more formal reports place detailed supporting information in appendices as a reference for readers who require these details. This organization allows the reader to quickly review and understand the major VA results, while still providing the important details that support the VA. Major and minor report headings (numbered in the example, but any standard heading protocol may be used) are followed by a recommendation on the responsible VA team member for the section in parenthesis. These responsibilities can be delegated by the responsible team member to another member of the team if desired. Report headings and suggested content include:

1.0 Executive Summary (VA Project Leader)

This section, generally no more than two pages long, should summarize the project goals, methods, and results. The section normally ends with a description of the results of the VA or the next step in the process.

2.0 Introduction (VA Project Leader)

This is usually a short opening statement of one or two paragraphs that describes some basic information that is relevant to why the VA was performed, such as a policy citation that requires periodic VAs, a recent event that triggered the VA, or in response to a request by an enterprise executive or regulatory agency.

2.1 Background (VA Project Leader)
A short paragraph that provides an overview of the project technical and administrative details that establishes the context of the VA for the reader. This section may include the names and functions of the VA team members, dates of the VA, and other pertinent details.

2.2 Purpose (VA Project Leader)
The purpose of the VA is usually a restatement of the project goals that comes from the project master document or contract.

2.3 Scope (VA Project Leader)
The scope of the VA describes the specific parts of a facility that were evaluated, how the VA results will be reported and to whom, relevant polices that support the performance of a VA, and any limitations that were placed on the VA. Examples of limitations include evaluation of only one asset type, time available to conduct the assessment, specific areas or functions that were excluded from the VA, and restrictions on who may see the results.

2.4 Data Collection and Analysis Tools (VA Analyst)
This part of the report should describe the techniques, tests, or other means used to collect data at a site. These descriptions are fairly detailed and provide the reader enough information to reproduce the tests, if desired. Analysis tools include a description of the process, software tools, computer simulations, or other methods used to support the analysis of data. This section is often a standard description of the tools, which is reused in many VA reports.

3.0 PPS Objectives (VA Analyst)

This paragraph should introduce the general purpose of the facility, a general description of assets that require protection, and an introduction to the threat level expected at the site. This is a short paragraph that introduces the succeeding sections, which provide more details about these areas.

3.1 Facility Overview (VA Project Leader)

A short overview of the facility, including major products and operations, number of employees, operating hours, geography, weather, surrounding area, and other useful information that will help a reader who is unfamiliar with the facility understand it. This section generally includes some pictures of the site.

3.2 Assets and Consequence of Loss (VA Analyst)

In this section, the assets that have been identified as targets of an adversary attack are described. Depending on how a VA is defined by the facility, this may be part of the VA or part of risk assessment. If the assets were identified as part of the VA, the assets and criteria should be listed in a table, from highest to lowest overall consequence of loss. This information should be supplemented by the locations of all the assets considered during the VA. If assets were identified and prioritized before the VA, this information can be summarized, and locations listed. During a VA, all or a subset of assets may be considered. Consequence of loss is a good way to frame the value of the asset to the facility and enterprise.

3.3 Defined Threat (VA Analyst)

This section should describe the defined threat(s) at the facility. This information should be presented in categories such as high, medium, and low, or by using a descriptive label, such as vandal, criminal, insider, or extremist. In addition, the weapons, tools, motivation, number, and other capabilities of each threat should also be listed here. Often, a table is used to summarize this information. It is recommended that the threat is agreed upon before starting the VA. Usually, the threat is established during a risk assessment.

4.0 PPS Characterization (VA Project Leader)

This section should include a brief descriptive narrative of the existing PPS at the facility. It should address the detection, delay, and response elements in use, at a high level. Specific details are provided in subsequent sections. Pictures of the overall site are also used here.

4.1 Detection Function (VA Project Leader)

Detection elements that are present can be summarized in this section, including hardware, procedures, and personnel. This is also a good place to describe where the facility perimeter starts (exterior fences or a building wall). For each of the following sections, pictures can be used to document VA team observations.

4.1.1 Exterior Sensors (SME-Sensors)

Describe any exterior sensors in use and then list observations and their effects on the system. For example:

Observation: There is a two-fence isolation zone around the main area that forms a perimeter. The zone is approximately 10-feet wide and is covered in gray gravel. There are a number of places where weeds are growing between and around the two fences. There is a fence sensor on the outer fence, no sensors between the two fences, and no video assessment of the zone.

Effect: The fence sensor on the outer fence is not operational. Even if operational, sensor placement on the outer fence makes it easy for an adversary to approach and tamper or defeat the sensor. There is no intrusion sensing between the two fences, and the zone is not wide enough to allow video assessment of a fast-moving adversary, if more sensors and video assessment were added. Weeds growing between the two fences are a visible indication of the lack of attention to maintenance of the protection system.

Numbering the observations consecutively (i.e., starts at 1, then sequentially numbers all observations for all PPS elements) through the entire report will make it easier to refer to these points in the Analysis and Recommendations sections of the reports. At the end of this section, each exterior sensor in use should be listed, and an estimate of performance should be given using qualitative or quantitative measures. This can be facilitated through the use of a table listing sensors in one column, and performance estimates in another. There may be multiple performance estimates if multiple threat levels and facility states are used.

4.1.2 Interior Sensors (SME-Sensors)

Similar to the discussion on exterior sensors and information is presented the same way. As an example:

Observation: The presence and implementation of PIR sensors at the exterior doors are not consistent. Some have PIR sensor coverage just inside the doors, and other doors did not have PIR sensors. All sensors had visible alarm indicator lights. These sensors are not integrated with video to provide timely assessment.

Effect: Boundary penetration at exterior walls must be contiguous to be effective. If it is not, there are vulnerabilities in this layer. Leaving the alarm indicator lights visible will indicate to an adversary when he has been detected and will give information about the detection coverage to insiders.

At the end of this section provide estimates of probability of detection, P_D, for all sensors, using all threats and facility states.

4.1.3 Alarm Assessment (SME-Video)

Describe how alarms are assessed (manually using humans, video surveillance, or video assessment), document observations and effects, and provide performance estimates. An example:

Observation: The mixture of lamp types and mountings indicate several iterations of lighting design. Light measurements were taken along the west side of the building and along the front to get a typical reading from the different types of lights. Data showed the average light on the west side is 5 foot-candles (fc) and

that the light-to-dark ratio is 7:1, which is acceptable. The readings along the front indicate a lower average light level of 1 fc and a light-to-dark ratio of 6:1, both of which are also acceptable. Several lights were burned out along the fence line. The light level was not measured close in to the buildings because of shadow areas.

Effect: Exterior cameras require consistent and even lighting to provide the best resolution. It is not good design practice to mix different types of lighting. Uneven light distribution reduces the quality of live and recorded video. The cameras have enough light to see most places along the fence, but, because of high light-to-dark ratios close to the building, there will be areas in which details and human-size targets will not be seen. This is precisely the area in which alarm assessment would take place. The PTZ cameras looking into the lights reduce video image quality, making it difficult to see details in the scene. Light levels would be higher if maintenance of the lights was better.

At the end of this section, provide an estimate of probability of alarm assessment, P_{As}.

4.1.4 Entry Control (SME-Entry Control)

Provide an overview of the entry control system in a paragraph or two, then list observations and effects. This may need to be broken into sections addressing personnel, vehicle, and contraband detection aspects. For example:

Observation: For access through vehicle gates, a guard visually checks the driver and all passengers for a badge.

Effect: A crude facsimile of an authorized badge could be used to pass the perimeter with almost no chance for detection. Dependence on easily counterfeited photo badges makes passage through these entry points easy. In this case, a vehicle bomb could be allowed access to the inner perimeter of the facility. This is close enough to cause significant damage to buildings and personnel.

At the end of this section, provide an estimate of P_D for personnel, vehicles, and contraband, as appropriate, considering all adversary attack tactics (physical, deceit, technical).

4.1.5 Alarm Communication and Display (SME-AC&D)

Describe the AC&D subsystem equipment, location, procedures, and operator effectiveness. Use observations and effects to show how the subsystem is degraded. For example:

Observation: Approximately 10 to 15 feet from the front of the operator console are 15 large monitors mounted in the wall to supplement the alarm assessment capabilities of the operator. There is one 36-inch monitor in the center, eight 20-inch monitors on each side of the 36-inch monitor, and two 26-inch monitors on each end. A local TV station was playing on the 36-inch monitor. Only some video of the main area was visible on monitors because the video switcher has not been working for over 6 months. Sensor alarms are annunciated, but no associated video is presented on the 5-inch assessment monitors located in the operator console. The control center relies on phone calls from personnel to verify that they caused an alarm or on roving patrols to assess alarms.

Effect: Lack of alarm assessment prevents anyone from knowing what the actual state of security is across the complex. It would be difficult under the current operating conditions to differentiate an actual attack from normal operation. In addition, having the 36-inch TV tuned to commercial TV stations should cause concern about the concentration of the operators in evaluating the alarms, who do not need any additional distractions.

Using the data obtained through observations and effects, provide an estimate of the probability of assessed detection, P_{AD}. This value may be degraded beyond the product of probability of detection and probability of assessment if the AC&D subsystem is very ineffective.

4.2 Delay Subsystem (SME-Delay)

Provide a one or two paragraph description of the barriers that are used at the facility, including terrain, entry portals, doors, windows, and building materials, then describe specific barriers for each category of delay.

4.2.1 Terrain (SME-Delay)

Describe the surrounding terrain, if there is an exterior perimeter in use, or if a vehicle is part of the threat capability. For example:

Observation: The main area is surrounded by an earth berm just outside the outer perimeter fence.

Effect: In some places, the berm allows an adversary to bypass the perimeter fence sensors. The berm casts long shadows during the day and at some locations at night, making video alarm assessment impossible.

4.2.2 Personnel/Vehicle Entry Portals (SME-Delay)

Describe delay elements present at portals that prevent people or vehicles from entering before being granted authorized access or in the case of a stealth or force attack. As an example:

Observation: There are pop-up vehicle barriers located at all vehicle portals that are left in the down position during operating hours.

Effect: The barriers are not effective against any vehicle attacks during operational hours. They take several seconds to deploy and it is unlikely that the personnel manning the gate can deploy them in time to stop a vehicle.

4.2.3 Buildings (SME-Delay)

Describe the materials used in building construction, including walls, roofs, windows, utility ports, or ducts. For example:

Observation: Many of the walls appear to be concrete floor-to-ceiling. Most exterior doors are standard hollow metal emergency doors.

Effect: The delay times present at the complex do not contribute much to overall system effectiveness because they are not preceded by detection. Concrete walls are difficult to penetrate quickly, but there is no detection, so this is not as helpful as it could be. The exterior doors are easy to penetrate by the defined threat.

At the end of this section, provide estimates of delay times for all barriers that the defined threat will encounter along the appropriate paths. There may be multiple estimates if there is more than one threat level or category. This can be facilitated through the use of a table listing all the barriers, and then the estimates of delay for each threat.

4.3 Response Subsystem (SME-Response)

Describe the overall response at the site, including the response strategy, the length of time it takes for responders to arrive (if immediate response strategy), the weapons or other equipment security responders have, a review of training and procedures for responders, and a description of how security personnel communicate to the main dispatch and among themselves.

4.3.1 Response Force Communications (SME-Communication) Describe the communication system, and overall procedures for how the system is used during normal, abnormal, and attack conditions. For example:

Observation: The response radios do not work in all areas. There are dead spots between the annex and the main building and in some spots in the basement of the main building.

Effect: The AC&D station loses communication with units in these areas. There is no procedure for maintaining periodic contact with security guards who have been dispatched. This can be a vulnerability, because of lack of communication, and is an officer safety issue. In the time it takes to discover an officer has not reported in, an adversary may have completed an attack.

4.3.2 Response Force (SME-Response)

Observation: Response to alarms in the main building is not consistent and uses a variety of response personnel. The first responder may wait outside an area for a point-of-contact to arrive, or choose to enter, or some combination of these to both assess an alarm and respond. Some responders are armed, and some are not.

Effect: There is no set procedure for who will respond, what they will do on arrival, and how response is coordinated. It is difficult to coordinate response force tactics with variously equipped respoders arriving on scene. In the event of an adversary attack, these diverse units have not trained together, may not be equipped properly, and do not know how to deploy and communicate effectively.

Provide an estimate of the probability of communication, P_C, and response force time (as appropriate) at the end of this section. If the response uses a delayed strategy, refer to the Video Subsystem section for performance estimates. If neutralization is used, provide an estimate of probability of neutralization, P_N.

5.0 Analysis Results (SME-Analyst)

This section should introduce the analysis process, by listing the process steps and any analysis tools used. This is a convenient place to state which analysis approach is used—compliance-based, qualitative or quantitative performance-based. In addition, include which overall performance measure is used to represent system effectiveness (interruption only, interruption and neutralization (P_E), risk).

5.1 Baseline Results (SME-Analyst)

This section should remind readers that the first part of the analysis is meant to establish the baseline performance of the system. If this baseline meets protection objectives, no major upgrades are required, although some minor procedural upgrades may be appropriate. This is a key principle—the system must be analyzed to show the current state, and then upgraded only if performance is not acceptable. This technique will emphasize the differences between current performance and performance after upgrades.

5.1.2 Overall System Effectiveness Summary (SME-Analyst)

This section should summarize baseline analysis results using appropriate system effectiveness measures. This summary should include results across all facility states, particularly if there is reduced system performance during these times. An overview of site-specific vulnerabilities is described in this section. Specific details are addressed in subsequent sections.

5.1.3 Path Analysis (SME-Analyst)

This section includes an ASD of the site (see, for example, Figure 11-8) and describes the path analysis results for different facility states. Multiple ASDs need not be used; text descriptions can describe how PPS elements are affected by the facility states, and how this changes overall system effectiveness. This is also a good location to introduce certain attack scenarios, as a lead-in to the next section. It can also be useful to describe why only some paths are used in the analysis by noting that the available paths depend on the defined threat tactics, tools, and capability.

5.1.4 Scenario Analysis (SME-Analyst)

This section addresses credible attack scenarios that include attacks on PPS elements or the response force. These scenarios supplement the path analysis described previously, which considers only scenarios where the adversary directly attacks the asset. Different facility states favor different scenarios and these differences should be described. All scenarios are based on the defined threat tools and capabilities.

5.1.5 Neutralization (SME-Analyst)

If used, this section describes how neutral-ization was estimated and shows the probability of neutralization analysis. Inclusion of this section assumes that interruption and neutralization are performance measures of the overall system, and this section should show the product of the two values, under different facility states.

5.2 Upgrade Analysis (SME-Analyst)

This section should introduce the functional improvements to detection, delay, and response that were analyzed to predict which upgrades to the PPS would be most beneficial to the facility. If baseline performance is acceptable, this section is not required.

5.2.1 Upgraded System Effectiveness Summary (SME-Analyst)

This section should summarize upgrade analysis results using functional performance upgrades. This summary should highlight improvement in protection across previously weak facility states and will address the overall site-specific vulnerabilities described in Section 5.1.2.

5.2.2 Path Analysis (SME-Analyst)

This section illustrates how the functional upgrades improve the previously described weak paths. The ASD may or may not change, depending on the upgrades. If the ASD changes, a new ASD should be used to focus reader attention on the improvements.

5.2.3 Scenario Analysis (SME-Analyst)

This section shows how the potential upgrades will reduce successful attacks on PPS elements or the response force. It is likely that the same scenarios as the baseline will be used, but some additional credible scenarios may also be required.

5.2.4 Neutralization (SME-Analyst)

This section shows the analysis of how neutralization was improved by using the functional upgrades. System effectiveness using P_I, P_N, P_E, or risk should be shown for different facility states.

6.0 Recommendations (VA Project Leader)

This section describes how team recommendations are presented, and how they should be used. There are many ways to categorize recommendations. Some enterprises use cost; some use length of time to implement a recommendation. The best recommendations use a combination of the two and rely on overall system improvement as the final measure. It is suggested that the time period within which improvements can be made be used because this helps in planning upgrades. For example, short-term recommendations could represent those that can be achieved within 6 months; medium-term those that can be accomplished within 12 months; and long-term are those that are

anticipated to take more than 12 months. The time period can be varied as appropriate. Rather than provide tables for short-, medium-, and long-term recommendations, only one example table is provided here (see Table 12-1). It is vitally important to point out that these recommendations are not a multiple choice list of selectable options (i.e., four short-term, two medium-term, and one long-term out of each group), but that for the predicted improvement in performance, all of the recommendations must be implemented. This point should be strongly stated. Recommendations may address equipment, procedures, or personnel issues. For example, one short-term recommendation might be to develop contingency plans for faulty equipment or higher-alert states.

This section may also address other risk management options that can more cost effectively be used to protect assets. Because this book specifically addresses VAs, this analysis is limited to PPS

Table 12-1 *Sample Short-Term Recommendations.*

Links to	Recommendation
Baseline Analysis, Overall System Effectiveness	Provide training to all security organization personnel who have a role in design, selection, maintenance, oversight, and operation of the PPS. This training should be an introduction to security principles, with a heavy emphasis on system integration, vulnerability analysis, and performance measures.
Observation 14	Reattach the fence sensor cable to the fences where ties have fallen off and reconnect the cables to the processors so it is not so obvious that they don't work. Remove weeds and debris from the fences.
Observation 15	Determine operating status and condition of all sensors. This is a simple pass/fail test to determine which sensors might be used in a new design. At the same time, disable all alarm indicator lights for sensors.
Observation 27	Re-aim exterior cameras at the main area toward fences or doors so video surveillance is more useful. Because the pan and tilt control cables are not functional, this may have to be done manually. Currently, cameras are aimed at locations where an intruder can tell that there is little chance of being observed.

Note that either an observation or an analysis result is linked to the specific recommendation and that these recommendations do not represent a pick list of choices. All recommendations must be implemented to ensure overall system effectiveness.

upgrades. Analysis of other risk management alternatives may also be included here, if credible supporting data are available.

For most facilities, it is also usual to include notes on the estimated cost of each set of recommendations, what facility operations may be affected by the improved system, the need for modifications of facility policies to achieve the desired result, and other key points that the VA team wants to emphasize. It should be noted that any cost estimates are very rough at this stage, because the actual design team must still address all of the selection, construction, installation, and other details that will ensure successful implementation of the upgrades.

6.1 Short Term (VA Project Leader)
Insert a table or text that summarizes recommendations and link for short-term improvements.

6.2 Medium Term (VA Project Leader)
Insert a table or text that summarizes recommendations and link for medium-term improvements.

6.3 Long Term (VA Project Leader)
Insert a table or text that summarizes recommendations and link for long-term improvements.

7.0 Conclusions (VA Project Leader)

This section should summarize the VA results in a few sentences. In addition, it can be useful to include some potential next steps, particularly if the system is weak and will need considerable improvements. Other information might include next steps, who to contact for questions or further information, and who will get copies of the report and when.

8.0 Appendices

The appendices that are included are a function of the type of report, the audi-

ence, and the uses of the report. This is a partial list; not all listed are appropriate for all facilities and others can be added as needed:

A Overview of VA Methodology
B VA Team Roles and Responsibilities
C Supporting Data and Notes
D Facility States/ASDs
E Computer Models and Data Listing
F Neutralization Analysis Overview
G Neutralization Detailed Scenarios
H Neutralization Raw Data
I Supplemental Data/Information

Protecting Results

A major aspect of reporting is clarifying how the final report will be protected. By its very nature, a VA report is a powerful document and should not be shared indiscriminately. Protection of the final report, as well as the appropriate distribution, should be defined as part of the master project agreement. It is recommended that one organization have final control of the document and who it is shared with, even though other organizations may have copies.

Reporting Summary

There are various methods of reporting the VA results, ranging from short informal discussions to lengthy reports that include all the raw data collected by the VA team. In typical use, the VA team provides a briefing of their findings before departing the site; this is followed by a written report that formalizes the evaluation activities. The specific reporting method is defined in the master project agreement and conforms to the reporting standards used across the enterprise. Commercial enterprises may use shorter, less detailed reports; many government facilities must use specific reporting procedures and formats. The key to good reporting is to provide a clear and understandable flow of information to the reader that clearly supports the presence and impact of any system vulnerabilities. This information should be tailored to the target audience. For example, a shorter executive summary would be more practical for senior managers of the enterprise, and lengthier, more detailed reports would be valued by security managers and their staff.

Using the Vulnerability Assessment

Once the VA is completed, there are a variety of responses or next steps that can take place. By far, the most common approach is for the facility to pursue improving the PPS and following the recommendations of the VA team. As noted in Chapter 11, upgrades to the PPS proposed during the VA are usually limited to functional improvements (i.e., performance upgrades that must be achieved to improve overall system effectiveness). Some enterprises leave implementation of recommendations to the managers responsible for the facility. For the purposes of this discussion, it is assumed that the facility will implement the recommendations made in the VA, and the general process that should be followed to accomplish this will be described. Ignoring recommendations does nothing to protect assets and this decision does not require any additional discussion. It is more helpful to describe implementation of upgrades and the keys to successful implementation, at least at a high level.

Recall that in Chapter 1, the concept of systems engineering was described. Consistent with this discussion, a VA can be thought of as the analysis of system requirements that must be done before system design and implementation. The same things that made a particular PPS weak in the first place can limit the effectiveness of any upgrades, if they are not carefully considered. This process may be relatively short and easy, if the recom-

mendations involve only procedural or minor equipment changes, such as replacing one type of closed-circuit television camera with another. If the system requires major equipment upgrades, however, the proper approach to the upgrade design will ensure a cost- and performance-effective result. Just as with evaluation, a performance-based approach can be used in design and implementation. To keep the discussion simple, only the design stages that are used will be discussed. For any given system, these stages may be quickly accomplished or can take much longer; either way, some key concepts should be considered.

Design Stages

Often, a VA team does not possess all of the capability required to design an effective system, although they are quite knowledgeable about how the system should perform. This is why a separate team of designers is often used to plan the upgrades. In addition to the technical depth this group of experts brings to the upgrade, a better result can be achieved if one group creates the design, and a separate, independent group conducts the analysis. This avoids any conflict of interest, pride of ownership issues, and provides an effective check and balance on the final upgrades.

The goal of the design team is to develop upgrades that give the performance predicted in the upgrade analysis phase of the VA. This can be difficult to accomplish and can take several iterations between the designers and the facility to clarify goals and constraints and to create the best system that can be installed for the available funding. The three general stages of design activity include conceptual, preliminary, and final design. Although this discussion is focused on the use of a VA for improving an existing facility, the same process is used for design and evaluation of a new facility. For new facilities, VA analysts and designers work together closely to model the proposed PPS at the site and then iterate on which PPS elements will give the most cost-effective solution. Once they agree, the system designers work through the design stages to define the specific final design.

A conceptual design is the first iteration of the elements required to upgrade a PPS. This design relies on concepts or potential candidates for new PPS elements, hence the name *conceptual*. At this stage of design, many ideas that could be used in the final system are considered, and the impacts of these alternatives are characterized in terms of cost, performance effectiveness, operational impact, and time to implement, to name a few. This is generally called a tradeoff analysis, where the overall benefit of using one option over another is evaluated against all requirements (functional, constraint, and performance). At this stage, there are usually many discussions between the design team and their counterparts at the facility, so that progress can be made in reducing all the potential solutions to a smaller set of viable alternatives.

Once the potential solutions are reduced to a smaller set, the preliminary design stage begins. This is rarely such a sharp transition, but rather occurs almost seamlessly as all the conceptual solutions are considered, and either eliminated or carried forward, based on the tradeoff analysis. At this stage, more specific details of installation, maintenance, and integration are considered, so that the small number of options can be narrowed down to the best option in each functional area (detection, delay, and response).

At this point, the final, or detailed design, begins. This stage is characterized by consideration of every construction and installation detail, as well as training and procedural changes that may be required. Each PPS hardware element is located for precise position at the facility,

detailed drawings are created, and phasing of installation activities is planned. At completion of this stage, a detailed drawing package and all system requirements will exist. This package can then be sent out for bid, or can be implemented by facility personnel. Major upgrades are normally sent out for bid by security system contractors or integrators; minor upgrades may be performed by facility personnel.

If the final design will be sent out for competitive bid, a few high level details should be included in the bid package to help bidders understand what final product is desired. Detailed drawings should be supplemented by the performance that is required of the installed components. For example, the requirement might be to have an exterior microwave that has a probability of detection of 0.9 (or high performance if a qualitative analysis is used) against a running intruder during day, night, and bad weather conditions. This should be clearly stated in the requirements and specification documents that supplement the drawing package. It is also prudent to state that final payment for the installed system will be made only after both the installed components and the overall system have been tested and found to meet the specifications (acceptance testing). The requirements document should also describe the acceptance test procedure that will be used for each component and the overall system, so there is clear communication of expectations. This process requires more attention and oversight than the more traditional form of contracting, where the lowest bid wins and only limited, if any, testing takes place. The latter approach explains why so many security upgrades are installed that do not improve the system. If the measure of system effectiveness is dollars spent, this approach will work; however, more active oversight of the design stages and bid package preparation by the facility will pay big dividends at the end of the upgrade project.

Project Closeout

In cases where the VA is the end of the project, regardless of whether the recommendations will be implemented, there are certain activities that should be conducted to successfully close out the project. The amount of rigor applied to project closeout will vary with the project scope, the enterprise, and the VA provider. These details are normally described in the master project document, as discussed in Chapter 3.

In general, there are financial, administrative, and technical details of the project that must be considered before the project can be considered complete. Financial closeout generally involves a final accounting of project funds and the return of any unused monies to the customer. Administrative details include verifying with the customer that all deliverables have been completed, any equipment or drawings that were borrowed from the facility are returned, and project team members have a release schedule for when their project commitment is complete. Technical closeout details include the collection of all team members' notes, electronic files, data, pictures, and other project documents, for storage in a secure location or delivery back to the customer (as per the terms of the master project document). Archiving of all project documentation is particularly important if the VA is conducted by the enterprise security organization. This documentation can be used as the starting point for any future security reviews, evaluations, or audits that can reduce the time and cost of these efforts.

One additional aspect of project closeout is an internal team review of the project. Use of this technique is limited to large projects, but this can be accomplished quickly, even for small companies or projects. The internal team should review what went well, what could have been done better, what additional support might have helped do the project faster or better, and what actions could have reduced project costs. In addition, it is always a good idea to compare actual project costs to the estimated costs provided during the project proposal. This information can be used to help gauge future similar projects and to monitor the variance between actual and estimated costs. By monitoring this variance, a company can perfect project estimating, which can be a competitive and operational advantage.

Summary

This chapter described how to report and use VA results. Reporting can take one of two basic forms—oral briefings or written reports. The method of reporting should be specified in the master project agreement. The VA report should provide information to facility management that will show that the PPS is effective or show what functional improvements may be needed to increase system effectiveness. Often, the VA is the initial step in a longer PPS upgrade project. When this happens, the VA provides the basic functional requirements of an improved system. Various design stages, including conceptual, preliminary, and final, are followed that eventually lead to a specific design that can be implemented. After the VA report is delivered to the customer or facility, the project team must complete various administrative and technical activities before the project is officially completed. This includes delivery of all technical, financial, and status reports; return of borrowed equipment; and archiving of all project documentation. In addition, a brief review of the project, what went well, what did not, and how future projects could do better is recommended. This should include a comparison of estimated and actual project costs to aid in better cost estimates for future evaluations.

Appendix A

Project Management Forms and Templates*

PROJECT SUMMARY (An overview document of no more than two pages to be kept in organization files and updated at least yearly)

TITLE: Working title of project

PROJECT NUMBER: Job number, project number, or equivalent that is used to capture budget and charging information.

PROPOSAL NUMBER: Some organizations have a system to track proposals.

PROGRAM MANAGER: Responsible senior manager for the project.

PROJECT MANAGER: Responsible middle manager or staff member.

PROJECT LEADER: Responsible staff project lead. May be the same as Program and Project Manager.

SPONSOR: Name of principal customer sponsor, company or agency, and contact information.

PROJECT DESCRIPTION: One to two sentences on overall project goal, then a brief description of project tasks. Include information on VA scope, objectives of project

PROJECT JUSTIFICATION: Examples— required VA, supplemental, change in threat, new equipment replacement, etc.

DELIVERABLES/MILESTONES: High level review of project work breakdown structure by general tasks and major milestones.

Task/Milestone   Deliverable

FUNDING PROFILE: Funding profile by fiscal year, in dollars.

FY07	*FY08*	*FY09*
$10K	$30K	$30K

SCHEDULE: High level review of timetable of major tasks.

Task   Date

RISK: A concise discussion of various elements of risk associated with the project. This should include cost, performance and schedule risk, as well as any political, resource, or other known risk. (See Risk Assessment Worksheet)

*The appendices in this book are also available for download at http://books.elsevier.com/companions/0750677880

Project:

Max. Programmatic Risk Class: _____

RISK ASSESSMENT WORKSHEET

Notes:

Programmatic Risk Class	Customer Requirements	Project Technical Complexity	Project Management Complexity	Operational Impact	Key Personnel
PRC-1 (High Formality)	Requirements are not well established. High potential for changing requirements.	New, undeveloped, or unproven technology and/or methodology.	Multiple internal and external organizations with expected management difficulty (or large project).	Failure jeopardizes reputation. Failure could have significant adverse impact on environmental safety or health.	Loss of key personnel results in potential inability to complete the project.
PRC-2 (Medium Formality)	Only a few remaining questions regarding requirements. Foreseeable changes will not affect success.	Modification of existing technology and/or methodology.	Multiple internal and/or external organizations.	Failure jeopardizes programmatic performance.	Loss of key personnel requires a renegotiation with the customer.
PRC-3 (Low Formality)	Requirements well established.	Existing/known technology and/or methodology.	Project with simple interfaces (or small project).	Failure has little effect on future work. Failure would have no impact on environmental safety or health.	Loss of key personnel has negligible impact on meeting established requirements.

Completed by: _____

Name	Organization	Date

INSTRUCTIONS:

1. Circle PRC for each category.
2. Place maximum PRC for this worksheet in upper left block.
3. Use this risk assessment to determine formality of risk management documentation.
4. Submit worksheet with Project Summary package.

Appendix B
Initial Briefing Template

**Site X
Vulnerability Assessment
(VA)**

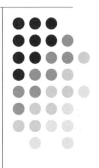

Presenter name
Presenter organization
Presenter phone
Presenter phone/email

Overview

- Purpose
- Scope
- Assumptions
- VA Methodology
- Schedule
- Questions

Purpose & Scope

- Complete a VA of Site X
- Evaluate the PPS as required by <insert policy reference or other basis>
- Establish baseline performance of the system and propose functional upgrades if not effective

Assumptions/Limitations (examples)

- Uses previously defined threats and assets
- Risk level must be less than <specify level>
- Considers installed system, not planned upgrades
- Limited time for VA—5 days

Defined Threat

- Describe threat spectrum or single defined threat. For example:

Level	Tactic	Weapons/Equipment	Number
Low	Theft	Unarmed, Hand Tools	1-2, No Insider
Medium	Sabotage	Handguns, Hand & Power Tools	2-4, Possible Insider
High	Sabotage	Armed, Hand/Power Tools, Thermal Tools, Explosive Charges	3-5, Possible Insider

Assets

- List assets that are targets of VA:
  - Target 1
  - Target 2
  - etc

VA Methodology

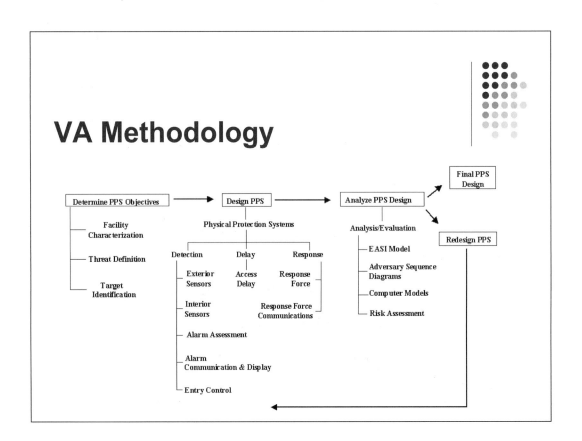

Concepts

- Defined protection objectives
- Performance-based
- Evaluate PPS
  - Detection
  - Delay
  - Response
- Analyze integrated system, not individual components

Benefits of Performance-based Assessments

- Based on performance, not mere presence, of components
- Clearly shows effects of vulnerabilities
- Links solutions to effectiveness
- Better risk management and resource utilization

Protection Principles

- Detection before delay
- Alarm assessment ends detection
- Balanced protection
- Protection-in-depth
- Immediate response required for critical assets

Relationship of PPS Functions

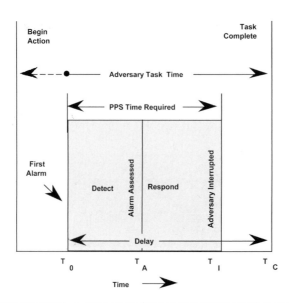

Analysis

- Describe if qualitative or quantitative analysis
- Describe performance measure used
  - Interruption, neutralization, system effectiveness, risk
- Describe tools used
  - Data collection
  - Tests
  - Path analysis
  - Scenario analysis

VA Schedule

- Day 1
  - Initial briefing
  - Facility tour
  - Workspace setup
- Day 2
  - Collect necessary maps & drawings
  - Data collection—sensors, video system
- Day 3
  - Data collection—entry control and AC&D
  - Begin analysis

VA Schedule

- Day 4
  - Data collection—delay and response
  - Finish analysis
  - Prepare briefing
- Day 5
  - Brief results
  - Depart site

Questions/Discussion

- ???

Appendix C
Threat and Facility Worksheets

THREAT WORKSHEET

Estimating Likelihood of Attack (P$_A$) Worksheet Pg 1/3

Date:	Recorded by:
Facility Identifier:	
Threat Type:	

Definitions:
Threat Type – the specific adversary group or level being addressed.
Attack – malevolent human attack that would result in the estimated level of consequences.

Capability: Is the adversary group capable of conducting a successful attack on this facility? To answer the question, consider: Is the adversary group . . . Located near or is able to gain access to the facility? Expected to have the material resources to attack this facility? Expected to have the technical skills to attack this facility? Expected to have the planning/organizational skills to attack this facility?	*If YES,* continue	*If NO,* P$_A$ = VL Stop

For the following sections, select the answer that most accurately describes the item contained in the left-most column of each row. Note the "score" associated with that answer and enter the numeric value in the right-most column under "Score."

History/Intent				**Score**
Historical interest	If there is documented evidence that historically, this adversary group has shown interest in this type of facility or this specific facility, Score = 5.	If there is speculation, but no evidence that this adversary group has shown interest in this type of facility or this specific facility, Score = 3.	If there is no evidence that this adversary group has ever shown interest in this type of facility or this specific facility, Score = 1.	
Historical attacks	If there is documented evidence that this adversary group has conducted similar attacks in the past at this facility or this type of facility, Score = 5.	If there is speculation, but no evidence that this adversary group conducted similar attacks in the past at this facility or this type of facility, Score = 3.	If there is no evidence that this adversary group has conducted similar attacks in the past at this facility or this type of facility, Score = 1.	

Estimating Likelihood of Attack (P$_A$) Worksheet Pg 2/3				
Date:			**Recorded by:**	
Facility Identifier:				
Threat Type:				
				Score
Current interest in facility	If current information suggests interest in the facility, Score = 10.	. . .	If there is no current information that suggests interest in facility, Score = 2.	
Current surveillance	If current intelligence documents surveillance at specific site, Score = 10.	If current intelligence documents surveillance at other similar facilities in the United States or abroad, Score = 6.	If current intelligence does not involve specific facility, similar facilities in the United States or abroad, Score = 2.	
Documented threats	If this site has received documented threats of attack from this threat, Score = 10.	If this site has received documented threats of attack, not from this particular threat type but similar groups, Score = 6.	If this site has not received documented threats from this threat type or other adversary groups, Score = 2.	
Relative Attractiveness as Target				
Consequence	If level of estimated consequence for attack is consistent with goals of this threat type, Score = 10.	If level of estimated consequence caused by attack is not definitely consistent with goals of threat type, but possibility exists, Score = 6.	If level of consequence caused by attack is not at all consistent with goals of this threat type, Score = 2.	
Ideology	If attacking this site is consistent with ideology/motivations of this threat type, Score = 10.	If attacking this site is not consistent with ideology/ motivations of this threat type but possibility exists, Score = 6.	If attacking this site is not at all consistent with ideology/ motivations of this adversary group, Score = 2.	

Estimating Likelihood of Attack (P_A) Worksheet Pg 3/3			
Date:		**Recorded by:**	
Facility Identifier:			
Threat Type:			
			Score
Ease of attack	If perception exists that physical protection system is relatively easy to defeat or doesn't exist and/or the undesired event is easily accomplished at this site, Score = 5.	If perception exists that the physical protection system at the site provides moderate protection and/or there is moderate difficulty in accomplishing the undesired event at this site, Score = 3.	If perception exists that the site has a robust, effective protection system and/or the undesired event is extremely difficult to accomplish at this site, Score = 1.
Total Score for Adversary Group (sum all scores)			
Likelihood of this Threat Type attacking this facility: **If the Total Score for this adversary group is:** **60 or greater, PA = Very High (VH)** **Less than or equal to 47 and greater than or equal to 59, PA = High (H)** **Less than or equal to 46and greater than or equal to 32, PA = Medium (M)** **Less than or equal to 31 and greater than or equal to 19, PA = Low (L)** **18 or less, PA = Very Low (VL)**			P_A

Other Notes:

Site Description Form
Physical Protection System

Site Name:
Location:
Point-of-contact (POC):
POC Phone:
POC Email:
VA Date:
Team Members:

Physical Protection System Details:
1. Facility Characterization
2. Threat Identification
3. Target Identification
4. Analysis and Evaluation

1. Facility Characterization:

Physical Conditions:

Facility Operations:

Facility Policies and Procedures:

Regulatory Requirements:

Legal Issues:

Safety Considerations:

Facility Goals and Objectives:

Physical Facility Conditions

Site Boundary and Buildings:

Room Locations within Buildings:

Entry Points:

Existing Physical Protection Features:

Infrastructure Details

Heating:

Ventilation and Air Conditioning:

Communication Paths and Types:

Power Distribution System:

Unique Environmentally Controlled Areas of the Facility:

Locations of Hazardous Materials:

Exterior Areas:

Physical Site Conditions

Topography:

Vegetation:

Wildlife, Background Noise (airport), Highways:

Climate, Weather, Rainfall, Hurricanes, Snow:

Soil Conditions:

Physical Protection Features

Fences:

Sensors:

Cameras:

Alarm Communication and Display Center:

Barriers:

Response Force Availability:

Response Force Time:

Facility Operations

Major Products of the Facility:

Process that Support these Products:

Operating Conditions (Facility States, Work Hours and Emergency Operations):

Type and Number of Employees:

Supporting Functions

Procurement Procedures:

Computing Resources and Distribution:

Maintenance Activities:

Asset Tracking:

Location of Senior Executives:

Workflow, Employee Parking:

Shift Changes:

Shipping and Receiving:

Accounting Functions:

Garbage Disposal (large vehicle access):

Hunters and Hiking Access:

Visitors and Public Access:

2. Threat Identification

Table 1-1 *Outsider Adversary Information H (high) M (medium) L (low)*

Outsider Adversary	Threat 1	Threat 2	Threat 3	Threat 4	Threat 5
Theft					
Sabotage					
Ideological					
Economic					
Personal					
Number					
Weapons					
Equipment Tools					
Transportation					
Technical Expertise					
Insider Assistance					
Other?					

Table 1-2 *Insider Adversary Information (Often, Occasionally, Never)*

Insider	Access to Asset	Access to PPS	Access to Vital Equipment	Theft Opportunity	Sabotage Opportunity	Collusion Opportunity
PPS Designer						
Control						
Operator						
Maintenance						
Guard						
Manager						
Other?						

3. Target Identification

List Targets at this Facility:

Table 1-3 *Analysis Matrix of Threat and Consequences for Target 1*

Level of Consequence			
High			
Medium			
Low			
Probability of Occurrence	**Low**	**Medium**	**High**

Table 1-4 *Analysis Matrix of Threat and Consequences for Target 2*

Level of Consequence			
High			
Medium			
Low			
Probability of Occurrence	**Low**	**Medium**	**High**

Table 1-5 *Analysis Matrix of Threat and Consequences for Target 3*

Level of Consequence			
High			
Medium			
Low			
Probability of Occurrence	**Low**	**Medium**	**High**

4. Analysis and Evaluation

Identify Current System Deficiencies:

Evaluate Improvements:

Perform Cost vs. Effectiveness Comparisons:

Appendix D
Data Collection Sheets

Exterior Sensors

VA ID: Date:

Data collected by:

Threat: H/M/L   **Estimated P_D:**

Isolation Zone: sketch "typical" zone   sketch unique zones (add pages if needed):

outer fence _____

_____

inner fence

Sensors:

Type:

Configuration:

Installation:

Maintenance: good/adequate/low   trouble reports/month:___ avg time to fix:___

Complementary?

Continuous line?

Sensitivity:

Detection pattern:

Detection by personnel: never/occasionally/always

Junction boxes:

Nuisance alarms:

Sources:

Estimated frequency (per zone or total per day):

Estimated false alarm frequency:

Area between fences:

Distance between

Dirt/gravel/grass/other

Even terrain/low spots/washouts/slope/etc

Standing water/vegetation/etc.

Fences:

Loose/tight fabric

Signs/hog rings/other noise sources:

Interference/bridging/tunneling/culverts:

Height:

Environment:

Temperature range:

Snow, rain, fog, etc.:

Humidity:

Background noise:

Pavement/roads/soil:

Tamper protection: Y/N   Type:

Line supervision: Y/N   Type:

Self-test: Y/N

Anti-capture: Y/N   Type:

Integrated with CCTV: Y/N

Comments (attach additional sketches or pictures available. Correlate to report):

Interior Sensors
VA ID: Date:
Data collected by:
Threat: H/M/L   **Estimated P$_D$:**

Interior Sensors: sketch   sketch unique zones (add pages if needed):

Room/Building Function: Maintenance/Equipment Room/Office/Vault/CAS/
other:_____
Sensors:
   Type:

   Configuration:
   Installation:
   Maintenance:
   Complementary?
   Target location:
   Sensitivity:
   Detection pattern:
   Optimal placement?
   Indicator light:
Nuisance alarms:
   Sources:
   Estimated frequency (per zone or total per day):
   Estimated false alarm frequency:
Daytime use:
   Sensors in access/operational
Integrated CCTV:
Environment:
   Temperature range:
   Local heating/windows/ducts/fans/vents:
   Doors open inward/outward:
   Humidity:
   Seismic/vibration sources:
   Room contents (furniture, carts, etc.):
   Overhang/pipes/conduits/fixtures:
   Lighting: fluorescent, incandescent, none, other
Tamper protection:
Line supervision:
Self-test:
Anti-capture:

Comments (attach additional sketches or pictures available. Correlate to report):

Exterior Assessment Subsystem
VA ID: Date:
Data collected by:
Threat: H/M/L   **Estimated P$_{As}$:**

Exterior Video Assessment: sketch   sketch unique zones (add pages if needed):
Outer fence _____

_____

Inner fence

Manual assessment (human) or CCTV
Cameras:
    Type: B&W/color   analog/digital   fixed/PTZ   #/zone:____
    Format: H resolution in lines:____   from vendor/by test
    Height:
    Installation:
    Maintenance:
    Type of tower:
    VMD included:
    Camera housing/mount:
    Lightning protection:
    Junction boxes:
Lighting:
    Type: HPS/LPS/Mercury/IR/none/other:____   height:____   above/below camera
    Light:dark ratio:___   estimated/measured   Lighting outside fences/zone:
    Ground reflectance: ____   Pole location: inside inner fence/outside outer fence/
        between
Integrated/aligned with sensors:
Environment:
    Temperature range:
    Snow, fog, rain, wind, etc:
    Humidity:
Tamper protection:
Line supervision:
Communication links/paths:
Video resolution:
    Circle, square, triangle   far field (black/white side):
        Day: Night:
        Black side/dark spots:
        White side/bright spots:
    Detect/classify/identify   calculated/by observation/both
    Focus: sunrise/sunset/day/night   IR cut filter installed: Y/N
Recording:
    Pre-alarm/post-alarm/none
    Frames per alarm:____   Time between frames:___
Switching:
    Manual/Sequential/Automatic on alarm

Comments (attach additional sketches or pictures available. Correlate to report):

Interior Assessment Subsystem

VA ID: Date:

Data collected by:

Threat: H/M/L   **Estimated P$_{As}$:**

Interior Video Assessment: sketch   sketch unique zones (add pages if needed):

```



```

Manual assessment (human) or CCTV?

Cameras:

      Type: B&W/color   analog/digital   fixed/PTZ   #/zone:____

      Format: H resolution in lines:____   from vendor/by test

      Height:

      Installation:

      Maintenance:

      Type of tower:

      VMD included:

      Camera housing/mount:

      Wiring protection:

Lighting:

      Type: Incandescent/Fluorescent/IR/none/other:____ height:____   above/below
                                                                                                                        camera

      Lights on 24/7/day only/other

Integrated/aligned with sensors:

Target location:

Environment:

      Temperature range:

      Localized heat/vents/windows/ducts:

      Humidity:

      Movement of items in area: frequent/occasional/random/never

Tamper protection:

Line supervision:

Communication links/paths:

Video resolution:

      Detect/classify/identify   calculated/by observation/both

      Focus (day/night):

Recording:

      Pre-alarm/post-alarm/none

      Frames per alarm:____   Time between frames:___

Switching:

      Manual/Sequential/Automatic on alarm

Comments (attach additional sketches or pictures available. Correlate to report):

Entry Control–Vehicles
VA ID: Date:
Data collected by: **Estimated P$_D$:**
Threat: H/M/L

Vehicle portal: sketch
outer fence with gate _____

_____

inner fence with gate

Request to enter: buzzer/guard observation/CCTV/phone/credential/other
Vehicle search:
     Vehicles allowed: Government only/personal/trucks/delivery/all
     Manual by guard: Y/N
     Search all entering vehicles/visitor only/contractor only/other
     Technology used: Inspection under vehicle/explosives detection/dogs/other
                    Search on entry/exit/both
     Gate type: sliding manual/sliding auto/open out/slide up
Driver ID check/exchange: Y/N   Describe:

Vehicle entry control procedure (describe):

Packages in vehicle search: Y/N
     all packages/visitor only/random/other
     Manual or technology type:
Operational hours: 24/7, daytime only, special use
     Traffic flow/throughput: Heavy/moderate/occasional
CCTV assessment: Y/N   Day/Night
     Sensors: Y/N
Barriers:
     Type (pop-up/ fixed/moveable):
Observation by personnel/guards: never/occasionally/always

Comments (attach additional sketches or pictures available. Correlate to report):

Entry Control–Personnel
VA ID: Date:
Data collected by: **Estimated P$_D$:**
Threat: H/M/L

Personnel Portal: sketch
outer fence _____

inner fence

Request to enter: buzzer/guard observation/CCTV/phone/credential/other
ID credential check/exchange: Y/N   Describe:

Visitor control procedure (describe):

Package search: Y/N
    all packages/visitor only/random/other
    Manual or technology type:
Operational hours: 24/7, daytime only, special use
    Traffic flow/throughput: Heavy/moderate/occasional
    Estimate entries/exits per hour (day or week):
Sensors:
    Type:
    Location:
    Placement:
    Metal detector: Y/N   Fixed/portable/other
CCTV assessment:
    Sensors: Y/N   Day/Night
Barriers:
    Turnstiles: Y/N   material:
    Wall material:
    Window material:
    Door material:
    Roof/other surface material:
Observation by personnel/guards: never/occasionally/always

Comments (attach additional sketches or pictures available. Correlate to report):

AC&D subsystem
VA ID: Date:
Data collected by:
Threat: H/M/L   **Estimated P$_{AD}$:**

sketch console: sketch room (add pages if needed):
Top (facing operator)

System Hardware:
    System vendor: Software vendor/version:
    OS/version: Network-based: dedicated/intranet/extranet/
                                          Internet
    Monitor placement:
    Operator Display Monitor: color/b&w size:
    Number of Video assessment monitors: Number/location of surveillance monitors:
    Secondary AC&D available: Y/N   Location:
    Other equipment: radios/badging/access control/fire
    Ergonomics:
    Associated equipment:
Operator workload:
    Number of operators:___   Functions:
    Alarm monitoring/assessment/door control/patrol communication/other
    Initiate equipment tests/log data/create reports/other
    Ease of use: Operator understanding of system:
Alarm Communication:
    Time to display alarm (secs): immediate/1-5 /5-10/10-15/15-20/>20
    Transmission system: Display: __ alarms:____secs
    Number of nodes:
    Communication protocol: Line supervision:
Alarm Display:
    Text/map/both/other
    Integrated with video: timely assessment/delayed assessment/surveillance/none
    Information displayed: system status/zone status/location/PPS component/procedures
Alarm Assessment:
    Live video/recorded video   Speed to display video: Synced with alarm data:
    Image quality:
    Time to assess alarm: Time to assess 5 alarms:
    Assessment actions: single keyboard/multiple keyboards/other
Maintenance:
    Tests: Frequency: Logs:
    Repair requests: Avg time to repair:
    Temperature range: Humidity:
System protection:
    Password protected: Y/N   HW Configuration changes:
    Duress protection: Y/N   SW configuration changes:

Comments (attach additional sketches or pictures available. Correlate to report):

Delay—Exterior/Terrain
VA ID: Date:
Data collected by:
Threat: H/M/L   **Estimated Delay Times (by element):**
                                       Distances:
                                               Across perimeter:
                                               To buildings/other structures:

Sketch:

Outside perimeter:
    Wooded/clear   natural barriers: flat/rough/rugged
    Overpass/culverts/tunnels/bridging/etc: Y/N
    Close to public roads:
    Restricted roads: Y/N   How are they restricted:
Inside area:
    Paved: Y/N/some   speed bumps/other traffic controls:

Observation by personnel/guards: never/occasionally/always

Comments (attach additional sketches or pictures available. Correlate to report):

Delay—Building or Room
VA ID:
Data collected by:
Threat: H/M/L

Date:

Estimated Delay Times (by element):
Surface: wall1_____wall2____wall 3____
           Floor_____roof____
Door: door1____door2_____door3___
Ducts: duct1_____duct2_____duct3____
Other:

Sketch:

Building location/number/function:

Barriers (describe material, thickness, use of multiple material layers, overburden, etc):
    Surfaces (walls, roof, floor):
    Doors:
    Windows:
    Installation:
    Maintenance: good/adequate/low
    Before/after detection
Entry control:
    Type: Card reader/biometric/PIN/all
    Locks: Y/N   Which doors:
                                     Type: padlock/electric/cipher/dial/key/other
Ducts present (>96 in²): Y/N
    Barrier: fixed/moveable   If moveable, sensor/position monitor: Y/N
    Sensored: Y/N   Grate: Y/N
CCTV assessment: Y/N   Sensors: Y/N   Lighting: Y/N
Balance:
    Are doors/surfaces/window/other barriers balanced? Y/N
Operations:
    What procedures are performed:
Asset description:
    Are assets ever left in structure overnight: Y/N
    How are they protected (building locked, guard posted, etc)
Equipment in area:
    Cranes/forklifts/hoists/etc:
    How is it locked out or protected:
    What is required to make equipment operational:
Observation by personnel/guards: never/occasionally/always

Comments (attach additional sketches or pictures available. Correlate to report):

Delay—AC&D location(s)
VA ID:
Data collected by:
Threat: H/M/L

Date:

Estimated Delay Times (by element):
Surface: wall1____wall2____wall 3____
　　　　Floor____roof____
Door: door1____door2____door3___
Ducts: duct1____duct2____duct3____
Other:

Sketch:

Building/room location/number/function:

```

```

Barriers (describe material, thickness, use of multiple material layers, etc):
　　Surfaces:

　　Doors:
　　Windows:
　　Ducts:
　　Installation:
　　Maintenance: good/adequate/low
　　Before/after detection
Entry control:
　　Type: Card reader/biometric/PIN/all
　　　Locks: Y/N　　　　　　　Which doors:
　　　　　　　　　　　　　　　Type: padlock/electric/cipher/dial/key/other
CCTV assessment: Y/N　　　Sensors: Y/N　　　　Lighting: Y/N
Any delay bypass present (ducts, passageway, halls, other doors, etc):
Are delay elements balanced: Y/N
Observation by personnel/guards: never/occasionally/always

Comments (attach additional sketches or pictures available. Correlate to report):

Delay—Equipment room

VA ID:

Data collected by:

Threat: H/M/L

Date:

Estimated Delay Times (by element):

Surface: wall1_____wall2____wall 3____

Floor_____roof____

Door: door1_____door2_____door3___

Ducts: duct1_____duct2_____duct3____

Other:

Sketch:

Building location/number/function:

Barriers (describe material, thickness, use of multiple material layers, overburden, etc):

Surfaces (describe skin, thickness, material between layers):

Doors:

Windows:

Ducts:

Installation:

Maintenance: good/adequate/low

Before/after detection?

Entry control:

Type: Card reader/biometric/PIN/all

Locks: Y/N

Which doors:

Type: padlock/electric/cipher/dial/key/other

CCTV assessment: Y/N

Sensors: Y/N

Lighting: Y/N

Equipment cabinets: Y/N

How protected:

Entry controls:

What equipment available to aid adversary:

Any delay bypass present (ducts, passageway, halls, other doors, etc):

Are delay elements balanced: Y/N

Observation by personnel/guards: never/occasionally/always

Comments (attach additional sketches or pictures available. Correlate to report):

Delay—Guard Station

VA ID: Date:

Data collected by:

Threat: H/M/L   Surface: wall1____wall2____wall 3____

                                      Floor____roof____

                             Door: door1____door2____door3___

                             Ducts: duct1____duct2____duct3____

                             Other:

Sketch: Building location/number/function:

Barriers (describe material, thickness, use of multiple material layers, overburden, etc):

    Surfaces (describe skin, thickness, material between layers):

    Doors:

    Windows:

    Ducts:

    Installation:

    Maintenance: good/adequate/low

    Before/after detection?

Entry control:

    Type: Card reader/biometric/PIN/all

    Locks: Y/N   Which doors:

                              Type: padlock/electric/cipher/dial/key/other

CCTV assessment: Y/N   Sensors: Y/N   Lighting: Y/N

Duress alarms: Y/N

Any delay bypass present (ducts, passageway, halls, other doors, etc):

Are delay elements balanced: Y/N

Observation by personnel/guards: never/occasionally/always

Comments (attach additional sketches or pictures available. Correlate to report):

Delay—Communications Hub

VA ID: Date:

Data collected by:

Threat: H/M/L   **Estimated Delay Times (by element):**

Surface: wall1_____wall2_____wall 3_____

Floor_____roof_____

Door: dor1_____dor2_____dor3___

Duct: duc1_____duc2_____duc3_____

Other:

Sketch: Building/room location/number/function:

Barriers (describe material, thickness, use of multiple material layers, overburden, etc):

    Surfaces (describe skin, thickness, material between layers):

    Doors: Access controls:

    Windows:

    Ducts:

    Installation:

    Maintenance: good/adequate/low

    Before/after detection

Entry Control:

    Type:

    Locks: Which doors:

                           Type: none/padlock/electric/cipher/dial/keyed cylinder/other

CCTV assessment: Y/N   Sensors: Y/N   Lighting: Y/N

Equipment cabinets: Y/N

    How protected:

    Access controls:

Any delay bypass present (ducts, passageway, halls, other doors, etc):

Are delay elements balanced: Y/N

Observation by personnel/guards: never/occasionally/always

Comments (attach additional sketches or pictures available. Correlate to report):

Response
VA ID: Date:
Data collected by:
Threat: H/M/L   **Estimated Response Time:**

Primary Response force:
    Type: Security guard/medical/safety/other
        Immediate or delayed response
    On-site/off-site
    Availability: on-site 24-7/called in as needed/night only/other
    Supplemented by:
    Number:
        Total: Multiple teams (number of teams, personnel per team):
    Armed: Type:
    Intermediate weapons:
    Hardened vehicles: Hardened fighting positions:
    Other equipment:
    Communication with external agencies:
Training:
    Radio procedures
    Intermediate force weapons:
    Weapons proficiency:
    Other equipment proficiency:
    Physical Fitness:
    Practice deployment exercises:
    Cover/concealment training:
    Ambush training exercises:
    Documented:
    Retraining period:
    Practice exercises with external agencies:
Procedures:
    Post Orders:
    Written policies:
    Use of force authorized: Y/N   Use of force policy established:
    Weapons requalification period:
    Deployment procedure:
    Chain of command:
    External liaison agreements:
Response strategy:
    Denial/containment
    Target knowledge:
    Other tactics:
Response force time (scenario dependent):
    Denial:
    Containment:
    Detection:
    Observe/report:

Comments (attach additional sketches or pictures available. Correlate to report):

Response Communications
VA ID: Date:
Data collected by:
Threat: H/M/L   **Estimated P$_C$:**

Sketch overall system:

Equipment:
Primary Communication: radio/cell phone/telephone/other   alternate:
    Repeaters: Locations:
    Comm Hub location:
    Transmission system:
    Duress alarms:
    Clear voice/encrypted/digital/spread spectrum radios
    Patrol vehicle:
Procedures:
    Use of codes:
    Authentication:
    Anti-jamming:
    Practice exercises:
Maintenance:
    Radios:
    Batteries:
    Antennas:
    Hubs:
    Repeaters:
    Patrol vehicles:
Communication nodes/paths:
    Main to patrols:
    Vehicle Patrol to vehicle patrol:
    Roving Patrol to main:
    Posts to vehicle:
    Posts to main:
    Central relay points or distributed:
    Dead spots:

Comments (attach additional sketches or pictures available. Correlate to report):

Appendix E

Alarm Communication and Display Subsystem Criteria

Requirement Description
Communications
The system shall continuously monitor the state of health of data communications between other security subsystems.
Failures of and tampering with, critical components associated with alarm detection, transmission, and annunciation shall be continuously detected and reported as events to the console.
The system shall detect and report any loss of communications or suspected tampering within the event timing parameters (see Event Handling section).
The system shall be redundant with physically separated communications paths.
All communications protocols shall be robust and reliable with automatic detection and recovery of errors, tolerance of single-point failures with automatic resynchronization of data after the auto-recovery.
Communications lines that exit the protected area shall be encrypted.
Event Annunciation
The system shall accurately display the correct current state of every component and subsystem.
The system shall treat on line functions (e.g., alarm processing, system status) with a higher priority than background functions (e.g., access control).
The system shall not automatically abort or preempt the operator out of any functions.
The system shall create events to report an alarm condition or set of related alarm conditions requiring operator notification.
The system shall be able to display and log details of alarm events.
The system shall display and log the type of event, the location of the event, and the time of the event.
The system shall provide information about a sensor on operator request.
The sensor information shall include any site specific sensor identifier, the current sensor priority, the sensor type, the current sensor state (alarm, tamper), the current sensor mode (access, offline), and the location of the sensor.
The mode of a sensor shall determine what events are displayed to the operator.
When the sensor is SECURE, any intrusion detection, tamper, malfunction, or communications loss shall be displayed.
When the sensor is in ACCESS, any tamper, malfunction, or communications loss shall be displayed. Intrusion detections shall not be displayed.
When the sensor is OFFLINE, no intrusion detections or tampers shall be displayed.
The system shall be capable of annunciating a minimum of eight alarm events per second.
The initial event shall be displayed within 1 second of the event activation.
No alarm event shall be lost.
The system shall be capable of uniquely identifying using both text and graphic maps: (1) the mode of any sensor, (2) the status of any event, and (3) the status of any sensor.
The system shall be capable of prioritizing all events.

Requirement Description
The system shall annunciate and display events in the order of their priority, and second by order of their time of occurrence.
The system shall provide the capability to assign the same priority to different events.
Security events shall have a higher priority than access control events.
Continuous activation of any event (alarms, communication losses) shall not prevent operators from handling other events.
Existing events shall not preclude the announcement of new events to the operator.
The system shall allow an operator to remove a sensor from service when it is malfunctioning.
The system shall provide a duress alarm that can be initiated by a console operator. This duress alarm shall not be indicated by the initiating console, but will be displayed on any other system consoles.
The system should allow an operator to handle any event out of priority order.
The system should allow an operator to document the actions and decisions regarding alarm events (i.e., associate a cause with an event).
Display Console Interface
The operator shall receive instant audiovisual feedback that a command has been initiated.
The commands used when interacting with the system shall be appropriate in the current system context and easy to understand.
The messages presented to the user by the system shall be easy to understand and clear on how the operator shall respond.
The user interface shall be designed that it may be operated without reference to manuals during normal operation.
The user interface shall present only essential or useful information.
Inputs required from the operator to initiate a command shall be consistent in performing similar command types.
The system response times shall be consistent when performing similar activities.
Any graphics display shall be interactive.
The system shall use prompts to guide an operator through complex operations.
Operator commands shall be functionally clustered.
The system shall not require more than two monitors to display system information.
The system shall support an acknowledge action. This optional action establishes that the operator is at the console and is aware of the security event.
The system shall support an assess action. This action indicates that the operator is assessing the security incident and taking appropriate action. Assess may also be used to acknowledge events.
The system shall support a reset or clear action. This action indicates that the operator has completed activity on the security event. An event can only be cleared if all alarm conditions contributing to the event are no longer present.
The system shall provide a color scheme for displaying events.
The color scheme shall uniquely identify unacknowledged events, acknowledged events, sensor states, and sensor modes.

Requirement Description
The system shall annunciate all events requiring an operator response with audible and visual signals at the console.
The audible signal shall be louder than background noise.
The system shall not allow the operator to permanently disable the audio.
The system shall provide a site-wide map available to the operator. This site-wide map shall identify the global state of all sensors and security events currently active on the site.
The system should provide a one-click access to the site wide map.
The system should have the ability to resound audio if no acknowledge or assess action has been taken within a configurable number of seconds.
The system should allow a capability to acknowledge more than one event with a single command.
The user interface should use techniques to aid in making decisions (i.e., the system should list possible alternatives when a decision is called for).
The system should always keep the operator aware of where he/she is in the command hierarchy.
The user interface should be consistent in that, what the operator learned in one context applies in another.
Video
The system shall interface to a video subsystem to provide CCTV assessment and surveillance capabilities.
The video ASSESSMENT subsystem shall support at least one and not more than six video monitors for presenting alarm event video information.
The system shall record video frames at a sufficient speed to capture the cause of the alarm.
Video presentation of an event incident on video monitors shall display both the current live video information and the recorded video information.
Video presented on the monitors shall be coordinated with the events being handled by the operator (i.e., sector 1 video is presented when handling sector 1's alarm).
The operator shall be able to select video information associated with another incident out of priority order.
The recorded image shall be identified such that the time, date, and location being viewed are contained within the recorded video frame(s).
The subsystem shall have the capabilities to report a signal line cut from the camera.
The system shall be capable of displaying any camera image to a video monitor at any time.
Any video being displayed on the assessment monitors shall not be removed from the monitor unless commanded by the operator.
Surveillance control functions shall have a manual keyboard to control any pan, tilt, zoom, focus, or other camera surveillance type functions that are options available on a camera.
Surveillance control functions should be available to the operator through the user interface.

Requirement Description
In the event of failure of a primary or secondary display console an alternate manual keyboard should be available to select any camera image to a video monitor.
The system should allow any live or recorded image to be archived to a removable media.
Monitors for video surveillance only, if used should be separated from assessment monitors to help delineate the functional use of the different monitors.
Access Control
Passage through portals shall be accomplished from entry control devices associated with that portal.
If PIN data is used by the system, such data shall be protected in storage and transmission so that unauthorized persons cannot determine the PIN associated with a given badge.
The system shall restrict an individual's access to only areas, buildings, and rooms where his presence is authorized.
The system shall automatically mask a door alarm for a predetermined amount of time on authorized entry into an area.
The system shall grant passage within 3 seconds upon successful completion of access control procedures.
The system shall provide positive feedback at a portal to indicate that passage is granted or denied.
If multiple access control procedures are required, the system shall provide instructions and positive feedback to guide users through the appropriate actions.
The system shall log all access attempts.
The system shall accommodate two-person rule. Two authorized users must successfully complete the access control procedures at a portal within a specified time period to allow entry or exit from a controlled area.
The system should display a security event if a configurable number of consecutive passage failures for that badge occur from a portal or group of portals configured for that function.
The system should display a security event if a deactivated badge is used to attempt access on a portal or group of portals configured for that function.
The system should provide anti-passback protection for any security area so configured.
The system should include functions to restrict access based on the time of day, day of the week, and holiday status.
Redundancy
The system shall consist of a primary system and a secondary system.
The secondary system shall provide continuous security functionality and be capable of providing effective response to security events in the event of a primary system failure.
The secondary system shall be able to take control from the primary system, announcing a security event at both displays when any of the following occur:
Control shall switch to the secondary system when the primary system or console fails.

Requirement Description
Control shall switch to the secondary system when the primary operator initiates a duress event.
Control shall switch to the secondary system when the primary operator fails to acknowledge a security event in a predetermined time period.
Control shall switch to the secondary system when the secondary operator manually switches the secondary into control.
Changing of primary or secondary status shall not cause the system to lose new or existing security events.
The system shall provide continuous visual indications at both primary and secondary system, of which system is in control.
The system shall provide a mechanism of isolating the primary or secondary system without disrupting the operation of the other system.
Duress events shall not be annunciated at the initiating console.
Configuration Information Management
The system shall allow only authorized individuals to create or change the system configuration.
The system shall provide a user interface that allows a user to create, delete, query, and modify system configuration items.
The system shall maintain an audit trail of system configuration changes that identifies who made the changes, what those changes were, and when the changes occurred.
The system shall provide the capability to configure a sensor to require two-person concurrence for sensor mode changes.
The system shall provide the capability to configure portals to require two-person concurrence before entry is granted.
The system shall grant individuals access to security areas.
The system shall be configurable such that an entry control device associated with a sensor can change the mode of that sensor.
The system should provide the capability to specify the entry and exit criteria for granting access into an area. This includes specification of badge, pin, biometrics, or other access criteria.
The system should provide the ability to configure portals to accommodate escorted visitors.
System configuration should be possible without interfering with primary and secondary console operations.
Printing/Logging
The system shall prevent operators from deleting log information.
The system shall log all security events.
The system should provide the capability to print reports such as system log files or audit trail files.
The system should log all events.
The system should provide advance warning when storage space available for the log entries is limited. This warning should provide sufficient time for the log files to be archived before the files are over-written.

Requirement Description
When log file space is exhausted, the system should overwrite the log file, the oldest log information being overwritten first.
System Privileges/Password Control
The system administrator shall have the ability to assign compartmentalized access for any or all system functions.
Compartmentalized access shall be protected by use of a password, biometric, or other identifier.
The system shall report and log attempts to modify system files or bypass system access security.
Sensor Mode Control
An operator shall be capable of changing the mode of a sensor.
The system shall log and notify operators when a sensor's mode is changed.
The system should allow a user to change the mode of a sensor from an associated entry control device.
Device Control
The system shall be able to control devices such as door lock, self-testing sensors, vehicle gates, and other devices.
Ergonomics
The console shall be configured so that commands can be easily activated. The operator shall not have to stretch or move from a normal operating posture to activate commands.
The system displays shall be placed in the center of the console within normal line of site.
Video monitors for assessment shall be placed in a position that requires only slight eye or head movement from normal line of site.
Response force communications equipment shall be within easy reach from the normal operating position.
Power
The system shall continue to operate normally after a power loss, with no loss of functionality until backup generators can be brought on-line. This time is recommended to be at least 1 hour.
The system shall sense and report a switch to backup power on any subsystem.
The system shall be protected from bad power such as surges, spikes, and low voltage conditions.
The system shall shutdown in an orderly way such that it will start up normally when power is reapplied.
The system shall automatically restart when power is reapplied.
The system should log a system restart.
The system should be able to determine the battery status (on a random basis) of the backup power and provide a security event indicating if there is a potential for a battery failure.

Requirement Description
Maintenance
The supplier shall provide maintenance documentation and troubleshooting procedures with the system.
The supplier shall provide training for operators, system administrators, and maintenance personnel.
The system shall not have remote diagnostic capability.
Specialized tools, equipment, and software necessary for system maintenance shall be provided with the system.
Archive/Backup
A means to generate off-line reports from the archived data shall be provided.
The system should provide the capability to archive system configurations to removable media.
The system should provide the capability to backup system software and files to removable media.
System Software
The software configuration management process shall include provisions for version control, numbering, and periodic releases.
The software configuration management process shall also include provisions for documentation and tracking software problems and their resolution.
The operating systems used by system computers should be current and supportable.
The source code and associated documentation for all applications software and build procedures should either be provided by the supplier or held in escrow by a third party.
Software tools required for development of the system software should be provided or held in escrow by the supplier.
The system software should have a documented software configuration management process.

Appendix F
Representative Delays

Table F–1 Penetration Times—Fences

Barrier Description	Penetration Equipment	Equipment Weight (kg)	Penetration Time (Minutes)			
			Min.	Mean	Max.	Standard Deviation
2-m chain-link mesh with outriggers	Ladder	5.0	0.1	0.2	0.3	0.04
4-mm × 50-mm mesh	Tarpaulin	2.0	0.1	0.2	0.3	0.04
	Pliers	1.0	1.0	2.0	3.0	0.41
	Manual bolt cutters	3.0	0.5	1.0	1.5	0.20
	Circular saw	10.0	0.5	1.0	1.5	0.20
	Manual bolt cutters, gloves (more cuts)	3.5	0.75	1.5	2.25	0.31
	Circular saw (more cuts)	11.0	0.75	1.5	2.25	0.31
	Gloves	0.5	0.1	0.2	0.3	0.04
Vinyl-coated 3-mm × 50-mm mesh	Manual bolt cutters	3.0	0.5	1.0	1.5	0.20
	Pliers	1.0	1.0	2.0	3.0	0.41
	Circular saw	11.0	0.75	1.5	2.25	0.31
2-m chain-link mesh without outriggers	Ladder	5.0	0.1	0.2	0.3	0.04
Vinyl coated, 1.8-mm × 40-mm mesh	No equipment	0.0	0.05	0.10	0.15	0.02
	Manual bolt cutters	3.0	0.5	1.0	1.5	0.20
	Pliers	0.5	1.0	2.0	3.0	0.41
	Vise grip pliers	0.5	0.30	0.60	0.90	0.12

Table F–2 *Penetration Times—Gates*

Barrier Description	Penetration Equipment	Equipment Weight (kg)	Penetration Time (Minutes)			
			Min.	**Mean**	**Max.**	**Standard Deviation**
Chain-link mesh pipe						
2.4-m × 4-m chain-link gate on metal pipe frame, chained and padlocked	Truck	1,500.0	0.05	0.1	0.15	0.02
	Pliers	1.0	1.0	2.0	3.0	0.41
Chain-link mesh pipe						
1.2-m × 2.4-m gate, 11-gauge × 5-cm mesh on 4.8-cm metal pipe frame, chained and padlocked	Sledgehammer	5.0	0.5	1.0	1.5	0.20
	1.8-m pry bar	10.0	1.0	2.0	3.0	0.41
	Bolt cutters	3.0	0.75	1.5	2.25	0.31
	Hacksaw	0.2	1.0	2.0	3.0	0.41

Table F–3 *Penetration Times—Walls*

| Barrier Description | Penetration Equipment (kg of explosives) | Equipment Weight (kg) | Penetration Time (Minutes) | | | |
			Min.	Mean	Max.	Standard Deviation
Concrete—10-cm Thick, Reinforced						
Concrete—210 kg/cm^2 one layer, 6.4-mm dia., 15-cm × 15-cm mesh	Sledgehammer, hand bolt cutters	10	2.0	4.0	6.0	0.82
	Sledgehammer, cutting torch	30	2.5	5.0	7.5	1.02
	Circular saw, sledgehammer	5	4.3	8.6	12.9	1.76
	Rotohammer, chisel, punch, sledgehammer, hand bolt cutters, generator	50	3.2	6.4	9.6	0.57
	Explosives (1.0), sledgehammer, manual bolt cutters	20	1.4	2.8	3.2	0.37
	Explosives (3.0), hand bolt cutters	10	1.0	2.0	3.0	0.41
	Explosives (5.0), hand bolt cutters	7	0.9	1.8	2.7	0.37
	Explosives (10)	10	0.8	1.6	2.4	0.33
	Sledgehammer, hand hydraulic bolt cutters	20	2.4	4.8	7.2	0.98
Concrete—210 kg/cm^2 one layer No. 5 rebar, 15-cm centers	Sledgehammer, cutting torch	30	2.0	4.0	6.0	0.82
	Rotohammer, chisel, hand hydraulic bolt cutters, generator	50	3.9	7.8	11.7	1.59
Concrete—15-cm Thick, Reinforced						
Concrete—210 kg/cm^2 one layer, No. 4 rebar, 20-cm centers	Sledgehammer, hand bolt cutters	15	4.0	8.0	12.0	1.63

Barrier Description	Penetration Equipment (kg of explosives)	Equipment Weight (kg)	Penetration Time (Minutes)			
			Min.	Mean	Max.	Standard Deviation
	Explosives (1.0), sledgehammer, hand bolt cutters	14	1.5	3.0	4.5	0.61
	Explosives (3.0), hand bolt cutters	5	1.15	2.3	3.45	0.47
	Explosives (5.0), hand bolt cutter	7	1.0	2.0	3.0	0.41
Concrete—20-cm Thick, Reinforced						
Concrete—210 kg/cm^2 one layer No. 5 rebar, 15-cm centers	Rotohammer, drill, sledge, chisel, punch, cutting torch, generator	65	7.0	14.0	21.0	2.86
	Explosives (2.0), sledgehammer, hand hydraulic bolt cutters	30	2.6	5.2	7.8	1.06
	Explosives (3.0), hand hydraulic bolt cutters	20	1.5	3.0	4.5	0.61
	Explosives (5.0), hand hydraulic bolt cutters	22	1.5	3.0	4.5	0.61
	Explosives (12)	12	1.2	2.4	3.6	0.49
Concrete—30-cm Thick, Reinforced						
Concrete—210 kg/cm^2 one layer, No. 4 rebar, 15-cm centers	Explosives (5.0), hand bolt cutters	8	1.3	2.6	3.9	0.53
	Explosives (7), hand bolt cutters	9	1.4	2.8	4.2	0.57
	Explosives (12), hand bolt cutters	14	1.5	3.0	4.5	0.61

(Continued)

Table F–3 *Penetration Times—Walls—Cont'd*

Barrier Description	Penetration Equipment (kg of explosives)	Equipment Weight (kg)	Penetration Time (Minutes)			
			Min.	Mean	Max.	Standard Deviation
Explosives (16),	18 hand bolt cutters	1.5	3.0	4.5	0.61	
Concrete—46-cm Thick, Reinforced						
Concrete—350 kg/cm^2 three layers No. 6 rebar, 15-cm centers	Explosives (16), hand-held power hydraulic bolt cutters, generator	282	3.0	6.0	9.0	1.22
Concrete—350 kg/cm^2 two layers No. 4 rebar, 15-cm centers	Explosives (20), hand bolt cutters	22	2.0	4.0	6.0	0.82
Concrete—60-cm Thick, Reinforced						
Concrete—350 kg/cm^2 four layers No. 6 rebar, 15-cm centers	Explosives (30), gas-powered hydraulic bolt cutters	59	4.4	8.8	13.2	1.80

Table F–4 Penetration Times—Doors

Barrier Description	Penetration Equipment (kg of explosives)	Equipment Weight (kg)	Penetration Time (Minutes)			
			Min.	Mean	Max.	Standard Deviation
Sheet Metal						
Standard industrial pedestrian door, 1.6-mm metal, panic hardware, cylinder lock, rim set, butt hinges with removable pins	Explosives (1.0)	1.0	0.75	1.5	2.25	0.31
	Sledgehammer, cutting torch, oxy-lance, fire-resistant suit	171.0	1.6	3.2	4.8	0.65
	Cordless drill	2.7	1.5	3.0	4.5	0.61
	Pry bar	7.0	0.1	0.2	0.3	0.04
	Fire ax	4.5	1.9	3.8	5.7	0.78
	Hammer, suction cups, punch, chisel	4.0	1.0	2.0	3.0	0.41
	Suction cups, sledge, cutting torch	25.0	0.5	1.0	1.5	0.20
	Explosives (.5)	2.5	1.0	2.0	3.0	0.41
	Lock picking tools	0.2	0.10	2.5	5.0	1.0
	Pipe wrench	1.0	0.2	0.4	0.6	0.08
	Explosives (2.0)	2.0	1.0	2.0	3.0	0.41
Standard industrial pedestrian door, hollow steel 1.6-mm narrow glass one side, louvers near bottom	Hammer	2.0	0.15	0.3	0.45	0.06
	Fire ax	4.5	0.80	1.6	2.40	0.33
Sheet Metal						
Standard industrial pedestrian door, hollow steel, 1.3-mm half glass expanded metal 2.8-mm grill	Grappling hook, wire cable, truck	1,520.0	0.3	0.6	0.9	0.12
	Manual bolt cutters	4.5	0.5	1.0	1.5	0.20

(Continued)

Table F–4 *Penetration Times—Doors—Cont'd*

Barrier Description	Penetration Equipment (kg of explosives)	Equipment Weight (kg)	Penetration Time (Minutes)			
			Min.	Mean	Max.	Standard Deviation
Standard industrial vehicle door, hollow steel panel, 1.6-mm	Explosives (0.5)	0.5	0.45	0.9	1.35	0.18
	Sledgehammer, cutting torch, oxy-lance, fire-resistant suit, water	385.0	0.80	1.6	2.40	0.33
	Sledgehammer, cutting torch, fire-resistant gloves, water	275.0	1.5	3.0	4.5	0.61
	Truck	2,025.0	0.3	0.6	0.9	0.12
	Pry bar, wooden plank	9.0	.75	1.5	2.25	0.31
	Fire ax	4.5	1.10	2.2	3.30	0.45
	Explosives (1.0)	1.0	.75	1.5	2.25	0.31
Standard industrial vehicle door, roll-up steel, corrugated 1.6-mm	Explosives (0.5)	0.5	.50	1.0	1.5	0.20
	Sledgehammer, cutting torch, oxy-lance, f ire-resistant suit, water	385.0	1.0	2.0	3.0	0.41
	Sledgehammer, cutting torch, oxy-lance, fire-resistant suit	171.0	0.65	1.3	1.95	0.27
Sheet Metal						
	Truck	2,025.0	0.35	0.7	1.05	0.14
	Pry bar, wooden plank	9.0	1.0	2.0	3.0	0.41
	Fire ax	4.5	1.10	2.2	3.30	0.45
	Explosives (1.0)	1.0	.75	1.5	2.25	0.31

Table F–4 *Penetration Times—Doors—Cont'd*

Barrier Description	Penetration Equipment (kg of explosives)	Equipment Weight (kg)	Penetration Time (Minutes)			
			Min.	Mean	Max.	Standard Deviation
Steel Plate						
Magazine door, 6.4-mm steel plate, one padlock	Explosives, linear-shaped charge (0.5)	0.5	0.40	0.8	1.20	0.16
	Sledgehammer, cutting torch, fire-resistant gloves, water	248.0	2.0	4.0	6.0	0.82
	Circular saw	16.0	2.1	4.2	6.3	0.86
	Suction cups, sledgehammer, chisel	4.5	0.6	1.2	1.8	0.24
	Sledgehammer, cutting torch, oxy-lance, fire-resistant suit, water	385.0	1.25	2.5	3.75	0.51
Steel Plate/Void/Steel Plate						
Heavy door with two large-hinged hasps for padlocking, 19-mm steel, 10-cm air space, 1.3-mm	Explosives (4)	10.0	0.75	1.5	2.25	0.31
	Sledgehammer, cutting torch, oxy-lance, fire-resistant suit, water	385.0	3.1	6.2	9.3	1.27
	Sledgehammer, cutting torch, oxy-lance, fire-resistant gloves	165.0	0.3	0.6	0.9	0.12

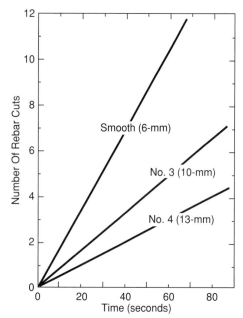

Figure F–5 Cutting Rates for
Reinforcement Bar Using 1-Meter
Boltcutters

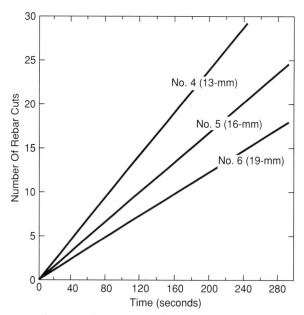

Figure F–6 Cutting Rates for Reinforcement Bar Using Portable Oxygen/Acetylene
Cutting Torch

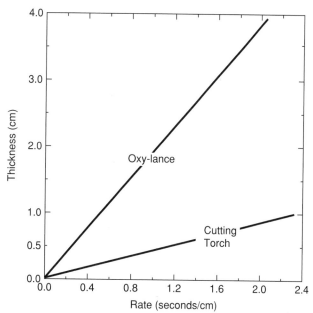

Figure F-7 Cutting Rates for Mild Steel Sheet & Plate Using Oxygen Acetylene Cutting Torch or Iron Oxygen Burn Bar

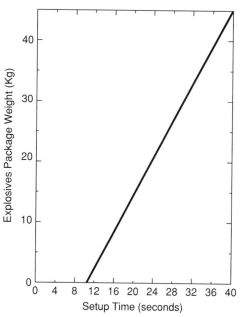

Figure F-8 Time Required to Set an Explosives Package as a Function of Package Weight

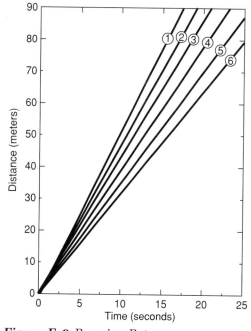

Figure F-9 Running Rates

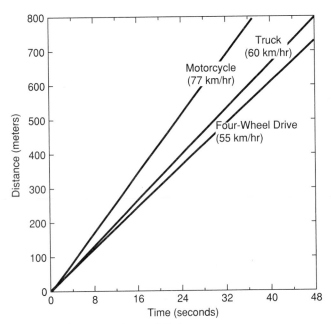

Figure F-10 Vehicle Rates for Experienced Drivers

Appendix G
Results Briefing Template

VA Results for Site X

Project Leader
Organization

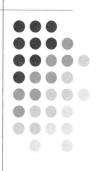

Overview

- Project Team
- Review Threats and Assets
- Data Summary
- VA Results
- Recommendations
- Next Steps

Project Team

- List all on-site representatives and VA team, areas of expertise/responsibility
- May need to add facility personnel who assisted to initial list

Threat

- Same as initial brief (unless modified)

Assets

- List assets that are targets of VA (may be modified from initial list)

Detection Subsystem/Data

- Key notes/observations
- Organize slides by component area— sensors, video, entry control, AC&D

Insert pictures of detection components that support observations

Delay Subsystem/Data

- Key notes/observations
- Organize slides by component area— windows, doors, walls, active/passive barriers, etc

Insert pictures of delay components that support observations

Response Subsystem/Data

- Key notes/observations
- Organize slides by component area—communication, response time, tactics, procedures, training, etc

Insert pictures of response components that support observations

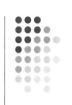

Site ASD

(Note: may need multiple diagrams for different facility states)

Offsite

PER   VEH

Traversal Area

A | Basement |

DOR   SUR

B | Target Area |

GNL

Target

Baseline Results

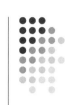

- Summarize analysis of current system using appropriate performance measure (P_I, P_N, P_E, risk, combination)

Graphs or Other Summarized Results

(Notes: Generally shown for each threat. May need additional for different facility states.)

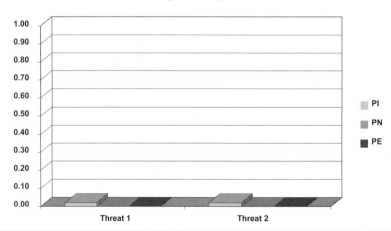

Upgrade Analysis

- Summarize functional improvements, not specific devices
- Detection, delay, response subsystems

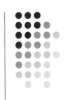

Upgrade Graphs

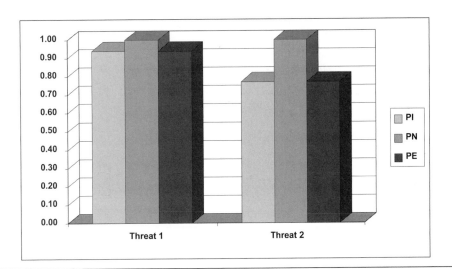

Analysis Notes

- Describe any special conditions or issues

Recommendations—Short term

- List immediate detection, delay, and response improvements

Recommendations—Medium Term

- List longer time-frame detection, delay, and response improvements

Recommendations—Long Term

- List long-term/major detection, delay, and response improvements

Next Steps

- List if appropriate
- Can include transition from VA to conceptual design

Questions

- ???

Index

Note: Entries followed by "f" denote figures' "t" tables.